COMMUNICATION AND PREJUDICE

COMMUNICATION AND PREJUDICE

Theories, Effects, and Interventions

Third Edition

By Alexis Tan

Washington State University

SAN DIEGO

Bassim Hamadeh, CEO and Publisher
Carrie Montoya, Manager, Revisions and Author Care
Kaela Martin, Project Editor
Christian Berk, Production Editor
Jess Estrella, Senior Graphic Designer
Alexa Lucido, Licensing Manager
Natalie Piccotti, Director of Marketing
Kassie Graves, Vice President of Editorial
Jamie Giganti, Director of Academic Publishing

3970 Sorrento Valley Blvd., Ste. 500, San Diego, CA 92121

To Riz, and children everywhere, our hope for tomorrow

Contents

Acknowledgments

After more than a decade's hiatus from teaching undergraduate students because of the demands of administrative work, I ventured back into the classroom in the fall of 2012 to teach a junior-senior level class on "Stereotypes and Communication." As I prepped for the class, two things became apparent to me: First, stereotypes were too limited as a topic because stereotypes are fundamentally a subset of a larger cognitive/affective phenomenon, and that larger concept is prejudice. So I re-conceptualized the course as "Communication and Prejudice." Secondly, I could not find a suitable text that discussed principles from social science research (and there is a lot of it) in a manner that would appeal to undergraduates. This then, was the genesis of this textbook. I wrote it to guide and inform my teaching. Thank you, to my students, who provided the motivation, as well as useful suggestions on topics, tone, and voice.

Thank you also to the splendid team from Cognella Academic Publishing who published a preliminary edition in Fall 2013 in record time without compromising quality. This first edition, also, published in record time, is a product of the collective efforts of Kristina Stolte, Acquisitions Editor; Sarah Wheeler, Senior Project Editor; Jess Busch, Senior Graphic Designer; and Chelsey Rogers, Marketing Program Manager. For the third edition, thank you to Cognella colleagues including Kaela Martin, project editor; Christian Berk, production editor; and Carrie Montoya, Manager, Revisions and Author Care.

I remember a professor and mentor from graduate school at the University of Wisconsin who was fond of saying that we (aspiring scholars) "stood on the shoulders of giants." That is indeed true of this book. Thank you to my colleagues in the social sciences—communication, social psychology, political science, sociology—whose research and theories are the building blocks for each and every chapter, and who have shaped my own work. I should also mention my graduate students—many who collaborated with me on studies discussed in this book—who kept the ideas coming, and who made research fun and exciting.

And, thank you to Gerdean for always being there and to Marco, Riz, and Deb also, for being there. My siblings, nephews, and niece in California and the Philippines, whether they know it or not, provided many insights on what it means to live and thrive in a multicultural world. My gratitude to them too.

1

Introduction to Communication and Illustrative Examples of Prejudice

During my lifetime I have dedicated myself to this struggle of the African people. I have fought against white domination, and I have fought against black domination. I have cherished the ideal of a democratic and free society in which all persons live together in harmony and with equal opportunities. It is an ideal which I hope to live for and to achieve. But if needs be, it is an ideal for which I am prepared to die.

—Nelson Mandela, 1964, at his sentencing to life imprisonment.

I magine a world where people got along regardless of race, ethnicity, religion, gender, sexual orientation, or any other marker of group membership that distinguishes "us" from "them"; where cultural differences were respected and valued rather than just "tolerated"; and where prejudice and discrimination were nonexistent. Sadly, regardless of the pronouncements of religious and political leaders around the world, the enactment of civil rights laws in the United States, and the celebration of humanity's "oneness" in song and popular culture (note Bob Marley and John Lennon), this ideal world does not exist. True, expressions of explicit prejudice are generally not acceptable ("I am not racist, *but … .*") with few exceptions (note White supremacist groups). However, a cursory examination of today's news from the United States and abroad would reveal that many of the conflicts between people and cultures can be traced, indeed, to prejudice and discrimination.

This book is about prejudice and communication. At this point, let's define *prejudice* as negative feelings toward a group and its members based on incomplete and biased information. Although prejudice may be positive, it is often negative. Prejudiced evaluations may be based on incorrect, incomplete, or unbalanced information from direct experience, peers, family, teachers, community members, the internet, or the mass media. Prejudice is often expressed in stereotyping. A *stereotype* is a belief that a group has certain attributes. Stereotypes are overgeneralizations, automatically projected to all members of the group, and, like prejudice, they are often negative. There are many psychological and sociological reasons why people are prejudiced, which I will discuss in chapters to come. However, my focus will be on communication—how we process information that we send and receive; how we transmit and interpret information in face-to-face interactions; how we send messages via the media, including the internet; and how we are affected by these messages. As you shall see, communication is a common vehicle for the transmission of prejudice, and in many instances it can cause and reinforce prejudice. But communication can also reduce prejudice. Therefore, the main themes of this book are (a) the effects of communication on prejudice, and (b) communication interventions to reduce prejudice. My objective is to provide you with an understanding of how communication can cause *and* reduce prejudice. In providing you with this understanding, I will base my explanations on social science theories and research. The concepts and principles I discuss will be based on scientific research, that is, as much as is possible, objective, and replicable. They will also be based on theories of media effects and human behavior that explain, rather than just describe, communication and prejudice. I do not claim to be completely unbiased. My biases will occasionally show in my interpretation of the research findings and in my recommendations. I believe that prejudice is wrong, dysfunctional, and immoral. At the same time, I believe that prejudice, particularly when based on unconscious biases, is fundamental to the human condition and cannot be completely eliminated. However, prejudice can be controlled using a number of communication strategies so that its harmful consequences for individuals and societies can be minimized.

Prejudice Everywhere?

What a depressing thought: Prejudice is everywhere! But indeed, research and casual observation might suggest that this is so. We disparage and attribute negative traits to others who are not like us. The more different these people are from us, and the more obvious these dissimilarities are, such as when they are visual, the more we dislike the other people.

Consider these examples from real-world events that have been reported in the media:

Example 1: Muslim Imams (Religious Leaders) Are Asked to Leave Flights

As reported by the Associated Press (2011), several Muslim leaders were asked to leave two commercial flights after they had passed through security at the airports. The imams, dressed in traditional Arab clothing, were on their way to a national conference. They were already seated when they were asked to leave the planes by airport personnel.

In a similar incident, personnel for another airline refused to let an Arab American board a plane even after he had passed through security. His son was removed from the same plane after the aircraft returned to the airport gate. The father told the AP, "I feel disrespected. It made us feel like criminals. ... My question is, Why? Why am I not allowed to fly? I'm a Muslim, not a terrorist. It's wrong."

None of the Muslims involved were charged with criminal activity and all were later cleared for flying.

A TSA spokesperson told the AP that his agency had nothing to do with the incidents.

In evaluating this incident, here are some questions we should ask ourselves:

- Did the airlines have the right to deny access to the Muslim passengers in the interest of national security? In the interest of passenger safety? After all, highly intoxicated people are often barred from flights.
- Is this an example of blatant prejudice and discrimination based on identification as a Muslim?
- Should the airlines be found guilty of violating the passengers' civil rights? Or should they be found innocent?

Example 2: Golf Club Admits First Women Members

The *Associated Press* (2012) reported that the Augusta National Golf Club, home of the Masters, invited former Secretary of State Condoleezza Rice and South Carolina financier Darla Moore to become the first women members in its eighty-year history. Both women accepted.

Several organizations, including the National Council of Women's Organizations, had urged the club to admit women as members but the former club chairman resisted, even at the risk of losing television sponsors, saying that Augusta National might one day admit a woman, "but not at the point of a bayonet" (*Associated Press* 2012).

In a related incident, the *Spokesman Review* reported in 2013 that several women who were members of a local country club in Spokane, Washington, won a judgment against the country club after they were excluded from some activities and facilities because they were women. One of the litigants reported, for example, that she was not allowed to enter a room at the club exclusively assigned to men when she wanted to speak to her husband, who was in the room.

Questions

- Did the Augusta National Golf Club have the right to restrict membership to men? Did the country club in Spokane have the right to restrict access to certain activities and facilities to men? After all, they are private clubs. And aren't there other organizations and activities that restrict memberships to women or to members of specific racial groups?
- Were these policies based on sexism, and were they indicators of prejudice and discrimination against women?

Example 3: National Public Radio "Appalled" by Former Executive's Criticism of Republicans and the Tea Party

As reported by *Yahoo! News* (2011), former NPR executive Ron Schiller was shown in a hidden camera video saying that the current Republican Party had been "hijacked" by people who are "not just Islamophobic, but really xenophobic", and suggesting some Tea Party followers are "seriously racist, racist people." He also said that he's proud of NPR's firing of Juan Williams for expressing fear of flying with people in "Muslim garb."

NPR spokesperson Dana Ravis Rehm said, "We are appalled by comments made by Ron Schiller in the video, which are contrary to what NPR stands for." Mr. Schiller later announced that he was leaving NPR for another job.

The hidden-camera video was released by conservative filmmaker James O'Keefe (Yahoo! News 2011).

Questions

- Was Mr. Schiller expressing prejudice against Republicans and the Tea Party movement?
- Was NPR spokeswoman Dana Davis Rehm justified in saying that NPR was appalled by Mr. Schiller's comments?

Example 4: Republican National Convention Attendees Removed for Reportedly Heckling Black Camerawoman

Slate.com (2012) reported that two people attending the Republican National Convention (RNC) in Tampa Bay threw nuts at a Black CNN camerawoman and said, "This is how we feed the animals."

After multiple witnesses reported the incident, RNC security and police immediately escorted the two people out of the convention hall.

Question

- Why do you think the two people in the story above threw nuts at the camera operator?

Example 5: "Are Racists Dumb?"

HuffPost Science (2012) reported results of a study published in *Psychological Science* that suggest that people who score low on IQ tests in childhood are more likely to develop prejudicial beliefs and socially conservative politics in adulthood. Authored by researchers from Brock University in Ontario, this study is discussed in Chapter 6 ("Where Do Prejudices Come From?") of this book.

Questions

- Do you believe that conservatives tend to be less intelligent?
- Is this just prejudiced opinion masquerading as science?

Example 6: Bill O'Reilly Says Harlem Restaurant Just Like Other Restaurants

The Associated Press (September 9, 2007) reported that Fox News Channel's Bill O'Reilly (no longer with Fox News) told a radio audience that after eating dinner at a well-known Harlem restaurant, he "couldn't get over the fact" that there was no difference between Sylvia's and other restaurants. "It was like going into an Italian restaurant in an all-White suburb in the sense of people were sitting there, and they were ordering and having fun. And there wasn't any kind of craziness at all," he said.

O'Reilly said that his experience at Sylvia's pointed to racial progress. "And that's really what this society is all about now here in the USA. There's no difference." He added, "That's right, there wasn't one person in Sylvia's who was screaming, 'M.F.-er, I want more iced tea.'"

Media Matters for America, a liberal media watchdog, distributed a transcript and an audio clip of O'Reilly's comments on the internet.

The AP quoted Bill Shine, senior vice president for programming at Fox News Channel, as saying, "This is nothing more than left-wing outlets stirring up false racism accusations for ratings. It's sad."

Questions

- Were Bill O'Reilly's remarks racist?
- Do you agree with Bill Shine that criticisms of O'Reilly's remarks were left-wing, false racism accusations for ratings?

Example 7: Jurors Reportedly Call Japanese American Lawyer "Mr. Kamikaze"

The *Spokesman Review* (2009) reported that jurors in a malpractice trial reportedly made derogatory comments about the heritage of one of the plaintiff's attorneys. According to the newspaper, a Washington State University professor told a presiding judge that five of his fellow jurors called attorney Mark Kamitomo "Mr. Kamikaze," "Mr. Miyashi," and "Mr. Miyagi," a character in *The Karate Kid*. Mr. Kamitomo was representing a family who sued a physician for malpractice. The jury found no malpractice; a Superior Court judge ordered a new trial after two of the twelve jurors gave sworn statements about other jurors' comments about Mr. Kamitomo. The doctor appealed, seeking to reinstate the jury's decision.

Questions

- Were the jurors' remarks racist?
- Were complaints about the jurors' remarks taking political correctness too far?

Example 8: Racial Harassment Complaints at University of California at San Diego

According to *The Chronicle of Higher Education* (2012), a Facebook invitation for an off-campus party at the University of California at San Diego asked women to dress as "ghetto chicks," and said that watermelon, chicken, and malt liquor would be provided. The party was called the "Compton Cookout." The invitation, along with other past incidents including public displays of hanging nooses and a Ku Klux Klan-style hood, prompted student protests. The president of the University of California system responded to the incident on his Facebook page: "It has no place in civilized society, and it will not be tolerated—not on this particular campus, not on any University of California campus," he wrote.

Questions

- Why did the students responsible for these incidents behave as they did?
- Do you agree or disagree that these acts were racist?
- If you agree that they were racist, what can a university do to prevent their occurrences?

Example 9: University of Texas Criticizes "Catch an Illegal Immigrant Game" Planned by Students

The Chronicle of Higher Education (2013) reported that the Young Conservatives of Texas (YCT) student group at the University of Texas (Austin) planned to stage a "Catch an Illegal Immigrant" game to encourage "a campus-wide conversation about illegal immigration." The group proposed to give $25 gift cards to students who "caught" people walking around campus wearing "illegal immigrant" labels.

According to *the Chronicle of Higher Education*, William C. Powers Jr., the University's president, said the proposed event was "completely out of line" with the university's values. He added, "Our nation continues to grapple with difficult questions surrounding immigration. I ask YCT to be part of that discussion but to find more productive and respectful ways to do so that do not demean their fellow students."

The YCT subsequently agreed not to hold the game.

The YCT at the University of Texas (Austin) in the past had been similarly criticized for holding an "affirmative action bake sale" in which it sold items to students at prices that varied depending on their race and gender.

Questions

- Was the game racist and prejudicial, or was it an effective way of encouraging a "campus-wide conversation about illegal immigration"?
- Should YCT have carried on its plans to hold the game?

Example 10: Four Students at San Jose State University Accused of Harassment

The Associated Press (2013) reported that four White students at San Jose State University faced police charges after taunting their Black freshman dorm-mate with racial slurs, hanging a Confederate flag in their dormitory suite, barricading the dorm-mate in his room, and placing a U-shaped bicycle lock around his neck.

According to the Associated Press, the Reverend Jethroe Moore II, president of the San Jose/Silicon Valley NAACP, said, "This is not simply hazing or bullying. This is obviously racially based terrorism targeted at their African-American roommate. The community will not stand idly by and allow for any student of color to be terrorized simply due to the color of his skin."

The Reverend Moore II and other civil rights leaders called on prosecutors to file felony hate-crime charges against the accused four students.

Questions

- Were the acts of the White students hazing, or were the acts hate crimes?
- Why did the White students act in this way?
- How should they be dealt with?

Example 11: Dutch Santa Claus's Helpers in Blackface Elicit Protests

The Associated Press (2013) reported that protestors in the Netherlands called a Dutch Christmas tradition racist. The protestors were referring to "Petes": dozens of Dutch Santa Claus helpers or servants who wear blackface, red lipstick, and frizzy Afro wigs. Petes leave cookies, chocolate, and other treats for children in mid-November until December 5. According to the protestors, Petes are "blatant racist caricatures" and should be banned.

Supporters of the holiday tradition said that Pete is a "positive figure of fun," and that the dissent is "a sign of political correctness gone overboard."

According to the Associated Press, about ninety percent of the Dutch have European ancestry, and a large majority felt that there is no racial insult intended by Black Pete.

The AP also reported that Verene Shepherd, head of the UN Working Group of Experts on People of African Descent, said on Dutch TV she "does not understand why it is that people in the Netherlands cannot see that this is a throwback to slavery and that, in the twenty-first century, this practice should stop."

Questions

- Is Black Pete a racist caricature, or is he simply a positive figure of fun?
- What should the Dutch do about the Petes?

Do These Examples Express Prejudice?

From the perspectives of the people or organizations accused of prejudice in the examples above, their words and actions do not express prejudice but simply are commonsense responses to the realities they were facing or innocent responses to the situations without any malicious intent. Here are some possible "justifications" that they may have invoked:

- "In the aftermath of 9/11, the airlines have every reason to take extraordinary measures to prevent terrorist attacks. Some Muslim organizations have declared the United States to be a primary target."
- "Women have special privileges and activities at golf and country clubs. Sexism is not a reason for special privileges and activities made available to men only."
- "Aren't some Democrats—like some Republicans—'Islamophobic'? Not all Tea Party members are racist. I was talking the realities. Besides, I was quoted out of context."
- "We were throwing nuts to express our displeasure at television journalists in general, not because she was African American."
- "By saying that an African American restaurant is just like any other American restaurant, I was paying a compliment. Give me a break!"
- "I was paying a compliment to the Japanese American lawyer. Mr. Miyagi was an honorable character in *The Karate Kid.*"
- "We [students] were just trying to have some fun. We did not intend to insult or harm anybody."

From these possible responses to accusations of prejudice, it's not difficult to see that most people actually do not consider themselves to be prejudiced. And, in fact, research has shown that a very small minority of

Americans, less than twenty percent, reveal themselves to be prejudiced in tests of explicit prejudice—that is, when they are asked in very direct language whether they think other groups are inferior or less deserving of the rights and privileges they enjoy (Greenwald and Krieger 2006; Nosek 2005). But implicit biases are another matter. Research shows that even the most professed egalitarians among us have implicit biases, measured indirectly by association tests discussed in more detail in Chapter 3 (What Is Prejudice?). Implicit biases are our unconscious judgments of people from groups other than those with which we identify closely, such as other racial groups or religions. We are not conscious of these biases, but our behaviors and words are often guided and even directed by them. About eighty percent of the two-million–plus people who have taken an Implicit Associations Test (discussed in Chapter 3) have implicit biases (Nosek, Greenwald, and Banaji 2005). The percentage in the general population is probably higher, considering that people most likely to take the test are, in the first, place, those interested in reducing their own prejudices.

Let's assume, for the sake of argument, that the people accused of prejudice in Examples 1 through 7 are indeed not explicitly prejudiced. However, based on the research, it is quite likely that they were acting on hidden or implicit biases, and their actions and words had very real and damaging effects on their subjects. A major question, then, and a key focus of this book, is whether and how these implicit biases can be controlled to minimize the damage to other people.

"I Am Not Prejudiced, But ..."

Because almost all of us do not admit to our prejudices, or may not even be aware of them, how do we explain beliefs and actions that consider others to be less desirable or less valuable than ourselves? Understanding how we rationalize our biases is a crucial step toward understanding the role of communication in reinforcing and, conversely, reducing prejudice. Many of the strategies we use to rationalize our prejudices are indeed communication-based, or, more particularly, they use semantics that mask negative feelings and evaluations of other groups.

A study of how college students "mask" their unconscious biases gives us some indication of how a relatively well-educated and egalitarian group rationalizes prejudice. The authors of the study (Bonilla-Silva and Forman 2000) found that White college students expressed more prejudice toward racial minorities in face-to-face interviews than they did in their responses in survey instruments that included direct questions on their feelings regarding the same minorities. The students used what the authors called "race-talk" in the interviews to avoid appearing racist. That is, they would profess to be supportive of minorities and then continue on with the "buts." For example, students were asked if they were in favor of or opposed to interracial marriage. As reported by Bonilla-Silva and Foreman (2000), here are some responses.

A male student:

Uh ... (sighs) ... I would say that I agree with that, I guess. I mean ... *I would say that I really don't have much of a problem with it, but when you, ya know. If I were to ask if I had a daughter or something like that, or even one of my sisters, um ... were to going to get married to a minority or a Black, I ... I would probably...it would probably bother me a little bit* just because of what you said. ... Like the children and how it would ... might do to our family as it is. Um ... so I mean, just being honest, I guess that's the way I feel about that. (61)

A female student:

I certainly don't oppose the marriage, not at all. Um ... *depending on where I am, if I had to have a concern, yes, it would be for the children.* ... Ya know, it can be nasty and then other kids wouldn't even notice, I think ... *I could care less what anyone else does with their lives, as long as they are really happy.* And if the parents can set a really strong foundation at home, it can be conquered, *but I'm not sure, in some places, it could cause a problem.* (60)

Responses to the interracial marriage and other questions asked in the interviews illustrate how people use rhetorical strategies to present a socially desirable "self." Most people, particularly those who are well-educated like college students, recognize that our (American) society does not approve of racism. Therefore, to be consistent with a desired self-image to be nonracist, we publicly profess to support nonracist policies and practices and then use rhetorical strategies to mask our true feelings (in this case, beliefs that some races should not intermarry). To present a nonracist image, we do not explicitly say that we oppose close contact with minorities, as in interracial marriage, but we qualify our support with rhetorical strategies such as *apparent agreement* (a formal statement of support), *apparent admission* (qualifying support by citing instances of nonsupport, such as, in the quotes above, "the children"), *displacement* (concerns for the children and for how interracial marriages would be accepted in some places), and *indirectness* (interracial marriage is fine "as long as they are really happy") (Bonilla-Silva and Forman 2000). By utilizing these linguistic strategies, we effectively qualify our professed nonracist beliefs and reveal possible hidden biases.

So, is anybody out there prejudiced? According to the Associated Press (2014), Cliven Bundy, a Nevada rancher involved in a "fight" with the government over grazing rights on federal land, referred to Black people in an interview with the *New York Times* as "the Negro" and wondered if they were "better off as slaves" than "under government subsidy." He recalled driving past homes in Las Vegas and seeing Black people who "didn't have nothing to do." At a news conference after the *Times* interview, Bundy repeated the same sentiment, asking, "Are they slaves to charities and government subsidized homes? And are they slaves when their daughters are having abortions and their sons are in prisons?" The AP reported that the official Bundy ranch Facebook page said that Bundy was a "good man, he loves all people, he is not a racist man."

In this chapter, I have presented a rationale for studying prejudice and communication, proposing that communication is a common vehicle for transmitting prejudice, can reinforce and cause prejudice, but can also reduce prejudice. Citing real-world examples of prejudice, I have illustrated how prejudice might be explained away because explicit prejudice is not socially acceptable and not readily admitted to by most of us, although, as research shows, almost all of us do have implicit biases that direct our evaluations of and behaviors toward people who are not like us. Many of the strategies we use to mask our prejudices are based on rhetorical strategies of self-justification to save face. Therefore, language and communication are central to our understanding of how prejudice is reinforced and can be reduced.

In the next chapter, we will take a closer look at communication—its definitions, its measures, its theories, and how it is related to prejudice.

Workbook

Define, describe, or illustrate; summarize the results of the studies:

1.   Stereotypes, prejudice, discrimination: definitions

2.   Incidents described in the book are examples of what?

3.   Masking unconscious biases: apparent agreement, apparent admission; displacement, indirectness

2

Communication and Prejudice

A main thesis of this book is that communication is central to the development, reinforcement, and maintenance of prejudice in individuals and societies. At the same time, communication is a key tool for reducing prejudice. In this chapter, let's take a closer look at communication and how it impacts prejudice.

(Author's note: Portions of this chapter are adapted from my textbook, *Mass Communication Theories and Research,* 2nd ed., 1986, Macmillan Publishing Co.)

Communication as a subject of scientific inquiry is not unique to the field of journalism and mass communication. Psychologists, sociologists, political scientists, anthropologists, mathematicians, engineers, sociologists, and speech communicators all study communication. This is not surprising, because communication is the fundamental social process of humans. It is needed to build up any form of social or group structure. Thus, disciplines concerned in any way with humans—individuals, groups, communities, societies—include the study of communication. This has led to many definitions and uses of the concept. Let's consider typical definitions from various fields.

Charles Cooley gave this sociological definition:

By communication is here meant the mechanism through which human relations exist and develop—all the symbols of the mind, together with the means of conveying them through space and preserving them in time. It includes the expression of the face, attitude and gesture, the tones of the voice, words, writing, printing, railways, telegraphs, telephones, and whatever else may be the latest achievement in the conquest of time and space. (Cooley 1966)

Two engineers, Claude Shannon and Warren Weaver, defined communication in this way:

The word communication will be used here in a very broad sense to include all the procedures by which one mind may affect another. This, of course, involves not only written and oral speech, but also music, the pictorial arts, the theatre, the ballet, and in fact all human behavior. (Shannon and Weaver 1949)

A biologically based definition was given by E. Colin Cherry:

Communication ... is that which links any organism together. Here "organism" may mean two friends in conversation, newspapers and their reading public, a country and its postal service and telephone system. At another level it may refer to the nervous system of an animal, while at another it may relate to a civilization and its culture. When communication ceases, the organism breaks up. (Cherry 1957)

S. S. Stevens, a behavioral psychologist, defined communication as follows:

The discriminatory response of an organism to a stimulus. This definition says that communication occurs when some environmental disturbance (the stimulus) impinges on an organism and the organism does something about it (makes a discriminatory response). If the stimulus is ignored by the organism, there has been no communication. The test is differential reaction of some sort. The message that gets no response is not a communication. (Stevens 1966)

A simple definition was given by Harold Lasswell:

A convenient way to describe the act of communication is to answer the following questions: Who says What in Which Channel To Whom With What Effect? (Lasswell 1948)

Wilbur Schramm, a pioneer in mass communication research, offered this definition:

When we communicate we are trying to share information, an idea, or an attitude. Communication always requires at least three elements—the source, the message, and the destination. (Schramm 1954)

This list of classic definitions—older but nonetheless influencing current definitions—is by no means complete. However, it is a representative sampling of definitions from the very broad to the specific. The definitions by Cooley and by Shannon and Weaver include in the study of communication all forms of human interaction or behaviors that can affect another person, intentionally or unintentionally. These include not only communicating using a verbal language, but also gestures, facial expressions, paintings, pictures, the arts, and technology. Stevens offers still a broader definition. To him, communication occurs whenever an organism reacts or responds to some object or stimulus in the environment, which may not even be from another person. Thus, a person taking shelter from a thunderstorm, or blinking the eyes in response to a flash of lightning, is communicating.

To Cherry, communication binds two persons (or organisms) together in a relationship that can exist only so long as communication continues. Schramm specifies the nature of this relationship—it is sharing of information. He defines information, as Shannon and Weaver did, as "any content that reduces uncertainty." Lasswell identifies the necessary components in communication as source, message, channel, receiver, and effect. Although these definitions vary in the number and kinds of behaviors that would be included in the study of communication, they all share a concern with effect or response—communication occurs only if the organism (e.g., a human) reacts to the message or stimulus in some way.

A Transactional Model of Communication

Most definitions of communication discussed above are transactional and purposive. Transactional communication is when all parties are actively involved in the process and have the chance of gaining something (such as attainment of a goal) from participating. Communication is purposive when it is goal-directed; that is, all parties participate because they would like to gain something by participating in the process. Tan (1986) proposed the transactional model of communication shown in Figure 2.1.

In this model, communication begins with a source, the initiating agent of the transaction. The source could be one person, a group of persons, a community, or a society. A social group consists of two or more people who interact with one another and who share at least one common unifying bond, such as common interests or common goals. Examples would be student groups on a university campus, such as fraternities, sororities, athletic clubs, debate societies, women in communication groups, and clubs based on academic interest. A community is a relatively small social unit, usually larger than a group and made up of many groups, comprised of individuals interacting with each other who share common values and have a sense of shared

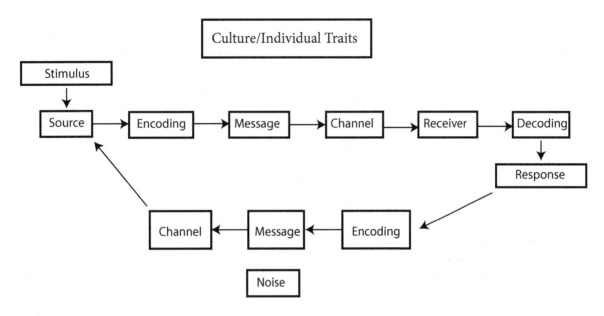

Figure 2.1 A Transactional Model of Communication.

emotional connection, integration, and cohesion (see, e.g., McMillan and Chavis 1986). We could speak of a community of students at a university, a community of communication scholars interested in prejudice and communication, or a community of environmental activists. A community need not occupy the same physical space; it could develop virtually through the internet. A society consists of large social groups made up of individuals who share a common culture, institutions, laws, political authority, and social stratification (Lensk, 1974). Members of a society are less attached to each other than are members of a community; they are motivated to societal membership primarily out of self-interest, such as preservation of resources. Individuals, groups, communities, and societies can all generate messages to communicate: an individual by carrying on a conversation with another individual, a group by oral statements in a meeting, a community by an announcement in a newsletter, or a society through official statements of its leaders via the mass media.

In this transactional model, communication begins when a source reacts to a stimulus in the environment. A stimulus is any object, person, event, thought, or emotion that incites the source to action. It could be in the source's immediate environment or sensory field (i.e., it can be seen, felt, or heard); it is recognized by the source who consciously responds by initiating communication or sharing a response with a receiver, who may be another person, group, community, or society. Communication will have occurred if the source shares a response to the stimulus with a receiver. If the source notices or is aware of a stimulus but does not share a response, communication has not occurred. The key element is that the source is consciously or knowingly responding to a stimulus and is consciously sharing this response with a receiver. For example, in writing this book, I am responding to former students in a Communication and Prejudice class who wanted a different textbook from the one we were using. My response was to write a sample chapter and send it to students, and to ask them to evaluate it. I was the source responding to student comments (the stimulus) and sending a message (the sample chapter I wrote) back to them. Here's another example: I am in a clothing store that sells expensive clothes. I begin to sort through possible purchases, and a sales clerk who was at the checkout stand leaves his station, approaches me, and offers assistance. I notice a young man with a handful of shirts and slacks at the same checkout stand, waiting to be helped. I tell the clerk to help him first. Clearly, at any given moment, a communicator could respond to an infinite number of stimuli in the environment. The selection of which stimuli to respond to is selective, and depends on a conscious purpose on the part of the communicator. This form of communication is also known as *purposive* communication.

In a purposive model of communication, a source will be directed by goals that are conscious, deliberate, and in most cases, self-serving. These goals are shown in Figure 2.2 (Tan 1986). The first goal is to inform the receiver of threats and opportunities in the environment, or simply to provide "knowledge" that will help the receiver adapt to or deal with the environment. An example is a news report of home burglaries in a neighborhood. This information warns residents of a threat so that they will be able to deal with it, such as by locking doors. A second goal is to teach the receiver how to apply knowledge or other information transmitted by a source. Teaching then goes beyond imparting information. The purpose of teaching, as seen in Figure 2.2, is to deliver information so that the receiver can apply skills and knowledge necessary to function effectively in the community, or in a broader sense, to learn appropriate behaviors and roles for acceptance in the community. An example is my teaching you (hopefully) with this book how to apply interventions to reduce prejudice in your everyday life. Another example is parents teaching their children to value multiculturalism. A third purpose of communication is to persuade, that is, to change attitudes, beliefs, and behaviors of the receiver in a direction determined by the source, and, usually, for the source's benefit. Examples are advertisements for a product, political advertisements, or a flyer you may have received for or against gun control. A fourth purpose is to please (usually through entertainment) and to satisfy receiver needs. Entertainment programming in television is a good example. Generally these programs do not consciously (or intentionally) seek to inform, teach, or persuade. Their purpose is to satisfy the receivers' need to be entertained, although, in reality, the bottom-line goal is to make money for advertisers, producers, and the companies that deliver the programs to the audience.

Because communication is transactional, meaning that sources and receivers will engage if each party gets a reward (or avoids punishment) from engagement, receivers will have corresponding goals, shown in Table 2.1, for participating. The list shown in Figure 2.2 is not exhaustive. Neither are the discrete purposes mutually exclusive; in reality, they often overlap. However, the list gives you an idea of the major purposes or goals of communication that are conscious and deliberate.

TABLE 2.1   Purposes of Communication (From Tan 1986)

Communicator's Goals	Receiver's Goals
1. To inform	1. To learn of threats and opportunities; to understand the environment
2. To teach	2. To acquire skills and knowledge; to learn community values, behaviors, and rules
3. To persuade	3. To reach decisions; to make choices
4. To please, to satisfy receiver needs	4. To enjoy, relax, be entertained, be distracted from problems

Unconscious Communication

So far, we have considered communication as a conscious, purposive act. But it's also possible for communication to occur unconsciously in a nondeliberate way. In fact, we learn and express most of our prejudices unconsciously, as we shall see later in this chapter. A large body of research in psychology has recently shown that humans are not always (some would say not often) in conscious control of our actions. That is, our actions and thoughts are influenced by suppressed thoughts (as in memories), experiences, and implicit biases that we may not be aware of but nevertheless that influence our behaviors (e.g., Bargh et al. 2012). These unconscious predispositions are "primed" by the presence of stimuli in our environment, influencing responses to the stimuli. In unconscious communication, the source is not aware that it is responding to a stimulus, which may be a thought or emotion from memory or past experiences, but there is a response nonetheless. Communication occurs when the response is directed at a receiver. Unconscious communication, from this viewpoint, consists of the subtle, unintentional, unconscious, involuntary cues that provide information to another individual (Chandler 2008). These cues often convey emotion such as liking or disliking, and can be verbal (in language) or nonverbal, such as in facial expressions and body language. As an example, have you ever said something to another person and then wondered, *What did I say and why did I say that?* Another example: I listen attentively to a request from a student to take a makeup test, while with another student, I am dismissive and short. I do not mean to be attentive to one and short with the other, but my teaching assistant, who observes the interaction, says that I am. Then I wonder, *Why am I responding to these students differently, when I should be treating them in the same way? Am I involuntarily expressing these communication cues—indicative of liking and disliking—because of some unconscious bias?* Most likely I am. As we shall see later in this chapter, prejudice is often communicated unconsciously.

Encoding the Message

Regardless of whether communication is conscious or unconscious, the response to the stimulus will have to be transformed into signs shared by the source and receiver for communication to occur. This process is called *encoding*. A *sign* is an object existing in the real world, meaning that the receiver can see, touch, hear, or otherwise consciously know that it is in the receiver's environment. It is an object the source uses to designate the stimulus and the source's response to the stimulus, which was the impetus for communication in the first place. Put simply, a sign conveys meaning and information from the source to the receiver (see, e.g., Thibault 1996) and can be composed of sounds, gestures, letters, images, pictures, or other symbols, or just about any object or behavior that the source uses, consciously or unconsciously, to represent its response to the stimulus. For example, I am using words, combinations of words, phrases, sentences, and paragraphs to encode my message (communication and prejudice) to you in this book. An architect used the Vietnam Veterans Memorial in Washington, DC, a piece of architecture, to convey respect for and admiration of Vietnam veterans. Some White supremacist groups use the Nazi double cross symbol and Hitler's image to express their belief in White supremacy and admiration for Nazi beliefs that races should be kept separate. The film director Ang Lee used moving images and visuals to tell a story about the oneness of life in *Life of Pi*. For communication to occur, source and receiver should, at the most fundamental level, share or recognize the signs that are used in encoding. Examples include language, symbols, or gestures recognized and shared by both source and receiver. Although signs are intended by the source to represent a "real" object or event, their interpretation or meaning depends very much on the cultures of the source and receiver. *Culture* is a system of shared beliefs, values, behavioral norms, and worldviews in a community that is handed down from generation to generation. As the research in intercultural relations and communications has shown us, the worldviews or ways of interpreting the environment can be very different between cultures or even between subcultures, such as within the United States. When source and receiver do not interpret or attach the same meanings to signs encoded by the source, communication won't be successful.

Words are often used as signs. Although intended to objectively signify the same object, a word can have different meanings attached by source and receiver depending on experiences and values that they bring to the communication interaction. Take the word "terrorist." You and I and almost every other American will agree that a terrorist is a person who is to be despised and who deserves to be prosecuted as a criminal because he or she commits crimes against humanity, that is, kills and injures innocent people in the name of a political or religious cause. This is certainly the meaning that we attach to the word "terrorist" and the meaning that I was using in a talk in the Middle East on stereotyping and the media. I was speaking at an academic conference in Amman, Jordan, which was attended by media researchers and professionals mostly from the Middle East. I was making a point about how American media often stereotype non-Americans inaccurately and unfairly to appeal to the largest audience, American news and entertainment need "villains" to add drama and excitement to their programs. To illustrate, I presented results of a study I had just completed, which showed, first, that Arabs were often stereotyped as terrorists in the media and, second, that this stereotype was accepted to be "true" by large segments of the American public. A gentleman in traditional Arab dress raised his hand during the question-and-answer period, and, speaking in Arabic (which was translated simultaneously into English and delivered to me by earphones), told me that in some communities in the Middle East, the word "terrorist" actually meant "hero" and "martyr," and being called a terrorist by Americans and the American media was actually an honor and not an insult. Therefore, in some Arab communities, the stereotype of Arabs as terrorists, and as depicted in American media, was not a negative portrayal at all. He completed his remarks by stating that, unequivocally, he was not a terrorist and did not approve of terrorism, given American usage of the word. I thanked him for his remarks, and said that the meanings attached to the word "terrorist" can indeed be variable, depending on the culture of the source or receiver, and that meanings of signs are subject to different interpretations.

As we have seen, a sign can be just about anything in the environment of the source and receiver that both can perceive—or sense that it is "there." Because our focus in this book is communication, we shall limit our discussion of signs to verbal, nonverbal, and visual communications.

Verbal Communication

Humans are uniquely qualified among animal species to adapt to (or even master) the environment by building communities consisting of members who cooperate and act collectively. This ability is made possible through the use of an advanced signal—such as language (see, e.g., Evans and Levinson 2009). A general definition of *language* is that it is a formal system of signs and rules that relate particular signs to particular meanings (Thibault 1996). We confine our discussion here to a definition of language as verbal—that is, it is a code that uses words, phrases, and sentences to convey meanings (Evans and Levinson 2009) and that can be transmitted orally using voice (speech) or in written form. A useful tool for understanding how verbal language can be used by a source to transmit different meanings is the Linguistic Category Model (LCM) (Maas 1999; Ruscher 2001). The LCM says that a source, in constructing a message such as describing an observed event to a receiver, has a choice of several linguistic categories with different levels of abstraction. Each linguistic category transmits a very different meaning than any of the other categories do. These categories, from the most concrete (i.e., description of the observed event that is closest to the "facts") to the most abstract, are listed and defined below (Ruscher 2001).

- *Descriptive action verb:* Refers to specific behavior without interpretation. For example, John shoves Bill; Susan touches Jim's arm.
- *Interpretative action verb:* Refers to a specific behavior but with interpretation. For example, John hits Bill; Susan caresses Jim.
- *State verb:* Infers an actor's cognitive or emotional state in describing motivation for a specific behavior. For example, John despises Bill; Susan loves Jim.
- *Adjective:* Refers to an actor's character trait or internal disposition without referring to the specific behavior. For example: John is aggressive; Susan is affectionate.

As can be seen from this list of linguistic categories at the disposal of the source, very different meanings can be transmitted to the receiver, depending on which category is used. A source's use of linguistic categories, whether conscious or unconscious, is influenced by the source's perception of the actor in the observed event (the stimuli instigating the communication). The more strongly the actors are perceived negatively or positively, the more likely the source will use a higher level of abstraction to describe the actors or the observed event. Thus, language is a powerful tool to convey meanings that go beyond describing people or their behaviors.

Nonverbal Communication

In human communication, meanings are conveyed not only by words but also by physical signals accompanying the words, or nonverbal signals. These nonverbal signals transmit information about the thoughts, feelings, and intentions of the source when the message is encoded and sent to the receiver, as well as the thoughts, feelings, and intentions of the receiver as he or she decodes the message. It's been estimated that about two-thirds of all human communication is nonverbal (Hogan and Stubbs 2003). In general, nonverbal communication has five primary functions (Argyle 1988):

1. To express emotions accompanying the experiential state of the source as he or she is encoding the message and of the receiver as he or she is decoding the message.
2. To express interpersonal attitudes, such as feelings the source has toward the receiver.
3. To manage the interaction between source and receiver to accompany speech, such as leaning forward to make a point.
4. To augment self-presentation, such as standing erect with hands behind the back, to project authority.
5. To define rituals or greetings, such as a handshake, bow, or hug.

In addition to expressing the source's feelings about the receiver, nonverbal signals also express the experiential state, or emotions felt, by the source as he or she encodes the message, which may not necessarily be directed at the receiver (see, e.g., Friedman and Elliot 2008). For example, my nervousness—an experiential state—in speaking before you may be expressed by my drumming my fingers on the lectern and the excessive movement of my arms and feet. The range of nonverbal signals is limitless, but, in general, the following behaviors are involved in nonverbal communication:

- *Facial expressions* refer to voluntary (conscious) or involuntary (unconscious or not controlled by the source) movements of the mouth, lips, eyes, nose, forehead, and jaw. The human face is estimated to be capable of more than 10,000 different expressions (Ekman 2004). The expression of emotions through facial movements varies across cultures, but the facial expressions for happiness, sadness, anger, fear, surprise, disgust, shame, and interest are similar across cultures throughout the world (Ekman 2004). Facial expressions of emotion can be negative or positive. Negative emotions are generally expressed by tightening of the jaw, furrowing of the forehead, squinting of the eyes, or "lip occlusion" (lips seemingly disappearing or appearing smaller). Positive emotions are generally expressed by loosening of the furrowed lines on the forehead, relaxation of the muscles around the mouth, and widening of the eyes (Navarro 2008). Because the expression of facial emotions is influenced by culture (some cultures are more expressive than others), and because some people can manipulate their facial expressions to convey emotions they don't feel in pursuit of self-presentation goals (e.g., a leader wanting to appear calm before her followers), the interpretation of facial expressions is far from an exact science and should not be overinterpreted. However, it is informative to know that in some contexts, facial expressions can and do transmit meanings not carried by verbal messages.
- *Paralinguistics* refers to variances in vocal delivery that are separate from language, Examples are tone of voice, loudness, inflection, and pitch, which can all influence how the verbal message is interpreted by the receiver. Again, the meanings assigned to paralinguistics are influenced by culture. Speaking in a loud voice may be seen as projecting authority and confidence in one culture but as impolite and disrespectful in another.
- *Gestures* refer to conscious (deliberate) or unconscious movements of the hands, arms, body, head, face, and eyes. Gestures may be used to convey a message (meanings) independently of words, provided there is agreement within a culture as to their meanings. Examples are the "Shaka" sign in Hawaii and the peace sign in the late 1960s and early 1970s. Gestures can also be used by the communication source to add meaning to verbal messages, such as with hand waving or pointing. As with other forms of nonverbal communication, the use and meanings assigned to gestures are culture-specific.

Gestures that convey positive emotions in one culture may be interpreted as improper and offensive in another (see, e.g., Pease 2004). Here are some examples: In Western cultures, gesturing with the hand is an acceptable signal to "come here, please." The same gesture is offensive in many Asian countries because it is commonly used to call dogs. In Western cultures, it is generally impolite to stick out one's tongue at another person; in Polynesia, the gesture is a sign of greeting and reverence (Kirch 1979). Of course, in the modern era of global communications facilitated by the internet and accessible travel, the cultural specificity of meanings assigned to gestures may be moving to universal understanding and acceptance, for better or for worse. The point is, these gestures convey meanings, intended or unintended by the source, and should be deciphered within the context of culture.

- *Body language and posture* complement gestures and convey additional meanings to words. Examples are slouching, towering, spreading legs, thrusting the jaw, putting shoulders forward, arm crossing, and leg crossing. Postures, whether conscious or unconscious, can convey emotions (liking or disliking) that the communication source feels toward the communication receiver, differences in status, and attention level or interest (Bull 1987). An "open" body stance such as a forward lean expresses liking and interest, while a defensive body stance such as leaning backward expresses dislike. Again, these interpretations are culturally based and influenced heavily by studies in Western societies. Whether there is a universal system of body language and posture is debatable. We should therefore refrain from overgeneralizing these interpretations. The point is that we should pay attention to additional meanings that body language and posture express, but always in the context of cultures of the source and receiver.

- *Proxemics* refers to how people use and perceive the physical space around them (Hargie and Dickson 2004). In general, the less space between the source and receiver, the more intimate the interaction is, and this is indicative of interest and liking. However, the interpretation of space is influenced by culture. What is appropriate space—and the intimacy interpretation of less space—in one culture may not be true in another. Although generalizations to entire cultures are often hazardous and inaccurate, research in intercultural communications nonetheless has suggested some differences in how cultures regard space. For example, some studies indicate that preferred distance between people engaged in some form of person-to-person interaction is much closer for Latin Americans, the French, Italians, and Arabs compared to White Americans, in general. According to Kirch (1979), here are some general guidelines for close-distance groups: One foot is for lovers, one-and-a-half to four feet is for family and friends, and four to twelve feet is for strangers. The principle suggested is that, again, within what is commonly accepted in the cultures of source and receiver, shorter distance expresses more liking and interest.

- *Eye contact or gazing* is defined as looking at the other person while talking and listening. In Western societies, liking and attentiveness are expressed by the duration of mutual gazing; the longer the gaze, the more liking and intimacy between the communication participants (Hogan and Stubbs 2003). However, in many other cultures such as Hispanic, Asian, Middle Eastern, and Native American, eye contact is considered to be a sign of disrespect or rudeness, and a lack of eye contact does not necessarily mean a lack of interest (Kirch 1979). Also, studies of gender differences in Western societies indicate that heterosexual women may avoid eye contact with men because eye contact can be misinterpreted as a sign of sexual attraction (Kirch 1979).

- *Haptics* is the study of how touching in communication adds meaning to words and visuals. Common touching in Western societies includes handshakes, holding hands, kissing (cheek, lips, hand), backslapping, high fives, a pat on the shoulder, and brushing an arm (Knapp & Hall, 2009). The interpretation of the meanings of touch is dependent on the context of the interaction, the relationship between source and receiver, what touch is used, and culture. Touching that is appropriate in one culture may be disrespectful in another. For example, in the West, a handshake conveys "Thank you," "It's a deal," or "Glad to meet you," among other meanings. While the handshake is becoming universally accepted to convey these meanings, a bow of the head may be more appropriate in Japan and China; a slight kiss ("buzz") on the cheek between men may be more appropriate in the Middle East. And, certainly, in Islamic countries, any form of touching, including a handshake, between men and women in a business or social context is generally inappropriate or even forbidden. To illustrate, here's an example: On my way to give a lecture in a Middle Eastern country, I was met at the airport by my female guide, who was to facilitate the process of clearing customs and immigration. She spoke perfect English and was very efficient. I was out of the airport in record time, and she escorted me to a car that was to take me to my hotel. She was wearing a "hijab"; that is, her head was covered by a scarf. To say goodbye and express a big thank-you, I just about grabbed her hand to shake it, out of habit. She recoiled and put her hand on her side. With a big smile, she told me that she appreciated my thanks but could not shake my hand. This was a lesson that I wish I had learned in my US State Department briefing—or, I suppose I should have known better!

In this section, I have presented to you how nonverbal communications can convey conscious (deliberate) and unconscious (not deliberate) meanings to verbal communication. The main points I would like to leave you with are that (1) most meanings in communication are indeed expressed nonverbally, and (2) the meanings expressed by nonverbal communication are heavily dependent on culture—these meanings differ from culture to culture, and depend on the context of communication. Research has identified some general differences between cultures, particularly between East and West. As America becomes more multicultural, and as global communication facilitates more direct and indirect interactions between cultures, the meanings of nonverbal signs should be evaluated in every communication interaction, particularly those having to do with liking or disliking. At the very least, communication sources and receivers should be aware that meanings are indeed conveyed by nonverbal signs.

Visual Communication

Is a picture really worth a thousand words? Most communication relies heavily on visuals to make a point or simply to express feelings. To understand the encoding process fully, we must consider the use of visual signs or visual communication.

Visual communication is commonly defined as the transmittal of meanings by using still and moving images received by the eye. Although visual signals include both words (also received by the eye) and pictures, we shall confine our discussion of visual communication to still and moving pictures, because we covered words in a previous section on verbal communication. By one estimate, Americans are bombarded by up to five thousand visual images in a day (Lester 2006). These images include pictures in magazines, newspapers, books, posters, and billboards; moving images in television and the movies; and the images we receive on the internet. With digital technologies, just about anyone with a digital phone and camera can send and receive images across geographical and time boundaries.

Considering the ubiquity of visual images, some scholars suggest that a visual culture worldwide, particularly among young people, has emerged, with people using images more than words to communicate, and people being more responsive to visual images than to written text (e.g., Lester 2006). This view is supported by studies showing that "pictures have a direct route to long-term memory, each image storing its own information as a coherent 'chunk' or concept" (Medina 2008, 2), implying that pictures are better remembered than words are. Also, some researchers suggest that humans are hardwired to respond to visual stimuli, considering that, historically, humans relied on vision to survive and adapt to the environment, for example, to choose a mate and to identify predators and food sources (Medina 2008). As a result, vision is our most dominant sense, and we absorb information much more successfully when visual signals are used, particularly when combined with words. To illustrate, one study found that three days after receiving a message, research participants remembered ten percent of what they had heard (orally only), twenty percent of what they had read, and sixty-five percent of a message consisting of oral and visual signs (Lester 2006).

Besides improving retention significantly, visual signs have these other characteristics that potentially can make a message more effective or can otherwise facilitate the encoding process:

- A large number of images can be transmitted in a short time (Lester 2006). Consider how much visual information can be conveyed in a twenty-second television commercial.
- Visual images, compared to words, project greater realism, force, and immediacy. Studies show, for example, that emotions are more readily aroused by photos and moving images than by words (Smith 2005).
- Visual images are capable of evoking involuntary (uncontrolled, unconscious) responses in receivers (Blair, Judd, and Chapleau 2004). Consider, for example, the warm, pleasant feelings evoked by pictures of puppies and children. These emotions are elicited by the images, not necessarily by the accompanying message.

In summary, visual images are a powerful tool for encoding messages, and should be included in the analysis of communication, particularly in the study of communication and prejudice.

Sending the Encoded Message; Decoding by the Receiver

Once the source's response to an internal or external stimulus has been encoded into a sign or system of signs shared with the receiver, we have a "message," which has an existence and form outside of the source. The *message* represents the source's response and provides meaning to the response. It can be verbal, nonverbal, or visual: This book (and any particular sentence, paragraph, or chapter in it) and my lectures are messages to you; today's newscast is a message from the television station or network; and a movie is a message from writers, producers, and a production company. These messages consist of systems of symbols that can be physically sent to and retrieved by the receiver. The means by which the message is transmitted is the *channel of communication*. Examples include the printed page, air (which transmits voice), the internet, digital communication, movies, television programs, and the newspaper. Communication continues when the transmitted message reaches and is accepted by the receiver— you read my book, you listen (with varying degrees of attention) to my lecture, and an audience watches a television program or movie. Communication cannot occur if the message is not "sensed" by the intended receiver, such as when its existence is ignored or if its existence does not materialize in the receiver's realm of experience (the television program is censored, so it is not shown). Once received, the message is interpreted or decoded by the receiver. *Decoding* consists of, first, the receiver's being aware of the message; second, the receiver's understanding the signs used to encode the message (such as understanding the language used); and, third and most important, the receiver's assigning meaning to the message. The meanings assigned by the receiver depend heavily on the receiver's past experience with the source and the topic of the message; the values and accepted belief and behavioral systems in the receiver's environment; and the receiver's needs, emotional states, and expectations from the communication interaction. In other words, meanings assigned by the receiver are heavily influenced by that person's culture (values, norms) and individual states (needs, emotions). Effective communication—that is, mutual satisfaction of source and receiver goals—occurs when the cultural orientations of source and receiver are similar, so that equivalent or similar meanings are assigned to the message. Communication breakdown (ineffectiveness) occurs when the receiver assigns meanings to the message that are different from the meanings intended by the source. Upon decoding the message, the receiver may choose to send a response back to the original source. Thus, the process begins all over again.

Noise

An important element in our transactional model is the concept of noise. Shannon and Weaver (1949), in their engineering model of communication, defined *noise* as any cause of message distortion as the message is transmitted from source to receiver. They were concerned with the amount of information (measured in bits) transmitted; perfect communication happened when the amount sent equaled the amount received. In our transactional model, we are more concerned with the meaning of information sent and received. Effective communication is measured by the amount of overlap between meanings sent and meanings received. The greater the overlap, the more effective the communication is. *Noise* in our model is therefore defined as any source of distortion in the meanings assigned by the source to the signal and meanings assigned to the signals by the receiver. Common sources of noise can be found in the source and the receiver.

Within the source, semantic noise can cause distortion of the meaning of the message. *Semantic noise* refers to the use (or misuse) of verbal, nonverbal, and visual signs. A textbook such as this one, when written in technical, esoteric jargon, is semantic noise. *Cultural noise* refers to interpretations of the environmental stimuli and signs used by the source that are highly subjective because of cultural values and worldviews, and that do not take into account the culture (perspective) of the receiver. Examples can be found in international advertising, when images that are appropriate in the home country are used in another country where the same images may not be understood or, worse, may be offensive.

There are several sources of noise in the receiver influenced by that person's culture. Receptivity to and interpretation of the message will be heavily influenced by the receiver's culture—previous experiences with the topic of communication and with the source; values, worldviews, and behavioral and attitudinal norms accepted within the community. Three decoding processes will be influenced by culture:

- *Selective exposure to the message:* The receiver has a choice to attend to or ignore the message. A general principle, from the selective exposure hypothesis, is that we will attend to and not reject messages that we agree with, that have high reward and low punishment value, and that are accessible (Tan 1986). *Rewards* can be self-gratification (arousal of positive emotions, entertainment, diversion from problems), or the fulfillment of other goals, such as to learn a new skill or to be informed. *Punishments* can be the arousal of negative emotions, such as fear or guilt. *Accessibility* refers to ease with which the message can be decoded, and is facilitated by symbols and signs, including language, that are familiar and easy to understand. Repetition of the message also facilitates accessibility.
- *Selective perception* refers to how the message is interpreted, or the meanings assigned to the signs. Again, culture and self-interest of the receiver influence perception of the message. We will assign meanings to the message that reinforce our values and worldviews, which may be very different from the source's values and worldviews. For example, very different interpretations will be given to the immigration bill recently passed by the Senate. Supporters will perceive the new law as just and good for the country; those opposed will see the new law as opening the "floodgates" to potentially undesirable immigrants.

The sources of noise discussed above are obstacles to effective communication. While we can learn to be more effective communicators by reducing source noise, such as in the use of words and visuals, receiver noise is more difficult to control. Therefore, we should be aware of how our receivers might misinterpret our messages. A starting point is to "take the other's perspective," that is, to be aware of the other's culture.

Levels of Analysis

Our transactional model of communication can be analyzed at four levels, depending on the size of the unit to be analyzed. These levels, from smallest to largest, are the intrapersonal, interpersonal, social system, and cultural levels (Tan 1986).

The Intrapersonal Level

At the intrapersonal level of analysis, also called the micro level, communication is considered to originate and reside primarily in the individual person. At this level, we are interested in how the source encodes the message, how the receiver decodes the message, and the meanings assigned by source and receiver to signs used in the message. Thus, we study the cognitive processes in encoding and decoding, including selective attention, selective perception, and selective retention. We also study effects of communication, such as attitude, belief, and behavioral change. Typically, we study these processes in individuals and then we aggregate or average individual results to a group to which the individual belongs.

The Interpersonal Level

At the interpersonal level, we are interested in how the *social context*—defined as other people in the immediate environment of source or receiver—affects the encoding and decoding of messages. The influence of other people, particularly people who are important to the communicator ("significant others") on the communication process is underscored by this quote from George Herbert Mead (1934):

> The self is something which has a development; it is not initially there at birth but arises in the process of social experience and activity, that is, develops in the given individual as a result of his relations to that process as a whole and to other individuals within that process.

Put simply, the "self"—who an individual is, and his or her identity, personality, beliefs, attitudes, and worldview—is shaped by other people and interactions with them. How a person communicates, whether when encoding or decoding a message, is very much a function of the self and is therefore subject to social influence. In interpersonal analysis, we are interested in the influence of group norms on attitudes and beliefs, on how messages are encoded and decoded, and on how we present ourselves (self-presentation) to others in the group. We are also interested in communication styles of leaders and opinion leaders, and, in general, how group decisions are reached through face-to-face or virtual interpersonal communications. With the accessibility of digital communications and social media on the internet, the definition of interpersonal communication today includes communication in virtual groups who, instead of communicating face to face, communicate online.

The Social System Level

At the social system level, the unit of analysis is a collection of individuals and small groups with physical properties or structures that control individual behaviors. While *social groups* are defined primarily by the interpersonal settings in which communication occurs, a *social system* is defined by the social structures that control individuals. Social structures can be found in the physical or tangible properties of the system (see, e.g., Parsons 1966). Examples are courts of law; a social stratification system; a language system; and federal, state, and local governments. These structures can reward and punish individuals in the system for compliance or noncompliance with "rules" in the system (e.g., laws). A social system can be a unit of coworkers (e.g., a labor union); a corporation (e.g., a media company), or a nation-state.

Analysis of communication at this level looks at how messages are encoded and decoded by social systems, such as how television networks and newspapers produce entertainment and news for their audiences, and how these systems influence communication behaviors of individuals and social groups within the system.

The Cultural System Level

Cultural system level analysis shares many of the characteristics of social system analysis. A cultural system is also a social system. However, while social system analysis is concerned with the influence of system structures on individuals within the system, cultural system analysis focuses on one process: the transmission of culture (Appelbaum 1970). Here is a sociological definition of culture:

> Culture is the integrated sum total of learned behavior traits which are manifest and shared by the members of a society. (Hoebel 1960)

Culture therefore includes the values, beliefs, and behaviors that are shared and accepted by members of a social system. For any social system to continue existing, its culture—including "rules" that guide behaviors, attitudes, and beliefs—is transmitted from generation to generation. The major mode of transmission is communication, interpersonally or mediated by a medium such as the mass media or internet, and using signals and signs that are shared or understood within the system.

At the cultural system level, we analyze how culture is transmitted through communication, and how culture affects communication. We ask, for example, how values and opinions are influenced by news and entertainment media; how the media are influenced by values and attitudes in the social system; and how culture in general affects individual communication behaviors.

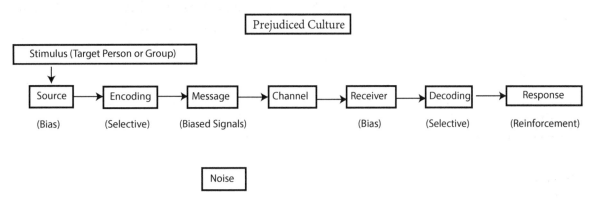

Figure 2.2 Prejudiced Communication.

Communication and Prejudice

Now that we have an understanding of the basic communication processes, let's apply the transactional model to the analysis of prejudice. Figure 2.2 repeats the top half of Figure 2.1, with the insertion of prejudice at critical points to show how the entire communication process is affected by prejudice. Recall our definition of *prejudice* as negative emotions directed at a group and its members that are based on selective experiences and incomplete or inaccurate information.

A Culture of Prejudice

There is compelling evidence, discussed in Chapter 3, that human beings are nurtured to be prejudiced by their communities for a variety of reasons, mostly having to do with self-preservation and self-enhancement. Therefore, prejudice is an inescapable fact of life, and is transmitted from generation to generation by a host of socialization agents, including family, peers, schools, the mass media, and social groups, and is manifested in the signs and symbols, language, group norms, and, to a lesser extent, social structures and rules in the community. Individual members of the community internalize the messages reinforcing prejudice, and, in effect, are microcosms of the culture of prejudice in their communities.

Stimulus

In this elaborated model (Figure 2.2), the stimulus that evokes the source to initiate communication is a "target" group and its members. A target group is a group with which the source does not identify and that is outside of the source's social circle, meaning that there is little interaction with the target group's members. The target group or a member may be in the immediate sensory field of the source, or it may be represented in signals (words, photos, moving images), or it could be simply a thought. The point is, the target group, however it is represented, stimulates the source to encode a message.

The Source

A basic assumption of our model is that almost all of us are biased or have prejudices acquired from socialization into our communities. Although we rarely admit to explicit prejudice, unconsciously we harbor preferences for groups with which we identify, and we have negative evaluations of groups with which we don't identify. (This concept is developed further in the next chapter as differences in evaluations of "in-groups" and "out-groups.") Because we are biased, our response to the stimulus will be favorable if the stimulus is an in-group, and negative if it is an out-group. Therefore, our response will be prejudiced against the out-group.

Encoding

Because the source is biased, its encoding of the message will be based on selective processes of attention, perception, and recall. The source will select, interpret, and recall information, consciously or unconsciously, to support his or her feelings toward the target group.

The Message

The message resulting from encoding will likewise use signals and signs to reinforce the source's feelings toward the target group. Consider the Linguistic Category Model (LCM) discussed earlier. Recall that the model identifies several categories of linguistic elements, from concrete to abstract, to describe behaviors of people. Research tells us that how we feel about the actor (our prejudices) influences the level of abstraction and its direction (positive or negative) that we use to describe his or her behavior.

Here's an example:

Abstraction level	James, a member of an out-group (negative prejudice).
Descriptive action verb	James pushed Tim.
Interpretative action verb	James hit Tim.
State verb	James hates Tim.
Adjective	James is violent.

The LCM says that we are more likely to use abstract language to describe behaviors of individuals or groups against whom we are prejudiced, compared to individuals or groups whom we favor. Thus, in the example above, a push leads to the description of James as violent. The lesson, of course, is for the observer to stick to descriptive action verbs as much as is possible. But, because of our prejudices, this is not always easy to do.

Receiver/Decoding/Response

Because the receiver is biased, his or her decoding or interpretation of the message will use strategies, consciously or unconsciously, to support those biases. These are the same processes used by the source: selective attention, perception, and recall. Messages that support the biases will be attended to, signs will be interpreted to support the biases, and supportive information will be remembered—all serving to reinforce existing biases. These processes facilitate the transmission of prejudice within a culture, and make efforts to change the culture challenging at best.

Communication as a Solution

Although prejudice is very much embedded in human cultures, there is growing evidence that most people— regardless of race, ethnicity, gender, religion, or other demographic category—do not want to be prejudiced and will not admit, explicitly, to being prejudiced. While it's true that almost all of us have implicit biases, most people do not want to be biased—it's not acceptable in most societies, and the consequences of prejudice are often costly for individuals and societies. The focus of recent research has been on how to *control* our biases so that our actions are not influenced by them. Most of these interventions use communication as the primary strategy. The same communication processes that contribute to the development and reinforcement of prejudice can be used to reduce prejudice. They are discussed in Chapters 12 and 13 of this book.

Workbook

Define and illustrate:

1. Definitions of communication: Cooley, Shannon and Weaver, Stevens, Lasswell, Schramm, transactional model

2. Communication goals, source and receiver

3. Unconscious communication

4. Encoding

5. Signs

6. Linguistic Category Model

7.   Non-verbal communication: functions and forms

8.   Visual messages

9.   Noise: selective exposure, selective perception, selective retention

10.   Levels of analysis, communication: intrapersonal, interpersonal, social system, cultural

11.   Communication and prejudice, influence of culture

3

What Is Prejudice?

I n this chapter, I take a look at classic (older) and more recent definitions of prejudice. I also discuss implicit biases, targets of prejudice, and who can be prejudiced.

Classic Definitions of Prejudice

The scientific study of prejudice has a long history in psychology, beginning with the book *The Nature of Prejudice*, by Gordon Allport (1954). According to Allport (1979), prejudice is "a feeling, favorable or unfavorable, toward a person or thing, prior to, or not based on actual experience" (6). Note that this definition includes both positive and negative feelings toward persons or things. For example, I have positive feelings toward college students and negative feelings toward White supremacists. The key element in this definition is that these feelings are not necessarily based on sufficient knowledge, evidence, or experience. Therefore, prejudice is an affective predisposition that influences how we evaluate and behave toward people and things (such as organizations and products). *Affective* refers to feelings and emotions; these feelings direct evaluations and behaviors in advance of the actual encounter with the targeted group or "thing"—therefore, they are predispositions.

Although prejudice can be positive or negative, much of the attention in research has been on negative prejudices, because these prejudices are manifested in generalized feelings that cause wars; violence against individuals; unfair treatment of people based on their group membership such as in race or gender; and, in general, hate (see, e.g., Dozier Jr. 2002). An example of negative prejudice is, in Allport's words, "negative ethnic prejudice," defined as "an antipathy based upon a faulty and inflexible generalization. It may be based toward a group as a whole, or toward an individual because he is a member of that group" (1979, 9).

To understand the consequences of prejudice, let's look at how prejudice might be expressed by individuals and institutions such as a government. Allport (1979) presents a five-phase model of "acting out our prejudice." These phases, from the least to most damaging to the targets of prejudice are antilocution, avoidance, discrimination, physical attack, and extermination.

Antilocution

The mildest form of prejudice, *antilocution*, is talk or conversations that express unwarranted (i.e., not supported by objective information) negative feelings about other people because of their membership in a group.

This talk often happens in small groups consisting of people who agree with the negative assessments of the group being talked about. For example, several professors talking about their students may refer to sorority and fraternity members as "party animals" who are in college to have fun, not to get an education, or to student athletes as "dumb jocks." Another example is a group of male faculty members evaluating a female candidate for a faculty position in the sciences as a "risky" hire because she will probably want to raise a family in the next few years and won't be able to devote her full attention and energies to the rigorous demands of research and teaching. These assessments of fraternity and sorority students, student athletes, and a female candidate for a science faculty position are prejudicial because they are not necessarily based on fact and are generalizations based on group membership. Antilocution is expressed in use of prejudicial language, usually in "safe" circles consisting of other individuals who agree with the prejudicial statements and who are not likely to challenge them. Therefore, antilocution reinforces and maintains prejudice, making prejudice more resistant to change.

Avoidance

As an expression of prejudice, *avoidance* is voluntary separation of the prejudiced individual from the targets of his or her prejudice. This separation is accomplished by a conscious effort to avoid contact with the targets of prejudice regardless of the inconvenience or difficulty. For example, a White family moves from Seattle (where there are "too many Asians") to Coeur d'Alene, Idaho (where "our kind of people live"), or, an Asian PhD in computer science avoids shopping at Walmart because "I might get mugged in the parking lot." Although the prejudiced individual does not directly harm the targets of prejudice, avoidance nonetheless contributes to the reinforcement of unwarranted negative feelings and evaluations because it precludes new information through personal contact that might challenge those prejudices.

Here's an example of avoidance.

White Supremacist Wants to Establish All-White Community; Finds Out That He Is Part Black

MSN News (August 24, 2013) reported that Craig Cobb, identified by the Southern Poverty Law Center as a "hard-core white supremacist anti-Semite," has been buying land in a tiny North Dakota ghost town and selling lots to other white supremacists. Cobb lives in a "ramshackle" two-story house in Leith, ND, and has purchased at least twelve other lots. He was once reported to say, "Racism is my religion."

Cobb wrote in an announcement made on a supremacist message board in May 2012:

"For starters, we could declare a Mexican illegal invaders and Israeli Mossad/IDF spies no-go zone. If leftist journalists or antis come and try to make trouble, they just might break one of our local ordinances and would have to be arrested by our own constable. See?"

Cobb added that he hoped new residents of his enclave would always fly at least one "racialist" banner such as a Nazi flag.

According to the *Los Angeles Times* (2013), Cobb found out during a taping of Trisha Goddard's talk show that he is part Black. He had submitted DNA for testing, and the results revealed during the taping of the show indicated that he was "eighty-six percent European and fourteen percent sub-Saharan African." As the audience cheered and laughed, Cobb protested, saying, "Wait a minute, wait a minute, hold on, just wait a minute. This is called statistical noise."

Goddard said, "'Sweetheart, you have a little Black in you." Cobb replied, "'Listen, I'll tell you this, oil and water don't mix." Goddard moved to fist bump Cobb, calling him "'Bro." Cobb declined to fist bump.

Cobb later told The Bismarck Tribune that he doubted the accuracy of the test and said he planned to take more DNA tests and publish the results. "I'll find out with real science and get the whole DNA map," he said.

Bobby Harper, a Black resident of Leith, told the Tribune, "I knew there was one other Black person in town. Is he going to want to kick his own self out of town and discriminate against himself?"

Discrimination

Discrimination occurs when an individual, group, community, or society actively excludes members of another group access or participation in desired activities (Allport 1979; Ponterotto 2006). Discrimination may be enacted by an individual, such as excluding another person because of his or her race from a social gathering. More often, discrimination is practiced by organizations and agencies of government, carried out in business and communities, instituted and supported by individual members or authorities with influence and authority, and enacted formally (e.g., supported by laws and policy) or informally (agreed on by leaders via antilocution). Examples, present and past, are segregation in education, employment, politics, social privileges, and recreational opportunities (see, e.g., Jones 1997). Ponterotto (2006) points out that in the United States, "discrimination based on race, gender, religion, ethnicity, age, and so forth is illegal; nonetheless, it happens every day" (15).

Here are some situations that may illustrate discrimination.

In the early 1990s I was called upon as an expert witness by the NAACP and the Lawyers for Civil Rights to testify on their behalf in a lawsuit that was being tried in Washington, DC. The plaintiffs alleged that a large real estate development agency in Washington, DC, was discriminating against African Americans by excluding them from promotions of new real estate developments in the area, including the absence of African American models in advertisements. This practice, the plaintiffs maintained, was de facto discrimination because a large majority of the population in the area was African American. I testified that the research indeed shows that people are attracted to messages, including advertisements, that prominently feature members of their own race. The defense had its own expert witness who testified that the race of models in the advertisements, based on focus groups recruited at a shopping mall, was not an important determinant of attention to the advertisements. The plaintiffs won the case, and the defendants were required to change their promotional practices and to pay the plaintiffs a large sum of money.

Also in the early 1990s, I was invited by an academic organization in South Africa to speak on intercultural communications. This was before the dismantling of apartheid. I am brown-skinned, born in the Philippines. Gerdean, my wife, was also invited to join me on the trip. Gerdean is Caucasian, originally from Montana. Our hosts, mostly university professors and some government officials, were very gracious and apologetic of policies and practices based on apartheid, including the prohibition of interracial marriage and cohabitation between persons of different races. They made it clear that they did not agree with these policies, and that there was a movement in the country to eliminate apartheid. I asked whether my wife and I would be allowed to stay in the same hotel room. With obvious embarrassment, one of our hosts said that this would not be a problem because "distinguished" visitors of color to the country like me are considered "honorary Whites."

Now consider the events reported by the following news stories.

Voting Rights Fight Continues

Stateline.org (2013) reported that Attorney General Eric Holder was moving "aggressively" to renew federal control over Texas elections to prevent implementation of a redistricting plan that a federal court had found to be "intentionally discriminatory."

Holder's actions against Texas were made even after the Supreme Court's ruling on the Voting Rights Act invalidated Section 5, which required states and municipalities with a history of discrimination to obtain pre-approval (for elections) by a federal court or the Justice Department. Discrimination could include any election changes that discourage groups from voting, such as location of polling places and voter ID laws. According to Stateline.org, all or parts of sixteen states, mainly in the South, were subject to the preclearance requirement.

Holder was basing his actions against Texas on a "bail-in" provision in a separate section of the Voting Rights Act, which allows the federal government or citizens to ask a federal judge to require preclearance if they can prove a state law is intentionally discriminatory. In Texas, a federal court had already found that the redistricting plan was intentionally discriminatory.

Question

- Is the US Justice Department justified in pursuing legal action against states with "a history of discrimination," or is it overstepping its authority given the Supreme Court ruling?

Racial Biases in Alabama's Greek System?

The New York Times (September 18, 2013) reported that a Black student at the University of Alabama in Tuscaloosa said that a sorority had "bowed to alumnae influence and considered race when it evaluated potential new members." According to the *Times*, "racial biases in Alabama's Greek system have been an open secret for decades," although many national Greek organizations say they have banned discrimination.

The *Times* reported that several hundred mostly White University of Alabama students and faculty members marched near the President's Mansion, demanding an end to segregation in the university's fraternities and sororities.

The university's president acknowledged that the university's Greek system remains segregated and told advisers of traditionally White sororities that she was ordering "an extended admissions process."

Question

- Was the segregation in the Greek system at the University of Alabama indicative of discrimination, or was it the result of self-selection? Blacks and Whites on many campuses often seek memberships in fraternities and sororities that are segregated.

Physical Attack

The fourth phase of prejudice expression, according to Allport (1979), is *physical attack*. When individuals or groups of individuals injure other people because of their membership in another group, or destroy property of the targeted group, prejudice expression takes on a violent phase. These acts are classified as "hate crimes" in many US states and are often prosecuted. For examples of hate crimes, see the website of the Southern Poverty Law Center (SPLC), a prominent antiprejudice, nonprofit organization that has successfully supported the prosecution of hate crimes across the United States. For example, the SPLC, through a series of lawsuits, successfully caused the Aryan Nations Brotherhood (led at that time by Richard Butler) to declare bankruptcy and abandon its "headquarters" in Hayden Lake, North Idaho. There are still remnants of White supremacy groups in North Idaho, probably no more than you can count on the fingers of both hands. The good citizens of Coeur d'Alene and Hayden have come together to actively fight racism and erase the area's reputation as a safe haven for White supremacists. Still, a handful of racists have caused confrontations that fall under the "physical attack" phase of discrimination. For example, the former director of a human rights organization found a noose dangling from her porch, some individuals picketed a roadside taco stand with signs saying "Honk to Keep Idaho White" (no one honked, and community members lined up to buy tacos from the stand), and public property was defaced with Nazi signs and racial slurs. I should note that the cities of Hayden and Coeur d'Alene investigated these incidents and actively pursued the perpetrators.

Here's how a newspaper report described a possible "physical attack" expression of prejudice in Coeur d'Alene, Idaho:

According to the *Coeur d'Alene Press* (August 30, 2011), a local man was charged with felony malicious harassment for his part in an alleged hate crime. The man (X) was charged with confronting and threatening Y as Y walked by X's apartment on his way to a community beach. X is White and Y is African American.

According to police reports, here is what Y told officers:

While on his morning walk to the beach, X stared at him. On his way back to his room at a local motel, X reportedly asked Y, "Are you (expletive) lost?"

Y told police that X had a small girl in his arms, and described X as having several tattoos, including a Swastika symbol.

Y asked X what he had said, and X repeated it and used racial slurs toward Y. Y asked X if he was going to beat him up with a child in his arms. X put the child back in the apartment and returned outside, and a verbal confrontation ensured.

Other people from the apartment joined X in his yard. Y then ran to a nearby friend's house, got a baseball bat, and returned to the street corner.

After another argument, neighbors came outside. Y walked back to his residence and called police who arrested X later that morning.

Y told the *Coeur d'Alene Press* that his reaction to the racial taunts (to get the bat) was "dumb, my pride got in the way. Usually I ignore it, it's silly."

According to the *Coeur d'Alene Press*, here is what X told police:

X asked Y if he needed directions because Y had walked back and forth around the block, as though he had been lost. X said he had not sworn or threatened Y.

X's fiancée told the newspaper that X isn't a racist, and does not have Aryan ties. She said X is enrolled and works at a local college, which court records also indicate.

The Press reported the presiding judge as saying, "The seriousness of the offense is significant here before the court. I don't think ($50,000, the bond amount) is unreasonable."

According to the newspaper, X had two felonies on his record, including theft and a felon in possession of firearms. If convicted, X faced five years in jail and up to $5,000 fines on one count of felony malicious harassment or hate crime. With two convicted felonies on his record, X qualified as a persistent offender and could have faced up to life in prison if convicted of the hate crime.

Extermination

The final phase of Allport's (1979) continuum of expressions of racial prejudice, and clearly the most destructive, is extermination. Ponterotto (2006) defines *extermination* as the "systematic and planned destruction of a group of people based on their group membership" (15). When applied to racial and ethnic groups, extermination is often referred to as "ethnic cleansing" or genocide. Mann (2005) catalogs instances of ethnic cleansing throughout history to the present, including the Nazi attempt to exterminate Jews, resulting in more than six million Jews being murdered because of their religion; the displacement and enslavement of millions of Africans to the "New World" (America); and the systematic marginalization of American Indians, who numbered about nine million at the time of Christopher Columbus's invasion, to two million today (Herring 1999). More recent examples include attempts to eliminate entire ethnic populations in Eastern Europe (Bosnian Serbs versus Bosnian Muslims) and Rwanda (Tutsis versus Hutus) (Ponterotto 2006).

Although extermination is enacted by governments and formal organizations, this extreme expression of prejudice begins at the individual and small-group levels with prejudiced communication derogating the targeted group. Allport (1979) provides this example in analyzing the Nazi attempt to exterminate Jews:

It was Hitler's antilocution that led Germans to avoid their Jewish neighbors and erstwhile friends. This preparation made it easier to enact the Nuremberg laws of discrimination which, in turn, made the subsequent burning of synagogues and street attacks upon Jews seem natural. The final step in the macabre progression was the ovens at Auschwitz. (15)

Thus, we can see that communication ("antilocution") is at the heart of, and is often the commencement of, more destructive expressions of prejudice.

Contemporary Definitions of Prejudice

Most current definitions of prejudice are based on Allport's (1954; 1979) definition. Recall that Allport included in his definition of prejudice both an attitude component (negative feelings) and a belief component (the assignment of negative traits to the targeted group). While some current definitions have retained the attitudinal and belief components of prejudice (see, e.g., Ponterotto 2006), others have assigned the attitudinal component to prejudice, the belief component to "stereotypes" (discussed in Chapter 7), and a behavioral component (overt action to exclude) to "discrimination" (see, e.g., Hecht 1998). In this three-component analysis, a belief (a stereotype) that a group has a negative trait (say, is "prone to terrorism") leads to prejudice or a negative feeling (e.g., fear or hatred) about the group, which leads to increased scrutiny in airport security checks (discrimination). Generalizations are made from target group evaluation to the individual without exclusions, so that an individual belonging to the targeted group is automatically assigned the stereotype and is the recipient of resulting negative feelings and discrimination. In theory, the three components are related in a causal chain—negative stereotypes should lead to prejudice, which should lead to discrimination. However, research has not established a strong link between these three components. The correlation between prejudice and discrimination is generally about .29 (meaning that only about 9% of discrimination is explained by prejudice) (Hecht 1998; Schutz and Six 1996). The correlation between stereotyping and prejudice is even smaller, generally no higher than .16 in some studies, meaning that only about 2.5% of prejudice is explained by stereotyping. Why the low correlations? Brewer (1994) offers this explanation: the "cognitive, affective, and behavioral orientations to individuals and social groups represent different, independent response systems whose interrelationships are more complex than previously thought" (321). In other words, stereotypes, prejudice, and discrimination are each influenced by a number of social and environmental factors that may be operating independently of each other. Stereotypes, for example, may be influenced by negative portrayals in the media, prejudice may be influenced by a personal encounter, and discrimination may be influenced by a perceived threat. Therefore, an individual may hold negative feelings toward another person, even in the absence of a a prior negative stereotype, and discrimination may be expressed without accompanying prejudice when a real threat is perceived. To better explain human behavior related to prejudice, Hecht (1998) suggests a more "holistic" approach:

> If the entire human action—whether called prejudice or discrimination—is examined, there may be cognitive, emotional, and behavioral elements to it, and these should be placed within the social and historical context of intergroup relations, economic conditions, and the wide array of factors discussed as causes of prejudice. (9)

Another explanation of the low correlations between stereotyping, prejudice, and discrimination is the difficulty in obtaining accurate and valid measures of stereotyping, prejudice, and *intent* to discriminate (discrimination or overt exclusion is more amenable to direct observation). Most societies in the world, and certainly the United States, profess egalitarian values that are contrary to prejudice. Therefore, to be "socially desirable" in their own societies because prejudice is disfavored, most people will not admit to explicit prejudice or negative stereotyping. Indeed, recent research has shown a declining number of Americans who admit to prejudice toward other races when prejudice is measured in questionnaires and interviews. On the other hand, a large body of research shows that most of us (up to eighty percent of Americans) have *implicit biases*, or prejudicial feelings that are not consciously held, when indirect association tests are used (discussed in Chapter 4). Correlations between stereotypical beliefs, negative feelings, and related behaviors are higher when measured indirectly or unobtrusively.

In more recent studies, strong links between explicit and implicit prejudice and evaluations of people and related actions have been demonstrated using more refined measures and experimental procedures, where cause and effect are more validly established and in conditions less susceptible to social desirability responses. These studies are discussed in more detail in Chapter 5, "Consequences of Prejudice." Here are a few examples of results of these studies:

- Implicit biases against women predict that women candidates for a job in the sciences will be evaluated less favorably than will men with the identical qualifications.
- Job candidates with names that sound African American will receive fewer callbacks and invitations to interview than will candidates with identical qualifications but names that sound White.
- Implicit and explicit prejudices against African Americans predict a higher probability that African Americans will be identified as violent criminals.
- Implicit and explicit prejudices against African Americans predict a higher likelihood that mock jurors will assign blame to African American defendants.
- Negative stereotypes of the elderly predict implicit and explicit prejudices, which predict avoidance of older people.
- Negative stereotyping of African American women predicts explicit and implicit biases, which lead to assignment of African American women to less desirable occupations.

Therefore, the theoretical and logical links between stereotyping, prejudice, and discrimination may be valid after all, a position I take in this book, and the reason that I am discussing stereotypes, prejudice, and related behaviors as three separate and distinct but related components.

Here is a definition of prejudice that I use in this book:

Prejudice often is thought of as an attitude consisting of affect and belief or at least the affective or evaluative reaction to group differences. (Hecht 1998, 8)

The emphasis in this definition is on the affective or evaluative component of prejudice (negative feelings) as reactions to group differences.

Stereotypes, discussed in Chapter 7, are the cognitive component, the belief that a group possesses certain traits or characteristics that are generalized to all members of the group.

Discrimination, the behavioral component discussed later in this chapter, is the overt (visible) exclusion of group members from desired activities and overt harmful actions taken against the group.

Levels of Analysis of Prejudice

Prejudice can be analyzed at the individual, interpersonal, group, and institutional levels. Breaking down prejudice to these levels helps us understand the role of communication in causing and remedying prejudice, because most current definitions of the communication process use the intrapersonal (individual), group (interpersonal), and mediated and institutional levels of analysis (see Chapter 2).

Individual Level

At the individual level, we analyze how a person acquires, maintains, and might change negative feelings toward a group and how these feelings are generalized to all members of the group. We look at the influence of information acquired through the media, other people, and interpersonal contact, no matter how incomplete or inaccurate this information might be. The focus is on how the individual acquires and processes this information. We also look at the influence of parents, peers, the school, and other people and groups important to the person through a process of socialization. In addition, we look at the psychodynamics within the person: self-esteem; identity; vulnerability to perceived threats; tolerance for ambiguity; close-mindedness or open-mindedness; and, as some recent research suggests, cognitive abilities ("intelligence"). A prejudiced individual will express prejudice in use of derogatory language, avoidance, hostile behaviors, and, in extreme cases, violence. These manifestations of prejudice are expressed by the individual acting alone. Intrapersonal communication processes, such as information processing, are key to understanding the person's prejudice and related behaviors.

Interpersonal Level

At the interpersonal level, the focus is on use of language in face-to-face and virtual (as in through the internet) conversations with other individuals, usually like-minded individuals. Analysis at this level corresponds to Allport's (1979) antilocution phase of prejudice. In conversations with others, the individual seeks validation of his or her prejudices; negative feelings and stereotypes directed toward the target group are sharpened and exaggerated. To understand how interpersonal communication reinforces and might change prejudice, we have to understand the role of language in reinforcing prejudice and how identity issues, such as self-presentation, are shaped by language.

Group Level

At the group level, individuals coalesce informally to pursue common goals in support of their prejudices. This "coming together" of like-minded people often happens after face-to-face conversations in which their prejudices are reinforced and is often expressed in overt actions aimed at harming the target of their prejudices. Examples are the five or six members of a White supremacist group who picketed a taco stand with signs saying, "Honk to Keep Idaho White," or, the fraternity at a University of California campus that organized an "African-American–themed" party, complete with stereotypical dress and activities. Analysis at the group level would include analysis of how conversations lead to action, leadership roles, "groupthink," and how information is used.

Institutional Level

At the institutional level, we analyze how formal structures and organizations of society—including local and national government agencies, business, education, and the media—practice, maintain, and change policies and actions based on prejudice. Hecht (1998) suggests that we look at a society's rituals, rules, and laws. Examples are policies that overtly or covertly exclude a group from membership (as in a country club) or employment (manifested in a "glass ceiling" for women and racial minorities); racial profiling in security checks and police traffic stops; or a legal system that disproportionately gives harsher sentences to African American men, the poor, and other minorities. At the institutional level, we look at how culture and institutionalized policies and practices support prejudice and how institutions can be agents of change. Communication, particularly mediated or mass communication, is central to change strategies.

These levels of analysis help us break down prejudice into manageable components. For example, intervention strategies to reduce prejudice will vary for each level, as discussed in Chapter 13. Also, the consequences of prejudice increase in harmful severity from the individual to the institutional levels. Research I discuss throughout the book is conducted at one level or another; therefore, results are best interpreted if we keep in mind what level is being addressed.

Targets of Prejudice

Because prejudice is directed at other people belonging to a group, it is useful to understand and identify who these "other people" are. In general, we direct our prejudices toward "out-groups," groups to which we do not belong and with which we do not identify. In contrast, we belong to "in-groups," whose members share important (to us) characteristics and qualities and with whom we identify. Distinctions between out-groups and in-groups can be based on social or biological factors, such as race, ethnicity, age, gender, religion, and social class, or on more mundane categories, such as sports teams, political affiliation, or even teams determined by the flip of a coin. Identification with an in-group is a source of social identity—who we are—and enhances our self-esteem or sense of self-worth. One way of reinforcing social identity based on in-group identification is to enhance the positive qualities of our in-group and to enhance the negative qualities of the out-group. The latter strategy, then, often results in prejudice. Thus, out-groups are targets of our prejudices.

Social Identification Theory

The dynamics of in-group and out-group relations are based on social identity theory (Tajfel 1979; Tajfel and Turner 1986). Social identity theory says that a large part of our sense of who we are (social identity) is based on group memberships and that we enhance our self-worth (self-esteem) by differentiating between groups with which we identify (in-groups) and groups with which we do not identify (out-groups). These differences are often based on traits, behaviors, and predispositions that we value, such as intelligence and motivation to work hard. As you would guess, we assign negative characteristics to out-groups and positive characteristics to in-groups regardless of "objective" information. According to social identity theory (Tajfel and Turner 1979) the mental processes involved in evaluating "us" versus "them" occur in the following order (McLeod 2008):

- *Categorization:* We categorize objects and people to simplify and make sense of a complex world, placing them in groups based on identifiable characteristics, such as race, religion, occupation, age, or gender. We also place ourselves in one or more of these categories, thus creating a sense of how we fit into this complex environment.
- *Social identification:* Once we have defined the categories, we adopt the identity of groups to which we belong, conforming to the norms of the groups such as opinions held and behaviors toward other groups. Because we could belong to many groups, the strength and salience of identification will vary according to the situation, but certain groups will generally be more central to a person's social identity than others will. For example, for some people, race or ethnicity may be the central source of identity; for others, it may be religion; still for others, it may be social class or education. For each category, there will often be one or more competing categories, that is, other groups that will differ on a shared characteristic and that may be perceived to be competing for the same resources. Examples are different races and ethnicities (Whites and Blacks in America; Hutus and Tutsis in Rwanda); different religions (Catholics and Protestants in Northern Ireland; Jews and Muslims in the Middle East); different memberships in student organizations in college ("Greeks" and non-Greeks); and political affiliation (Democrats and Republicans in the United States). Because we belong to several of these categories, our social identities will be shaped by more than one group; however, one group may be more dominant or influential than the others are.
- *Social comparison:* The next step is to compare the group or groups with which we identify (in-groups) with other groups (out-groups). Because our self-esteem is tied closely to our in-groups, we assign positive qualities to our in-groups and negative qualities to out-groups, resulting in prejudice.

Target Group Categories

Social identity theory explains how prejudice is linked to our social identities, which are influenced significantly by group memberships. Based on this explanation, out-groups, in general, are targets of prejudice. An out-group could be any group with which we don't identify. However, the following groups as targets of prejudice have been the foci of research, public attention, and policy because prejudices against them have affected large numbers of people, have disrupted social and political processes in many countries, and have led to destructive actions (e.g., physical violence, war) around the world.

- *Race and ethnicity:* We often target our prejudice toward people from other races and ethnicities. Race is defined as "a sub-group of people possessing a definite combination of physical characteristics, of genetic origin, the combination of which to varying degrees distinguishes the sub-group from other groups of mankind [sic]" (Krogman 1945, 49). The commonly recognized physical characteristics defining race are skin pigmentation, nasal index, lip form, and the color distribution and texture of body hair (Simpson and Yinger 1985). In the United States, commonly recognized races are Caucasoid (White Americans), Mongoloid (Asian Americans, Pacific Islanders, and Native Americans), and Negroid (Black Americans) (Sue 2004). The US Census Bureau uses the following racial categories:

"Hispanic, Latino or Spanish Origin?
___No
___Yes—Mexican, Mexican American, Chicano
___Yes—Puerto Rican
___Yes—Cuban
___Yes—another Hispanic, Latino or Spanish origin: Print ___
"Person's Race: Mark X in one or more boxes.
___White
___Black
___American Indian or Alaska native
___Asian Indian   ___Japanese   ___Native Hawaiian
___Chinese   ___Korean ___ Guamanian or Chamorro ___ Filipino ___ Vietnamese
___Other Asian: Print ___   Other Pacific Islander: Print ___
___Some other race: Print: ___
(Source: US Census Bureau 2010)

Many scholars have criticized this biologically based definition of race. As summarized by Ponterotto (2006), here are some criticisms:

1. Human beings share about 99.9% of our genes (Bonham, Warshauer-Baker, and Collins 2005). Therefore, we are very much alike in genetic origin, regardless of racial category.
2. Within one racial category, we can observe many nongenetic differences, such as language, religious customs, values, worldviews, or cultures in general.

Because of these problems in defining race, many scholars caution against using race to categorize people, suggesting that race is not a biologically valid construct but a socially constructed one. According to this view, race is given meaning in a particular society (e.g., the United States) by social relations, historical context, and power relations (see, e.g., Omni and Winant 1986; Ponterotto 2006). In other words, the meanings (e.g., ascription of positive and negative traits and behavioral tendencies) we assign to racial categories are artificial and depend on meanings agreed upon by the groups or people in control and with power within a social structure. These meanings change over time, and vary with geographical location. Despite these difficulties with the biological definition, race continues to be a commonly used construct to classify people in the United States and is probably "here to stay" because of social acceptance and historical usage (Carter and Pieterse 2005). Put simply, we have been "conditioned to use race to organize our thinking about people and the groups to which they belong" (Jones 1997; Ponterotto 2006, 7). As such, racial categorization is often a target of prejudice not only in the United States but in many countries around the world.

Ethnicity takes into account an observation that people from the same race who share similar physical characteristics are different in many ways. Rose (1976) defines *ethnicity* as groups of individuals who share a unique social and cultural heritage, such as language, customs, and religion, passed on between generations. Given this definition, generalizing negative traits (or for that matter, positive traits) to people based on their race can be erroneous and misleading. Ethnicities within a race can be differentiated according to characteristics such as culture that are more important than physical characteristics such as skin color. It is easy to see the fallacy of attributing general traits or behavioral tendencies (which lead to prejudice) to typical racial categories. Look at the racial classification "Mongoloid," which includes Asian Americans, Pacific Islanders, and Native Americans (see, e.g., Atkinson, Morten and Sue 1998; Sue 2004). Note that there are significant differences in the cultures, languages, religions, and worldviews of these different groups subsumed under "Mongoloid," and it is a mistake to lump them altogether in one racial category. The Asian American racial category is another misnomer. At least twenty different nationalities (citizenships in nation states) are included in this "racial" category. Although many Asians share some physical characteristics (brown or "yellow" skin, slanted eyes, "depressed" noses), they represent many different cultures, including different languages, values, religions, and worldviews. On the other hand, we sometimes group people into ethnic categories without differentiating the various races represented in the ethnic category. Jews, for example, are not a "race," because many racial groups are represented among the Jewish people. Jews, therefore, are an ethnic group, not a race (Ponterotto 2006). Similarly, Muslims are not a race; many racial groups are represented among Muslim people who share a similar culture, religion, rituals, and worldviews. Muslims, therefore, can be considered an ethnic group.

In the United States, race and ethnicity are often and erroneously used interchangeably to classify people. Given common and institutional usage in the "street," government, education, and business, meanings assigned to the racial categories go beyond physical attributes to include personality traits and behavioral predispositions, which become the bases for prejudice. These "social constructions," or common definitions of race, are influenced by mainstream society and groups in control of social, economic, and political institutions, including the media. A social psychological explanation for using racial categories to evaluate people is our need to make sense out of a complex environment by using the "least effort" possible. Racial physical characteristics are readily visible; they therefore provide a convenient marker to differentiate people, that is, "us" from "them," and "in-groups" from "out-groups." A sociological explanation is that race provides institutions, governments, and businesses with convenient categories for subdividing large populations into manageable subgroups, again on the bases of visible physical characteristics, to preserve power, authority, dominance, and control (see, e.g., Jones 1997).

Although, as we have seen, racial categories are not an accurate way to define people, we study race as a target of prejudice because many people around the world indeed direct their prejudices toward people of a different race. We refer to racial prejudice as *racism*, defined as resulting "from the transformation of race prejudice and/or ethnocentrism through the exercise of power against a racial group defined as inferior, by individuals and institutions with the intentional or unintentional support of the entire culture" (Jones 1997, 117, as cited by Ponterotto 2006). Several key elements of this definition are (1) the emphasis on a behavioral component—the exercise of power—resulting from prejudice, a negative feeling or assessment; (2) the use of power as an instrument of racism; and (3) the support of a culture or society, which can be intentional or unintentional.

James M. Jones, a noted scholar of racism, differentiates three levels of racism, which resemble the levels of prejudice discussed earlier in this chapter. As quoted by Ponterotto (2006), Jones (1997) defines the individual racist as

One who considers [that] the black people as a group (or other human groups defined by essential racial characteristics) are inferior to white because of physical (i.e., genotypical and phenotypical) traits. He or she further believes that these physical traits are determinants of social behavior and of moral or intellectual qualities, and ultimately presumes that this inferiority is a legitimate basis for that group's inferior social treatment. An important consideration is that all judgments of superiority are based on the corresponding traits of white people as norms of comparison. (417)

This definition of individual racism focuses on Whites as the perpetrators of racism and Blacks and other racial groups as targets, given that, even today, the power structure in the United States is controlled by Whites—White men in particular (Sue 2004)—and notwithstanding the election of President Barack Obama to a second term. Given our discussion of out-groups and in-groups, racism can be directed by any group (not only Whites) at any other group (not only Blacks or other people of color). In some countries in Asia, such as Japan and China, racism directed at Whites has been analyzed.

A second level of racism, according to Jones (1997), is *institutional racism*, defined as

Those established laws, customs, and practices which systematically reflect and produce racial inequalities in American society. If racist consequences accrue to institutional laws, customs, [and] PR practices, the institution is racist whether or not the individuals maintaining those practices have racist intentions. Institutional racism can be either overt or covert (corresponding to de jure and de facto, respectively) and either intentional or unintentional. (438)

A third level of racism is *cultural racism*, defined by Jones (1997) as

The cumulative effect of a racialized worldview, based on belief in essential racial differences that favor the dominant racial group over others. These effects are suffused throughout the culture via institutional structures, ideological beliefs, and personal everyday actions of people in the culture, and these effects are passed on from generation to generation. (472)

Institutional and cultural racism looks at, first, who has power in a given society and, second, whether this power is used to exclude other racial and ethnic groups from sharing in resources that are available to people with power. In institutional racism, this exclusion is accomplished through formal or informal policies and practices of groups and offices of government, business, education, and other instruments of society. *Cultural racism* is the sum total of individual and institutional racism, and describes a society wherein the devaluation of racial groups is embedded in the value system of members of a society, demonstrated in actions and policies, generally accepted, perpetuated by groups with power, and passed on from generation to generation. A culture of racism can be challenged with a change in the power structure, when people who have been excluded gain a voice and authority in the society, through violent (e.g., a revolution) or nonviolent (e.g., elections) means; when values are changed through formal education and via the mass media; and when new laws and policies are enacted to assure equal participation by all in the community.

Some scholars would argue that many of these conditions challenging racism are indeed present in the United States today and that racism no longer or minimally exists. Others would argue that cultural racism is still very much present in American society. The evidence, it seems, points to the truth being somewhere in between. Consider this national poll on prejudice conducted by the Associated Press (AP) in collaboration with researchers from Stanford University, the University of Chicago, and the GFL Group, a commercial polling agency:

The AP poll was an online survey of a random sample of 1,071 American adults nationwide completed in 2012. It showed that four years after we elected our first African American president, racial prejudice at the individual level was more widespread than it was when Mr. Obama was first elected president in 2008. Of this sample, which is generalizable to the entire adult US population within plus or minus 3.78 percentage points, 51% of all Americans expressed anti-Black attitudes (or prejudice), compared with 48% four years ago. Most of the poll respondents (67%) were White, non-Hispanic. Prejudice was measured in the poll by asking the respondents to answer items from the Modern Racism Scale (discussed in detail in Chapter 4). People who endorse modern racism believe that "(a) racism against Blacks is a thing of the past; (b) Blacks are too pushy and demanding of their rights; (c) this pushiness results in the use of unfair tactics; and, consequently, (d) the advances and gains Blacks have made are undeserved" (McConahay 1986). Also according to the poll, a larger majority (57%) of non-Hispanic Whites expressed anti-Hispanic attitudes in 2012 than they did in 2008 (52%).

Another poll by the Pew Research Center (2013) shows that 35% of Blacks say they have been discriminated against in the past year, compared to 20% of Hispanics and 10% of Whites. Majorities of Blacks say they are treated less fairly than Whites by the police, in courts, in local public schools, and on the job. Overall, 44% of Whites and 79% of Blacks say "a lot more" remains to be done to achieve racial equality.

These poll results measured prejudice at the individual level, and show that more than 50% of Americans indeed are willing to express explicit prejudice toward Blacks and Hispanics. More difficult to measure would be prejudice at the institutional and cultural levels. Although laws exist to protect the civil rights of racial groups in the United States, anecdotal and official statistics show that covert or de facto prejudice still exists at the institutional and cultural levels. Here are a few examples.

Several studies have shown a "preference for Whiteness" in the United States, even within the same race. One study by Joni Hersch of Vanderbilt University looked at the wages of more than two thousand legal immigrants to the United States. After accounting for country of origin, proficiency in English, occupation, and education, Hersch found that immigrants with the lightest skin earned an average of 8–15% more than did similar immigrants with darker skin (Hersch 2011). Another study by William Darity Jr. and Patricia Mason of the University of North Carolina showed that the greatest wage differential between American Blacks and Whites was between Whites and Blacks with dark or medium-dark skin, where the differential was 10 to 15% (Darity Jr. and Mason 1998).

According to one study, Blacks are more likely than Whites are to receive the death penalty. Also, Blacks with darker skin and "stereotypically Black features" are more likely to receive the death penalty than are Blacks who are "less stereotypically Black," but only when the victim is White. The study's author, Jennifer Eberhardt of Stanford University, showed students photos of Black defendants and asked them to rate each person on "how stereotypically Black" he looked. Of the defendants rated as "stereotypically Black," 57.6% had received the death penalty, compared to only 24.4% of defendants judged to be "less stereotypically Black" (Eberhardt et al. 2006).

According to the Human Rights Watch of Washington, D.C., "most drug offenders are white. Five times as many whites use drugs as Blacks. Yet Blacks comprise the great majority of drug offenders sent to prison" (Human Rights Watch 2008). Black men are thirteen times more likely to be sent to prison on drug charges than are White men.

David Cole, in his book *No Equal Justice: Race and Class in the American Criminal Justice System* (1999), points out that from January 1995 through December 1997, 70% of the drivers stopped by state troopers on Interstate 95 in Maryland were African Americans, yet only 17.5% of all cited speeders were African American (as cited in Cole 1999).

- *Gender:* Another group targeted for prejudice in the United States and many countries around the world is women. Prejudice toward women is often referred to as *sexism*, defined as "specific acts or behaviors that denigrate women" (Rakow and Wackwitz 1998, 99). Sexism is a worldwide problem, resulting in the ascription of traits to women that devalue their worth to society, and in actions that exclude them from full participation as productive and responsible members of society.

In the United States, studies have shown that women are judged to be less competent than men in male-dominated jobs that typically pay more and are more prestigious, such as medicine, science, and engineering.

Women are also perceived to be less capable of male-stereotypic behavior, such as being assertive, goal-oriented, and analytical. On the other hand, women are rated highly on stereotypically female traits, such as being nice, nurturing, and communal traits that most societies see as qualifications for roles such as wife and mother, and for low-status, low-paying, female-dominated jobs. In most societies, high-status, high-paying, male-dominated jobs require characteristics stereotypically ascribed to men (Eagly and Mladinic 1994). Not surprisingly, US labor statistics show significant underrepresentation of women in fields such as science and engineering, and in the upper echelons of business and politics.

The Organisation for Economic Co-operation and Development (OECD) has created a Social Institutions and Gender Index (SIGI), which measures prejudice against women on several variables (OECD, 2012). With headquarters in Paris, France, the OECD is an organization of thirty-four countries, including the United States, whose mission is "to promote policies that will improve the economic and social well-being of people around the world" (OECD 2012). The OECD developed the SIGI to measure gender equality worldwide using indices of norms, values, and attitudes that exist in a society in relation to women. Grouped into several institutional categories, these indices are as follows (**https://genderindex.org/sig/**):

A. Discrimination in the Family

1. *Legal age of marriage:* measures whether women have the same rights with respect to the legal minimum age of marriage
2. *Early marriage:* measures the prevalence of early and forced marriage
3. *Parental authority:* measures whether women have the same right to be a legal guardian of a child during marriage, and whether women have custody rights over a child after divorce
4. *Inheritance:* measures whether widows and daughters have equal rights to their male counterparts as heirs
5. *Divorce:* measures whether women have the same rights as men.
6. *Household responsibilities:* measures whether men have the same responsibilities as women

B. Restricted Physical Integrity

1. *Violence against women:* measures the existence of women's legal protection from rape, assault, and sexual harassment, the prevalence of domestic violence, and attitudes toward domestic violence
2. *Female genital mutilation:* measures the prevalence of female genital mutilation
3. *Reproductive integrity:* measures the extent to which women can exercise reproductive autonomy
4. *Missing women:* measures gender bias in mortality due to sex-selective abortions, infanticide, or insufficient care given to baby girls

C. Restricted Access to Productive and Financial Resources

1. *Missing women:* measures gender bias in mortality due to sex-selective abortions, infanticide, or insufficient care given to baby girls
2. *Fertility preferences:* measures gender bias in fertility preferences using the share of males as the last child

D. Restricted Resources and Entitlements

1. *Access to land:* measures women's access to agricultural land
2. *Access to credit:* measures women's access to bank loans and other forms of credit
3. *Access to property other than land:* measures women's access to other types of property, especially immovable property

E. Restricted Civil Liberties

1. *Freedom of movement:* measures the restrictions limiting women's freedom of movement and access to public space
2. *Political voice:* measures the level of discrimination against women with respect to political participation
3. *Citizenship rights:* measures whether women have the same rights as men to participate in the political system
4. *Access to justice:* measures whether women have the same rights as men in the court system

Using the SIGI measures, the OECD ranked 86 countries on gender equality or prejudice against women in 2012. The top countries showing the least prejudice (or most equality), from 1 to 10, were Argentina (1), Costa Rica, Paraguay, South Africa, FYR Macedonia, Cuba, Trinidad and Tobago, Brazil, Dominican Republic, and El Salvador (10). The lowest-ranking countries were Gabon (77), Guinea, Nigeria, Chad, Benin, Somalia, Yemen, Congo Democratic Republic, Sudan, and Mali (86). The United States, Canada, and Western European countries were not ranked. Although the SIGI uses measures generally accepted to measure prejudice against women in the Western world, it is instructive, through our Western lens, in showing the extent to which women are devalued in many countries of the world. The United States probably would be near the top of the list in terms of gender equality. Prejudice against women in the United States is more subtle and is expressed primarily in unequal access to high-paying, high-prestige professions, and in the ascription to women of traits that qualify them primarily for stereotypically female roles, such as wife and mother, and for low-paying, low-prestige jobs (Eagly and Chin 2010).

- *Sexual orientation:* Prejudice directed at gays and lesbians is often referred to in research as *heterosexism*, defined as "an ideological system that denies, denigrates, and stigmatizes any non-heterosexual form of behavior, identity relationship, or community" (Herek 1990). Heterosexism includes discriminatory behaviors against gays and lesbians in employment, housing, and services, as well as hostility to gay and lesbian lifestyles, behaviors, and communities. Although the majority of Americans have recently supported gay and lesbian equal employment rights (89% in 2010), legalization of consensual same-sex relations (54% in 2010), and lifestyles (57% in 2008) (Herek 2009; Gallup Poll 2010, 2008), prejudice against gays and lesbians is expressed more subtly in negative stereotyping and openly in hate crimes resulting in injury or death, as reported in this May 21, 2013, news item by the Associated Press:

The Associated Press (2013) reported that a gay man was killed as he walked with a companion through New York's Greenwich Village after he was taunted with homophobic slurs. A suspect held in police custody without bail had not entered a plea.

According to the AP, gay bashing had continued to increase in New York in recent years. In another case, three men connected with a twenty-eight-year-old man online, lured him to a rest stop with a promise of a date, and chased him into traffic; he was hit and killed.

The AP also reported that there has been an increase in bias-related crimes overall in New York, from thirteen in 2012 to twenty-two in 2013 (as of May). Officials said they were not sure whether the increase reflected more violence or more aggressive reporting.

The AP reported that thousands marched the streets of Manhattan to protest the latest killing, chanting, "We're here! We're queer! Homophobia's got to go."

- *Age:* Prejudice toward people perceived to be old is referred to in research as *ageism*, defined as "prejudice and discrimination against older people on the basis of age" (Nelson 2005). Another more recent definition is as follows: "Ageism is defined as negative or positive stereotypes, prejudice and/or discrimination against (or to the advantage of) elderly people on the basis of their chronological age or on the basis of a perception of them as being 'old' or 'elderly.' Ageism can be implicit or explicit and can be expressed on a micro-, meso- or macro-level" (Iversen, Larsen, and Solem 2009). This more recent definition allows for the possibility that prejudice against the elderly may be positive (as it is in some countries because of cultural traditions—in Japan, for example), although the emphasis in research and this book is on the more prevalent, negative prejudice. Also, this definition includes analysis of ageism at the interpersonal (micro), interpersonal (meso), and institutional (macro) levels.

One problem in studying ageism is the inexact specification of who is "old." Studies have indicated that the perception of who is old depends on the age and gender of the perceiver, cultural norms, and historical perspectives (Lyons 2009). For example, most economically developed countries generally accept the chronological age of 65 years as the definition of an "older person" (World Health Organisation 2009). Younger people, aged 20–29 years, consider people aged 60–69 years elderly, while people over 50 years of age define 80 years old as elderly (Musaiger and D'Souza 2009). Men are more likely to cite a younger chronological age as "old age" than women are, and women are generally perceived by men to reach old age at a younger chronological age than men do. For example, participants (both men and women) in one study considered 40–49 years as elderly for women, and 70–79 years as elderly for men (Musaiger & D'Souza 2009; Lyons 2009). Also, older males are perceived more favorably, with fewer negative stereotypes, than older women, who are perceived to have more negative stereotypes (McConatha et al. 2004; Tan et al. 2004). Historically, old age was considered to begin at 40 years in the early nineteenth century, whereas in the last decade 65 years has been referred to as the upper end of middle age (McConatha et al. 2004; Lyons 2009.)

The Age Discrimination in Employment Act of 1967 (ADEA) "prohibits employment discrimination based on age with respect to employees 40 years of age or older as well" (Feder 2010). For many, 40 would hardly be described as "old," considering the increase in longevity of people in the United States and many other countries because of improved health care, diet, and healthy lifestyles. So instead we use some "markers" to characterize people as "old," including being retired, being a Baby Boomer (born between 1946 and 1964), having a general type of appearance (gray hair, stooped posture), and having decreased activity levels. People with one or more of these markers can be targets of prejudice. As noted by Nelson (2005), age prejudice is "one of the most socially condoned and institutionalized forms of prejudice; older adults in the United States tend to be marginalized, institutionalized, and stripped of responsibility, power, and ultimately their dignity".

Ageism—or negative prejudice—is expressed in negative evaluation of older people by ascribing to them negative traits—decreasing intellect, slower cognitive functioning, hearing problems, senility, rigidity, incompetence, uselessness, resistance to change, lack of creativity, cautiousness, slowness to make judgments, lower physical capacity, disinterest in technological change, and difficulty in being trained (see, e.g., Nelson 2005). Ageism is also expressed in negative portrayals in the media; patronizing language, such as "overaccommodation" (being overly polite, speaking more loudly and more slowly), and "baby talk" in interpersonal conversations; and employment discrimination. In the workplace, firms are more than forty percent more likely to interview a young adult job applicant than they are an older job applicant (Lahey 2005). In terms of competency for the highest public office in the United States, a recent national survey of American voters found that a majority would be less likely to vote for a president past a given age, with only forty-five percent saying that age would not matter (Pew Research Center 2007). Although quite common in the United States and other countries, ageism is not a well-researched topic. In a search of research articles in psychology, one researcher found more than 3,000 documents for racism, 1,385 documents for sexism, and only 294 documents for ageism (Nelson 2005). Therefore, we know much less about the causes, processes, and prejudice reduction interventions for ageism, compared to what we know about racism and sexism.

In this section, I have identified four common targets of prejudice: racial or ethnic groups, women, gays and lesbians, and older people. These categories are easily identifiable as "out-groups" by an "in-group" because of perceived differences in skin color and facial characteristics (race or ethnicity), physical appearance (women, older people), or "lifestyle" (gays and lesbians). As such, they present easy targets for prejudice when people are motivated to reinforce their social identities by denigrating an out-group and enhancing the value of an in-group.

These targets of prejudice also are often marginalized in many societies, excluded from activities that could lead to a greater share of resources and from centers of power and influence, and are, therefore, compared to groups in power, easy targets for prejudice.

Who Can Be Prejudiced?

Some scholars subscribe to the idea that prejudice, particularly institutional prejudice, can only be directed by people belonging to groups in power toward people in groups without power in any given society (see, e.g., Sue 2003). In American society, people in power, according to some scholars, are predominantly White men (Sue 2004). Therefore, following this analysis, White men are the major perpetrators of prejudice in American society.

While not completely dismissing this analysis, I take a more general view of who can be prejudiced in any given society. True, the power structure should be considered, and people in power have a vested interest in keeping that power by keeping others "in their place." However, following a social identity perspective, *anyone* can be prejudiced. All of us identify with in-groups and can easily identify our out-groups. Therefore, it is theoretically feasible (and often happens in the real world) that we will direct prejudice against out-groups to strengthen our identities with the in-group. This distinction between out- and in-groups does not have to be based on race or ethnicity, gender, sexual orientation, or age. It can be based on *membership* in any category of people, from groups artificially created by the toss of a coin to, indeed, race or ethnicity, gender, sexual orientation, or age. Some in-group/out-group distinctions identified by my students in Communication and Prejudice classes include Greeks/non-Greeks; athletes/non-athletes; in football, offensive linebackers/other "skill" positions; White men/everyone else; frat men/non–frat men; sorority women/non–sorority women; engineering and science majors/liberal arts and communication majors; students from rural towns/students from large cities. These categorizations of students provide the bases for group identities, the ascription of negative traits, and, therefore, prejudice.

Jones (1997), a social psychologist noted for his research on prejudice and racism, offers a similar analysis to mine as to who can be prejudiced:

> The problems posed by prejudice and racism belong to all of us. Problematizing one group or another is a hindrance to finding solutions to the discord wrought by prejudice and racism. By framing the issue in terms of the total cultural fabric, we see clearly that we cannot solve a problem this complex and ingrained in society by singling out a particular group—whether the group be white men, say, or Latina immigrants. (531)

Workbook

Define, describe, or illustrate; summarize the results of the studies:

1.   Forms of prejudice: antilocution, avoidance, discrimination, physical attack, extermination

2.   Links between prejudice, stereotyping and discrimination

3.   Levels of analysis, prejudice: individual, interpersonal, group, institutional

4.   Social identification theory: processes

5.   Race and racism: definitions, AP poll, study results

6.   Social Institutions and Gender Index: what does it measure? components

7.   Heterosexism, ageism, sexism: definitions, examples

8.   Who can be prejudiced? Jones, Tan

4

Measures of Explicit and Implicit Prejudice

To study prejudice, we must be able to conceptually and operationally define prejudice. Conceptual definitions are "dictionary" definitions that use concepts or abstract ideas to define another concept. In this chapter, the concept of interest is *prejudice* which we have defined as "a feeling, favorable or unfavorable, toward a person or thing, prior to, or not based on actual experience" (Allport 1979, 6). But how do we detect prejudice when it happens?

This is a question of operational definitions, which specify how a concept is measured. In social science research operational definitions should accurately measure the real thing (concept of interest). A measure that does this has validity. Also, a measure should give the same results consistently if there is no change in the concept. A measure that does this is reliable. In the case of prejudice, a valid measure will assess negative feelings toward a group, not another concept such as emotional instability of the person being measured (perpetrator of prejudice), or the desire to be socially acceptable (giving a response that will be accepted by the perpetrator's group). A reliable measure will give the same results when taken today and again tomorrow, assuming no changes in the respondent's prejudice. Validity and reliability are measured by how well the measure of interest correlates with other equivalent measures or manifestations of the concept. The correlation coefficient can range from 0 (or near 0) to 1. It can be negative or positive. The higher the positive correlation coefficient, the higher the measure's validity and reliability.

Most research on prejudice in the social sciences, including communication, has focused on measuring prejudice at the individual (intrapersonal) level. To measure explicit prejudice, researchers ask individuals, through questionnaires and interviews, how they feel about a particular out-group. To measure implicit biases, researchers ask individuals to make timed associations between a member of an out-group and positive or negative words and objects.

Measures of Explicit Prejudice

In general, measures of explicit prejudice identify the target groups and ask the respondent in very direct language how he or she feels about the target group. Here are a few examples:

The Bogardus Social Distance Scale (Bogardus 1933; Karakayali 2009)

The Bogardus Social Distance Scale is a general measure of prejudice that can be applied to any out-group. The scale assumes that social distance—how far or near an individual is willing to accept a member of an out-group into his or her social space—is an indicator of prejudice. The closer the distance, the less prejudice, and, conversely, the greater the distance, the more prejudice. The scale asks people to indicate whether they would accept a member of a group into one or more of these relationships:

- As close relatives by marriage (score 1)
- As close personal friends (2)
- As neighbors on the same street (3)
- As coworkers in the same occupation (4)
- As citizens in my country (5)
- As only visitors in my country (6)
- Would exclude from my country (7)

These relationships are listed in descending order of social distance, from the closest (as close relatives by marriage) to the farthest (would exclude from the country). A person's score is the score for the closest relationships he or she checks, with a lower score indicating less distance. Thus, a person checking "as close relatives" would receive a score of 1; "as only visitors," 6; and "would exclude," 7.

The Bogardus scale is one of the most enduring and used prejudice scales in the United States. It has been used in hundreds of studies to measure the level of acceptance of various racial and ethnic groups in the United States. A common finding is that individuals generally will express closer distance for groups that are similar to their own group in physical characteristics, culture, values, history, and worldviews.

For example, a national sample of 2,916 students enrolled in twenty-two colleges and universities was surveyed in 2001 using the Bogardus Social Distance Scale (Parrillo and Donoghue 2013). The students were 70% Caucasian, 10% Black, 8.6% Hispanic, 6.4% Asian, and 6.5% another race. Although the social distance rankings were generally nonprejudicial to any particular group, with scores ranging from 1.07 (closest, indicating low prejudice) to 1.94, racial and ethnic groups most similar to White Americans were rated the closest. Here are the top 10 and lowest 10 scores and rankings, from closest to most distant: White Americans (score [S] 1.07, rank [R] 1), Italians (S 1.15, R 2), Canadians (S 1.20, R 3), British (S 1.23, R 4), Irish (S 1.23, R 5), French (S 1.28, R 6), Greeks (S 1.33, R 7), Germans (S 1.33, R 8), African Americans (S 1.33, R 9), and Dutch (S 1.35, R 10). The lowest ranked groups (most distant) were Dominicans (S 1.51, R 21), Japanese (S 1.52, R 22), Cubans (S 1.53, R 23), Koreans (S 1.54, R 24), Mexicans (S 1.55, R 25), Indians (from India) (S 1.60, R 26), Haitians (S 1.63, R 27), Vietnamese (S 1.69, R 28), Muslims (S 1.88, R 29), and Arabs (S 1.94, R 30).

Although these scores show that the students differentiated between groups in their social distance rankings, the differences are small and probably not statistically significant, meaning that the differences may be due to chance. Also, the scores are on the positive end of the scale, closer to 1 (no prejudice, closest distance) than to 7 (most prejudice, most distant). Even the score for Arabs (1.94) denotes that most respondents would accept Arabs "as my closest personal friends." These results may reflect a self-concept of college students defined by egalitarianism and acceptance of people from all races (i.e., absence of prejudice). Also, college students in particular may be more sensitive to socially desirable responses. Among peers—other college students—being egalitarian and not prejudiced is a desirable response. Explicit measures of prejudice generally elicit socially desirable responses, therefore masking the true feelings and attitudes of respondents.

The Modern Racism Scale (MRS)

The Modern Racism Scale (MRS) measures White Americans' prejudice against Blacks (McConahay 1986). Whites who endorse modern racism believe that "(a) racism against Blacks is a thing of the past; (b) Blacks are too pushy and demanding of their rights; (c) this pushiness results in the use of unfair tactics; and, consequently, (d) the advances and gains Blacks have made are undeserved" (Neville et al. 2000). Here are the items in the MRS scored on a five-point Likert scale from 1 (strongly disagree) to 5 (strongly agree):

"Over the past five years, Blacks have gotten more economically than they deserve."

"Over the past few years, the government and news media have shown more respect for Blacks than they deserve."

"It is easy to understand the anger of Black people in America."

"Discrimination against Blacks is no longer a problem in the United States."

"Blacks are getting too demanding in their push for equal rights."

"Blacks should not push themselves where they are not wanted." (McConahay 1986)

As you can see from these items, the MRI explicitly asks people (mostly White Americans) how they feel about Blacks. Reliability or consistency of responses is acceptable at .82 (McConahay 1986). However, validity is a problem. Although the MRI has been extensively used to measure prejudice against Blacks, some researchers (e.g., Sears and Henry 2005) have asked whether it is too susceptible to socially desirable responses; that is, especially among people with at least some college education, the socially desired responses will be to support Blacks, and therefore the scale will underestimate the "real" extent of prejudice against Blacks.

The Symbolic Racism Scale (SRS)

The Symbolic Racism Scale (SRS) was developed by Henry and Sears (2002) in response to critiques of the MRS. The SRS is worded so as to lessen the tendency for respondents to give socially acceptable responses, and to make it more adaptable to other racial minority groups by substituting the group of interest for "Blacks" in the questionnaire items. The SRS has been shown to be reliable (with coefficients of .7 or higher) and to correlate well with other measures of prejudice (Henry and Sears 2002). Here are the measures in the SRS, from Henry and Sears (2002):

"It's really a matter of some people not trying hard enough; if blacks would only try harder, they could be as well off as whites." (strongly agree, somewhat agree, somewhat disagree, strongly disagree)

"Irish, Italian, Jewish and many other minorities overcame prejudice and worked their way up. Blacks should do the same. (strongly agree, somewhat agree, somewhat disagree, strongly disagree)

"Some say that black leaders have been trying to push too fast. Others feel that they haven't pushed fast enough. What do you think?" (trying to push too fast, going too slowly, moving at about the right speed)

"How much of the racial tension that exists in the United States today do you think blacks are responsible for creating?" (all of it, most, some, not much at all)

"How much discrimination against blacks do you feel there is in the United States today, limiting their chances to get ahead?" (a lot, some, just a little, none at all)

"Generations of slavery and discrimination have created conditions that make it difficult for blacks to work their way out of the lower class." (strongly agree, somewhat agree, somewhat disagree, strongly disagree)

"Over the past few years, blacks have gotten less than they deserve." (strongly agree, somewhat agree, somewhat disagree, strongly disagree)

"Over the past few years, blacks have gotten more economically than they deserve." (strongly agree, somewhat agree, somewhat disagree, strongly disagree)

Although the items in the SRS are less indicative of blatant prejudice against Blacks, they still are subject to socially desirable responses, although to a lesser extent than in the MRS. Therefore, like most explicit measures of prejudice, the SRS may still be underestimating the real extent of prejudice in people.

P.J. Henry and D.O Sears, "The Symbolic Racism Scale," *Political Psychology*, Vol. 23, No. 2, pp. 260-261. Copyright © 2002 by International Society of Political Psychology.

The Color-Blind Attitude Scale (CoBAS)

The Color-Blind Attitude Scale (CoBAS) was developed by Neville et al. (2000) to measure "color-blindness" in American society, a constellation of attitudes that says race should not and does not matter. As such, the CoBAS does not directly measure racial prejudice, and is an attempt to measure a mind-set that theoretically predicts prejudice and therefore should be less susceptible to socially desirable responses. The CoBAS measures three attitudinal dimensions: (a) unawareness of racial privilege, (b) unawareness of institutional discrimination, and (c) unawareness of blatant racial issues (Neville, Roderick, Duran, Lee, and Browne 2000). In other words, a color-blind person does not think there is a problem of prejudice and discrimination against some racial groups in the United States, and this unawareness is indicative of racial prejudice. The American Psychological Association (APA) presents this analysis:

> The color-blind approach ignores research that shows, even among well-intentioned people, skin color ... figures prominently in everyday attitudes and behavior. Thus, to get beyond racism and other similar forms of prejudice, we must first take the differences between people into account. (APA 2002, 2)

Here are some sample items in the CoBAS[1], scored on a five-point Likert scale from strongly disagree to strongly agree:

"Everyone who works hard, no matter what race they are, has an equal chance to become rich."

"Race plays a major role in the type of social services (such as type of health care or day care) that people receive in the US."

"It is important that people begin to think of themselves as American and not African American, Mexican American, Italian American or any other racial group in the US."

"Due to racial discrimination, programs such as affirmative action are necessary to help create equality."

"Racism is a major problem in the US."

The CoBAS has good reliability (.7 or higher) and correlates well with more direct, explicit measures of prejudice such as the MRS. While it is less subject to social desirability than are the MRS and the SRS, it is not a measure of prejudice. Rather, it is a measure of an attitude that is related to, or predicts, prejudice. However, it is a useful measure in prejudice studies as long as the link to prejudice is established[1].

The Attitudes Toward Women Scale (AWS)

The AWS measures attitudes toward the rights and roles of women (Spence, Helmreich, and Stapp 1973). Although four decades old, it continues to be used extensively to measure gender-related attitudes indicative of prejudice toward women (see, e.g., Aosved and Long 2009). Here are some sample items from the test[2], scored on a four-point Likert scale with possible responses of agree strongly, agree mildly, disagree mildly, or disagree strongly. To score these items, assign a 0 to agree strongly; 1 to agree mildly; 2 to disagree mildly; and 3 to disagree strongly except for items tagged with "R" which should be reversed scored (strongly agree = 3; disagree strongly = 0). A high score indicates less prejudice towards women and support of a pro-feminist, egalitarian attitude while a low score indicates more prejudice and a traditional, conservative attitude.

"Swearing and obscenity are more repulsive in the speech of a woman than a man."

---

1   See Neville et al. (2000) for all items in the scale.
2   See Spence et al. (1973) for all items in the scale.

"Under modern economic conditions with women being active outside the home, men should share in household tasks, such as washing dishes and doing laundry." (R)

"It is insulting to women to have the 'obey' clause remain in the marriage service." (R)

"A woman should be free as a man to propose marriage." (R)

"Women should worry less about their rights and more about becoming good wives and mothers."

(Spence, Helmreich, and Stapp 1973)[2].

This scale is reliable with a reported coefficient of .85 and correlates well with other measures of sexism, indicating validity (Aosved, Long, and Voller 2009). However, it has been criticized for measuring primarily old-fashioned sexism (which today most people would not admit to) rather than the common, subtler, modern sexism more likely to be found today.

The Ambivalent Sexism Inventory (ASI)

The Ambivalent Sexism Inventory (ASI) was developed by Glick and Fiske in 1996 to measure hostile and benevolent sexism toward women, with benevolent sexism representing subtler, modern sexism. As defined by Glick and Fiske (1996), *hostile sexism* "is an antagonistic attitude toward women, who are often viewed as trying to control men through feminist ideology or sexual seduction." *Benevolent sexism* is a "chivalrous attitude toward women that feels favorable but is actually sexist because it casts women as weak creatures in need of men's protection."

Here are some sample items in the ASI[3]; responses are on a five-point Likert scale from disagree strongly to agree strongly. Benevolent sexism items are labeled as "B"; hostile sexism items are labeled as "H":

B 1. "No matter how accomplished he is, a man is not truly complete as a person unless he has the love of a woman."

H 2. "Many women are actually seeking special favors, such as hiring policies that favor them over men, under the guise of asking for 'equality.'"

B 3. "In a disaster, women ought not necessarily to be rescued before men." (R)

H 4. "Most women interpret innocent remarks or acts as being sexist."

H 5. "Women are too easily offended."

(Glick and Fiske 1996)

To score the ASI, assign a score of 5 to agree strongly responses and 0 to disagree strongly responses, except for items labeled with "R," which should be reverse-scored (disagree strongly = 5, agree strongly = 0). Then average or sum the scores. The higher the score, the more prejudice toward women, or the more sexism expressed.

The ASI, particularly the benevolent sexism items, is more appropriate for today's American society and is less susceptible to socially desirable responses than are other sexism scales. The developers of the scale, Glick and Fiske (1996) report favorable reliability and validity coefficients[3].

---

3   See Glick and Fiske (1996) for all items in the scale.

The Modern Homophobia Scale (MHS)

The Modern Homophobia Scale (MHS) was developed by Raja and Stokes (1998) to measure prejudice against lesbians and gay men. It is an improvement over many other previous scales measuring sexual prejudice, which did not differentiate between gays and lesbians and instead referred to them as "homosexuals," that is, as one group. The MHS consists of twenty-four items for lesbians and twenty-two items for gay men, which measure institutional sexual prejudice, personal discomfort, and beliefs that homosexuality is "deviant and changeable" (Aosver and Long 2009). The items are scored on a five-point Likert scale, from 1 (do not agree) to 5 (strongly agree). Items with an "R" should be reverse-scored so that strongly agree = 1 and do not agree = 5. Lower scores indicate higher levels of sexual prejudice. Here are some sample items. In the actual test, separate items are presented for lesbians and gay men.

> "I wouldn't mind going to a party that included (lesbians/gay men)."
> "I wouldn't mind working with a (lesbian/gay man)."
> "I am comfortable with the thought of two (women/men) being romantically involved."
> "I welcome new friends who are (lesbians/gay men)."
> "I don't think it would affect our relationship if I learned that one of my close friends was a (lesbian/ gay man)."
> "(Lesbians/Gay men) should undergo therapy to change their sexual orientation." (R)
> "It's all right with me for two (women/men) to hold hands."
> "(Male/Female) homosexuality is a psychological disorder." (R)
> (Raja and Stokes 1998).

The MHS scale has good reliability ($r = .95$) and correlates well with other measures of sexism, an indicator of good validity. Although still quite explicit in asking respondents about prejudice against gays and lesbians, it is an improvement over other existing scales in that it breaks down prejudice into institutional and personal prejudice, and differentiates between lesbians and gay men rather than referring to them as one group (i.e., "homosexuals").

To illustrate the difficulty in operationalizing homophobia, here is a news report from 2013 about the decision of the Boy Scouts of America to accept openly gay boys as Scouts (Selle 2013):

> Coeur d'Alene, Idaho, May 25, 2013: The Kootenai County Sheriff said Friday that he is compelled to drop the department's Boy Scouts of America charter because the organization is promoting a lifestyle that is against state law.
>
> "It would be inappropriate for the sheriff's office to sponsor an organization that is promoting a lifestyle that is in violation of state law," Sheriff Ben Wolfinger said.
>
> Sodomy is against the law in Idaho, he added.
>
> Boy Scouts of America voted to open its ranks to openly gay boys on Thursday during the National Council's annual meeting at a conference center not far from Boy Scout headquarters in suburban Dallas. Of the roughly 1,400 voting members of the council who cast ballots, 61 percent supported the proposal drafted by the governing Executive Committee. The policy change takes effect Jan. 1.
>
> In the resolution that was passed, it states: "Scouting is a youth program and any sexual conduct, whether homosexual or heterosexual, by youth of Scouting age is contrary to the virtues of Scouting."
>
> While the National Council said the ban on openly gay adult leaders is still in effect, Wolfinger said media reports indicate that the Boy Scouts will eventually lift that ban as well.
>
> "It's in *USA Today*, this just opens the door to having openly gay scout leaders," he added.

The controversy arising from the Boy Scouts' decision to accept openly gay boys as Scouts raises an empirical question for objective and scientific analysis. Does prejudice against gays play a role in objections to the decision? Are we overlooking rational reasons for objections because of the pressure to appear nonprejudiced?

The Fraboni Scale of Ageism (FSA)

The Fraboni Scale of Ageism (FSA) measures prejudice toward the elderly (Fraboni, Sallstone, and Hughes 1990). It includes twenty-nine items on people's attitudes toward and beliefs about older people. Responses are scored on a five-point scale from 1 (strongly agree) to 5 (strongly disagree). Scores are summed for the twenty-nine items; higher scores indicate lower levels of prejudice against the elderly. Here are some items from the FSA; items with an "R" should be reverse-scored:

"Teenage suicide is more tragic than suicide among the elderly."
"Many elderly people just live in the past."
"Feeling depressed when around elderly people is probably a common feeling."
"Many elderly people are happiest when they are with people their own age."
"I sometimes avoid eye contact with elderly people when I see them."
"I would prefer not to live with an elderly person."
"Elderly people complain more than other people."
"Most elderly people should not be allowed to renew their driver's licenses."
"Elderly people should be encouraged to speak out politically." (R)
"Elderly people deserve the same rights and freedoms as other members of our society." (R)
"Elderly people can be very creative." (R)
"I personally would not want to spend much time with an elderly person."
(Fraboni, Sallstone, and Hughes 1990)

The FSA is reliable ($r = .86$) and correlates well with other measures of ageism (Fraboni et al. 1990). It measures institutional and personal prejudices against the elderly, an improvement over other measures that measure only personal or individual prejudice.

In this section, I have discussed several measures of explicit prejudice directed toward race, women, gays and lesbians, and the elderly, as well as a social distance scale that can be adapted to measure prejudice against any out-group. These scales (collection of individual items) all measure prejudice at the *individual level* using questionnaires that can be filled out by the respondent (self-administered) or with questions that could be asked in an interview. More commonly, the measures are self-administered. The items measure an individual's level of prejudice, at least to the extent that he or she is conscious (aware) of them, and able to and willing to express them. Typically, individual responses are summed or averaged for all respondents in the sample group, and aggregate scores are presented as indicative of a defined group's prejudice (e.g., college students) toward a target. Or, individual scores within a sample are correlated with other individual variables, such as level of education, frequency of contact with the target group, gender, and other personality and demographic variables, to identify predictors of prejudice. As such, analysis at the individual level (intrapersonal) provides useful information on why people (individuals) are prejudiced, and how their prejudices can be controlled or minimized. Analysis at the individual level is the focus of this book, and provides the basis for most of the discussion to come on causes of prejudice, consequences of prejudice, and interventions.

Prejudice can also be measured at a more macro (group and institutional) level. These macro measures usually use statistics of observable and recorded (or potentially recordable) events, actions, and consequences from within a defined community, such as a city, region, or country, on the representation of the groups targeted for prejudice in the institutions and practices of the community, and in the sharing of desired resources. A good example is the Social Institutions and Gender Index (SIGI) developed by the Organization for Economic Co-operation and Development (OECD) to measure prejudice against women around the world. Recall from Chapter 3 that the OECD measures social and community (subsumed under the category of "institutional") policies and practices affecting women, such family codes, physical integrity, civil liberties, and resources and entitlements. Other examples of institutional measures are rates of incarceration and length of sentences for crimes, educational attainment, representation at executive levels in business, drop-out rates in school, per capita distribution of resources such as school aid, and health care delivery. Comparisons of these data for groups within a society (e.g., racial groups) and controlling for other variables (e.g., community size, population distribution) provide a basis for inferring the existence of prejudice against target groups (out-groups) in the community. The challenge, as with individual measures, is to rule out other possible causes for the observed and inferred prejudice.

The individual measures we have discussed (and this is also true for most institutional measures) are based on the assumption that people are aware of our prejudices and are willing to express them in words and actions. This assumption is not always tenable, particularly in societies where egalitarian values are, at least on the surface, widely accepted, as in, for example, the United States. As such, a new wave of research in psychology and communications has focused on another type of prejudice—implicit biases or implicit prejudice.

To illustrate the difficulty in analyzing whether explicit prejudice is driving overt actions, consider this news report about a judge's ruling on racial profiling in Arizona.

> According to the *New York Times* (2013), a federal judge in Arizona ruled that the Maricopa County sheriff and his deputies had violated the constitutional rights of Latinos by targeting them during raids and traffic stops in Phoenix and throughout the county. The judge said that the sheriff relied on racial profiling and illegal detentions to target Latinos, using their ethnicity as the main basis for suspecting that they were in the country illegally even when many of the people targeted were citizens or legal residents of the United States. The judge also ruled that the sheriff's deputies unreasonably prolonged the detentions of people who were pulled over.
>
> The judge said that the sheriff, who symbolized Arizona's strict approach to immigration enforcement, turned much of his focus to arresting immigrants who he and his deputies suspected were in the country illegally, in most cases for civil violations, at the expense of fighting crime.
>
> The *Times* reported that the judge's ruling came more than eight months after a seven-day, nonjury trial. The sheriff has repeatedly denied the allegations. He did not face jail time or fines as a result of the ruling. Instead, he and his deputies were prohibited from using race or Latino ancestry as a factor in deciding whether to stop a vehicle or as a factor in deciding whether Latino occupants of a car are in the country without authorization.
>
> The lawyer for the sheriff's office said the office intended to appeal, and that the office's position was that it "has never used race and never will use race to make any law enforcement decision."
>
> According to the *Times*, the sheriff, known for jailing inmates in tents and making prisoners wear pink underwear, started strict immigration enforcement in 2006 when Arizona voters expressed frustration with the state being the nation's busiest "illegal entryway."

Consider the ruling of the judge that the sheriff was engaging in racial profiling of Hispanics. Do you agree? How much of the sheriff's actions are caused by prejudice against Hispanics? Or was he simply exercising common sense in performing his duties? Are statistics on when racial profiling happens an individual or institutional measure of prejudice?

Measures of Implicit Prejudice

My scores on explicit measures of prejudice indicate that I have absolutely no prejudices toward people of other races, gays and lesbians, women, the elderly, or any out-group I can think of. Does this mean I am prejudice-free? Hardly. I am aware of what these tests measure. Given my self-image as a prejudice-free person who has actively campaigned for equal rights for just about any group you can think of, I know what responses to the test items are expected of me and will be consistent with my self-image. Therefore, these explicit measures may not be accurately measuring how, *subconsciously*, I may feel about some out-groups.

I catch myself, occasionally, in actions and decisions that are not consistent with being prejudice-free: jumping to the conclusion that the Black man who is in a photo accompanying a news story is the perpetrator of the crime rather than the victim; assuming the man I am having a conversation with is the CEO of a business rather than the woman who is with him; speaking loudly and slowly with an elderly person; avoiding eye contact with an openly gay man I am talking to; asking an Asian American student what country is she from; wondering whether a Hispanic man I've just met is "legal" or not. And here's another example from my own experience:

> After a workout in our dojo, our sensei (karate instructor) takes me aside and asks me if I want to teach a class at a community center in a neighboring town. We are in West Texas, a bastion of conservative political and religious thought, where gun racks in pickup trucks are a common sight and a "macho" male-centric culture is the norm. My taking up karate was very much a survival response in my new environment.
>
> "Yes, of course," I say without hesitation. "I enjoy teaching kids."
>
> "Well, your students won't be kids."
>
> "That's fine, adults are fun too."
>
> "Your students will be members of the Wild Boars."
>
> I pause. That's a motorcycle gang. Images of the Hell's Angels. Burly men with White Power and Nazi tattoos, unkempt hair and beards, probably drug dealers and murderers and racists, too. "Why would we teach them the martial arts? Won't we be just contributing to their ability to hurt others? They already have guns, knives, and who knows what else," I ask, trying to find a way out. What I was actually trying to say to my instructor was, Why me? A brown-skinned Filipino with a ponytail. Why not one of our White black belts to teach these rednecks?
>
> "Their officers said they wanted to stay in shape and learn self-defense," my sensei says. "Remember what Buddha says..." he adds.
>
> A week later, I park in front of the "community center," except that it wasn't the community center but the gang's clubhouse. Twenty or so men, mostly in their thirties and forties, of all shapes and sizes, were waiting for me, some sitting on the floor, others standing or leaning on the walls, most engaged in animated conversation. I am wearing my black gi (martial arts uniform) and my well-worn brown belt (I know more of this stuff than any of you will ever know, [I thought]). No one notices when I enter the room.
>
> "Hello," I say loudly without shouting. (Wouldn't "YO" be more appropriate, I ask myself.)
>
> Most of the conversation stops. They turn toward me. Are those questioning looks in their eyes? I'm the only person of color in the room. Thank goodness for Asian stereotypes, I say to myself.
>
> I introduce myself and ask them to form two lines facing me, to take off their shoes and boots (we're in Texas). I ask each one to introduce himself and to say why they are interested in karate and what they did for a living. I get the usual answers to my first question—to stay in shape, for self-defense, one even says "for balance" in his life, another "for inner peace." Answers to my second question provide the surprise. There are accountants, store owners, farmers, ranchers, schoolteachers, even a lawyer or two. So, these aren't the Hell's Angels after all.
>
> I enjoy teaching the class and having a beer or two with some of my students after our workout. (Tan 2013)

This experience, and many more like them, have led me to the very uncomfortable and disconcerting realization that I have unconscious prejudices and biases that sometimes influence my actions, perceptions of people, and decisions in ways that I am not even aware of. And my hidden prejudices are confirmed by results of the Implicit Association Tests (discussed later in this section) I have taken.

Implicit prejudices are biases for or against people or objects that are not under the conscious control of the individual making the bias evaluations. Therefore, the individual is not aware that he or she is making these evaluations based on biases that are "unconscious, unthinking, automatic, impulsive and intuitional" (Greenwald and Banaji 1995). Implicit biases operate at an unconscious level; we are not even aware that we have them (unless pointed out by an external source such as the Implicit Associations Test). However, these biases direct our perceptions and judgments of people and objects, as well as our actions toward them. Quite often, implicit prejudices are manifested impulsively and are activated automatically in the mere presence of the target object or person without conscious intention or awareness (Bargh, Schwader, Haily, Dyer, and Boothby 2012).

Implicit prejudice is based on implicit attitudes and implicit stereotypes (Greenwald and Krieger 2006). Implicit attitudes are unconscious (not intentionally controlled) affective, or like/dislike or favorable/unfavorable, evaluations. Implicit stereotypes are the unconscious assignment of traits to groups that we generalize to the individual member. Implicit prejudices can be positive (in favor of or preference for a group or object) or negative (against a group or object). Although implicit prejudice is unconscious, it directs many of our overt actions and judgments, such as evaluation of job candidates, ascription of guilt to defendants in court, assignment of blame in crime, personal interactions with people, evaluations of ability of school children, delivery of health care, and many others, discussed in Chapter 5. When these actions and evaluations are discriminatory, that is, resulting in an imbalance in the distribution of resources or the meting out of punishments in a society, then implicit prejudices, although an individual-level construct, can have dysfunctional and deleterious effects in a society, particularly on the groups targeted for these actions and evaluations. Compared to explicit prejudice (which most people won't admit to), implicit prejudices are more difficult to control because they "operate under the radar," and are discernible primarily when they are manifested in overt evaluations and actions. Also, measures of implicit attitudes have been shown to have a significantly higher correlation with discriminatory behaviors than measures of explicit prejudice (see, e.g., Greenwald and Krieger 2006).

How then are implicit prejudices measured? In 1995, Greenwald and Banaji developed the Implicit Associations Test (IAT: available online at http://implicit.harvard.edu/implicit/demo/index.isp), which has been taken voluntarily by more than two million people worldwide, mostly by people in the United States.

The IAT measures how we unconsciously and automatically assign valence (positive or negative feelings or attitudes) and traits or stereotypes (positive and negative) to groups of people and objects. Using a computer keyboard, the respondent, by clicking the appropriate keys, associates valence and traits to identified groups or objects presented on a computer screen. Thus, the IAT indirectly measures relative strengths of associations between concepts and attributes (Greenwald, McGhee, and Schwartz 1998). A strong association will require less time, because it is easier to give the same response (clicking on the keyboard) to items representing two concepts when they are well associated than when they are not. For example, consider two concepts: African Americans and European Americans and two general evaluations (valence), pleasant and unpleasant. It is easier to give one response to unconscious associations in our minds because of stereotypes that we may not even be aware of than it is to give one response to unconscious associations that are contrary to stereotypes that we may not be aware of. The IAT effect is the difference in time that it takes a respondent to make the associations between concepts and words representing valence or traits. In the example above, if it took me a lot less time, measured in milliseconds, to associate pleasant words with European Americans and unpleasant words with African Americans, compared to the time it takes me to associate pleasant words with African Americans and unpleasant words with European Americans, I will have revealed an implicit bias for European Americans over African Americans (a common finding from IAT tests, by the way). According to Greenwald, McGhee, and Schwartz (1998), the IAT is resistant to the self-presentation effect (giving the socially desirable response) and depends less, compared to explicit measures, on conscious cognitive processing of the respondent. Therefore, the IAT measures biases that are not discernible from explicit measures.

The IAT is scored by computing the time difference (in milliseconds) between the time taken to complete the "stereotype non-congruent test" (e.g., European Americans and negative words; African Americans and positive words) and the time taken to complete the stereotype congruent test (e.g., European Americans and positive words; African Americans and negative words). A positive difference indicates that it took the respondent longer to complete the non-congruent test, implying that it was harder for him or her, in our example above, to associate positive words with African Americans and negative words with European Americans, an indication of implicit biases against African Americans. The IAT scores can range from –2 to +2; scores of .15 are considered to be indicative of a "slight bias"; .35 indicates a "moderate bias"; and .65 indicates a "strong bias" (Greenwald et al. 1998).

A more valid and reliable score than the millisecond difference scores was developed by Greenwald, Nosek, and Banaji in 2003. This is the "D" measure, which, unlike the millisecond difference measure, is less susceptible to individual differences in test taking such as cognitive skill. The "D" measure, also referred to as "log-transformed latencies" (Greenwald et al. 2003), divides the individual millisecond difference by an overall "latency" standard deviation, resulting in a measure that takes into account individual variability in taking the test (see Greenwald et al. 2003 for a more complete and technical discussion). For our purposes, suffice it to say that the "D" measure is the preferred one.

The IAT has fifteen versions at this time:

- Race IAT
- Asian IAT
- Arab-Muslim IAT
- Skin-Tone IAT
- Native IAT
- Age IAT
- Religion IAT
- Sexuality IAT
- Weight IAT
- Disability IAT
- Gender–Science IAT
- Gender–Career IAT
- Obama–McCain IAT
- President IAT
- Weapons IAT

These individual IATs can be classified into valence IATs, which associate concepts with positive or negative valences, and stereotype IATs, which associate the social stereotypes with concepts. Since 1998, several IAT tests have been available as self-administered tests on a website (http://implicit.harvard.edu) to anyone willing to have individual results anonymously included in analysis of aggregated results (Greenwald and Krieger 2006; Nosek 2005). Of 2.2 million American adults taking a race IAT test, 65.3% favored European Americans, compared to 10.6% favoring African Americans, with 24.1% neutral, for a bias index of 55% (the percentage favoring an advantaged group minus the percentage favoring a disadvantaged group). Of 1.15 million American adults taking the age IAT, 81% favored the young compared to 4.7% favoring the old, with 14.3% neutral, for a bias index of 76% (Greenwald and Krieger 2006).

Additional analysis of the race IAT showed a bias for Whites over African Americans among respondents who were White (65% bias index, or BI), Hispanic (50% BI), and Asian American/Pacific Islanders (60% BI). Black Americans showed a slight bias for African Americans (–2% BI; 34% favored African Americans, 32.4% favored Whites, and 33.6% were neutral). Also, bias for Whites over African Americans was found among people under 25 (58% BI), 25 to 44 (50% BI), and 45 and older (49% BI); females (52% BI) and males (59% BI); and conservatives (67% BI), moderates (56% BI), and liberals (48% BI). Therefore, the bias for Whites over African Americans was held by all respondents regardless of race (except for Black American respondents), gender, and political ideology (Greenwald and Krieger 2006; Nosek, Greenwald, and Banaji 2007).

These tests were taken voluntarily by people who were probably interested in discovering their own hidden biases and therefore more likely to be less biased than a general population. Consequently, the voluntary nature of the tests and the self-selected sample may actually underrepresent the biases in the general adult American population toward African Americans and the elderly.

Similar data were collected by the IAT research team (see, e.g., Greenwald and Krieger 2006; Nosek 2005) from IAT research website tests, which had smaller samples ranging from 144 to 263 American adults. Here are some of results, reported as bias indices:

- 51% BI, Whites over Asians
- 67% American places over foreign places
- 60% straight people over gay people
- 57% Jews over Muslims
- 93% rich people over poor people
- 53% thin people over fat people
- 73% USA over Japan

The data set reported by Nosek et al. (2007) and Greenwald and Krieger (2006) compares bias indices computed from explicit measures of prejudice (self-reports of endorsed attitudes) and the IAT. This analysis shows a BI of 24% for explicit measures and 64% for the IAT; also, 42% of respondents expressed neutral attitudes on the explicit measures compared to only 18% on the IAT. These results show that far more bias is revealed by the IAT and that people are more likely to express neutrality in explicit tests than they are in implicit tests.

The IAT also reveals associations that we make between people and traits and objects. Here are some results (as reported in Greenwald and Krieger 2006):

- Most people associate women more strongly with liberal arts and men with science, and women with family and men with careers.
- Most people associate Asian Americans with foreign landmarks, and European Americans with American landmarks.
- Most people associate Black faces with weapons, and White faces with harmless objects.
- Most people have a bias for lighter over darker skin tone.

Most of the IAT studies have reported results from adult populations in the United States. Similar results have been reported from several Asian, European, and Australian groups (Nosek 2005). More recently, a children's IAT has been developed (Baron and Banaji 2006) using sounds and pictures rather than words and pictures, and smiling and frowning faces rather than positively or negatively valenced words. Among the results, six-year-olds have biases similar to those of ten-year-olds and adults on the race IAT (Baron and Banaji 2006).

The IAT is not without its critics. One criticism is the "arbitrary" cutoff points for associating a score with descriptors of bias (Blanton, Jaccard, Gonzales, and Christie 2006). The IAT score can range from –2.0 to + 2.0, with any score above +.65 or below –.65 described as a strong indicator of bias for the advantaged group, such as White Americans (+), or the disadvantaged group, such as African Americans (–). According to Blanton (2005), there is "not a single study showing that above or below that cutoff, people differ in any way based on that score." To this criticism, Nosek (2005) says that most social psychological measures are arbitrary metrics, that the descriptors are intended to guide interpretation of the raw scores, and that people taking the test are advised not to overinterpret results. Also, Greenwald et al. (2009) point out that the IAT is a significantly better predictor of behavior than explicit tests are. Therefore, regardless of the labels attached to the scores, the scores themselves have predictive validity.

Another criticism of the IAT is that the test is sensitive to its social context; that is, people's scores change depending on external influences. Though this may be true to some extent, Greenwald and Krieger (2009) point out that the IAT is still a better predictor of behaviors than explicit tests are, indicating that it is less sensitive to external influence. Also, the "D" score discussed earlier controls for individual variances or influences in test-taking.

Even with these criticisms, the IAT continues to be a major influence in current research on prejudice because it is a better predictor of discriminatory or other prejudicial behaviors than explicit prejudice is. In the next chapter, I discuss what these behaviors are, and how explicit and implicit prejudices predict them.

Workbook

Define, describe, or illustrate; summarize the results of the studies:

1.   Correlation coefficient, reliability, validity

2.   Bogardus Social Distance Scale, Modern Racism Scale, Symbolic Racism Scale, Color-Blind Attitude Scale, Attitudes toward Women Scale, Ambivalent Sexism Inventory, Modern Homophobia Scale, Fraboni Scale of Ageism: What do they measure?

3.   Implicit prejudice and bias: definitions

4.   Implicit Association Test: What is it?

5.   Results of IAT

6.   Criticisms of IAT

7.   Response to criticisms of IAT

5

Consequences of Prejudice

Prejudice, as defined in Chapter 3, is an attitude or affective disposition (feeling) toward a person, group, or object that can be positive or negative. Whether explicit or implicit, prejudice is assumed to predict behaviors toward the targets of prejudice. In fact, our interest in prejudice is primarily because of its potential harmful effects when manifested in actions that are discriminatory and unfair. The ability of measures of explicit and implicit prejudice to predict behaviors that theoretically are related to prejudice is referred to in research as *predictive validity*. Thus, if a preference for Whites over Blacks in the Implicit Associations Test (IAT) predicts a preference for Whites over Blacks in hiring, the Black–White IAT has predictive validity. In testing for predictive validity of explicit and implicit measures of prejudice, researchers have identified several behavioral consequences of prejudice. These findings not only inform us on the predictive validity of the prejudice measures; they also provide guidance on social and legal policies, as well as on individual decisions that may be based on our biases. The research shows that, in fact, a large number of discriminatory behaviors are predicted by both explicit and implicit prejudices.

An analysis of 184 research studies by Greenwald, Poehlman, et al. (2009) showed that, overall, both IAT and explicit measures had predictive validity—that is, independently, they were significant predictors of social behaviors and judgments, including consumer preferences, Black-White interracial behavior, personality differences, clinical phenomena, alcohol and drug use, nonracial intergroup behavior, gender and sexual orientation evaluations, close relationships, and political preferences. For behaviors and judgments that were not socially sensitive, such as consumer preferences and political preferences, explicit measures were stronger predictors. However, for socially sensitive behaviors such as interracial and other intergroup behaviors, IAT measures were stronger predictors. These results establish the predictive validity of both explicit and implicit measures. Understandably, implicit measures (IAT) are stronger predictors in situations such as interracial interactions when socially desirable responses to explicit measures can mask the underlying or unconscious prejudices of people. Here are some behaviors and related judgments of people that research shows to be affected by explicit and implicit prejudices.

Hiring Practices and Evaluations

A number of studies have shown that employers are more reluctant to hire and invite for a job interview, and more likely to give negative evaluations to, people from groups that the IAT and explicit measures of prejudice show they are biased against. Most of these studies have compared how Black and White applicants are evaluated when they have equivalent qualifications, the only difference being race. In some studies, these evaluations are analyzed according to implicit biases of the hiring authorities uncovered in the IAT and, sometimes, according to explicit measures of prejudice. Here are some such studies.

1. Bertrand and Mullainathan (2004) sent out 5,000 résumés in 2001 and 2002, in response to more than 1,300 employment ads in Chicago and Boston newspapers. The ads were for a wide range of jobs, including sales, administrative support, clerical, customer service, and office and management positions. Half of the résumés were "higher quality" and the other half "lower quality," with the higher-quality résumés indicating more experience and "fewer holes" in the employment history. For half of the résumés, the applicant had a typically African American-sounding name, such as Lakisha Washington or Jamal Jones; the other résumés were from applicants with a typically White-sounding name, such as Emily Walsh or Greg Baker. The researchers selected distinctively African American and White names from birth certificates in Massachusetts, and pretested them in Chicago. Therefore, half of the résumés were equivalently high quality; the others were low quality and equivalent to each other. In addition, half of the high-quality and low-quality résumés were from applicants with African American names; half of the low-quality résumés were from applicants with White-sounding names. The difference between the résumés, high and low quality, was the name of the applicant, African American or White.

Bertrand and Mullainathan (2004) found that applicants with White names needed to send about ten résumés to get one callback, whereas applicants with African American names needed to send fifteen résumés, a difference of about fifty percent. Also, Whites with higher-quality résumés received nearly thirty percent more callbacks compared to Whites with lower-quality résumés, while the difference in number of callbacks for Blacks with higher-quality résumés compared to Blacks with lower-quality résumés was statistically not significant, except for "special skills such as a certification degree and ability to speak a foreign language." Bertrand and Mullainathan (2004) concluded that of "two identical individuals engaging in an identical job search, the one with an African-American name would receive fewer interviews" (1000) than would the one with a White name. Further, a higher-quality résumé helps White applicants significantly more than it does African American applicants. As interpreted by the researchers, "the gap between Whites and African-Americans widens with résumé quality. While one may have expected improved credentials to alleviate employers' fear that African-American applicants are deficient in some unobservable skills, this is not the case in our data" (992).

This study shows differential and discriminatory treatment of African Americans in the job market, but can the evaluations and actions of employers be attributed to prejudice? We can't tell, and can only surmise, because prejudice was not measured as a possible cause. The next two studies that follow provide direct and experimental evidence that prejudice, indeed, is a factor in hiring evaluations and decisions.

2. Ziegert and Hanges (2005) used a laboratory setting with college students as participants to study whether explicit and implicit prejudices influence evaluations of Black and White job applicants. In addition to prejudice, they also wanted to know whether organizational climate influenced these evaluations. They measured explicit prejudice with the Attitudes toward Blacks Scale (Brigham 1993) and the Modern Racism Scale (McConahy 1986), and implicit prejudice with the IAT. They manipulated organizational climate by giving half the study participants—randomly selected—a memo from the fictitious organization's president that advised the students participating in the study to hire the White candidate because most of the workforce was White. Students in the climate for equality condition did not receive these instructions. The students took the explicit prejudice tests and were asked one month later to evaluate the dossiers of job applicants with equivalent qualifications. Half of the applicants were identified to be Black, the other half White. Participants rated each applicant on a five-point scale, from 1 (should not have been referred) to 5 (excellent referral). After rating the applicants, the participants took the IAT.

Results showed that (a) participants in the climate for racial bias condition ("hire a White candidate") evaluated the Black candidates significantly lower than did participants in the climate for equality condition; (b) explicit prejudice did not influence candidate ratings in either of the climate conditions; (c) participants who showed a bias for Whites over Blacks in the IAT rated the Black candidates lower than White candidates, but only in the climate for racial bias condition.

These results show, first, that organization climate has a significant influence on hiring decisions and second, that implicit biases result in discriminatory evaluations of candidates, but only in a race-bias climate. This study was done with college students. Do implicit biases influence hiring evaluations and decisions in the real world, with real employers? Let's take a look at the next study.

3. Rooth (2010) studied whether explicit and implicit prejudices affect the evaluations of Swedish and Arab Muslim men for jobs in Sweden. He asked 193 employers to take an Arab Muslim performance stereotype IAT, an Arab-Muslim attitude IAT, and explicit measures of prejudice such as the Feeling Thermometer (a scale that measures feelings towards people or objects, from 0, very cold or unfavorable to 100, very warm or favorable). They were then asked to state how probable it would be that they would invite an applicant for an interview. Half of the applicants had Swedish-sounding names; the other half, Arab Muslim names. Rooth (2010) reports that there was a significant correlation between employer IAT scores indicating a bias against Arab Muslims and the probability that the employer would invite an Arab Muslim for an interview. Among recruiters who had at least a moderate negative implicit bias against Arab Muslims (56% of recruiters), the probability to invite job applicants with Muslim names (such as Mohammed or Ali) decreased by five percentage points. There was not a significant association between explicit prejudice scores and the probability that an Arab Muslim would be invited for an interview. Rooth concludes by saying, "There are recruiters who implicitly discriminate, but who would not explicitly do so" (529).

Taken together, the three studies we have reviewed so far provide evidence that (a) racial prejudice influences the evaluation of job candidates, and (b) implicit prejudice or bias is a stronger predictor of discriminatory evaluations than explicit prejudice. These studies have focused on people's race and ethnicity as targets of prejudice. Do women face similar prejudices in hiring decisions? There is evidence that they do. Let's take a look at one study that supports this conclusion.

4. Moss-Racusin et al. (2012) wanted to find out if university professors in the sciences would show gender bias in favor of men when evaluating student applicants for a laboratory manager position. This is an interesting question because professors, particularly those who are scientists, are trained to be objective in their work, and we would therefore expect them to be objective in evaluating the job candidates. On the other hand, people who have a self-identity as being objective, fair, and egalitarian are often susceptible to unconscious biases because they are less careful about being "on guard" about those biases (Monin and Miller 2001; Uhlmann and Cohen 2007). The researchers also wanted to know whether explicit biases against women as measured by the Modern Sexism Scale (Swim et al. 1995), would influence their evaluations. A number of previous studies have shown gender bias in hiring decisions: Women are evaluated to be warm, nurturing, and likeable, but less competent than men, particularly in high-prestige and high-paying jobs typically populated by men, and implicit biases exacerbate the bias for men in these fields (see, e.g., Foschi 2000). These findings held for both men and women employers: Women were just as likely as men to show gender bias in favor of men. Based on these previous studies and the finding that people who believe they are objective without biases are susceptible to the automatic expression of hidden biases, Moss-Racusin et al. (2012) expected to find a gender bias in favor of men among both men and women scientists, and that implicit biases against women would be negatively related to evaluations of the female job applicant.

To test these hypotheses, the researchers asked a nationwide sample of 127 professors in biology, chemistry, and physics from research-intensive universities to rate the application of an undergraduate student who was presented as applying for a science laboratory manager position. The application consisted of identical résumés, with half of the applicants assigned a female name and the other half assigned a male name. These two versions of the application (male or female applicant) were assigned randomly to the professors who would make the evaluations. The professors were asked to rate the competence and hirability of the applicant, to recommend a starting salary, and to indicate their willingness to mentor the applicant if hired. They were also asked to complete the Modern Sexism Scale.

Results supported all of the researchers' hypotheses. Both men and women evaluators rated the male applicant as significantly more competent and hirable than the female applicant, recommended a higher salary for the male applicant, and offered more career mentoring to the male applicant. Scores of the men and women evaluators on the Modern Sexism Scale were negatively related to evaluations of the female candidate, but not the male candidate; the more bias, the less competent and hirable the female candidate was perceived to be, and less mentoring offered to her.

This study shows that gender bias in hiring operates in the sciences, a male-dominated field, and that this bias is found in men and women. Additionally, implicit bias against women causes even more negative evaluations of women, confirming results from other studies.

Consider this report about a Black female scientist.

Scientist or "Whore" Question Points to Prejudice Toward Women in Science?

According to the *Chronicle of Higher Education* (October 25, 2013), a Black woman scientist with a PhD in biology received an e-mail asking if she would be interested in contributing to the life sciences blog, *Biology Online*. The scientist studies rodent behavior and wrote the popular *Urban Scientist* blog for *Scientific American*. She declined the offer when she learned that the blogging assignment would be unpaid. The blog's editor responded, "Are you an urban scientist or an urban whore?"

The *Chronicle* reported that the exchange between the scientist and the blog's editor generated a number of comments from science bloggers pointing to the continuing difficulties facing women with careers in science, especially women of color. An engineering dean at the City College of New York said in an e-mail, "The incident is indicative of the pervasive and well-documented devaluation and marginalization of women of color in science."

According to the *Chronicle*, *Biology Online* apologized to the scientist and announced that the blog's editor had been fired.

Question

- Was the "urban whore" comment " indicative of prejudice, or was the comment an unbiased response to a refusal to contribute to the blog?

Political Attitudes and Behaviors

Do explicit and implicit prejudices influence our preferences for political candidates from a different race and our positions on race-coded issues or issues that differentially affect people from different races? Two studies discussed below shed some light on these questions. They were done just before the 2008 presidential election, which provided a natural "laboratory" with Barack Obama running against John McCain. (Note: The 2012 election with President Obama running for reelection against Governor Romney provided a similar laboratory. I could find no published studies, however, probably because of the time lag between study completion and publication in research journals, which can be one year or more.)

1. Greenwald, Smith, et al. (2009) studied 1,057 registered voters before the 2008 presidential election. This sample voluntarily visited the Project Implicit website (http://implicit.harvard.edu) and completed the following tests and measures: self-report measures of citizenship, age, sex, race, and liberal-conservative ideology; two Black–White IATs; two Black–White thermometer scales; the Symbolic Racism Scale; a political conservatism scale; and intention to vote for Obama or McCain. Not surprisingly, the sample was not representative of the general population because participants voluntarily visited the Project Implicit website, indicating that they were interested in finding out about their implicit biases. Study participants were highly educated (64.9%) with BA, BS, or higher educational degrees; predominantly intended to vote for Obama (84.2%) over McCain (15.8%); were considerably more politically liberal than the American population (mean = −1.78 on a seven-point scale from −3, strong liberal, to +3, strong conservative); had a mean age of 35.1; and were 81.3% White, 6.3% Black, and 12.4% from other racial categories. Because a large majority of participants were for Obama and were self-reported liberals, the researchers weighted the sample so that results are reported for a theoretical sample with equal proportions of Obama and McCain supporters.

Here are some results of the analyses:

- The four race attitude measures significantly predicted vote intention. Respondents who showed a White preference in the thermometer scale, the Symbolic Racism Scale, and the two IATs preferred McCain to Obama, accounting for 21.4% (weighted scores) of candidate preference.
- The two implicit measures (IATs) predicted 13.0% of the vote preference (White preference predicted McCain preference).
- The explicit measures (Symbolic Racism Scale and thermometer scale) predicted 17.8% of the candidate preference (White preference predicted McCain preference).
- Conservatism accounted for the most variance in preference for McCain; the more conservative the respondent, the more likely he or she was to vote for McCain.

These results suggest that, to some extent, prejudice against Blacks (or preference for Whites) predicted preference for a White candidate over a Black candidate. This relationship held even when other possible influences on voting behavior, such as political conservatism, were controlled for. However, these results should not lead to the conclusion that prejudice against Blacks was the only reason—or even the major reason—that voters supported McCain over Obama. Prejudice was a factor, but not the only factor. Consider, for example, that while statistically significant, only 21.4% of the intention to vote for McCain was explained by the race prejudice measures. However, the finding that prejudice is a factor deserves our attention and further objective and scientific scrutiny. The next study I review provides additional perspective, particularly on the relationship between prejudice (racism) and support for public policy.

2. Knowles, Lowery, and Schaumberg (2010) studied whether explicit and implicit prejudice against Blacks was related to support for President Obama in the 2008 elections as well as support for his health care reform plan. Their study participants were 285 adults recruited from a Stanford University database. The sample was 83% European American, 15% Asian American, and 2% Latino; 32% male and 68% female; and ages 18 to 70 with a mean age of 34.3. They participated in the study online using a link to the project website. Each received a $15 gift certificate for participating. From October 28–30, 2008, study participants took a race Black–White IAT and the Modern Racism scale, a measure of explicit prejudice. Several days later (November 1–3, 2008) they rated then-candidate Barack Obama on four positive and three negative attributes on a five-point scale, from 1 = very uncharacteristic to 5 = very characteristic. The positive attributes were American, patriotic, presidential, and trustworthy; the negative attributes were elitist, uppity, and radical. The positive attributes were reversed-scored (1 = very characteristic; 5 = very uncharacteristic). Therefore, a high score indicated a negative evaluation of candidate Obama. After the elections (November 19–21, 2008), the study participants were asked to report whether they had voted for Obama/Biden; voted for McCain/Palin; voted Other; or Did Not Vote. And, finally, from October 1–3, 2009, participants were asked to rate their support for Obama's

health care reform proposal. Note that the prejudice, attitude, vote, and health care proposal support measures were taken at different points in time to minimize "sensitization" of the participants to the purpose of the study.

The researchers came up with the following results:

- Implicit prejudice against Blacks predicted a vote against Obama. Individuals who scored high on the IAT (1 standard deviation above the mean) were 42.5% less likely to vote for Obama. Controlling for explicit prejudice, they were 36.0% less likely to vote for Obama.
- Implicit prejudice predicted negative evaluations of Obama on the attitude rating scale.
- Implicit prejudice, even after controlling for explicit prejudice, predicted opposition to the Obama health care proposal.

To find out if implicit prejudice against Blacks was actually a cause of opposition to the Obama health care policy, the researchers conducted an experiment with 130 of the study participants in the last assessment (October 1–3, 2009). A randomly selected half of the participants evaluated the health care proposal, which was attributed to President Obama; the other half of the participants evaluated an identical health care proposal but this time attributed to former president Bill Clinton. Implicit prejudice predicted negative evaluations of and opposition to the health care plan when it was attributed to Obama, but not when the policy was attributed to Clinton. When attributed to Clinton, implicit prejudice was not related to support of the policy. The researchers conclude that "Obama's race—and not just the political or ideological character of his policies—underlies the relationship between prejudice and opposition to his health care reform plan" (Knowles et al. 2010, 422).

The studies on politics and prejudice above suggest that there is indeed a relationship between implicit bias against Blacks and support for President Obama and his policies. However, caution should be used in overinterpreting these results. There is no evidence that all who oppose President Obama and his policies are explicitly or implicitly prejudiced against him because of his race. What the studies show is that prejudice accounts for *some* of this opposition, 21.4% in the Greenwald et al. (2009) survey, and up to 42% in the Knowles et al. (2010) study. So, at least some of the opposition to President Obama and his policies can be explained by prejudice. We should be aware that there is an opposite view. Using focus groups in a study for the Democracy Corps organization, Greenwald, Carville, et al. (2009) found that race "did not ever become a central element, and indeed was almost beside the point, despite respondents' having had the full opportunity to bring race into their discussion" (1). Knowles et al. (2010), authors of the Stanford study above, disagree with this assessment. They point out that most people are unwilling to express their prejudices, particularly racial biases, in public because in most American society, it is not socially acceptable to be a racist; also, most people may not even be aware of their implicit biases. In their view, race has some role in "driving opposition to Obama and his policies" (Knowles et al. 2010, 420).

Racial Bias in the 2016 Election?

The election of President Donald Trump in 2016 prompted several scientific studies analyzing his unexpected victory. Most researchers used national surveys and laboratory experiments to first, identify predictors of support for Mr. Trump and secondly, to analyze the effects of public policy messages, such as on immigration, on Mr. Trump's supporters.

Surveys measured several variables besides the usual demographics cited in media reports (age, gender, education, race, income), among them the following:

- Political ideology: strongly conservative, conservative, neither conservative nor liberal, liberal, or strongly liberal. Conservatism and liberalism have many dimensions, including a social dimension (liberals support more government aid to the poor, are more likely to support immigration) and a structural dimension (conservatives favor the status quo, more deference to authority and rules, less government control over private lives) (Hodson and Busseri 2010).
- Authoritarianism: deference to authority, a rigid hierarchical view of the world, resistance to new experiences (Pettigrew and Schaffner 2018).
- Social dominance: preference for domination over lower status groups (Azarian 2018)
- Personal contact with other races
- Perceptions of relative economic deprivation: lack of social mobility, feeling "left behind" (Pettigrew and Schaffner 2018).
- Anti-immigrant sentiments: perceiving immigrants as a physical and cultural threat (Stephan and Stephan 2000).
- Racial resentment: perceiving non-White races as a physical and cultural threat (Pettigrew and Schaffner 2018).
- Sexism: prejudiced attitudes towards women (Glick and Fiske 1996).
- Color blind racism: denial that racism exists (Neville et al. 2000).

Most studies show that not surprisingly, the strongest predictors of support for Donald Trump over Hillary Clinton were political party affiliation and political ideology. However, other strong predictors were racism, racial resentment, and anti-immigrant sentiment, which in many surveys, accounted for up to twenty-five percent of the probability that a voter preferred Trump over Clinton (Pettigrew and Schaffner 2018). Other predictors of a Trump preference were sexism, authoritarianism, social dominance, and lack of personal contact with non-White races (Hooghe 2018). Perceptions of economic deprivation were a weak predictor of Trump support.

These results do not suggest that all supporters of Mr. Trump were racists. However, racism was a factor among some of his supporters.

Racial Cues and Trump Supporters

If some support for Mr. Trump in 2016 was influenced by racial bias, how would Trump supporters evaluate public policy that is cued to a racial minority? To answer this question, Luttig (2017) conducted an online experiment with seven hundred White adults who supported Trump or Clinton. Half of the Trump supporters and half of Clinton supporters were shown a photograph of a home with a "Foreclosed" sign in front accompanied by a photo of a Black man. The other half of Trump and Clinton supporters saw the same photo of the home with a "Foreclosed" sign, but this time with a photo of a White man. The men in the photos were matched for age and attractiveness; the only difference was their race. Trump and Clinton supporters were randomly assigned to either the Black photo or White photo conditions. The study participants were then asked whether they supported a government mortgage program to help people whose homes were foreclosed; whether mortgage aid would make them angry; and whether they blamed the homeowner for the foreclosure. Here are the results of the study:

- Trump supporters who saw the photo of a Black man indicated stronger opposition to mortgage assistance, more anger toward assistance, and a greater tendency to blame the home owner compared to Trump supporters who saw the photo of the White man.
- Clinton supporters who saw the photo of a Black man reported stronger support for mortgage assistance, less anger, and assigned less blame to the homeowner.

These results show that Trump supporters responded to racial cues negatively in support of racial biases, while Clinton supporters responded positively, controlling racial biases by supporting a racial minority. Further, the study provides evidence that racial bias influences positions on public policy issues, supporting previous research on health care and President Obama (Knowles et al. 2010).

Semantic Primes and Evaluations of Stereotype Targets

Do semantic primes— words— influence perceptions of targets of stereotyping? Research has shown that unconscious stereotypes are activated by semantic primes, particularly when attributed to a public figure and when widely reported in the media. A 2016 study analyzed whether candidate Trump's public statements about Mexican immigrants to the United States influenced public perceptions of Mexican immigrants (Schaffner 2018). In an internet experiment, half of a sample of American adults, randomly selected, read a number of quotes from public officials, including this one from Mr. Trump:

> "When Mexico sends its people, they're not sending their best. They're sending people that have lots of problems—They're bringing drugs. They're bringing crime. They're rapists. And some, I assume, are good people."

The other half of the study participants, randomly selected, read the same quotes except for Mr. Trump's statement on immigrants, which was deleted. After reading the quotes, study participants were asked: "In a few words, please let us know what comes to mind when you think of the following groups: Blacks, Mexicans, Whites, politicians, the middle class, and millennials." Researchers were interested in evaluations of Mexicans. Other groups were included to disguise the purpose of the study. Study participants typed in their comments in a small box in a computer screen. Comments were then analyzed by trained coders who classified the comments as negative or positive. Results showed that study participants who read the Trump quote wrote more derogatory and negative remarks about Mexicans, echoing Mr. Trump's words, compared to participants who did not read the Trump quote. These results were found primarily among Trump supporters, but also among independents and non-Trump supporters to a lesser degree. This study, then, provides evidence that statements from public figures can activate and reinforce unconscious biases towards racial minority groups, in this case, towards Mexicans.

Health Care Disparities

Several studies provide evidence of racial bias in health care. Blacks, in particular, receive poorer health care than Whites after controlling for income, education, access to insurance, age, lifestyle, and health condition (DeAngelis 2019). Consider the following data from recent studies:

- A study of four hundred hospitals showed that Black patients with heart disease received older, cheaper, and more conservative treatments than comparable White patients. They were also less likely to receive coronary bypass procedures and angiography, and were discharged earlier from the hospital at a stage when discharge was inappropriate (Bridges 2019).
- Black patients received fewer referrals for cardiovascular procedures than comparable White patients (Bridges 2019).
- Physicians prescribe less pain medication to Black patients compared to White patients.
- Black women are three to four times more likely than White women to die from pregnancy-related causes (Gawronski 2019).

These findings are explained by unconscious biases and stereotypes against Blacks held by physicians. A common misperception is that Blacks are less likely than Whites to follow instructions from physicians. This misperception, activated by the mere presence of a Black patient, directs diagnosis and treatment prescribed by the physician.

One would expect that physicians—medical doctors—would be immune from prejudices favoring one race over the other. After all, they undergo years of rigorous education and training in the sciences where objectivity and evidence-based decisions are the norm. Also, through a process of self-selection, physicians might be expected to be more "intelligent" and to have a higher sense of moral responsibility than the general population. And it's true—physicians exhibit no prejudices at all when *explicit measures* are used. However, measures of implicit prejudice reveal that physicians are no different from you or me. Between 2004 and 2006, more than 2,500 doctors took the race IAT. In general, White, Asian, and Hispanic doctors showed a significant preference for Whites over Blacks, the same as the general population. Black doctors showed no significance preference. These unconscious biases were two to three times higher than the doctors' expressed biases in explicit measures of prejudice (O'Reilly 2009).

We are interested in implicit biases in physicians because of the possibility that these biases might affect their interactions with patients, which in turn may affect trust and commitment to a treatment regimen on the part of the patient, thereby affecting outcome of the treatment. In fact, some studies show that doctors with more race implicit biases interact more poorly with minority patients (see, e.g., Blair, Steiner, and Havranek 2011). Another study looked at interactions from the patients' points of view. African American patients rated more biased doctors as lower in warmth and friendliness than less biased doctors (Blair et al. 2011; Ponner et al. 2010). Therefore, there is evidence that implicit biases among doctors influence the quality of their interactions with minority patients. But does implicit bias affect the actual medical treatment of racial minorities? The next study provides some evidence that the answer may be yes.

1. Green et al. (2007) studied 287 internal medicine and emergency medicine residents at four academic medical centers in Atlanta and Boston. They wanted to find out if implicit biases would influence the treatment that doctors would recommend for Black and White patients with chest pain. They conducted the study over the internet, first presenting a clinical "vignette" of a patient suffering chest pains and with "an acute coronary syndrome" (3); then asking the doctors to complete a questionnaire measuring explicit prejudice against Blacks and perceptions of cooperativeness of black patients; and, finally, asking them to complete a race (Black–White) IAT. Half of the doctors were randomly given the photos of two Black patients to accompany the vignette; the other half were randomly given photos of two White patients. The photos were matched for age and attractiveness. The vignettes were identical, describing "a 50-year-old male presenting to the emergency department with chest pain and an electrocardiogram suggestive of anterior myocardial infarction. ... Primary angioplasty is not an option and no absolute contraindications to thrombolysis are evident" (Green et al. 2007, 3). The research question is, will recommended treatment—that is, the preferred option of thrombolysis (a procedure to dissolve the bold clots) for Black and White patients—be affected by implicit prejudice—that is, implicit preferences for Whites over Blacks? Here are some results of the study:

    • Doctors reported no explicit preference for Whites over Blacks, or differences in perceived cooperativeness.
    • Doctors manifested implicit preferences for Whites over Blacks, and implicit stereotypes of Blacks as less cooperative with medical procedures and less cooperative generally than Whites.
    • As doctors' implicit biases in favor of Whites increased, the likelihood of their treating White patients and not treating Black patients with thrombolysis increased. The researchers concluded that doctors' unconscious biases may contribute to disparities in the treatment of racial and ethnic minorities. Their study dealt only with Black patients. Whether similar results would be found for other racial or ethnic groups should be tested in future research.

When the results were discussed with them, participating doctors expressed interest in controlling their implicit biases and agreed that the research experience was educational and a worthwhile experience.

Social Interactions

Do our prejudices affect how we interact person-to-person with people from other races and ethnicities, particularly when we have unconscious biases against them? Here is a related question: How do our implicit and explicit biases or prejudices affect our evaluations of social interactions that we observe, and that involve members of groups for whom we have unconscious and explicit biases, particularly when these interactions are ambiguous in terms of being positive or negative? For example, will our implicit biases lead us to call a shove by a Black man an aggressive act, while calling the same behavior a "friendly nudge" when done by a White man? In the previous section on health care disparities, we learned that physicians with unconscious biases toward a racial group interacted less warmly and were not as friendly with patients from the less favored group in doctor–patient clinical interactions compared to their interactions with a favored racial group. Will these tendencies be true in other types of interactions, and will they be exhibited by other groups of people besides physicians? The next two studies provide some answers.

1. McConnell and Leibold (2001) wanted to know whether explicit and implicit prejudices would influence person-to-person interactions between Whites and a Black or White person. They randomly assigned forty-two White undergraduates at an American university to either a White or Black female experimenter, who gave instructions and asked questions about a study the students were participating in. The students filled out a race Black–White IAT, the implicit measure of prejudice, and measures of explicit prejudice against Blacks, including semantic differential trait scales (beautiful–ugly, good–bad, pleasant–unpleasant, honest–dishonest, and nice–awful) and feeling thermometers for Blacks and Whites (ranging from 0, extremely unfavorable, to 100, extremely favorable). The students' interactions with the Black or White experimenter were videotaped. The videotaped interactions were then evaluated by trained judges who coded the interactions on behavior cues that convey positive or negative emotions and attitudes. These cues, based on categories validated in previous studies (e.g., DePaulo 1992) include "molar" or general cues, such as abruptness or curtness of participant's responses, participant's friendliness, and participant's general comfort level. The cues also included more specific behaviors, such as the amount of eye contact with the experimenter, the extent to which the participant's body leaned toward the experimenter versus leaning away, the openness of the participant's arms versus crossed arms, the expressiveness of the participant's arms versus not moving at all, physical distance between the participant and the experimenter, speaking time, number of smiles, number of speech errors, number of speech hesitations (e.g., "um"), number of fidgeting body movements (e.g., swinging feet and shifting positions), number of extemporaneous social comments made by the participant, and how much the participant laughed at the experimenter's jokes. These cues have been shown in previous studies to express positive or negative social interactions. As an additional measure of whether the interactions were positive or negative, the experimenters themselves (one Black, the other White) rated their interactions with the students on a nine-point scale (1 = not at all; 9 = extremely) on the following cues: degree of eye contact, abruptness or curtness of the participant's responses, the participant's friendliness, the participant's comfort level, and the experimenter's own comfort level. To minimize bias in the ratings of the interactions, the judges and experimenters were not aware of the purpose of the study.

Here are some of the results:

- Participants expressed more positive biases in favor of Whites compared to Blacks in the IAT, semantic differential, and feeling thermometer measures. The most bias was revealed in the IAT, followed, in order, by the feeling thermometer and the semantic differential.
- There were significant correlations between IAT scores (showing a bias against Blacks) and negative ratings of the interactions by judges and the experimenters themselves. Overall, the interactions of biased Whites were rated by judges and the experimenters to be more negative with the Black experimenter than they were with the White experimenter. For example, with biased Whites, the interaction

with the White experimenter compared to the Black experimenter was rated to have greater participant speaking time, more smiling, more extemporaneous social comments, fewer speech errors, and fewer speech interactions.

- Compared to explicit measures, the IAT was the stronger predictor of positive or negative interactions, predicting ratings from both the judges and the experimenters themselves. Explicit measure predicted only experimenters' ratings.

The authors concluded that implicit and explicit prejudices do indeed influence how we interact with people from other races. These interactions will be less positive, as indicated by several behavioral cues, when we have biases against the people we are interacting with. Further, we are not always aware of these biases, and we are often reluctant to express explicit biases, explaining why implicit biases were stronger predictors of negative social interactions.

2. Gawronski, Geschke, and Banse (2003) studied whether our explicit and implicit prejudices influence how we perceive ambiguous behaviors of people from races other than our own, particularly those races that are targets of negative bias. Their study was conducted in Germany. The presumed favored ethnic group in their study was Germans, the in-group; the presumed disfavored ethnic group was Turks. Participants in the study were seventy Germans, who were paid five dollars for participation in the study. They were asked to read a brief story that described an evening a young man spent with some friends at a disco. Half of the participants, randomly selected, were given a photo of a Turkish-looking young man to accompany the story, identifying him as the character in it. The other half of the participants were given a photo of a German-looking young man to accompany the story. The photos were evaluated in pretests for equivalence of attractiveness and age. After reading the story with the accompanying photographs, the research participants rated the young man's behavior on eight dimensions intended to measure positive or negative behavior identification on a five-point scale, from 1 (not true) to 5 (true). These dimensions were objectionable, brash, cheeky, obtrusive, insensitive, obstinate, arrogant, and bigheaded. The research participants also predicted the young man's behavior in nine hypothetical situations, a measure of dispositional inference, on a five-point scale (1 = very unlikely; 5 = very likely). Examples of these situations were as follows:

    a. "One evening, A is walking along a quiet street. There is no one on the street except an old man walking a few metres in front of A. Close to the street lamp, the old man's wallet falls out of his pocket without him noticing it. How likely is it that A grabs the wallet and does not return it to the old man?"

    b. "A is at the train station and waits for the train to come. On arrival of the train, a big crowd emerges and a man hits A strongly with his suitcase. How likely do you think it is that A will get enraged in response to this event?"

    c. "A few days ago, A was surprised to meet an old friend from high school. They immediately arranged a meeting at his friend's place. Now A is at his friend's place when he is asked by his friend whether he would like to smoke marihuana. How likely do you think it is that A accepts this offer?"

    d. "One cold winter evening A is on his way back home from a party. It's about midnight and he is a bit drunk. On the way to his car, he considers whether to walk two kilometers to his home or to drive with his car. How likely do you think it is that A drives even though he is drunk?"

Scores on the behavior identification and dispositional inference measures indicated positive or negative interpretations of the described behaviors for two different target persons: a German young man or a Turkish young man. High scores indicated negative evaluations; low scores indicated positive evaluations.

In addition to rating the behaviors of the target persons, research participants also completed an explicit measure of prejudice, the German version of the Subtle and Blatant Prejudice Scale (Pettigrew and Meertens 1995), a Race IAT (Greenwald et al. 1998), adapted for Turkish and German people (Gawronski et al. 2003).

Here are some results of the study:

- Participants described the behavior in the disco (behavior identification) as significantly less negative when the young man (target) was German than when he was Turkish.
- Participants with strong negative unconscious biases (IAT) against Turks rated the disco behavior as more negative when the target was Turkish than when he was German. Participants with low negative biases against Turks rated the behavior of the Turkish target equally less negative as the behavior of the German target.
- Participants rated the predicted behaviors (dispositional inference, a. to d. above) of the Turkish target more negatively than the predicted behaviors of the German target.
- Participants with strong unconscious biases (IAT) against Turks rated the target more likely to behave negatively when he was Turkish than when he was German. Participants with weak negative biases against Turks rated the Turkish and German targets equal in the likelihood for negative behavior.
- Implicit prejudice as measured by the IAT was a stronger predictor of behavioral and dispositional evaluations than explicit prejudice. There were no significant effects of the explicit prejudice measures with either the behavioral or dispositional evaluations.

These studies provide evidence that implicit prejudices do indeed influence how we interact with people from races or ethnicities about whom we have unconscious negative biases: The more negative these biases, the more negative our interactions with them, the more negatively we evaluate their behaviors in social interactions, and the more likely it is that we will predict negative behaviors by them. Although not tested directly in these studies, it is also quite likely that we will avoid any kind of interaction with them to avoid imagined and anticipated uncertainty, stress, and discomfort. These tendencies—to avoid contact with groups we unconsciously "don't like"—can be a real hindrance to developing more positive intergroup relations. As we will learn in this book's chapter on interventions, personal contact can be a powerful influence on negating prejudices and negative stereotypes.

Consider this news report about negative interactions between police and some racial minority groups.

Survey Finds Racial Differences in Evaluation of Seattle Police

The *Seattle Times* (2013) reported survey results showing almost two-thirds of Seattle residents believe police discriminate against racial minorities, and almost half think police officers use excessive force "very" or "somewhat" often. The random survey of nine hundred adult Seattle residents was commissioned by a federal monitor overseeing police reforms.

According to the *Times*, approval ratings of the Seattle police department differed between races. Whites and Asian Americans gave the highest ratings while African Americans and Latinos gave the lowest ratings. For example, twenty-seven percent of Latinos and Blacks say police officers used physical force other than handcuffing, compared to five percent of Whites. Blacks and Latinos also were less likely than Whites and Asian Americans to report being treated respectfully and have their questions answered; they were more likely to report being stopped by police officers.

According to the *Times*, the interim Seattle police chief said that the survey results were consistent with nationwide research that has shown similar dissatisfaction or suspicion among some racial groups over issues such as housing and other services. The chief also said that he would ask his staff to study results among Asian Americans who gave his department the highest approval rate at sixty-seven percent, to "determine what can be learned from it."

According to the *Times*, the survey showed that sixty percent of all survey respondents said the Seattle Police Department is doing a "good" or "excellent" job, and seventy-five percent said the police do a good job at keeping people safe.

- Were the police officers influenced by implicit biases in their differential interactions with different races, or were their interactions influenced by contextual and situational factors?

Evaluating Evidence in the Courtroom

Considerable research in law and the social sciences has analyzed whether defendants from minority races are treated equitably in the courtroom (see, e.g., Levinson and Young 2010; Rachlinski et al. 2009). Some studies suggest that race is a factor. For example, studies have found that Blacks, in particular, receive different treatment than Whites do:

- Judges in Connecticut set bail amounts that were twenty-five percent higher for Black defendants than for "similarly situated" White defendants, after controlling for eleven variables that might affect the bail amount, suggesting that race (Black or White) may be the determining factor (Ayres and Waldfogel 1994).
- Federal judges imposed sentences on Black Americans that were 12% longer than those imposed on Whites for comparable crimes (Mustard 2001).
- "Killers of White victims are more likely to be sentenced to death than are killers of Black victims," and "Black defendants are more likely than White defendants" to receive the death penalty (Banks et al. 2006, as cited in Rachlinski et al. 2009).

There are descriptive data, then, that show that Blacks in particular receive harsher treatment than Whites do in the courts. But is this differential treatment due to prejudice against Blacks—explicit and implicit—on the part of jurors and judges, or is it attributable to other factors that have nothing to do with anti-Black bias? Few studies have studied whether there is a direct link between judge and/or juror racial bias and their evaluations of defendants and the resulting decisions and actions. Some have suggested an indirect link.

1. Levinson and Young (2010) found that students in a mock jury study judged ambiguous evidence to "be more indicative of guilt" when the alleged perpetrator had dark skin tone than they did when the perpetrator had light skin tone. The mock jurors were also more likely to judge the defendant as guilty when he had dark skin tone than when he had light skin tone. When the mock jurors were asked at the end of the study if they remembered whether the defendant in the photo had dark skin, most said, "No." This finding, in addition to the absence of significant correlations between measures of explicit prejudice and whether skin tone affected evaluations of the defendant, led the researchers to suggest that prejudice against the darker-skinned defendant operated at an unconscious level: The mock jurors were not aware that they were making biased evaluations based on skin color.

2. Another study by Levinson, Cai, and Young (2010) of the same scenario as in example 1 above found that Black–White IATs did not predict the evaluations of the guilt of dark- and light-skinned defendants, but did predict the evaluation of total evidence for both dark- and light-skinned defendants: The higher the bias against Blacks, the more likely the total evidence was judged to be indicative of guilt for both defendants. In this second study, the mock jurors (university students) showed a significant association between Black and guilty in the IAT, meaning that they held an implicit association between Blacks and being guilty. Also, participants were more likely to associate unpleasant words with Blacks than they were with Whites in the IAT. According to Levinson, Cai, et al. (2010), results from these two studies show that, at least in the context of the experiments' using university student participants, unconscious biases against Blacks (darker skin tone) lead to more negative evaluations than those that occur for Whites (lighter skin tone) in a criminal case. This evidence, they admit, is indirect because there was no significant correlation between IAT scores and evaluations of the dark- and light-skinned defendants. The researchers suggest that more research should investigate

whether prejudices and unconscious biases directly influence the evaluation of evidence in criminal cases by judges and jurors. The next study asks whether unconscious racial bias affects trial judges.

3.   Rachlinski et al. (2009) recruited 128 judges from the eastern and western United States to participate in the study; 66% (85) were White, and 34% (43) were Black. The judges completed a race IAT (White–Black) and then read descriptions of three hypothetical cases: a juvenile shoplifter, a juvenile robber, and a battery. In the first two cases, the race of the defendant was not identified; in the third case, some of the judges were told that the defendant was Caucasian, and others that he was African American. The race of the defendants in the first two cases, although not identified explicitly, was identified subliminally or unconsciously using word primes for half of the judges; the other half saw words with no common theme. The subliminal Black primes (for half of the judges) were words that a previous study of police officers used to make unconscious connections between mostly negative and unsubstantiated stereotypes and Blacks. The Black primes were flashed on a computer screen at speeds that would not allow conscious recognition (Graham and Lowery 2004). The words were *graffiti, Harlem, homeboy, Jheri curl, minority, mulatto, negro, rap, segregation, basketball, Black, Cosby, gospel, hood, Jamaica, roots, afro, Oprah, Islam, Haiti, pimp, dreadlocks, plantation, slum, Tyson, welfare, athlete, ghetto, calypso, reggae, rhythm,* and *soul.* After the primes for the first two cases (shoplifting and robbery), the judges were asked (1) what disposition they would make in the case given seven options, from dismissal to a transfer to an adult court; (2) the likelihood that the defendant would commit a similar crime in the future; and (3) the likelihood that the defendant would commit a more serious crime in the future. For the third case, battery, in which the defendant was explicitly identified as White or Black, the judges were asked to render a verdict and to rate their confidence in the verdict.

4.   Bielen, Marneffe, and Mocan (2018) used 3D Virtual Reality (VR) technology to record criminal trials in a courtroom prosecuted by real-life prosecutors and real-life defense attorneys in this creative and unique study in Belgium. The alleged crimes prosecuted were burglary and assault cases. The trials were first recorded with a White defendant. The identical trials were then recorded with a defendant of Middle Eastern or North African descent who clearly had darker skin than the White defendants. The defendants were young men matched for dress and physical appearance except for skin color. The trial recordings were then shown to randomly assigned groups of law students, economics students, practicing lawyers and judges, who were mostly White. Also represented were Belgians of color. Study participants (evaluators) acted as the jury and judge, deciding on the guilt or innocence of the defendant and, if guilty, imposing a sentence. The researchers wanted to find out whether the evaluators would demonstrate racial bias against Belgians of color. Here are some results of the study:

- Overall, across all conditions, minority defendants were more likely to be convicted (by twelve percentage points) than White defendants.
- Overall, across all conditions, minority defendants were sentenced on average to prison terms 1.3 months longer than white defendants were—a 32% increase in prison time.

This study provides evidence that racial biases can direct courtroom evaluations when controlling for other possible environmental and actor (prosecutor, defense attorney) influences on decisions. Although the researchers did not measure racial biases, we can conclude that these biases directed decisions of the evaluators because the trials were identical except for race of the defendant.

The study design allowed the researchers to test whether implicit biases directly influenced the judges' decisions in two conditions: when the defendant was explicitly identified as Black or White, and when the defendant's race was not explicitly identified but primed subconsciously. Here are the results:

- White judges showed a strong White preference on the IAT, with 87% indicating a White preference over Blacks.
- Black judges showed no clear race preferences on the IAT; they performed the stereotype congruent trial (White/good and Black/bad) taking almost the same time as the stereotype incongruent trial (White/bad and Black/good).
- The White judges expressed a significantly larger White preference than the Black judges did.

- Judges in the battery case, where the race of the defendant was explicitly identified to be White or Black, were not affected by race of the defendant; they were equally willing to convict the defendant whether he was White or Black.
- In both the shoplifter case and the robbery case, when the race of the defendant was not explicitly identified, "judges who expressed a White preference on the IAT were somewhat more likely to impose harsher penalties when primed with Black-associated words than when primed with neutral words" (1217), while judges who expressed a Black preference were more likely to impose less harsh penalties.

Results of this study show that judges were not affected by race of the defendant when the external cues clearly pointed to race as a possible factor in their decisions. The researchers suggest that judges, because of the clear cues, were sensitized to the expectation that they are supposed to be impartial, and to treat all races equally. Therefore, they were able to control whatever unconscious biases they may have had, and, indeed, made decisions and evaluations that were not affected by the race of the defendant.

On the other hand, when external race cues were not present, that is, when race (the Black race in particular) was primed subconsciously by words rather than explicitly identified, the judges who showed White preference over Black in the IATs were influenced by the race of the defendant, giving harsher evaluations and penalties to the defendant primed as Black. This finding suggests that cognitive bias control mechanisms were not used by these judges because they were not consciously aware that first, they had unconscious biases and that second, they were dealing with a Black defendant. Therefore, the researchers concluded, judges can be influenced by unconscious biases when they are not self-motivated to control them.

In this chapter on consequences of prejudice, I have presented evidence that explicit and implicit prejudice can influence our evaluations of and behaviors towards other people and their groups. Most of these studies show that implicit prejudice is a stronger predictor of negative evaluations of targeted groups and corresponding behaviors. Most of us will not admit that we are prejudiced, but most of us do have implicit biases. In the next chapter, I discuss the *why* question. Why are we prejudiced?

Workbook

Define, describe, or illustrate; summarize the results of the studies:

1.   Predictive validity of explicit and implicit measures of prejudice

2.   Bertrand and Mullainathan (2004)

3.   Ziegert and Hanges (2005)

4.   Rooth (2010)

5.   Moss-Racusin et al. (2012)

6.   Greenwald et al. (2009)

7.   Knowles at al. (2010)

8.   Green et al. (2007)

9.   McConnell and Leibold (2001)

10.   Gawronski et al. (2003)

11.   Levinson and Young (2010)

12.   Levinson et al. (2010)

13.   Rachlinski et al. (2009)

14.   Pettigrew and Schaffner (2018)

15.   Hooghe (2018)

16.   Racial cues: Luttig (2017)

17.   Semantic primes

18.   DeAngelis (2019)

19.   Bielen, Marneffe, and Mocan (2018)

6

Where Do Prejudices Come From?

Consider that prejudice is universal—we find prejudice in just about every society in the world. In attempting to explain this phenomenon, social scientists look for conditions that might exist in individuals, groups, and societies. Individual-level analysis takes into account processes and traits that occur within a person as he or she adapts to the environment. This analysis, would, for example, consider how an individual makes sense of the environment, processes information, and chooses the strategies used to adapt to the environment. Analysis at the group level includes interactions between group members, how groups preserve identities, and how groups adapt to the environment. Social-level analysis includes the socialization process, or how social values, customs, and traditions are handed down from one generation to the next and how we learn to be a member of society. Also included at the social-level is analysis of how power and "order" are maintained in society.

Individual-Level Analysis

The Sociobiological Explanation

The sociobiological explanation says that humans are "hardwired" or programmed to be prejudiced, but that this program can be altered by the environment (see, e.g., Fiske 2000). Prejudice is the result of the evolutionary need for a species (e.g., the human race) to survive, hardwired into the genetic makeup through the process of evolution. To survive, a species has to protect its gene pool to keep the species pure, and one way of doing this is to keep other species away, to fear the unknown, and to defend the species aggressively from intrusions. A strictly biological explanation of prejudice—protecting the gene pool—has been criticized as being too deterministic—that is, biology affects behavior and there is little we can do about it (see, Fiske 2000). Considering that prejudice exists even in relatively homogeneous communities (same race, same religion), environmental and sociocultural factors must also be considered. In addition, researchers have observed that mixing of gene pools at least in plants and animals have often resulted in a "hybrid" effect, a more robust offspring that is more adept at adapting to the environment, such as in being more resistant to disease. And, if evolution is an explanation for the desire to keep a species pure, history tells us that this motivation has led to the practical elimination of species, at enormous cost in life and fortune. So isn't it equally reasonable to expect that survival, indeed the successful propagation of the human species irrespective of race or other biological and socially constructed categories, would be best served by intermingling, that is, by mixing and integrating.

Regardless of the apparent shortcomings of the biological explanation, there is recent evidence from studies of other species (not human) that prejudice may indeed be hardwired into our brains and DNA. In a study by Mahajan et al. (2011), *rhesus macaques*, a primate species, distinguished between members of their own social groups and members of other social groups and stared longer at out-group members than they did at in-group members. Longer stares, according to the researchers, were a manifestation of greater vigilance toward the out-group monkeys, who were considered to be threats to the in-group monkeys (own social group). Using a Looking Time Implicit Association Test, Mahajan et al. also found that macaques associated in-group members more with positive items (e.g., fruits) and out-group members more with negative items (e.g., spiders), meaning that the monkeys, like humans, automatically evaluate in-group members positively and out-group members negatively. Mahajan et al. suggest that "the architecture of the mind that enables the formation of these biases may be rooted in phylogenetically ancient mechanisms," that is, the instinct for survival.

The evolutionary and biological explanation of prejudice basically says that prejudice is inborn, and is something that we (humans) all have. Although this may be true, more recent explanations give more weight, in explaining differences in levels of prejudice in individuals, groups, and societies, to the influence of the environment. That is, we may be genetically programmed to be prejudiced, but this program is "malleable," and is heavily influenced, in particular, by the culture in which we live— the shared values, behavioral norms (accepted ways of behaving), worldviews, meanings we attach to symbols and words, and, in general, ways of thinking. The sociobiological explanation of prejudice, therefore, acknowledges a biological explanation, but assigns more influence on culture and the environment, on the influence of nurture resulting from interaction with other human beings and their institutions, such as schools, family, peers, government, and, not the least, the mass media. Central to social influence is communication that takes place between individuals, in groups, between groups, and in societies.

Cognitive Style

A large body of research has shown that cognitive style, an individual-level variable, is related to prejudice. Cognitive style can be generally defined as how we process information, particularly new information; how we make sense of the environment; and the ability to evaluate and adopt alternative perspectives (see, e.g., Hodson and Busseri 2012). The basic premises of this research are (1) prejudice is based on fear of the unknown; (2) to conquer this fear, a person should be open to new information through personal contact or mediated communication (e.g., the mass media and the internet); and (3) openness to new information is facilitated by a cognitive style that, generally, is capable of processing complex information. Researchers have found that several indicators of cognitive style are indeed related to prejudice. Here are some examples:

- Intolerance of ambiguity and a preference for simple answers are positively related to prejudice: The more intolerance and a greater preference for simplicity, the more prejudice (Jost et al. 2003).
- Greater cognitive rigidity (preference for "Yes" and "No" answers, for example; Rokeach 1948), less cognitive flexibility (openness to alternative perspectives; Sidanius 1985), and less ability to integrate complex information (Stankov 2009) are related to social conservatism (characterized by resistance to change and the maintenance of the status quo to provide psychological stability and a sense of order), which in turn predicts prejudice.
- Individuals with lower levels of general intelligence as measured by standardized tests are more likely to be prejudiced than individuals with higher intelligence scores (see, e.g., Deary et al. 2008; Schoon et al. 2010). This relationship between general intelligence and prejudice can be explained by findings that individuals with lower levels of general intelligence are less trusting of other people, less sensitive to interpersonal cues, less capable of identifying other people's behaviors and intentions, and less capable of abstract reasoning (Keller 2010; Murphy and Hall 2011).

These studies provide evidence that lower levels of general intelligence predict greater prejudice. However, it is not clear to what extent general intelligence is directly causing prejudice, or whether this relationship is indirect—that is, whether intelligence predicts some other components of cognitive style, which in turn predict prejudice. Addressing this issue, Hodson and Busseri (2012) proposed that lower cognitive ability as indicated by lower general intelligence test scores predicts "right-wing ideologies" and low levels of contact with out-groups, which in turn predict greater prejudice. Thus, in this "mediation model," the effect of low intelligence on prejudice is indirect—it is mediated by "right-wing" ideology, which the authors define as social conservatism and authoritarianism. Hodson and Busseri analyzed longitudinal data from the United Kingdom and data on college students from a study of prejudice against gays and lesbians in the United States (Keiller 2010).

In the UK study, the general intelligence of children 11 and 10 years old was assessed; the children were then surveyed again (same people) at ages 33 (4,267 men and 4,537 women) and 30 (3,412 men and 3,658 women), when social conservatism and racism were measured. This longitudinal design (over time) can tell us whether childhood general intelligence is related to social conservatism and racism later in life. The researchers defined general intelligence as "cognitive abilities," measured among 11-year-old participants by "verbal intelligence (similarities between words, 40 items) and nonverbal intelligence (similarities between shapes or symbols, 40 items)" (3) and, for the 10-year-old participants, measured by "matrix abilities (drawing missing aspects of shapes, 28 items), digital recall (recalling digits from number series, 34 items), word definitions (identifying the meaning of words, 37 items), and word similarities (generating words that are semantically consistent with presented words, 42 items)" (3). Social conservatism, measured when the children were ages 33 and 30, was defined as "resistance to change and a desire to maintain existing social stratifications," and more specifically as endorsement of socially conservative values such as "desire for law and order, punitive reactions toward wrongdoers, adherence to social conventions or traditions, and social control" (3). These beliefs were measured on an agree–disagree Likert scale with items such as "Give lawbreakers stiffer sentences," "Schools should teach children to obey authority," and "Family life suffers if mum is working full-time" (3). The researchers defined racism, measured when the children were ages 33 and 30, as negative affect ("antipathy") toward racial out-groups in general, rather than negative affect toward a specific group. To control for other factors besides general intelligence and social conservatism that might affect prejudice, the researchers also measured parental socioeconomic status when the participants were children (social prestige of occupation), personal socioeconomic status when the participants were adults (social prestige of education), and participants' level of education when they were adults. Socioeconomic status and education were controlled for statistically, so that their potential influence on prejudice would be factored out, allowing for the analysis of general intelligence and social conservatism as the remaining possible causes of prejudice, at least in this study.

Hodson and Busseri (2012) found the following results from the United Kingdom study:

- General intelligence at childhood predicted prejudice in adulthood. The lower the intelligence scores, the higher the prejudice scores: 62% of boys and 65% of girls who scored below the median of the intelligence test at age 10 showed above-median levels of prejudice in adulthood, compared to 35% to 38% of the children who scored above the median in the intelligence test.
- Social conservatism and prejudice are significantly related in adulthood: The more socially conservative, the more prejudice expressed by the adult sample.
- General intelligence in children is significantly related to social conservatism in adulthood: the less intelligence, the more socially conservative.
- The link between general intelligence in children and prejudice in adulthood is not statistically significant when social conservatism is accounted for, meaning that intelligence does not directly influence prejudice. Rather, the influence of intelligence on prejudice is indirect, and is mediated by social conservatism. Children who score lower on the intelligence test will be more socially conservative

adults than children who score high; adults who are socially conservative will be more prejudiced than adults who are not socially conservative. There is no direct link between intelligence and prejudice. However, intelligence is a significant influence on social conservatism, and, therefore, has a significant indirect effect on prejudice.

In explaining these results, Hodson and Busseri (2010) say,

> Thus, conservative ideology represents a critical pathway through which childhood intelligence predicts racism in adulthood. In psychological terms, the relation between g (intelligence) and prejudice may stem from the propensity of individuals with lower cognitive ability to endorse more right-wing conservative ideologies because such ideologies offer a psychological sense of stability and order. By emphasizing resistance to change and inequality among groups, these ideologies legitimize and promote negative evaluations of out-groups. (6)

The results of this particular study, while provocative, should not be overread. They do show a link between low intelligence and prejudice. However, this link, while statistically significant, is generally modest, when controlling for education and socioeconomic status, in the vicinity of r (correlation coefficient) of .25, meaning that about six percent of prejudice is explained by intelligence. Not all social conservatives are prejudiced, and not all social liberals are prejudice-free. At the same time, the results of this study should not be dismissed. If we adopt a definition of intelligence based on cognitive style rather than a biological predisposition, the link, no matter how small, provides guidance on how education, formal and informal, can teach people how to think abstractly regardless of political or social ideology. Abstract thinking, the research suggests, is a key element of being open-minded, and therefore less susceptible to prejudice. Also, a large amount of variance in prejudice is explained by other factors besides intelligence, such as the influence of culture and group dynamics. In the next section, I discuss how group identity and relations between groups can affect prejudice toward out-groups.

Most studies on intelligence and prejudice have used explicit measures of prejudice. Because most people, regardless of cognitive style, are susceptible to expressing socially desirable responses to prejudice measures, we can expect the same, if not stronger, results if measures of implicit bias are used. That is, lower levels of "intelligence" will also be strongly related to higher levels of implicit bias. The ability to be aware of one's biases, and the ability to control them, should be facilitated by a cognitive style that is open, less rigid, and capable of integrating complex and abstract information—a cognitive style that is indicative of higher levels of "intelligence." Therefore, people of higher intelligence should be better able to be aware of their biases and to control them, and should express less implicit bias than people with lower levels of intelligence, again, presuming that intelligence is defined as cognitive style rather than a biologically determined trait.

Group-Level Analysis

Although the propensity to be prejudiced as indicated by less capability and motivation to process new and contradictory information develops in individuals, the group remains at the center of our analysis of prejudice. After all, individuals express prejudice against other individuals because the latter are members of groups—out-groups, in particular. And, prejudice between groups facilitates the development and reinforcement of group identities and enhances the self-concepts of individuals belonging to groups. At the group level of analysis, we consider how perceptions of other groups by individuals and resulting interactions affect prejudice. We also look at how identification with the in-group by individual members affects prejudice.

The key element in intergroup prejudice (prejudice directed between in-groups and out-groups) is fear—fear that out-groups will take over power, authority, and control of resources from the in-group. The basis of fear is threat posed by the out-group, including real and perceived threats. Stephan and Stephan (2000) present an Integrated Threat Theory (ITT) that helps us understand how threats lead to prejudice.

An ITT model, from Stephan and Stephan (2000) with minor modifications, is shown in Figure 6.1.

In this model, the first set of variables predicts the second set (threats), which predicts prejudice toward an out-group. Let's look at some definitions, adopted with some modifications, from Stephan and Stephan (2000).

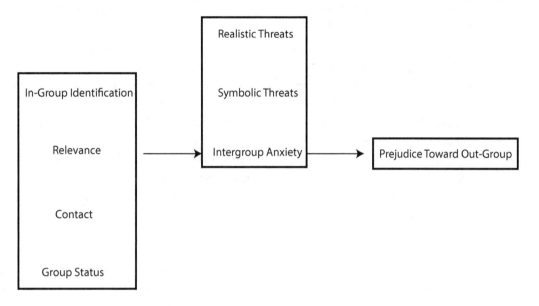

Figure 6.1 An Integrated Threat Theory of Prejudice (Stephan and Stephan 2000).

In-group identification is the extent to which the individual identifies with the in-group, which is determined by status within the group, perceived rewards from group membership, and, in general, the extent to which a particular group membership is a part of the individual's personal identity. For example, I have several personal identities: professor, husband, Filipino American, tennis player, martial arts practitioner, civil rights activist, and so forth. The strengths of my identification with each of these groups will vary, and most likely are situational. The ITT model predicts that the stronger the identification with a particular in-group, the stronger the perceived threats from an out-group, resulting in greater prejudice.

Relevance is the extent to which the perceived threats are perceived by in-group members to affect them personally by "costing" them significantly in material or psychological ways. For example, some American college students (in-group is American college students) may perceive international students as a threat because they perceive that international students take away coveted scholarships and financial support from them. The threat would be very relevant in fields favored by international students, such as science and engineering, but would be less relevant to students where there are fewer international students, such as the humanities and social sciences. The ITT model predicts that higher relevance predicts higher levels of threat, which leads to more prejudice.

Contact is face-to-face or vicarious interactions with members of the out-group. Face-to-face interactions occur in interpersonal settings, where participants occupy the same space and therefore are able to carry on a conversation with each participant physically present, and are able to observe each other's behaviors, with opportunities for immediate feedback. Vicarious contact occurs in mediated communication through the mass media or the Internet. Participants are in different locations and observe each other, often in narratives or stories, such as newscasts and entertainment programs. Direct and vicarious contact facilitates the transmission of information—accurate or inaccurate—of out-groups, which is the basis for impressions of, attitudes toward, and prejudice or lack of prejudice toward out-groups. Personal contact can facilitate positive intergroup relations and less prejudice when participants have equal status, work toward a common goal rather than competing, and when contact is approved by peers and group leaders. However, opportunities for personal contact with out-groups are limited, considering the motivation of in-group members to seek others who are "like them." Therefore, most intergroup contact occurs vicariously via the media. Most media portrayals are inaccurate or incomplete, and do not fulfill the requirements for optimum contact that could lead to less prejudice. The ITT model states that more contact, under optimum conditions, leads to less perceived threats from out-groups and therefore less prejudice.

Group status refers to which group is dominant and in control of power and resources. For example, in the United States, immigrants from Mexico have less power and resources than, let's say, law enforcement groups in some states. The out-group, in this example, Mexican immigrants, and the in-group, law enforcement groups, theoretically will see each other as threats (see the following discussion of threats). The ITT model predicts that as the degree of status inequality increases, the perceived degree of the severity of threats also increases, and prejudice will increase.

According to the ITT model, there are several types of threats that could be perceived by in-groups and out-groups. Most discussions center on how in-groups perceive out-groups as threats, primarily because most studies of prejudice focus on prejudice directed by groups with power (in-groups) against groups with less power (out-groups). The ITT model predicts that the greater perceived severity of these different types of threats, the more prejudice will be directed by the group feeling threatened toward the group perceived to be causing the threat.

Realistic threats are those perceived to threaten the very existence of the group, such as threats to political and economic power, territorial boundaries, wealth, natural resources, and the physical well-being of group members in general. Heightened perception of realistic threats sometimes leads to war and violent confrontations, driven by competition for valued and scarce resources.

Symbolic threats are those perceived to undermine the culture of a group, including its values, beliefs, worldviews, customs, behaviors, traditions, political system, and "way of life." These threats are based on the belief of group members that their "way," that is, culture, is superior to the culture of the threatening group, and is driven by the desire to maintain, propagate, and even extend the group's culture. The discussion on whether the United States should be a "melting pot" or a multicultural society is sometimes framed in terms of symbolic threats. Are the cultures of the many immigrant groups a threat to mainstream American culture, thereby undermining traditional values, beliefs, and standards of behavior? Do these perceived threats lead to more prejudice against these immigrant groups? The ITT model predicts that the wider the gap between cultures of in-groups and out-groups, the more severe symbolic threats will be perceived to be, and therefore the more prejudice will be directed toward the out-group.

Intergroup anxiety is the discomfort, stress, and negative emotions experienced in intergroup interactions, such as personal contact. Fear of the unknown leads to this anxiety, which in turn can be explained by uncertainty, lack of knowledge, negative stereotypes, and a natural tendency for humans to prefer the familiar (in-group) to the unfamiliar (out-group). In familiar surroundings around familiar people, we feel confident in how to behave and interact, whereas we feel anxious in unfamiliar surroundings with unfamiliar people. Anticipated and real interaction with out-groups is a threat—we avoid situations that lead to anxiety. Therefore, opportunities to learn about groups we don't know much about are limited by the threat of interactions. Vicarious interaction, such as through the media, is less threatening, but is also less likely to lead to less prejudice because much of this interaction is based on portrayals of groups that are incomplete, inaccurate, or based on negative stereotypes. The ITT model predicts that the greater the perceived differences between groups, the more anxiety in intergroup interactions, and the more prejudice directed at one another.

Prejudice, as discussed earlier, is affect or emotions directed at members of another group, and at the group itself. Most prejudice we study is negative, although prejudice can also be positive, in favor of a group such as in-groups.

Stephan, Ybarra, and Bachman (2011) tested the ITT model in a study of prejudice toward immigrants in the United States. Their study participants were college students in Florida, Hawaii, and New Mexico. The immigrant groups they studied were Mexicans in New Mexico, Cubans in Florida, and Asians in Hawaii. In surveys, they asked their college student research participants to fill out a questionnaire that measured realistic threats, symbolic threats, intergroup anxiety, stereotypes, and prejudice. The realistic threat index consisted of twelve items, including such threats as crime, disease, drugs, job loss, and economic costs for health, education, and welfare. For example, participants were asked to express their degree of agreement or disagreement with this statement: "Mexican immigrants are contributing to the increase in crime in the United States." The symbolic threat index consisted of twelve items measuring perceived differences between Americans and Mexicans in work, family, religious, and moral values. A sample item, with responses on a agree-disagree scale, was as follows: "Mexican immigration is undermining American culture." Intergroup anxiety consisted of twelve items that asked participants how they would feel in interactions with the immigrant groups. Examples were apprehensive, confident, worried, at ease, and anxious. The stereotype scale consisted of twelve traits that previous research had shown to be associated with negative stereotyping of immigrant groups. Participants were asked to estimate the percentage of an immigrant group possessing a trait, and to rate the favorability of each trait. Examples of traits were dishonest, unintelligent, clannish, hardworking, and friendly. Prejudice was measured using twelve emotional reactions to the immigrant groups. Participants were asked the degree to which they felt each of the emotions toward the immigrant groups. The emotions included hostility, admiration, disliking, acceptance, superiority, affection, disdain, and approval. These measures tapped into explicit prejudice, rather than unconscious biases.

Stephan et al. (2001) report results for each participant group (Florida, New Mexico, Hawaii) and for each immigrant group (Cubans, Mexicans, and Asians). Prejudice toward the immigrant groups was significantly predicted by realistic and symbolic threats in all the samples. In the New Mexico college sample, for example, the realistic and symbolic threats accounted for seventy-two percent of prejudice toward Mexican immigrants. Results of this study provide strong support for the ITT theory of prejudice. Perceived threats do explain prejudice. More research is needed to test the predictions of other components of the model, that is, the causal paths from in-group identification, relevance, contact, and group status to perceived threats, and whether this group of variables influences prejudice directly.

Social-Level Analysis

Prejudice is very much a creation of the environment—culture, in particular—as it is an individual phenomenon. The propensity to be prejudiced and accompanying behaviors are learned from people around us, reinforced and encouraged by organizations and institutions in our communities, and passed on from generation to generation. The process by which prejudice is learned is *socialization*, and the people and institutions who teach us, intentionally or unintentionally, are *socialization agents*. In this section, we will focus on the socialization of children who, compared to adults, are more likely to be influenced by socialization agents, because they are just beginning to develop their personalities and predispositions to their environment and other people. The main question is, when and how do children learn prejudice? Or, as noted psychologist Phyllis Katz (2003) asks, "Racists or tolerant multiculturalists: how do they begin?" (1).

Children recognize race from a very young age, as young as six months, and develop racial biases by age three. Katz and Kofkin (1997) found that infants at six months are able to place people in racial categories. They showed infants photos of unfamiliar faces from the infant's own race and photos of unfamiliar faces from another race. They found that the infants looked significantly longer at an unfamiliar face of a different race than they did at an unfamiliar face of their same race. Other studies have shown that toddlers as young as two years old categorize other children based on race and infer behaviors based on race (Hirschfeld 2008). In addition, three-to-five-year-olds express bias based on race (see, e.g., Aboud 2008; Hirschfeld 2008; Katz

2003; Patterson and Bigler 2006). In one study, three-to-five-year-olds in a racially diverse day care center identified themselves and other children according to race and used race as a criterion to include or exclude other children from their activities (Van Ausdale and Feagin 2001).

There is evidence, then, that children at a very young age categorize other children and people according to race and show biases based on race. The question is, how do they learn to be prejudiced at such an early age? Conventional wisdom and early research suggested that children have racial biases because they are directly taught to be biased, primarily by their parents. However, the evidence is mixed regarding parental influence. Some studies have found significant correlations between racial attitudes of parents and their children. Mosher and Scodel (1960) found that ethnocentrism expressed by mothers was positively correlated with ethnocentrism and social distance between African Americans and Jews expressed by their daughters. Carlson and Iovini (1985) found that social distance from African Americans expressed by fathers and sons was positively correlated. On the other hand, other studies have not shown a relationship between parental and children's racial attitudes (see, e.g., Aboud and Doyle 1996). These inconsistent results suggest that there are other influences besides parents on children's prejudices, and that the relationship between parental and children's prejudices may be moderated by other variables, such as the parent-child relationship (see, e.g., Sinclair, Dunn, and Lowery 2005).

More recently, researchers have expanded their search for influences on children's prejudices to other elements in the child's environment besides parents. Acknowledging that children have developing and immature cognitive structures, this approach analyzes how children pick up cues from their environments to make sense of and simplify a complicated world (Patterson and Bigler 2006). Children are capable of collecting information about how to navigate their environment by observing adults other than parents, such as teachers and adults they come in contact with in everyday life, their peers, and, not in the least, relationships between people and symbols in the media. Some researchers have suggested and provided evidence for the proposition that, in the United States, the predominant culture presented to children in their environments is, first, that race is a salient category, and, second, that race makes a difference in interpersonal relations—or that race matters.

How does race matter? Some researchers argue that "consciously or unconsciously, middle class White culture is presented as a norm or standard in the United States in terms of appearance, beauty, language, cultural practices, food and so on" (Winkler 2009, 3). This culture, which subtly implies that White is preferable, is presented in picture books, children's movies, television, and children's songs (Giroux 2001; Graves 1999; Katz 2003). In addition, the everyday experiences of most children can suggest that certain roles and relationships are based on race. For example, White children growing up in mostly White neighborhoods may notice that people have different heights, ages, and genders, but mostly all have the same skin color. They may then surmise that being among people with the same skin color is "right" and that they should avoid people with different skin colors, even if they are not told to do so explicitly by an adult (Aboud 2005). Similar assumptions about skin color can be made by children if they observe that most doctors they see are White or that most service people they see are Brown or Black (Bigler and Liben 2007). Thus, children learn by observation, and are capable of forming conclusions about race and skin color based on these observations. Although American culture is changing as more people of color assume positions of power and influence (starting at the top, with the US presidency), the norm is still that Whiteness is associated with privilege, power, and influence and that it is desirable to have or to identify with "Whiteness" (Katz and Kofkin 1997). A study illustrating the preference for Whiteness among Black and White children was done by Katz and Kofkin in 1997. They studied children at age thirty months, again (same children) at thirty-six months, and again at sixty months. The children were shown photos of unfamiliar White and Black boys and girls, and were asked to choose a potential playmate. At age thirty months, all the children expressed an interest in a playmate of their same race. At thirty-six months, "the majority of black and white children chose white playmates" (Katz and Kofkin 1997, 59); at age sixty months, the preference for White playmates, although declining slightly, was again observed for Black and White children. These results show a preference among the older children for Whiteness. The implication is that they have internalized, through subtle and direct cues in the environment, the standard that "White is good" and preferable. According to Tatum (1997), this message is prevalent in American society.

Although most current research has focused on environmental and cultural influences on the development of prejudicial attitudes in children, the role of parents should not be overlooked. Parental influence, under certain conditions, is a powerful force in shaping how children perceive people from different races. Sinclair, Dunn, and Lowery (2005) asked whether children who identify strongly with their parents will develop racial attitudes similar to their parents more than children who identify less with their parents will. They studied fourth and fifth graders, forty girls and forty-seven boys. The children answered a questionnaire that assessed identification with their parents and explicit racial attitudes. Identification with parents was measured by four items: how much they cared about making their parents proud (seven-point scale, from don't care at all to care a lot), how often they did what their parents told them (five-point scale, from never to almost always), how much they enjoyed spending time with the parent who answered the parents' questionnaire (seven-point scale, from do not enjoy at all to enjoy a lot), and how much they wanted to be like the parent who completed the survey (seven-point scale, from not at all to exactly the same). Explicit racial attitudes were measured with a modified version of the Multi-Response Racial Attitude measure (Doyle and Aboud 1995). Children were shown a picture of an unknown White boy and an unknown Black boy. They were then given a list of adjectives and asked to check those that they thought described the boy in the picture. The adjectives were helpful, good, friendly, wonderful, nice, kind, smart, happy, clean, healthy, selfish, bad, unfriendly, naughty, mean, cruel, stupid, sad, dirty, and sick. After completing the questionnaire, a Children's IAT was administered to groups of children in the school's computer labs. To measure racial attitudes of parents, the researchers sent them a questionnaire with the Intergroup Threat Scale (Stephan and Stephan 2002), a measure of explicit prejudice. This scale consisted of the following items, answered on a seven-point scale, from strongly disagree to strongly agree: (1) African Americans get more from this country than they deserve, (2) African Americans are a physical threat to the safety of most Americans, (3) African Americans should learn to conform to the rules and norms of American society, (4) the values and beliefs of African Americans regarding work are basically quite similar to those of most Americans (R), (5) the values and beliefs of African Americans regarding moral and religious issues are not compatible with the beliefs and values of most Americans, and (6) the values and beliefs of African Americans regarding family issues and socializing children are basically quite similar to those of most Americans (R). Items with an "R" are reverse-coded. The researchers compared parental explicit prejudice with children's explicit and implicit prejudices, and analyzed whether parental identification would affect these comparisons. Here are results of the study:

- Children did not express any explicit prejudice.
- Children showed implicit bias against Blacks, expressing a slight preference for Whites.
- Implicit and explicit biases of children were not correlated.
- Implicit and explicit biases of parents were not correlated.
- Children's implicit and explicit prejudices corresponded with the prejudices of their parents more when they highly identified with their parents than when identification was lower; the higher the identification, the stronger the influence of parents on prejudice of children.
- Among children who identified strongly with their parents, parental explicit prejudice predicted implicit prejudice among children, but only marginally predicted explicit prejudice.
- Among children who identified less with their parents, parental prejudice was not related to implicit prejudice, but was negatively related to explicit prejudice; that is, children with less parental identification took the opposite view from their parents on explicit prejudice—the more parental explicit prejudice, the less explicit prejudice in their children.

In explaining the last result, Sinclair, Dunn, and Lowery (2005) suggest the following:

It is possible, then, that children who identify with their parents may adopt the racial attitudes of their parents more on an implicit than an explicit level, whereas children who do not identify with their parents may actually reject their parent's attitudes, but only on an explicit level. (287)

In sum, the evidence suggests that prejudice in children is indeed influenced by a host of socialization agents including parents, peers, adults other than parents, and the cultural environment, defined by symbols and stories in the media and by communication in general. The emerging picture is that children are capable of internalizing cues from their cultural milieus by simplifying distinctions between people using the most obvious cues, such as skin color, and drawing conclusions as to which skin color is preferable. With continued changes in this environment, including the celebration of multiculturalism with its accompanying symbols, the hope is that prejudice based on race will diminish among children.

Figure Credit

Figure 6.1: W.G. Stephan and C.W. Stephan, "An Integrated Threat Theory of Prejudice," Reducing prejudice and discrimination. Copyright © 2000 by Lawrence Erlbaum Associates.

Workbook

Define, describe, or illustrate; summarize the results of the studies:

1.   Levels of analysis of the origins of prejudice

2.   Explanations of the origins of prejudice

3.   Hodson and Busseri (2012)

4.   Integrated theory of prejudice: definitions of components

5.   Stephan, Ybarra, and Bachman (2011)

6.   Development of prejudice in children

7.   Sinclair, Dunn, and Lowery (2005)

7

What Are Stereotypes?

While *prejudice* is negative or positive feelings or emotions toward groups and individuals who are members of targeted groups, *stereotypes* are beliefs that groups and their members possess positive or negative traits. Thus, prejudice is affective, or emotional, and stereotypes are cognitive, or the products of an assessment of the "truth" of an association between traits and groups. There is an assumption that stereotypes are based on some degree of "thinking," while prejudice is less thoughtful. Nevertheless, prejudice and stereotyping can result from, and be expressed after, deliberate, intentional, and controlled efforts, meaning that they can be "conscious." Prejudice and stereotypes can also be implicit and automatic, reflexive processes, and responses—in other words, "unconscious." Both prejudice and stereotypes can predict discriminatory behaviors toward individuals because of their group memberships and are intricately related, leading to two questions:

First, are prejudice and stereotypes separate and independent constructs? Research has shown that a person can be negatively prejudiced against a group without having negative stereotypes about the group. Conversely, a person can have negative stereotypes about a group without being prejudiced against that group (Hilton and von Hippel 1996). The reason is that prejudice and stereotypes have different origins—or, there are different sets of reasons for being prejudiced and for stereotyping. While there is some overlap, prejudice is not always based on the belief that the targeted group has negative traits. As we saw in the previous chapter, prejudice is learned from the cultural environment, which includes other clues as to the valence of out-groups besides the association of negative traits.

A second and related question is, which comes first—prejudice or stereotypes? The classic view is that stereotypes predict prejudice (Hamilton and Sherman 1994), that is, our association of positive or negative traits with a group will predict how we feel about that group, or, simply put, as long as stereotypes exist, prejudice will follow. The current view is that stereotypes sometimes come before prejudice (Hilton and von Hippel 1996). Studies reviewed in the last chapter show that children as young as six months old express some degree of prejudice—preferential responses to members of their in-groups. Children this young wouldn't be processing information required for the attribution of positive or negative traits to other people. Their "prejudices" can be explained by other factors besides stereotyping, such as observation of other people and symbols in their environment. The view we take in this book is that the relation between prejudice and stereotyping is bi-directional; each influences the other, and it's really not conceptually or practically important which comes first. Intervention strategies, for example, won't depend a lot on the direction of causality.

Defining Stereotypes

Labels are devices for saving talkative persons the trouble of thinking.

—Morley (1886, 142), as quoted in Gilbert and Hixon (1991)

The simplest definition is that a *stereotype* is a label. To be more precise, however, let's consider some common definitions (as quoted in Banaji and Greenwald 1994).

A stereotype is a fixed impression, which conforms very little to the fact it pretends to represent, and results from our defining first and observing second (Katz and Braly 1935, 181)

A stereotype is an exaggerated belief associated with a category (Allport 1979, 191).

A generalization about a group of people that distinguishes these people from others. Stereotypes can be overgeneralized, inaccurate, and resistant to new information (Myers 1990, 332)

A collection of associations that link a target group to a set of descriptive characteristics (Gaertner and Dovidio 1986, 415)

A cognitive structure that contains the perceiver's knowledge, beliefs, and expectancies about some human group (Hamilton ad Trolier 1986, 133)

The definitions above stress that stereotypes are generalizations of trait assignments to groups, and that these generalizations are often inaccurate. The next set of definitions stresses that stereotypes are generalizations of group characteristics to all members of the group, without providing for "individuation," or the assessment of a group member separately from the group category.

A categorical response, i.e., membership is sufficient to evoke the judgment that the stimulus person possesses all the attributes belonging to that category. (Secord 1959, 309)

In stereotyping, the individual: (1) categorizes other individuals, usually on the basis of highly visible characteristics such as sex or race; (2) attributes a set of characteristics to all members of that category; and (3) attributes that set of characteristics to any individual member of that category. (Snyder 1981, 183)

To stereotype is to assign identical characteristics to any person in a group, regardless of the actual variation among members of that group. (Aronson 1988, 223)

These definitions are the basis for most current definitions, but do not specifically address some components of stereotypes that are of interest to us, given recent interest in broadening the scope of stereotype research to conscious and unconscious processes, as well as interest in introspective strategies to reduce prejudice and negative stereotyping.

In this book, I use a general definition of stereotypes:

Beliefs about the characteristics, attributes, and behaviors of certain groups. (Hilton and von Hippel 1996)

This definition maintains the core concept of classical definitions, that is, that stereotypes are beliefs and the result of some cognitive processing. Its generality allows for refinement to include the following key elements:

- Stereotypes are overgeneralizations, which cause people to fail to notice individual differences among group members.
- Stereotypes can be positive or negative, although our attention will focus more on negative stereotyping, a major reason for dysfunctional interpersonal relations, ineffective communication, and social inequities. Also, stereotypes about out-groups are more likely to have negative connotations compared to stereotypes about in-groups (Hilton and von Hippel 1996).
- Stereotypes are selective. They are focused on group features that stand out and are most distinctive (Nelson and Miller 1995), that differentiate the most between groups, and that vary the least within groups (Ford and Stangor 1992). Consider the stereotype of Hispanic immigrants as "unpatriotic."

This trait stands out because there are many overt indications of being patriotic—willingness to learn English and American history, for one. And, patriotism can differentiate a "true" American from an "untrue" American; all Americans are expected to be patriotic with little variance.

- Stereotypes can be conscious or unconscious. *Conscious stereotypes* are those that the person is aware of, and that deliberately or intentionally guide his or her behaviors toward the target person or group. *Unconscious stereotypes* are those that a person is not aware of and that trigger automatic responses toward the target person or group. Unconscious stereotypes involve "the unintentional or spontaneous activation of some well-learned set of associations or responses that have been developed through repeated activation in memory" (Devine 1989, 6). Also, unconscious stereotypes do not require deliberate (or conscious) effort, and can be triggered by the mere presence of the target person or group in the environment (Bargh, Chen and Burrows 1996). Conscious stereotypes elicit voluntary responses from the person, while unconscious stereotypes elicit involuntary responses. For example, I may consciously believe that most Asians are good at math, so I will deliberately seek out a research assistant who is Asian, because my research requires quite a bit of number crunching. At the same time, I may not be aware that I have an unconscious stereotype of women as not being good at math, so in class I may unconsciously turn to a male student and ignore the raised hand of a female student when I have a question about a mathematical problem. I am conscious about my stereotype of Asians because this is a relatively benign stereotype and in fact may be considered positive by some (although this opinion is subject to debate—I do agree that any kind of stereotyping is injurious and should be avoided). On the other hand, I may try to deny and therefore force out of my consciousness my negative stereotype of women.

- Stereotypes have many dimensions including clusters of personality and behavioral and physical traits. Using factor analysis of individual traits, Tan et al. (2010) found three dimensions that they labeled "Work Ethic," "Aggression," and "Attractiveness." The Work Ethic factor included such traits as being hardworking, being honest, being polite, having good morals, and being generous. The Aggression factor consisted of the traits of being arrogant, violent, and aggressive. The Attractiveness factor was made up of the traits of being intelligent, beautiful, and (not) sloppy. Other researchers have identified similar dimensions of stereotypes. Sides and Gross (2013) suggest that the "first and primary" dimension should answer the question, "Will these other people hurt me or help me?" This dimension has been labeled as having "warmth" (Fiske and Cuddy 2002), "morality" (Wojciszke 2005), and "social desirability" (Phalet and Poppe 1997). The second dimension, which has been labeled as "competence" (Wojciszke 2005) refers to the ability of the target group members to accomplish their goals (Fiske et al. 2002). It includes the attributes of intelligence, skill, and creativity (Fiske, Cuddy, and Glick 2007). These two dimensions—warmth and competence—have been shown to be "reliably universal dimensions of social judgment across stimuli, cultures and time" (Fiske et al. 2007, 82).

- A person may be aware of the existence of stereotypes but may not endorse them. There is a difference between awareness and endorsement, which is sometimes confounded in measurement of stereotypes. In other words, "one may have knowledge of a stereotype," but "his or personal beliefs may or may not be congruent with the stereotype" (Devine 1989, 5).

- Although most stereotypes are based on inaccurate or incomplete information, some stereotypes may be based on accurate knowledge that a person may have about a group or differences between groups, and, therefore, may be "real" (Banaji and Greenwald 1994). The question, then, is how many members of a group must objectively have an attribute before a stereotype is to be considered "real." For example, some would agree with the stereotype that "Qataris are rich." This stereotype can be verified by checking the mean or median income in Qatar, but it does not answer questions such as the following in this context: "What is 'rich'?" "Who is a Qatari?"(natural born, most likely), and, "Is rich good or bad?" Regardless of whether the stereotype has some basis in objective facts ("accurate knowledge"), my view is that all stereotyping is harmful because stereotypes don't allow for evaluations of individuals independent of group affiliations.

In summary, a general definition of stereotypes with the specific elements discussed above provides a useful frame of analysis for this chapter. The central point is that stereotypes are cognitive representations of groups and their members. Consider my experience that I relate below:

I am zooming along a two-lane state highway, about forty miles from my hometown in Washington State. My nine-year-old son is asleep in the passenger seat, tired after playing in a tennis tournament. A state police cruiser going the opposite direction slows down as it gets closer. The officer flashes his lights and turns his vehicle around. I pull over. The state trooper approaches my window. I see that he has unhooked the fastener to his firearm holster.

"Do you know why I stopped you?" he asks, sounding a bit irritated.

"Sorry, officer, I don't know."

"Going a little too fast there," he says.

"Sorry, officer, I lost track." *I must have been going 10 miles above the speed limit*, I thought.

"Nice car. What is it?"

"Porsche."

"This car yours?" he says, with a frown.

"Yes."

"Do you mind if I look inside?"

Now, what am I to do? I ask myself. I vaguely remember that the law says search only with probable cause. What is probable cause? Probable cause for what? How does one determine probable cause? And perhaps I got it wrong. No big deal, I convince myself. By this time, my son is awake. I can see the concern—fear?—in his eyes.

"Go right ahead," I tell the officer.

The trooper looks through my son's tennis bag and our overnight bags. He asks for my driver's license, car registration, and proof of insurance, tells me to stay put, and goes back to his car.

He walks back to our car, and hands me my license and insurance card. He's friendly this time, and asks about the car. I tell him about it, and point to the speedometer, saying that they really shouldn't put speedometers in street cars that read up to 160 miles per hour. He is smiling as he tells me to take it easy and that he'll let me go with a warning this time.

Where Do Stereotypes Come From?

We like to solve problems easily. We can do so best if we can fit them rapidly into a satisfactory category and use this category as a means of prejudging the solution.... So long as we can get away with coarse overgeneralizations we tend to do so. Why? Well, it takes less effort, and effort, except in the area of our most intense interests, is disagreeable. (Allport 1979, 20–21, as quoted in Gilbert and Hixon 1991)

We hold stereotypes for many of the same reasons that we are prejudiced, except with stereotypes, there is more emphasis on the role of information. This is understandable, considering that stereotypes are based on beliefs, which are formed through cognitive processing of information. Several models, or representations of processes that we are trying to explain, can help us understand how stereotypes are formed.

The Cognitive Model

According to this model, stereotypes help us make sense of a complicated environment that has more information than we can comfortably process at any given moment. This function of stereotypes is called *cognitive economy*. The least effort principle underlies the cognitive economy function of stereotypes: the less effort required, the more comfortable we are. Therefore, we process as little information as possible to make sense of people and objects by using categories, because categorization requires less effort than evaluating individual persons and objects does. Applied to stereotyping, "the ability to understand new and unique individuals in terms of old and general beliefs is certainly among the handiest tools in the social perceiver's kit" (Gilbert and Hixon 1991, 509).

Cognitive explanations consider stereotypes as the result of incoming information, distilled and summarized, from significant others (e.g., peers, teacher, family members), the media, or personal contact with the stereotyped group (Allport 1979; Dixon 2006; Schneider 2004). Stereotypes are generalizations based on the contents and valence of the information (e.g., positive or negative portrayals in the media), the frequency of exposure, and clarity of the information (see, e.g., Bandura 2002). Considering limited human information-processing capacity (see, e.g., Lang 2000), we sort and organize incoming information into simplified cognitive schemas to describe groups of people and objects (Snyder and Meine 1994), resulting in stereotypes. Thus, stereotype formation in the cognitive model can be explained as limited and simplified processing of incoming information.

The Psychodynamic Model

According to the psychodynamic model, stereotypes fulfill individual needs (Hamilton and Sherman 1994), such as ego maintenance. Holding positive stereotypes of the groups to which we belong and with which we identify (our in-groups) and negative stereotypes of our out-groups enhances and maintains our feelings of self-worth.

The Sociocultural Model

According to the sociocultural model, stereotypes facilitate group identification and membership maintenance. Sharing stereotypes—beliefs about other groups—strengthens identification with in-groups and maintains membership. Cohesive groups have members who share values, beliefs, and goals, including stereotypes. At the community and societal level, stereotypes reinforce social values, structures, and symbols (see, e.g., Glick and Fiske 2001; Jost, Burgess, and Mosso 2001). Negative stereotypes provide some "rationalization" for maintaining the power structure and control of the allocation of resources. For example, if the prevailing stereotype of Martians in a society (such as a nation state) is that Martians are lazy, people in power can use this stereotype to restrict the immigration of Martians into its society.

How Are Stereotypes Measured?

To be able to study and understand stereotypes, we must be able to measure them; that is, we ask, "How do I know a stereotype when I see one?" Stereotypes may be explicit (conscious, voluntarily held, and deliberate) or implicit (unconscious, automatic, involuntarily elicited). Correspondingly, there are explicit and implicit measures of stereotypes.

Explicit Measures

1. *Free responses* (see, e.g., Monteith and Spicer 2002): Respondents are asked to "Describe—[name group]—using adjectives that come to your mind." Respondents are given a time limit—say, a couple of minutes—to list the adjectives. The most frequently listed adjectives are the stereotypes of the target group.
2. *Attribute checking* (see, e.g., Katz and Braly 1933): In this earliest measure of stereotypes, respondents are instructed as follows: "Here is a list of traits often used to describe people. Select those which

seem typical of _____ [name group]. Write as many of these words in the following space as you think are necessary to characterize people in this group adequately. You may add other traits not on this list." Respondents are then given a list of adjectives such as aggressive, intelligent, lazy, devoted to family, and patriotic. The adjectives listed most frequently by members of the respondent group are the stereotypes of the target group.

3. *Attribute ratings* (Brigham 1971): Respondents are given a list of traits or adjectives and then are asked to estimate the percentage of a group that has a particular trait. Traits with estimates of 80% or higher are considered stereotypes. Or, respondents are asked, "How likely is it that [name group] are [trait, such as 'assertive']—very likely, quite likely, somewhat likely, or not too likely?" Traits rated as very likely or quite likely are considered stereotypes.

4. *Semantic differential ratings* (Gardner 1973; Tan et al. 2000): The semantic differential measures the meaning of an object on a bipolar (opposites) adjective scale that is usually a seven-point scale. Applied to stereotypes, the semantic differential measure asks respondents to "rate the [group] on each of the attributes listed below by checking a space between the two opposing adjectives." The closer the space is to an adjective, the more the group can be described using that adjective. Several bipolar adjectives with seven spaces in between are then listed for the respondents. For example:

> Hardworking ___ ___ ___ ___ ___ ___ ___ Lazy
> Patriotic ___ ___ ___ ___ ___ ___ ___ Unpatriotic

Responses are scored on a seven-point scale; seven is the space closest to the positive adjective; one is the space closest to the negative adjective. Attributes whose ratings are significantly different (using a *t*-test) from the scale's midpoint (four on a seven-point scale) are considered to be consensual stereotypes, or stereotypes agreed on by the respondents taking the test.

5. *Group reality ratings* (Tan, Fujioka, and Tan 2000): Respondents are asked to estimate the percentage of the target group who display stereotypical behaviors. For example, "What percentage of [group] do you estimate to be

> In prison for violent crimes? ___%
> On welfare ___%
> Drug users ___%
> Drug dealers ___%

These estimates are then compared with official statistics that show what the actual percentages are in the real world. Behaviors or characteristics with estimates that are significantly higher than real-world estimates are considered to be stereotypes.

6. *Belief scales:* Respondents are asked to rate how descriptive stereotypical behaviors are of the target group. For example, Barreto, Manzano, and Segura (2012, 25) used this five-point scale in a national survey of Hispanic/Latino stereotypes. For each item, possible responses were "very well," "somewhat," "don't know," "not that well," or "not at all."

The surveyor asks, "Now I am going to read to you a few statements, and for each one, please tell me if you think it applies to Hispanics or Latinos very well, somewhat well, not that well, or not at all. So, thinking about Hispanics, in general, how well does [insert phrase] describe the group?"

- Have too many children
- Honest
- Less-educated
- Family oriented
- Culture of gangs and crime
- Religious, church-going
- Illegal immigrants
- Don't keep up their houses
- Take jobs from Americans

- Keep to themselves
- Refuse to learn English
- Use welfare or public assistance
- Neighborly and welcoming

With this scale, items that have mean scores significantly higher than the theoretical mean (three on a five-point scale) can be considered to be stereotypes. Also, items endorsed by a majority of respondents, 50% or higher, can be interpreted as stereotypes.

The interpretation of results from the explicit stereotype measures above has been a subject of debate among researchers. Several issues have been raised regarding these measures:

1. How sensitive are these measures to social desirability motivations among respondents? It is generally not socially acceptable to be prejudiced, racist, or sexist, so our desire to be accepted by others may lead us to avoid appearing prejudiced in our responses to these measures.
2. When does a trait endorsed by a group become a stereotype? Clearly, there will seldom be 100% agreement within an in-group that an out-group possesses a certain trait. So, is 80% or 50% agreement, or significant difference from the mean, sufficient for an endorsed trait to be considered a stereotype? There is very little in theory that could guide us in making this decision. Consequently, these decisions are often arbitrary, and results are presented descriptively, with traits ordered in terms of frequency of endorsement. Or, results are analyzed at the individual level. That is, an individual's scores are correlated to some other construct, say the individual's evaluation of a job candidate, and the conclusions are made on the basis of how scores (high or low on a numerical scale) are related to, or can predict, a related construct. For example, I may find that higher negative scores on a stereotype scale predict lower scores on a target person's job evaluation. I could then draw the conclusion that negative stereotyping is related to low job evaluations, without concluding that the respondent group had a stereotype of the target group. The analysis of stereotype scores is relative to the scores of other respondents in the group. The mean score may be positive, but a particular individual may have lower scores than other members in the group. A more appropriate conclusion in this case would be the less positive the stereotype, the less positive the job evaluation. Analyses like this help us minimize the social desirability disadvantage of explicit measures.

Implicit Measures

Implicit measures of stereotypes are a subset of the Implicit Associations Test (IAT) discussed in Chapter 4, Measures of Explicit and Implicit Prejudice. Most of the tests in the IAT measure implicit attitudes—positive or negative feelings toward groups—and are, therefore, measures of prejudice. Several tests measure the association of traits or behaviors with groups, and are, therefore, measures of implicit stereotypes. The stereotype IATs follow the same procedure and theoretical assumptions of the attitude IATs; that is, the strength of association between concepts is indicated by the relative speed in making those associations. Some stereotype IATs are the following, as described on the IAT website:

1. *Asian American stereotype:* Uses six headshot sketches of Asians, three female and three male; six headshot sketches of Whites, three female and three male; and six foreign landmarks (e.g., the Egyptian pyramids) and six American landmarks (e.g., the Statue of Liberty). Respondents generally associate American landmarks with Whites and foreign landmarks with Asians, implying implicit stereotypes of Asian Americans as foreign and unpatriotic.
2. *Native/White stereotype:* Uses the same stimuli as in the Asian American stereotype IAT, except six headshots of Native American faces and six headshots of White faces are used. Respondents generally associate American landmarks with Whites and foreign landmarks with Native Americans, implying implicit stereotypes of Native Americans as foreign.

3. *Weapons and faces:* Faces with dark and light skin are used as stimuli, along with seven weapons (e.g., battle axe, mace, revolver) and seven harmless objects. Respondents generally associate dark skin with weapons and Whites with harmless objects, implying an implicit stereotype of violence and aggression for dark skin.
4. *Gender science:* This stereotype test shows a link between liberal arts and females and between science and males.
5. *Gender career:* This stereotype test shows a link between females and family and between males and careers.

The stereotype IATs show that most people have implicit biases for and against certain groups. These biases can influence group evaluations as well as discriminatory behaviors, and are more likely to be revealed than in explicit measures of stereotypes.

Public Stereotypes of American Racial Groups

Various national and international surveys have tracked stereotypes of racial, ethnic, gender, age, and nationality groups over time. Because the main instrument of data collection is surveys, explicit measures are commonly used. Here are three recent studies that tell us about current stereotypes of racial groups in the United States.

Associated Press (AP) Racial Attitudes Poll (2012)

From August 30 to September 11, 2012, an AP-sponsored poll was conducted to gauge racial attitudes prior to the presidential election and four years after President Obama had been elected to his first term. The poll was conducted for AP by the GFL group, a commercial research firm, in collaboration with researchers from Stanford University and the University of Chicago. The poll randomly sampled the political and racial attitudes of 1,071 American adults nationwide. The survey was administered online, which previous studies have shown to be less sensitive to social desirability responses than phone interviews. The random sample was 62% female, 48% male; 67% White, Non-Hispanic, 12% Black, Non-Hispanic, 6% Other, Non-Hispanic, 14% Hispanic, 1% two or more races non-Hispanic. The margin of error was plus or minus 3.7%. The poll asked a series of stereotype questions, for example, "How well does each of these words [stereotypic trait] describe most [racial group]?" Possible responses were extremely well, very well, moderately well, slightly well, not at all, or refused/not answered. Here are some of the results (Associated Press Racial Attitudes Survey 2012).

Friendly

In the category of being friendly, these three racial groups were said to equally fit the ratings of "extremely well" and "very well": Blacks (32%), Whites (33%), and Hispanics (32%). However, among the minority of the sample responding "slightly well" or "not at all," Blacks were rated to be the least friendly (20%), followed by Hispanics (18%). Only 9% of respondents rated Whites to be somewhat or not at all friendly. For most of the sample, Blacks, Whites, and Hispanics were considered to be equally friendly. However, for a small subset of the sample, Whites were clearly considered to be more friendly, while Blacks and Hispanics were considered to be less friendly.

Determined to Succeed

Respondents rated Whites as the most determined to succeed (extremely well and very well, 40%). Much smaller percentages rated Blacks (24%) and Hispanics (31%) determined to succeed. At the other end of the scale, 31% rated Blacks somewhat or not at all determined to succeed, followed by Hispanics (20%). Only 9% of respondents rated Whites as not determined to succeed. Clear differences emerge on this trait. Respondents rated Whites as most determined to succeed more strongly than they did Hispanics and Blacks, and Blacks as less determined to succeed than Hispanics.

Law-Abiding

Respondents rated Hispanics to be least likely to be law-abiding (20% extremely well and very well). Blacks and Whites were rated equally likely to be law-abiding (32%). At the other end of the scale, 28% rated Hispanics to be somewhat or not at all law-abiding, followed by Blacks (20%) and Whites (12%). Therefore, among the three racial groups, Hispanics were considered the least likely to be law-abiding. At the other end of the scale, Blacks were rated to be less law-abiding than Whites.

Hardworking

Hispanics were rated to be the most hardworking (48% extremely and very well), followed by Whites (37%) and Blacks (31%). At the lower end of the scale, 25% of respondents said Blacks were somewhat or not at all hardworking, followed by Hispanics (11%) and Whites (10%). Thus, Hispanics and Whites were considered to be hardworking, and Blacks less so.

Intelligent at School

The ratings for intelligence at school show that Whites were clearly rated the most favorably (36% extremely well or very well; 9% somewhat likely or not at all). The ratings for Hispanics (20% and 29%, respectively) and Blacks (23% and 28%) indicate much lower ratings than Whites. Noteworthy is that close to one-third of respondents rated Blacks and Hispanics as somewhat likely or not at all likely to be intelligent at school, compared to only 9% giving Whites the same ratings.

Smart at Everyday Things

More respondents rated Whites higher on this trait (32% extremely well or very well; 14% somewhat well or not at all) compared to Blacks (26% and 26%, respectively) and Hispanics (22% and 27%). Thus, Whites were considered to be smarter at "everyday things" than Blacks and Hispanics.

Good Neighbors

More respondents rated Whites as good neighbors (40% extremely well or very well; 9% somewhat well or not at all) compared to Blacks (29% and 24%) and Hispanics (27% and 24%). Clearly, respondents considered Whites more likely to be good neighbors than Blacks or Hispanics.

Dependable

More respondents rated Whites as dependable (31% extremely well or very well; 12% somewhat well or not at all), followed by Hispanics (31% and 20%, respectively) and Blacks (27% and 27%). Thus, Whites had the highest ratings, and Blacks the lowest.

Keep up Property

Whites received the highest ratings (40% extremely well or very well; 10% somewhat well or not at all). Blacks (23% and 30%, respectively) and Hispanics (23% and 29%) received much lower ratings. Clearly, Blacks and Hispanics were perceived as less likely to keep up property than Whites.

Violent

A majority of respondents said that this trait describes the groups somewhat well or not at all—50% for Blacks, 53% for Whites, and 53% for Hispanics. However, 16% said that *violent* described Blacks extremely well or very well, compared to 10% for Hispanics and 6% for Whites. Most respondents were unwilling to characterize any group as violent; however, a minority described Blacks as more violent than Hispanics or Whites, and Hispanics as more violent than Whites.

Boastful

The most frequent response in the sample was that *boastful* did not describe (i.e., with responses of somewhat well or not at all) Hispanics (51%), Whites (43%), or Blacks (41%). However, 20% said *boastful* described Blacks and Whites extremely well or very well, compared to only 10% for Hispanics. In comparison to Blacks and Whites, Hispanics were perceived to be the least boastful.

Complaining

Hispanics were seen as the least complaining (52% somewhat well or not at all; 10% extremely well or very well), followed by Whites (38% and 17%, respectively) and Blacks (42% and 23%).

Lazy

A majority of respondents said that *lazy* somewhat or not at all characterized Hispanics (60%), Blacks (54%), and Whites (53%); 14% said *lazy* described Blacks extremely well or very well, compared to 5% for Whites and 6% for Hispanics. Thus, some respondents attributed "lazy" more to Blacks than to Whites or Hispanics, but the majority of respondents did not make this distinction.

Irresponsible

A majority of respondents did not characterize (somewhat well or not at all) any of the racial groups as irresponsible (Hispanics, 54%; Blacks, 52%; Whites, 51%). However, more respondents said that *irresponsible* describes Blacks extremely well or very well (12%) than this description does for Whites (6%) and Hispanics (7%).

The picture that emerges from the AP national poll of racial attitudes is that people are not stereotyping racial groups negatively when explicit measures are used. On each of the stereotypical traits measured in the poll, the most frequent responses were the mid-point (moderately well) or in the direction of positive stereotypes (intelligent, not violent). However, another indication of stereotyping is the relative ratings given to each of the groups, that is, a group rating compared to ratings of the other groups. If stereotyping indeed does not occur, we would expect all the ratings to be equal or close to equal. However, that is clearly not the case. Some racial groups are rated less positively or more negatively on some of the traits, and not all stereotypes of Hispanics and Blacks are negative. Here are some conclusions regarding attributions of traits that we could draw from the AP poll, according to the responses of a nationwide sample:

- Whites are *friendlier* than Blacks and Hispanics.
- Whites are more *determined to succeed* than Blacks and Hispanics. Blacks are least determined to succeed.
- Whites are more *law-abiding* than Blacks and Hispanics. Hispanics are least law-abiding.
- Hispanics are more *hardworking* than Blacks and Whites. Blacks are the least hardworking.
- Whites are more *intelligent at school* than Blacks and Hispanics, who are equally less intelligent at school.
- Whites are *smarter at everyday things* than Blacks and Hispanics; there is little difference between Blacks and Hispanics here.
- Whites are more likely to be *good neighbors* than Blacks and Hispanics, who are equally less likely to be good neighbors than Whites.
- Whites are more *dependable* than Blacks or Hispanics; Blacks are the least dependable.
- Whites are more likely to *keep up property* than Blacks or Hispanics, who are equally less likely to keep up property than Whites.
- Blacks are rated to be slightly more *violent* than Whites and Hispanics; Hispanics are more violent than Whites.
- Hispanics are rated to be least *boastful*; there is little difference between Blacks and Whites here.
- Hispanics are rated to be least *complaining*; there is little difference between Blacks and Whites here.
- Hispanics are rated to be the least *lazy*, followed by Whites, then Blacks.
- Blacks are rated to be the most *irresponsible*, with little difference in ratings of Whites and Hispanics.

These results are summarized here:

TABLE 7.1   Stereotypes of Whites, Blacks, and Hispanics (Data taken from AP Racial Attitudes Poll, 2012)

Stereotype Trait	Group With Highest Rating	Group With Lowest Rating
Friendly	Whites (W)	Blacks (B) and Hispanics (H), No Difference
Determined to succeed	W	B
Law-abiding	W	H
Hardworking	H	B
Intelligent at school	W	B and H
Smarter at everyday things	W	B and H
Good neighbors	W	B and H
Dependable	W	B
Keep up property	W	B and H
Violent	B	W
Boastful	B and W	H
Complaining	B and W	H
Lazy	B	H
Irresponsible	B	W and H

Based on relative ratings, Whites were perceived to have the most positive ratings on eight of nine positive traits and the most negative ratings on two (tied with Blacks) of five negative traits. The relative ratings can be used to infer the following stereotypes of each racial group:

Whites: friendly, determined to succeed, law-abiding, intelligent at school, smarter at everyday things, likely to be good neighbors, dependable, likely to keep up property, complaining, boastful.

Blacks: less friendly, less determined to succeed, less hardworking, less intelligent at school, less smart at everyday things, less likely to be good neighbors, less likely to keep up property, less dependable, violent, boastful, complaining, lazy, and irresponsible.

Hispanics: less friendly, less law-abiding, hardworking, less intelligent at school, less smart at everyday things, less likely to be good neighbors, less likely to keep up property, less boastful, less complaining, not lazy.

Several cautionary notes should be considered in interpreting these data:

- Most respondents rated the racial groups positively or neutrally on the five-point scale.
- The differences in ratings between groups are based on examination of percentages, and not on statistical analysis of differences between means or percentage.

Notwithstanding these limitations, the AP data provide evidence that, even with explicit measures, Americans are expressing stereotypical beliefs about racial groups.

Stereotypes of Muslims and Support for the War on Terror (Sides and Gross 2012)

In this large-scale national study, Sides and Gross (2012) used a national nonprobability sample of 39,000 respondents. Thirty-nine universities collaborated on the study, which was directed out of the Massachusetts Institute of Technology. Survey data were collected online from a cross-section of American adults in 2006 and 2007. The purpose of the study was to measure stereotypes of Muslims and racial groups in the United States, and to see if stereotypes of Muslims were related to opinions about the war on terror. The groups studied were Muslims, Muslim Americans, Asian Americans, Hispanic Americans, Blacks, and Whites. The stereotype traits studied were peaceful/violent, trustworthy/untrustworthy, hardworking/lazy, and intelligent/unintelligent. Sides and Gross (2012) called the first two traits "warmth" stereotypes, and the last two traits "competence" stereotypes. The stereotype traits were rated on a seven point scale, where 7 was the most unfavorable rating of a trait, 4 was the mid-point, and 1 was the most favorable rating. Here are some of the results:

- Most ratings clustered around the mid-point, indicating that respondents were not willing to explicitly express negative ratings of any group, particularly on the "intelligent/unintelligent" trait. However, there were several differences in ratings of groups, based on the distance of a particular rating from the mid-point.
- Asian Americans and Whites were rated to be peaceful; Muslims and Muslim Americans were rated to be the most violent, with little difference between the two, followed by Blacks. Hispanics were rated on violence close to the mid-point.
- Asian Americans and Whites were rated to be trustworthy. Muslims and Muslim Americans were rated to be untrustworthy (with little difference). Trustworthiness ratings for Blacks and Hispanic Americans were close to the mid-point.
- Blacks were the only group to be rated as lazy, although their negative ratings on this trait were close to the mid-point. All other groups were rated to be hardworking, with Asian Americans receiving the highest ratings, followed, in descending order, by Whites, Hispanic Americans, and Muslims and Muslim Americans (with little difference), whose positive ratings were close to the mid-point.
- All groups were rated to be intelligent. Asian Americans were rated to be the most intelligent, followed, in descending order, by Whites, Muslims, Muslim Americans, Blacks, and Hispanics. The positive ratings for Muslims, Muslim Americans, Hispanic Americans, and Whites were close to the mid-point.

We can draw several conclusions from this study:

- Stereotypes of Muslims and Muslim Americans were negative on the warmth dimension (peaceful/violent, trustworthy/untrustworthy), and fairly neutral, although leaning toward the positive end, on the competence dimension (hardworking/lazy, intelligent/unintelligent). This is not a surprising result, considering the state of American foreign affairs, and, to be discussed in Chapter 9, the negative portrayals of Muslims in American entertainment and news. Respondents did not distinguish between Muslims and Muslim Americans.

- Asian Americans and Whites were rated most positively on all traits, an interesting result for Asian Americans, considering their continued negative portrayals in news and entertainment.
- Blacks were rated most negatively. Their ratings on three traits fell on the negative end of the scale.
- Hispanic American stereotypes were rated neutrally (mid-point) on three traits, and positively as hardworking.
- The results of this study provide supporting evidence for the negative evaluations of Muslims by the American public. Previous studies have shown that many Americans "have unfavorable views of Muslims, Arab-Americans, and Islam" (Sides and Gross 2012; Nisbet, Ostman, and Shanahan 2007; Panagopoulos 2006).
- An ABC poll in 2006 showed that about one-third of respondents said that Islam "encourages violence"; 58% said that there are more "violent extremists" within Islam than in other religions.
- Pew surveys from 2002 to 2006 showed that only about half of respondents had a favorable opinion of Muslims.

Consider this news report:

Mosques Designated as Terrorist Organizations

The Associated Press (2013) reported that the New York Police Department has secretly designated entire mosques as terrorist organizations. This designation would allow police to use informants to record sermons and spy on imams, "often without specific evidence of criminal wrongdoing."

According to the AP, designating an entire mosque as a terrorist organization subjects anyone who attends prayer services to potential investigation and surveillance. Confidential police documents showed how the NYPD investigated New York Muslims in its search for terrorists, put information in secret files, and subsequently released most without filing any charges.

Stereotypes of Latinos (Barreto, Manzano, and Segura 2012)

In this study, the authors looked more closely at stereotypes of Latinos and Hispanic Americans. They defined Latino and Hispanic Americans as "people whose families are descended from Spanish-speaking nations in Latin America like Mexico, Cuba, Puerto Rico, Guatemala, and other countries in Central and South America. Many are born here in the US, but some are immigrants from other countries" (Barreto, Manzano, and Segura 2012, 24). The authors conducted a national survey of nine hundred non-Latino respondents over the phone in 2012. Respondents were asked how well stereotypic traits described Latino/Hispanic Americans on a four-point scale (very well, somewhat well, not well, or not at all). They found both positive and negative stereotypes of Latinos/Hispanic Americans. The corresponding sample percentages endorsing the trait (very well or somewhat well) are shown after each trait.

Positive stereotypes:

- Family oriented: 90%
- Hardworking: 81%
- Religious/churchgoing: 77%
- Honest: 76%

Negative stereotypes:

- Welfare recipients: 51%
- Less educated: 50%
- Refuse to learn English: 44%
- Too many children: 40%

- Take jobs from Americans: 37%
- Don't keep up homes: 33%

These results show that respondents strongly endorsed the positive stereotypes, and were less likely to express negative stereotypes. Considering that explicit measures were used, and that interviews were done over the phone, the negative stereotypes can be taken as having some validity, particularly because they reinforce results of other polls (e.g., AP Racial Attitudes Poll 2012). We can conclude with some degree of confidence that racial stereotyping by the American public continues, although people are reluctant to publicly express these views. This conclusion is based on supporting evidence from a number of studies that show that people make differential attributions of stereotypical traits based on race. We have focused on race because most studies have studied racial stereotypes. To be sure, public stereotyping based on gender, sexual orientation, age, and disability also deserves attention and discussion.

Stereotypes of Americans Abroad

We are interested not only in stereotypes that Americans have of each other, but also in stereotypes that people in other countries have of Americans. Considering the potential of stereotypes to affect evaluations of and behaviors toward target groups and their members, stereotypes of Americans abroad can impact US foreign diplomacy, business, and other interactions with foreign countries. Several studies give us some information on how we are perceived abroad.

DeFleur and DeFleur (2003)

This study surveyed 1,300 teenagers in twelve countries to find out their stereotypes of Americans. They used an eleven-point scale, from –5 (most negative) to +5 (most positive); 0 was neutral. Most of the stereotypes were negative; the higher the negative score, the more negative the rating. The negative stereotypes were as follows:

- Like to dominate other people –1.43
- Sexually immoral (American women): –1.18
- Very materialistic: –1.01
- Violent: –.87
- Does not respect people unlike themselves: –.3

The positive stereotypes were as follows:

- Strong family values: +.74
- Concerned about the poor: +.29

Ratings for "engage in criminal activity," "peaceful," "generous," and "strong religious values" were close to the 0 mid-point.

Considering overall ratings across all traits, Americans were rated negatively in nine of the twelve countries; at about the mid-point in two countries; and positively (slightly) in one country. Here are the country ratings:

Saudi Arabia: –2.13
Bahrain: –1.80
South Korea: –1.80
Lebanon: –1.65
Mexico: –1.5
China: –1.06

Spain: –.89
Taiwan: –.75
Pakistan: –.46
Nigeria: –.05
Italy: –.03
Argentina: +.69

The DeFleur and DeFleur (2003) study gives us a snapshot of American stereotypes by teenagers in several countries, and that snapshot doesn't paint a positive picture of Americans. Considering that their study was done more than a decade ago, an update would be very useful.

Tan, Dalisay, Han, Zhang, and Merchant (2010)

This study surveyed 378 students from urban and rural high schools in South Korea, a growing world economic power and US military partner, where American television and film are easily available. We measured stereotypes on a seven-point semantic differential scale, from 1 (most negative) to 7 (most positive). The positive stereotypes and their mean scores, in descending order from most positive, were as follows:

- Hedonic (seeking pleasure): 4.87 (Pre-testing indicated that to our high school student sample, seeking pleasure was a positive trait.)
- Humorous: 4.71 (Also a positive trait to high school students.)
- Honest: 4.12
- Hardworking: 4.11

The negative traits and their mean scores, in descending order from most negative (closest to –1.0), were as follows:

- Arrogant: –2.76
- Violent: –.3.02
- Aggressive: –3.26
- Prejudiced: –3.41

Ratings for having good morals and being polite were close to the mid-point.

Tan et al. (2010) conclude that the image of Americans in their sample of South Korean high school students is a mix of positive and negative traits, and can be explained by use of American media (discussed further in Chapter 9).

Tan, Dalisay, Zhang, and Zhang (2009)

The researchers studied stereotypes of Americans and the American government among 345 high school students in rural China and urban China (Beijing) in 2008. They measured stereotypes on a seven-point semantic differential scale, from 1 (most negative) to 7 (most positive). Results are shown in Table 7.2. Mean scores are shown; a higher mean indicates a rating closer to the positive trait, and a lower mean indicates a rating closer to the negative trait. Positive and negative traits are listed as pairs, with the positive trait listed first. The means are shown in descending order, from the most positively rated trait for Americans, to the most negative.

TABLE 7.2 Stereotypes of Americans and the American Government Among Chinese High School Students (Data taken from Tan et al. 2009)

Stereotype Trait (7-point scale; 7 = positive)	Americans	American Government
Rich (7)/poor (1)	6.15	6.57
Open-minded (7)/close-minded (1)	5.6	5.17
Polite (7)/impolite (1)	5.43	4.55
Good morals	5.23	4.13
Intelligent	5.17	5.22
Honest (7)/dishonest (1)	5.04	3.84
Beautiful (7)/not beautiful (1)	4.05	3.82
Not greedy (7)/greedy (1)	3.43	2.66
Not prejudiced (7)/prejudiced (1)	2.99	2.63
Not violent (7)/violent (1)	2.87	2.14
Not hedonistic (7)/hedonistic (1)	2.66	2.81
Humble (7)/arrogant (1)	2.5	1.93
Not aggressive (7)/aggressive (1)	2.36	2.09

These results show that Americans were stereotyped positively as being rich, open-minded, polite, intelligent, and honest, with good morals. Negative stereotypes were being arrogant, hedonistic (a negative trait among Chinese high school students, according to pretesting), violent, prejudiced, and greedy. At the midpoint of the scale was being beautiful.

The American government was stereotyped positively as being rich, open-minded, and intelligent. Negative stereotypes were being arrogant, aggressive, violent, prejudiced, greedy, and hedonistic. Mid-point stereotypes were being honest, beautiful, and polite, with good morals.

Overall, the American government was rated more negatively than American people on all scales (with differences statistically significant by t-tests at $p < .05$). In particular, the American government was rated to be considerably more arrogant, violent, dishonest, aggressive, and prejudiced and greedier than Americans.

These data show that it is an oversimplification to conclude that American stereotypes in China are negative, at least in this sample of high school students. While there are negative characterizations, Americans also were perceived to have positive traits, indicating that the concept "Americans in general" is perceived by the sample to be more complex than an overall negative stereotype can simply describe.

Pew Global Attitudes Project (2012)

The Pew Research Center and Foundation conducts periodic assessments of opinions of the United States in countries around the world. Using random samples of adults that range in size from a few hundred to thousands, respondents are asked about their opinions about a range of issues, most concerning the United States and foreign policy. In 2012, the global survey asked foreign respondents, "Please tell me if you have a very favorable, somewhat favorable, somewhat unfavorable, or very unfavorable opinion of the U.S." Although the question did not measure stereotypes directly, the opinions expressed can be influenced by stereotypes. Table 7.3 shows some results, collapsing responses into two categories (unfavorable and favorable). The percentages do not add up to 100, because some respondents did not answer the question or gave a no-opinion response.

TABLE 7.3 Opinions of the United States Abroad (Data taken from PEW 2012)

Country	Unfavorable (% of Respondents)	Favorable (% of Respondents)
Italy	22	74
Japan	27	72
Poland	26	69
France	31	69
Brazil	30	61
Britain	31	60
Spain	32	58
Mexico	31	56
Czech Republic	37	54
Russia	34	52
Germany	44	52
Lebanon	49	48
Tunisia	45	45
China	48	43
India	n.a.	41
Greece	61	35
Egypt	79	19
Turkey	72	15
Pakistan	80	12
Jordan	86	12

These results show that opinions about the United States in this sample of twenty countries are mixed. Eleven had favorable opinions, with 50% or more of the respondents saying "very favorable" or "somewhat favorable," while five had unfavorable opinions, with 50% or more of the respondents saying "very unfavorable" or "unfavorable," These opinions are clearly related to the geopolitics and international affairs of the United States. Our interest in this book is in pointing out the possible link between opinions and stereotypes, and the possible consequences of stereotypes on behaviors toward and evaluations of target groups.

Stereotypes of Older People

Numerous studies have shown that public stereotypes of older people in the United States and abroad are generally negative (Lyons 2009; Kite et al. 2005). Nosek et al. (2002), for example, reported that negative implicit stereotypes of older people relative to younger people were the strongest obtained in their studies in comparison to implicit race and gender stereotypes.

Positive stereotypes of older people do exist. Some examples are:

- Warm, sincere, kind and motherly (Cuddy et al. 2005; Barrett and Cantwell 2007).
- Wise, knowledgeable, experienced, patriotic, experienced (Barrett and Pai 2008).

Although positive stereotypes exist, most public stereotypes of older people are negative (e.g., Musaiger and D'Souza 2009). Palmore (1981), for example, found that seven out of the nine most frequent misconceptions of older people reflected negative stereotypes. Sauer (2006) reported that college students were three times more likely to use negative rather than positive descriptors to describe older people.

Here are some examples of negative stereotypes of the elderly:

- Shrewd, greedy, selfish, stubborn, grumpy (Barrett and Pai, 2008).
- Lonely, depressed, closed-minded, boring, wrinkled, forgetful, technologically challenged (Barrett and Pai, 2008).
- Pessimistic, difficult, grouchy, irritable (Tan et al. 2004).

Older men, in particular, have been described more often in comparison to older women as:

- Intolerant, suspicious, conflictive (e.g., Narayan 2008).

Tan (2011), a clinical neuropsychologist at Stanford University, points out several stereotypical myths about older people. These stereotypes are myths because, according to Tan, they do not correspond to the facts. Here are some of these myths, with corresponding rebuttals from Tan (2011, 1–2):

- Old people are incompetent.
  "Many elderly people, even in the early stages of dementia, can retain their abilities to understand and appreciate information they are given and reason to make important life choices. Physical disabilities are often mistakenly linked to intellectual deficits."
- All old people are the same.
  "There is more variety among older people than among any other age group."
- Most older people are senile (suffer from memory loss, disorientation, bizarre behavior).
  "About 80 percent of older adults are healthy enough to carry out their normal activities."
- As people age, their ability to learn often stops.
  "Learning patterns may change and speed of learning may diminish, but the basic capacity to learn is retained."
- Everyone who gets old will develop dementia.
  "Only 6–8% of people over age 65 have dementia, and 1/3 of those over age 85 have some dementia symptoms."
- All old people get depressed.
  "Most older adults, most of the time, are not depressed. Depression is NOT a normal part of growing old but rather an illness that needs to be treated. Age alone is not a risk factor for depression."

The myth that all older people are alike, if accepted, leads to stereotyping. Therefore, rejection of this myth reduces the likelihood of stereotyping.

Gender Stereotypes

Gender stereotypes have been studied as traits usually assigned to men and women in positions of authority such as in public office and in some professional careers. In the past few years, these stereotypes have been mixed, including positive and negative traits. Here are some examples.

Men and Women as Leaders in Public Office

Who make better leaders—men or women? To answer this question, the Pew Research Center (2008) asked a national random sample of 2,250 adults living in the continental United States whether several leadership and performance traits were "more true" for men or women. The results are summarized in Tables 7.4 and 7.5.

As Table 7.4 shows, the public, as represented by the national random sample, rated women more positively or better than men in five of eight leadership traits (honest, intelligent, compassionate, outgoing and creative.) They rated women equal to men in two traits (hardworking and ambitious), and lower than men in one trait (decisive). Also, the respondents' predominant response (highest percentages) for the traits intelligent and hardworking was "Don't Know" and "No Difference," a volunteered response not prompted in the interview. These results show that women were clearly rated superior to men in almost all of the leadership traits, with the strongest ratings (as indicated by the greatest differences between men and women) for compassionate, creative and honest. Of the four traits the respondents said were most important in a leader, women were rated higher than men in two (honesty and intelligence, ranked 1 and 2 in importance) and tied with men on two (hard work and ambition, ranked 3 and 4). Clearly, stereotypes of women, as measured by leadership traits, were more positive than stereotypes of men.

In terms of performance skills and dealing with policy matters, women were rated better or more positively than men in five of seven categories: working out compromises, keeping government honest, representing your interests, standing up for what they believe, and dealing with social issues (see Table 7.5). Men were rated more positively in two categories: dealing with crime and public safety and dealing with national security and defense (Table 7.5). It's clear that women in general had more favorable ratings than men. However, the highest response in four of the performance and policy skills categories (keeping government honest, representing your interests, standing up for what they believe, and dealing with crime and public safety) was "Don't Know" and "No Difference", a volunteered, unprompted response. Therefore, most respondents were unwilling to stereotype men and women on these traits, although among those who differentiated between men and women, women were rated more positively than men in three out of four performance skills.

The PEW survey also asked about four additional traits that might affect leadership abilities: emotional, manipulative, arrogant, and stubborn. Women were rated to be more emotional than men (85% women, 5% men), and to be more manipulative than men (52% women, 26% men). Men, in comparison to women, were rated to be more arrogant (70% men, 10% women) and more stubborn (46% men, 32% women).

The Pew survey also found gender differences in the ratings of men and women on twelve stereotype traits. Women saw themselves more positively than men on ten of twelve traits (less arrogant, less stubborn, more decisive, more ambitious, more outgoing, more hardworking, more honest, more intelligent, more creative, more compassionate), while evaluating men more positively on two (men were less emotional and less manipulative than women). Men rated themselves superior to women on just five of the twelve traits (decisive, hard work, ambition, not being emotional, not being manipulative), and inferior on seven (honesty, intelligence, compassion, creativity, being outgoing, being stubborn, being arrogant.)

When asked "Who makes a better political leader: men or women", 69% of all respondents said "equal"; 21% said "men"; 6% said "women"; and 4% said "don't know" (PEW 2008).

Taken together, results of the PEW survey indicate that women are viewed more positively than men in almost all of the traits and performance skills related to political leadership. However, when asked to give a summary evaluation of who makes a better political leader, more respondents chose men (21%) than women (6%) although most respondents (69%) said men and women could be equally effective.

The discrepancy between more favorable ratings of women on almost all leadership traits and a lower summary rating on overall leadership effectiveness can be explained in part by the traits included in the study. According to PEW (2008), a pro-male evaluation might have been observed if a broader range of leadership traits were included. Other research, for example, has shown that men are generally rated higher than women on traits valued by our society in key leadership positions, traits such as dominant, aggressive, and competent. On the other hand, women are seen as warm, nurturing, likable, and emotional, traits that are not as valued in top leadership positions (Eagly and Mladinic 1994; Moss-Racusin et al. 2012).

This interpretation is supported in evidence presented in other research. Dolan (2014), for example, reviewed research indicating that men, in comparison to women, are generally perceived as more competent, decisive, stronger leaders, and with greater ability to handle a crisis. Women, on the other hand, are generally viewed to be more compassionate, expressive, honest, and better able to deal with constituents.

Perceived gender differences have also been observed in ability to deal with issues. Women are perceived to be "more interested in, and more effective at dealing with, issues such as child care, poverty, education, health care, women's issues and the environment than men, while men are thought to be more competent at dealing with economic development, military, trade, taxes and agriculture" (Dolan 2014, 6).

The PEW (2008) survey results and research reviewed by Dolan (2014) indicate that while most stereotypes of women may be more positive than stereotypes of men, the overall public evaluation of ability for public office still favors men. When it comes to those traits and performance skills that many think to be important in a leader, men are favored over women.

And, negative stereotypes of women still linger. Here are some examples pointed out by Dolan (2014):

- A heckler calling on Hilary Clinton when she was running for the Democratic party's nomination for president to "Iron my shirt."
- A voter, asking Oklahoma Lt. Governor Jari Askins when she was running for governor of her state, whether, as a single, childless woman, she had enough life experiences to understand the concerns of the average Oklahoma family.
- Public debate during the 2008 presidential election (when Sarah Palin was the Republican candidate for vice president) about whether a mother of young children had the time to be vice president.

TABLE 7.4 Perceived Leadership Traits of Men and Women (Data taken from PEW, 2008)

Trait	Percent saying trait is truer for		
	Men	Women	Don't Know and Equally True
Honest	20	50	30
Intelligent	14	38	48
Hardworking	28	28	44
Decisive	44	33	23
Ambitious	34	34	32
Compassionate	5	80	15
Outgoing	28	47	25
Creative	11	62	27

TABLE 7.5 Perceived Performance Skills of Men and Women (Data taken from PEW 2008)

Performance Skill	"Are men or women in public office better at …" Percent saying		
	Men	Women	Don't Know and Same
Working out compromises	16	42	42
Keeping government honest	10	34	56
Representing your interests	18	28	54
Standing up for what they believe	16	23	61
Dealing with social issues	7	52	41
Dealing with crime and public safety	42	12	46
Dealing with national security and defense	54	7	39

Preferences for Men and Women in Positions of Authority

Gender stereotypes can influence the public's preference for men or women in positions of authority, such as in some careers. A PEW (2008) survey asked a nationally representative sample of 1,260 adults whether participants preferred a man or woman in several careers. The most frequent response for five of seven careers was "same": banker, 48 %; surgeon, 54%; lawyer, 48%; airline pilot, 50%; family doctor, 42% (Table 7.6). Among respondents making a choice between men and women, men were preferred as police officers (46% men, 15% women), surgeons (33% men, 11% women), lawyers (29% men, 21% women) and airline pilots (41% men, 6% women). Women were preferred as elementary school teachers (59% women, 7% men) and bankers (36% women, 16% men). Men and women were equally preferred as family doctors (28% men, 29% women). Interestingly, the PEW survey showed very little difference between male and female respondents on which gender they would prefer in each career tested. The exception was family doctor: most women preferred a woman doctor, while most men preferred a male doctor. These results suggest that gender stereotypes still influence evaluations of the suitability of some careers for women, although some of these stereotypes are moderating as indicated by the most frequent response of no preference in five of seven careers that were rated.

TABLE 7.6   Career Preferences for Men and Women (Data taken from PEW 2008)

Career	"Are men or women preferred as …" Percent saying		
	Men	Women	Same
Elementary school teacher	7	59	33
Police officer	46	15	36
Banker	16	36	48
Surgeon	33	11	54
Lawyer	29	21	48
Airline pilot	41	6	50
Family doctor	28	29	42

Figure Credits

Table 7.1: Source: AP Racial Attitudes Poll.
Table 7.2: Source: Alexis Tan et al.
Table 7.3: Source: Pew Research Center.
Table 7.4: Source: Pew Research Center.
Table 7.5: Source: Pew Research Center.
Table 7.6: Source: Pew Research Center.

Workbook

Define, describe, or illustrate; summarize the results of the studies:

1.   Stereotypes—definitions

2.   Origins of stereotypes

3.   Explicit measures of stereotypes

4.   Implicit measures of stereotypes

5.   AP racial attitudes poll (2012)

6.   Stereotypes of Muslims (Sides and Gross 2012)

7.   Stereotypes of Latinos (Barreto et al. 2012)

8. DeFleur and DeFleur (2003)

9. Tan et al. (2010)

10. Tan et al. (2009)

11. PEW Global Attitudes Project (2012)

12. Stereotypes of and myths about older people—p. 114

13. Gender stereotypes: leadership traits and performance skills (PEW 2008); Career preferences (PEW 2008).

8

Consequences of Stereotypes

We are interested in stereotypes because they potentially could affect our feelings toward others, our evaluations of them, as well as our behaviors toward them. The consequences of stereotyping are quite similar to consequences of prejudice because both processes fulfill similar functions for the individual, groups, and societies, that is, preservation and enhancement of self-interests. Prejudice and stereotyping accomplish this by providing a rationale, no matter how erroneous, for denigrating out-groups and their members. I discussed in Chapter 5 some consequences of prejudice, or negative feelings, toward others. In this chapter, I discuss consequences arising from cognitive categorization of people, or stereotyping. Although there are similarities in the studies providing evidence for consequences of prejudice and stereotyping, my focus here is on how categorization of people and their ascribed traits, rather than feelings toward them, affect the target person or group, interpersonal and intergroup behaviors, and opinions on social issues.

Consequences for Targeted Persons: Stereotype Threat

Numerous scholars have studied and written about the possible effects of negative stereotyping on members of targeted groups. An early premise was that targeted persons would internalize the negative stereotypes, feel inadequate, and consequently have low expectations of themselves (e.g., Allport 1979; Clark 1965; Grier and Coobs 1968). More recently, the emphasis has been on situational factors that could influence the effects of negative stereotyping. Pursuing this direction, Claude Steele developed the theory of stereotype threat, which he defines as "being at risk of confirming, as self-characteristic, a negative stereotype about one's group" (Steele and Aronson 1995, 797; Steele 2010). Thus, the awareness of a negative stereotype triggers the "fear of doing something that would inadvertently trigger the stereotype" (Steele 1999, 46), thereby affecting performance tied to the stereotype. For example, I may be made aware through cues in my environment of a negative stereotype of Asian Americans as being clumsy and boring speakers just as I am about to give my students a lecture. If I am aware of this stereotype consciously (I am told it, or read about it) or unconsciously (I am told that my students will evaluate my lecture, without mention of the stereotype), my performance in the lecture will be bad: I will stumble, and indeed will be clumsy and boring, because I will be anxious about fulfilling the negative stereotype and think about it while giving the lecture. The activation of corresponding negative behaviors is situational, rather than general. Being aware of this particular negative stereotype won't affect my tennis game. But why will performance be affected by stereotype threat? In an integrated model of stereotype threat, Schmader et al. (2008) suggest that stereotype threat causes poor performance on stereotype-related tasks because of three processes:

1. Stress arousal, which disrupts information processing and interferes with memory;
2. Performance monitoring, which interferes with attention, thereby disrupting focus and attention to the task at hand;
3. Self-consciousness arousal, which leads to attempts to suppress negative thoughts and emotions, which in turn disrupts information processing and attention to the task at hand.

According to Steele (1997), stereotype threat has the following features:

1. Stereotype threat is a general threat that can be experienced by members of any group for whom a negative social stereotype exists. It is not only members of stigmatized groups or groups experiencing discriminatory behaviors (such as some racial groups) that experience stereotype threat. The key point is that the threat should be specific enough so that it can be linked to a specific task at which the stereotype might be demonstrated. Some examples are as follows:

    - Blacks and the stereotype of being not intelligent in the classroom
    - Women and the stereotype of being poor at math and science
    - White men and the stereotype that "White men can't jump" in the game of basketball
    - Asian women and the stereotype that they are lousy drivers
    - Older persons and the stereotype that old people can't learn new skills

2. Stereotype threats are turned on when the task or setting provides a specific stereotype-related opportunity to validate the stereotype. Thus, the activation of stereotype threat is situational. In the examples above, stereotype threats will be activated in the following situations:

    - When Blacks take a test that is presented to them as an important indicator of intellectual ability
    - When women take a test in math with men
    - When White men play basketball with Blacks
    - When Asian women take a driving test for a driver's license
    - When an elderly person takes a class in computer programming

3. The type and degree of stereotype threats vary from group to group, depending on identification with the "domain" of the stereotype (what is covered by it), and the contents of the stereotype. For example, stereotype threat is more likely to operate for a young Black college student who highly identifies with college and academic achievement, for a woman who highly identifies with her major in science, and for a White man who highly identifies with being a good basketball player.

4. For stereotype threat to occur, a target person does not have to believe the stereotype. Here's an illustration from the African American social psychologist James M. Jones (1997), as quoted in Steele (1997, 618):

    > When I go to the ATM machine and a woman is making a transaction, I think about whether she will fear I may rob her. Since I have no such intention, how do I put her at ease? Maybe I can't ... and maybe she has no such expectation. But it goes through my mind. (262)

Does Stereotype Threat Affect Performance?

The short answer is *yes*. More than three hundred studies have confirmed that the threat of a negative stereotype can impair performance on stereotypic-related tasks and activities. Many studies have looked at intellectual performance of women in mathematics and Blacks on standardized tests.

Women and Math

A common social stereotype of women is that women are not good at math, and that their math ability is poorer than men's. The threat, then, is that a woman will confirm this stereotype and perform poorly in a math test, particularly a difficult math test. To test the hypothesis that math ability stereotype threat will result in poorer math test performance, Steele and his colleagues (Steele 1997) gave a difficult math test to women and men college students. Half of the participants (randomly assigned), men and women, were told that men generally performed better on the test. This was the stereotype threat manipulation, to make women aware of the negative stereotype. The other half of the participant pool was told that men and women performed equally well on the test. As expected, women who were made aware of the stereotype threat (i.e., told that men performed better) scored significantly lower than men in the same stereotype threat condition; women who were not made aware of the threat (i.e., told that men and women scored equally well) performed just as well as men in the no-threat condition. Steele (1997) interpreted these findings as support for the stereotype threat hypothesis, a result that has been supported in a large number of other studies.

African Americans and Standardized Tests

A social stereotype of Blacks, as seen in this chapter, is that Blacks are not as "intelligent at school" as Whites. The threat, then, is that an African American person would confirm this stereotype by not doing well academically, or, more specifically in the case of college students, in standardized tests of academic ability. When the threat is activated, performance on the tests would actually suffer, and scores of Black students will be lower than scores of White students; when the threat is not activated, there would be no difference between scores of Black and White students. To activate the stereotype threat among their Black college student participants, most of whom were from an elite Western university, Steele (1997) and his colleagues used several manipulations: (a) giving the most difficult items from the Graduate Record Examination Test (the act of taking the test would activate the stereotype threat), (b) telling the participants that the test was either a valid measure of intellectual ability (stereotype threat condition) or a laboratory problem-solving task (no stereotype threat), (c) asking the students to identify their race at the end of the study, and (d) completing a word completion test that activated Black stereotypes. As a validation check on whether negative stereotype threat was activated, Black and White participants were asked in some studies to complete a seven-point agree/disagree scale with items such as the following: "Some people feel I have less verbal ability because of my race," "The test may have been easier for people of my race," "The experimenter expected me to do poorly because of my race," "In English classes people of my race often face biased evaluations," and "My race does not affect people's perception of my verbal ability" (Steele and Aronson 1995).

Results from studies of stereotype threat and performance of Blacks on standardized tests measuring "academic intelligence" have been consistent (Steele 1997):

- Black students report stereotype threat (validation check), but not White students.
- Black students perform less well on the tests when stereotype threat is activated, compared to White students. There is no difference in performance between Black and White students when stereotype threat is not activated.

Does Stereotype Threat Affect Health?

Some studies of stereotyping of the elderly, although not directly testing the stereotype threat hypothesis, provide evidence that awareness of positive and negative stereotypes can affect the health of older people. Levy et al. (2002), for example, found that older people who accept and endorse positive stereotypes of the elderly were forty-four percent more likely than those who endorse negative stereotypes to recover after suffering from a severe disability. Participants were 598 individuals who were at least 70 years old and free of disability at the start of the study. Recovery was based on ability to perform four basic activities of daily living: bathing, dressing, moving without a wheelchair, and walking. Levy et al. (2002) also reported that results of other studies indicate that older people with positive stereotypes of the elderly show lower cardiovascular responses to stress, and tend to engage in healthier activities.

Another study followed 660 people 50 years or older over time (Levy 2002). Those who endorsed positive stereotypes of the elderly at the start of the study lived 7.5 years longer than those who believed in negative elderly stereotypes.

These results are consistent with the results of studies investigating the effects of stereotype threat on performance. Older people who were aware of negative elderly stereotypes and who believed them were more at risk of poor health and slow recovery from a disability than older people who endorsed positive stereotypes.

Reducing Stereotype Threat

Considering the implications of stereotype threat for performance of almost all of us in a wide range of activities, but particularly considering the implications for the most stigmatized (negatively stereotyped) groups in our society, considerable attention has recently been directed at identifying strategies to reduce stereotype threat. Here are some strategies that have been supported by research (see www.reducingstereotypethreat.org/).

Reframing the Task (e.g., Good, Aronson, and Harder 2008; Quinn and Spencer 2001; Steele and Aronson 1995)

Stereotype threat lowers performance because the stereotyped person perceives that the task (e.g., a test) can affirm the negative stereotype. Dissociating the task or test from the stereotype therefore can reduce the negative effects on performance of stereotype threat. For example, women can be assured that a math test is gender-fair, or that men and women perform equally well on the test; Blacks can be assured that a test is race-fair.

Increasing the Salience of Nonthreatened Identities; Reducing the Salience of Threatened Identities (e.g., Danaher and Crandall 2008; McGlone and Aronson 2006; Stricker and Ward 2004)

Human beings, because we are social, have different identities based on group memberships: race, gender, job, hobby, sports, sexual orientation, family membership, age, and so forth. Stereotype threat is activated when the negative stereotype is linked with a particular identity. Therefore, reducing the importance or pertinence (salience) of the threatened identity in a particular domain (setting where performance is tied to identity) will also reduce the effects of stereotype in poor performance. Some strategies are (a) moving questions about race and gender to the end of the test; (b) encouraging members of the stereotyped group to think of their other identities—for example, college students at a very good university instead of race or gender; and (c) encouraging group members to think of their characteristics shared by in-group and out-group members.

Self-Affirmation (e.g., Cohen, Garcia, Apfel, and Master 2006; Schimel, Arndt, Banko, and Cook 2004)

An effective strategy for insulating stigmatized individuals from stereotype threat is to affirm and reinforce their feelings of self-worth. The confidence gained from affirmation can negate the effects of stereotype on poor performance. Affirmation can be accomplished by encouraging people to think about their strengths (e.g., their positive traits) and values.

High Standards and Assurance of Capabilities for Meeting Them (Cohen, Steele, and Ross 1999)

To reduce the perception among stereotyped individuals that they will be judged according to negative stereotypes, they can be told that high standards are expected in the task or test, but, most important, that they are capable of doing well, This feedback signals to the group members that the negative stereotype won't be a consideration in their performance or evaluation of the performance.

Positive Role Models (e.g., Huguet and Regner 2007)

Providing examples of members of the stereotyped group who perform well in the task, or are presumed to perform well, reduces the negative effects of stereotype threat on performance. For example, simply thinking of a group member whose performance is superior improves performance among stigmatized groups. Positive role models can also be provided by teachers or experimenters, or vicariously in the media. The key is for the role model to be perceived as performing or as capable of performing well (with superior performance) on the task affected by the negative stereotype.

Consider this report from the *Chronicle of Higher Education*.

Stereotypes Obstruct Minority Male Students' Success in College, Report Says

The Chronicle of Higher Education (2013) reported results of a new study on Black and Latino male high school achievement in New York City. According to the study, positive stereotypes and positive self-concepts facilitate achievement, while negative stereotypes and negative self-concepts are related to failure.

The study's author, according to the *Chronicle*, began the report with this statement:

"Please stop mischaracterizing young men of color as hopeless thugs who care nothing about their education, communities, and futures. ... Black and Latino male teens, especially those who reside in America's largest cities, are persistently portrayed in media and elsewhere negatively; [these negative portrayals] affect society's expectations of them, and at times, their expectations of themselves."

He continued, "This caricature of young men of color in urban contexts is both pervasive and longstanding. It also is one-sided, terribly racist, and far from universal."

The report suggested that rather than focusing on reasons why male Latino and Black students fail in high school and college, attention should be directed at why most succeed. For example, the study points out, forty-two percent of male Latino students fail to complete college in four years, while fifty-eight percent of them graduate on time.

Consequences of Stereotypes on Opinions About Race-Coded Issues

Two models of policy reasoning explain how we make decisions about which side of a policy issue to take (Sniderman, Brody, and Tetlock 1991). The cognitive model, used by people who are more "sophisticated" on the issue because of the ability to process complex information (indicated, for example, by higher levels of education), says that complex cognitive reasoning rather than emotion guides policy decisions. On the other hand, the affective model, used by less sophisticated individuals, says that policy reasoning is guided more by feelings or emotions than by information. In the affective model, limited information drives the individual to use the simplest heuristic to policy reasoning, and often this is reasoning based on emotions which can be triggered by prejudice and stereotyping. In the cognitive model, previously coded information facilitates the policy decision by making it easier to process new information. Although these models make sense, Sniderman et al. (1991) suggest that for race-coded issues, sophisticated and less sophisticated individuals will use the affective heuristic, because race is an emotional issue for many. Race-coded issues "play upon race without explicitly raising the 'race card'" (Gilens 1996, 593). Examples of such issues are immigration, affirmative action, and welfare. Support for the proposition that emotions such as prejudice and related stereotypes will direct opinions on race-coded issues is provided by several studies.

Gilens (1996)

This study found in a national sample of adults that the single most important predictor of opposition to welfare was the belief that African Americans are "lazy," followed, respectively, by the belief that poor people are lazy, and by opposition to government activity in general. Education, party identification, and political ideology had minimal effects on opposition to welfare. Thus, negative stereotypes were the most powerful predictors of opposition to welfare for people of all educational levels.

Tan, Fujioka, and Tan (2000)

This study of 166 White college students found that negative stereotypes—the belief that African Americans are less intelligent and lazy, and prefer to be on welfare—predicted opposition to affirmative action policies. Thus, with a "sophisticated" sample (college students), the affective heuristic guided policy reasoning.

Timberlake, Howell, Baumann, Grau, and Williams (2012); Timberlake and Williams (2000)

This study of 2,150 adults in Ohio found that negative stereotypes of immigrants from Latin America predicted the belief that immigration would result in negative consequences, such as higher levels of unemployment, lower quality of schools, and higher levels of crime. Thus, the more negative the stereotypes, the more likely the belief that immigration would lead to negative consequences. Stereotypes were measured on five semantic differential scales: rich/poor, intelligent/unintelligent, self-sufficient/dependent/not dependent on government assistance, trying to fit in/staying separate from Americans, and violent/nonviolent.

Profiling Marginalized Groups

A major consequence of stereotyping is profiling, which in turn, unconsciously or consciously, direct many of our behaviors towards stereotyped groups. Profiling is discriminatory behaviors towards a group because of pre-conceived perceptions of group characteristics or traits and group behavioral tendencies, in other words, because of stereotypes (Satzewich and Shaffir 2009; Page and Shepherd 2008). Discriminatory behaviors are observed in differential treatment by a person or persons in power such as law enforcement officers, physicians and health care providers, educators, judges, and banking officials. Perceived members of marginalized groups, or groups without power are targets of profiling, and are treated more negatively than members of the mainstream group or group with power. Examples of negative treatment are denial of desired resources such as bank loans or access to education, and punitive behaviors such as arrests and longer sentences in the judicial system

Profiling is based on subconscious stereotyping, that is, placing an individual in a group category, and assigning traits or stereotypes that have been stored in long-term memory. The group member is a prime, a cue or signal, that activates the stereotype that then directs behavior towards the targeted individual. Profiling is facilitated when the targeted individual has easily recognizable physical characteristics that place him/her in a group. Because physical characteristics, particularly skin color, associated with race are easily recognizable, racial profiling has attracted the most attention from researchers and policy makers as a common problem in American society. Racial profiling is a subset of profiling of marginalized groups. It is discriminatory behavior directed at individuals because of their race. Much of the concern and research in the United States have focused on racial profiling of Black Americans because of their history of oppression, which still can be observed in many facets of modern life. Persico (2008) offers a general framework for the analysis of racial profiling. She identifies several domains in which racial profiling and resulting discriminatory behaviors can be analyzed. Here are those domains and related profiling actions.

- Lending discrimination: Stereotypes guiding behavior are that Blacks are poor, untrustworthy and irresponsible. Discriminatory behaviors are that stricter lending criteria are applied to Blacks, loan amounts are smaller, and interest rates higher.
- Hiring discrimination: Stereotypes are that Blacks are "lazy," untrustworthy, irresponsible, and less likely to "fit in." Discriminatory behaviors are that they are less likely to be interviewed and hired and will receive a lower salary.
- Health care discrimination: Stereotypes are that Blacks are less likely and less able to follow doctor's recommendations. Discriminatory behaviors are that they are less likely to be prescribed the best treatments; they will experience shorter and less "warm" interactions with health care providers.
- Enforcement discrimination: Stereotypes are that Blacks, particularly young men, are violent and aggressive and are likely to commit crimes. Discriminatory behaviors are more frequent traffic stops and searches; more scrutiny and less service in stores.
- Selective prosecution for alleged crimes: Stereotypes are that Blacks are more likely to commit crimes. Discriminatory behavior is more frequent prosecution.
- Sentencing discrimination: Stereotypes are that Blacks are more likely to commit and repeat crimes. Discriminatory behavior is longer sentences.

Research evidence supporting some of the assertions above are provided in the following sections of this chapter. Additionally, racial profiling occurs in everyday life. Consider these recent headlines from the Huffington Post and other online news sources (Huffington Post 2019; 2020):

- Ivy League Economist "Suspected of Terrorism" While Doing Math Aboard American Airlines Plane
- British Tourists Who "Looked Middle Eastern" Caught Up in Terror Scare in Canada
- British Asian Man Victim of Racial Profiling by US Border Officials
- White Man Calls Police on Black Mother and Child for Using Neighborhood Swimming Pool
- "I interviewed for a scientist position, but was asked about terrorism instead"
- Kroger Manager Accused of Racial Profiling After Calling Cops on Black Teens Buying Snacks
- Massachusetts Attorney General Probes Racism Allegations Against Boston Museum
- Texas Police Tried to Arrest a Black Man in His Own Yard After Misidentifying Him
- Black Hotel Guest Making a Call in Lobby Accused of Loitering, Loses His Room

In each of these incidents, a victim was subjected to discriminatory actions because of negative stereotypes associated with his/her perceived group. These are classic examples of racial profiling that can occur while going about what should be normal everyday activities.

Shopping While Black

Studies have consistently shown that Black Americans are racially profiled in small stores, box stores, specialty stores, and high-end stores (e.g., Pittman 2020). They are stereotyped, unconsciously or explicitly, to be poor, unable to pay, and with criminal intent. Controlling for education, age, gender, income and type of store, studies have shown that Black Americans are routinely ignored by store clerks ("invisible," no offers to help), receive inferior customer service (store clerks not helpful), and are followed and watched for criminal intent.

One recent study in New York City, for example, interviewed fifty-five Blacks in managerial and professional occupations, white collar jobs, and blue collar jobs about their experiences shopping in apparel and high-end stores. Eighty percent reported discrimination such as being watched more intensely than non-Black shoppers, being ignored, and being offered inferior service. Many reported they felt that they were perceived by store employees to be poor or unable to pay for the merchandise, or to be a shoplifter. These reports were reported by Blacks in all occupational categories and in all types of stores. Race was the most salient category in directing store employee responses (Pittman 2020).

Racial Profiling and Traffic Stops

Race of the driver influences law enforcement officers in decisions to stop and search vehicles, and whether to cite or give a warning. The Stanford Open Policing Project (Stanford 2020) analyzed 200 million traffic stops since 2015, and concluded that "significant racial disparities in policing" exist. Generally, police officers stop Black and Hispanic drivers at higher rates than White drivers for similar offenses. Following a traffic stop, Black drivers, compared to white drivers, are twenty percent more likely to get a ticket for similar offenses; Hispanic drivers are thirty percent more likely to get a ticket. Data from states such as California and North Carolina provide similar statistics (Stanford 2020). In Washington State, Black, Latino, Native American, and Pacific Islander drivers were stopped and searched at higher rates than White drivers. However, state troopers were actually more likely to find drugs, weapons and other illegal items when searching White drivers (*Spokesman Review* 2020). These data suggest that racial minority drivers are being profiled by law enforcement officers. Even when driving offense and neighborhood are controlled for in the analysis, minority drivers are stopped, searched, and ticketed more often than White drivers. For Blacks, the stereotypes likely directing the profiling are "violent" and "criminal." The causal relationships between driver race, stereotypes, and law enforcement responses are difficult to prove by analyzing statistics like presented above because we cannot control all factors that might affect law enforcement responses. One such response, for example, is driver behavior after being stopped. One study tried to address this weakness by conducting a field experiment. In this study, Black, Hispanic, and White drivers (who were confederates of the researchers) in similar cars "slightly" exceeded the speed limit on a state highway. Black and Hispanic drivers were stopped more often than White drivers, confirming previous analysis using statistical data (Starr 2016).

Identification and Misidentification of Criminal Suspects

Research has established that Blacks are stereotyped in America as "dangerous criminals" (see, e.g., Oliver and Fonash 2002), that Whites perceive greater fear of crime when Blacks are present than they do when Whites are present, and that violent crime is more strongly associated with Blacks than with Whites (Gordon, Michels, and Nelson 1996). Building on these findings, Oliver and Fonash (2002) studied whether Whites would more often misidentify Blacks as criminal suspects compared to Whites as suspects. In their laboratory experiment, White college students first took an Anti-Black Attitude scale (Katz and Haas 1988), a measure of prejudice toward Blacks. The study participants then read short newspaper stories accompanied by photographs of either Black or White suspects. Half of the stories were about violent crimes; the other half were about nonviolent crimes. Twenty minutes after reading the newspaper articles, the participants were shown ten photographs: four were the same photographs included in the news stories, three were photographs of Black men not shown in the news stories, and three were photographs of White men not shown in the news stories. The researchers then asked the participants to indicate, on a seven-point scale, whether they thought each photo was pictured in the news stories; the scale ranged from 1 (definitely not pictured) to 7 (definitely pictured). Here are some of the results:

- Correct identification for the violent crime stories did not differ for White versus Black suspects. That is, research participants identified Black and White suspects (matching photos of suspects shown after reading the news stories with the photos accompanying the news stories) with the same degree of accuracy.
- Correct identification for the nonviolent crime stories differed by race of the suspect. Research participants identified White suspects with a higher degree of accuracy than they did for Black suspects.
- Misidentification—identifying photos of a Black or White male who was not featured in the news stories as the photos of the suspects in the news story—was higher for Black males than for White males, but only for the news articles about violent crime. Blacks who were not featured in stories about violent crime were more often identified to be the suspect, compared to Whites. There were no differences in misidentification of Black and White males for the stories about nonviolent crime.
- Prejudice, as measured by the Anti-Black Attitudes Scale, was not related to greater misidentification of Blacks as criminal suspects.

These results provide some evidence that negative stereotyping of Blacks as "violent criminals" is related to greater misidentification of Blacks as suspects in violent crimes. Although Oliver and Fonash (2002) did not measure explicit or implicit stereotyping, a possible explanation is that the White participants were influenced in their judgments by unconscious stereotypes. Particularly for college students, prejudice such as racism is not socially acceptable, so these processes—the link between stereotyping and misidentification as suspects—were most likely operating subconsciously, triggered or primed by photos of Black men. The social desirability explanation, "I am not prejudiced," can account for the lack of a relationship between explicit racial attitudes and misidentification of Blacks as suspects.

Consider these incidents reported by the news media in light of the discussion above.

Black Teen Arrested After Buying $350 Designer Belt

NBCNewYork.com (2013) reported that a 19-year old college student is suing New York City and a luxury department store because he was handcuffed and locked in jail after buying a $350 designer belt. The college student, who has no prior arrests, told NBCNewYork.com that he saved up from a part-time job to buy the belt, and that he wondered, as he was taken to a cell in handcuffs: "Why me? I guess because I'm a young black man, and you know, people do a credit card scam so they probably thought that I was one of them. They probably think that black people don't have money like that."

According to the lawsuit, the checkout clerk asked to see the young man's identification when he went to the store to buy the belt. After the sale went through and he left the store, he was approached by police about a block away, and asked "how a young black man such as himself could afford to purchase an expensive belt."

The lawsuit stated that officers took the young man to the local precinct where he showed police his identification as well as his debit card and the receipt for the belt. Police still believed the young man's identification was fake, and called his bank, which verified it was his.

The young man's attorney told a newspaper, "His only crime was being a young black man."

Questions

- Were the police officers justified in the actions they took toward the young black man?
- How would you feel if you were in the young man's place? How would you deal with the situation?

Racial Profiling in New York City?

The New York Times (2012) reported that Black and Latino lawmakers in New York State were criticizing the "stop and frisk" policy of New York City police officers which they say is unfairly targeting minority men. This criticism of the policy was made public as debate continued about the fatal shooting of a Black man by a police officer in the Bronx, and the shooting of Trayvon Martin by a neighborhood watch volunteer in Florida. Both victims were unarmed.

According to the *Times*, several New York state lawmakers related personal experiences in which they have been stopped by police because, they believed, of their race.

A Brooklyn senator recalled several occasions when, as a high school student walking home in his neighborhood, he was stopped by police, patted down, told to empty his pockets, produce identification, and divulge his destination.

An assemblyman remembered greeting a woman when he was walking down a street, when, he said, officers in plain clothes approached him and demanded to know who he was, where he was going, and whether he had any guns or drugs.

A senator from Manhattan said that when he was fourteen, detectives threw him against a wall and patted him down when he was on his way to buy a newspaper for his father.

The *Times* also reported that Governor David Paterson, New York State's first African-American governor, said in an interview that he himself had been stopped three times by the police. "It's a feeling of being degraded," he said. 'I think that's what people who it hasn't happened to don't understand."

According to the *Times*, New York City's police commissioner defended the "stop and frisk" policy, saying it was an effective tool intended to reduce violence against Blacks and Hispanics. The police department said that it conducted 684,330 stops in 2011, and that eighty-seven percent of those stopped were Black or Hispanic. About ten percent of those stops led to arrests or summonses and one percent to the recovery of a weapon, according to the Center for Constitutional Rights.

Question

- Do you approve or disapprove of the "stop-and-frisk" practice in New York City? Why?

Stereotypes and the Decision "to Shoot"

When "primed," stereotypes can bias reactions to stimuli, particularly ambiguous stimuli in a direction consistent with the stereotype. *Priming* is the process by which a stereotype stored in memory is accessed by the individual, after being triggered by objects, events, or thoughts associated with the stereotype. Some examples of primes are perceiving the presence, physically or vicariously, of a target of the stereotype; observing behaviors linked to the stereotype; and perceiving objects linked to the stereotype. For example, take a common stereotype of Asian Americans as "foreign" and "unpatriotic." This stereotype may not be in the consciousness of an individual at any given time. However, it could be primed by the mere sight of an Asian American man, or by dining in a Chinese restaurant, or by seeing the Japanese flag hoisted at a Japanese consulate. Once primed, the stereotype can direct responses to stimuli linked to the stereotype.

A particular stereotype that has captured the attention of many researchers, in particular Correll and his colleagues (Correll, Park, Judd, and Wittenbrink 2007), is a stereotype that links Black Americans with danger. Correll et al. are particularly interested in whether this stereotype is related to spontaneous, split-second decisions to "shoot" or "don't shoot" in ambiguous situations. A basic assumption of this research is that Blacks are associated with danger (the stereotype). Consistent with this assumption, Correll et al. (2007) found that, using an implicit test of word associations, non-Black college students more quickly associated danger words with Black names than with Caucasian names. The danger words were *attack, criminal, danger, hate, threat, violence, war,* and *weapon*. These results provide validation of an implicit association of Blacks with danger.

To test the hypothesis that the "danger" stereotype of Blacks will result in quicker decisions by non-Blacks to "shoot" rather than "don't shoot," Correll et al. (2002) developed a video game featuring images of armed and unarmed, Black and White young men in backgrounds such as city streets and parks. The research participants—non-Black and typically college students—are instructed to shoot armed targets by pressing a button labeled "shoot," but not to shoot unarmed targets (pressing a second button labeled "don't shoot"). Half of the "targets," armed and unarmed, are Black, and half are White. Using this video game, results have been consistent in several studies as reported by Correll et al. (2010):

- "Participants typically shoot Black targets, armed and unarmed, more frequently than White targets."
- Participants more quickly shoot an armed target when he is Black than when he is White.
- Participants more quickly "don't shoot" an unarmed target when he is White than when he is Black.

These results assume an implicit stereotype linking danger with Blacks as the explanation for the quicker and more frequent response to "shoot" Black targets without actual measurement of the stereotype. Supporting this assumption is at least one study showing a direct link. Glaser and Knowles (2008) report that non-Black college students' scores on the IAT Blacks/Whites Weapons test correlated with the tendency to "shoot" armed Black men in the Correll video game. That is, the stronger an association of Blacks with weapons, the greater the tendency to "shoot" armed Black men.

More recently, studies have shown that racial bias in the decision to shoot or don't shoot can be reduced by training and repeated participation in the Correll et al. (2002) video game. Study participants including police officers who repeated the simulations at least once and who were informed of their race bias made fewer errors in their decisions to shoot when they repeated the game. Also, racial differences were significantly lower than in initial encounters (Correll et al. 2014). These results suggest that training to make police officers aware of unconscious biases can reduce discriminatory actions towards racial minorities, particularly in ambiguous and stressful situations. The mechanism by which unconscious biases are controlled is "cognitive control." When made aware of the effects of racial biases on actions, police officers can make a conscious effort to control those biases.

Consider this shooting incident in North Carolina.

Family of Man Shot by Charlotte Cop Wants Answers

The Associated Press (2013) reported that an unarmed man seeking help after a car crash was shot ten times by a Charlotte police officer who was charged with his death.

According to the AP, the man's car ran off the entrance to a suburban neighborhood, crashing his car into trees. He kicked out the back window and headed up a hill toward some houses. He then "started banging on the door" of a home to attract attention, according to the police chief. A woman answered the door thinking it was her husband coming home from work. She shut the door and called police when she saw the man. The police chief said he did not think the unarmed man made any threats.

The AP reported that police officers responded to the woman's call and found the man on a road that leads to a neighborhood pool. According to police, the man ran toward the officers who tried to stop him with a taser. Police said an officer shot the man when he continued to run toward them. The man died at the scene after being shot ten times. According to the man's family's attorney, the officer firing the shots did not identify himself as a police officer.

According to the AP, the man shot was a former Florida A&M University football player. His family said that he had moved to Charlotte to be with his fiancée, and was working two jobs, intending to go back to school and become an automotive engineer.

Stereotypes and Ageism

Negative stereotypes of older people influence how they are treated by others, ranging from subtle exclusion from social activities to blatant discrimination, as in the workplace. In general, most people are not even aware they have these negative stereotypes. Therefore, resulting behaviors often go unchallenged.

Older people, however, are aware of consequences of negative stereotyping. Research throughout the European Union indicates that age discrimination against older people is the most commonly experienced form of discrimination (Lyons 2009). In the United States, the majority of older people say they frequently encounter incidents of ageism (Palmore 2004). For example, McGuire et al. (2008) report that eighty-four percent of 247 adults aged sixty to ninety-two years in community dwellings said they had experienced at least one type of ageism.

Ageism or prejudice against the elderly can take many forms. Here are some examples (Lyons 2009):

1. Ageism in the workplace
   Negative stereotyping of older people affects recruitment, job security, promotion, salary, and retention or termination of employment (Kooij et al. 2008). In general, underrepresentation of older people in the workforce is increasing, and can be attributed in some part to policies and practices that favor younger workers over older workers (McVittie et al. 2003). Older people are generally perceived to be less efficient than younger workers, resistant to change, difficult to train, unable or slow to adapt to new technologies, too cautious, and with poor health, fitness, stamina, and computing skills (Lyons 2009; Cuddy et al. 2005). As a result of these negative stereotypes, older people are in many instances discriminated against in the workplace.

2. Ageism in health care
   According to Lyons (2009), studies show that many older people in Ireland and the United Kingdom are unhappy with the conduct of staff and the health services that they receive; feel disrespected and discriminated against because of their age; and may be denied access to services, mistreated or mis-diagnosed because of their age. A possible explanation is the stereotype that ill health is the norm for older people, resulting in the belief that it is acceptable for older people to suffer from many illnesses without adequate care (Lyons 2009).

3. Ageism as a factor in career choice
   In many countries (e.g., Australia, Brazil, England, Germany, Israel, and the United States), working with older people is the lowest preference as a career choice (Lyons 2009). For example, Happell (2002) found that less than two percent of nursing students in the study sample named care of older persons as their most desired future career, and over two-thirds ranked elderly care as one of their last three preferences. Careers in elderly care are often the least preferred because of the common perception that older patients do not get better; work in this area is therefore perceived to be of limited value and unrewarding (Lyons 2009). On the other hand, work with children is considered more worthwhile, more exciting and dynamic, with observable and useful outcomes, and is therefore preferred to working with the elderly (Happell 2002).

4. Ageism and social exclusion
   Social exclusion directed at older people can be defined in several dimensions (Barnes et al. 2006): social relationships (contact with family and friends); cultural and leisure activities (e.g., going to the theatre); civic activities (e.g., membership in community groups, volunteer work, voting); access to basic services (e.g., health services, shops); neighborhood exclusion (e.g., friendliness of local people); financial products (e.g. banks, pensions); and material goods (e.g., consumer products, central heating.) In general, social exclusion results from negative stereotyping of older people as frail, having diminished physical and mental capacities, and having little to contribute to society. A study in the United Kingdom indicated that half of a sample over fifty years old did not experience exclusion. However, about a third reported exclusion on one dimension, and 13 % reported exclusion on two dimensions (Barnes et al. 2006).

5. Ageism, elder abuse and neglect
   The most severe and blatant form of prejudice against the elderly, we can argue, is abuse and neglect. As defined by Ireland's Working Group on Elder Abuse (2002), elder abuse is "A single or repeated act or lack of appropriate action occurring within any relationship where there is an expectation of trust which causes harm or distress to an older person or violates their human and civil rights." Although

reported cases of elder abuse are generally low (e.g., 2.6% among older people in the United Kingdom, as reported by O'Keefe et al. 2007), the social exclusion of older people and negative stereotypes of the elderly that undervalue their worth in society can lead to abuse and neglect (Lyons 2009).

In this chapter, we have seen that stereotypes are not merely pictures in our heads: they have important consequences on our interactions and evaluations of other people. Stereotypes influence our opinions on policy issues; our evaluations of other people such as judgments of guilt or innocence of criminal suspects; and our decisions to take action, such as to "shoot" or "don't shoot" armed or unarmed "targets" in a video game. Just as importantly, stereotypes affect self-concepts and related performance of stereotyped individuals. The stereotype becomes a self-fulfilling prophecy, resulting in performance that is consistent with the stereotype.

In the next chapter, we take a closer look at stereotypes in the media and how media stereotypes can influence our own stereotypes.

Workbook

Define, describe, or illustrate; summarize the results of the studies:

1.   Stereotype threat definition; features

2.   Why stereotype threat causes poor performance

3.   Women and math (Steele 1997)

4.   African Americans and standardized tests (Steele 1997)

5.   The elderly, stereotype threat and health (Levy et al. 2002)

6.   Reducing stereotype threat: strategies

7.   Cognitive and affective models of policy reasoning

8.   Gilens (1996)

9.   Tan, Fujioka, and Tan (2000)

10.   Timberlake et al. (2012)

11.   Oliver and Fonash (2002)

12.   Priming

13.   Correll, Park, Judd, and Wittenbrink (2007)

14.   Stereotypes and ageism (Lyons 2009, pp. 130–131)

15.   Profiling and stereotypes

16.   Persico (2008)

17.   Pittman (2020)

18.   Stanford Open Policing Project (2020)

19.   Correll et al. (2014)

9

Media Stereotypes

A s we have seen, people learn stereotypes from their cultures through a socialization process involving other people and institutions in their communities. The media—television, movies, newspapers, magazines, and books—are major socialization agents, and their reach and consequent influence are even greater today because of the internet. Just about any group can be considered to be stereotyped in the media given the time, space, and creative limits on the presentation of the "real world" in an artificial medium. We focus in this chapter on the portrayals of groups that have less economic and political power, are generally less privileged in American society, and have shared a history of discrimination in the United States. These are Asian Americans, Latino Americans, African Americans, Native Americans, and Arab Americans.

Stereotypes in the media can be studied by using content analysis, by using critical analysis by an observer or group of observers, and by asking potential media audiences or members of the target groups to describe how the target group is described in the media. Our emphasis will be on contemporary rather than historical stereotypes, with *contemporary* meaning having occurred within the last two decades or so. I chose this time period because it coincides with the emergence of the internet as a worldwide conduit of entertainment and news. Excellent discussions of historical stereotypes can be found in other books, notably *Racism, Sexism and the Media* by Wilson, Gutierrez, and Chao (2013).

Some of the most comprehensive studies of media stereotyping have been done or sponsored by organizations of media professionals, academics, and concerned citizens such as the Asian American Journalists Association (aaja.org),the Media Action Network for Asian Americans (manaa.org), the National Association of Hispanic Journalists (nahj12.com), the National Association of Black Journalists (nabj.org), the Native American Journalists Association (naj.com), the Arab American National Museum (arabamericanmuseum. org), the *Associated Press* (ap.org), and the American Society of News Editors (asne.org). For their work to be credible, the researchers from these organizations use acceptable social science methods and unbiased observers, often working in collaboration with academic researchers. They point out media news and information content that portrays racial groups stereotypically, as well as content that portrays racial groups realistically and less stereotypically. Regardless of the method used or the authorship of the studies, there is agreement on how American racial groups, the elderly, and women have and are being stereotyped by the media.

Asian Americans

Consider the 1998 headline on the MSNBC website when White figure skater Tara Lipinski, an American, defeated Michelle Kwan, a second-generation American, for the Olympic gold medal. The headline read, "American Beats Out Kwan" (Sorensen 1998.)

Although some media stereotypes of Asian Americans can be considered to be "positive" (e.g., hardworking, intelligent), a common portrayal is that Asian Americans, regardless of the fact that they, their parents, their grandparents, and so on were born in the United States, are foreign and can never be "true Americans." Because mainstream American as portrayed in the media is mostly White, Asian Americans are seldom separated from the nationalities of countries of their heritage (often described as "Asians"), resulting in portrayals that emphasize distinctive accents and exotic cultural practices. Illustrating the view of Asian Americans as foreign, a commonly asked question is, "Where are you from?"

Another stereotypical portrayal is that all Asians are one racial and ethnic group, and are therefore all alike and all look the same, which fails to make the distinction between the more than twenty ethnicities that are considered "Asian" in the United States.

Consider this quote from Ronald Takaki, author of *Strangers from a Different Shore: A History of Asian Americans* (1989):

> There are no Asians in Asia, only people with national identities, such as Chinese, Japanese, Korean, Indian, Vietnamese, and Filipino. But on the other side of the Pacific there are Asian Americans. This broader identity was forged in the crucible of racial discrimination and exclusion: their national origins did not matter as much as their race. (as quoted in the *AAJA Handbook* 2000, 33)

(MANAA): Portrayals of Asian Americans in the Media and How to Balance Them

According to the Media Action Network for Asian Americans (MANAA;manaa.org), an advocacy group for Asian Americans in the media, the following are stereotypical portrayals of Asian Americans in the media (news and entertainment). Following each description is a recommendation for a "stereotype buster" (MANAA 2012). Because media portrayals commonly do not differentiate between Asians and Asian Americans, stereotypes of both groups are discussed. The list below is from MANAA (2012).

- *Asian Americans as foreigners:* Asian Americans and their cultures are apart from American society. *Stereotype buster:* Portraying Asian Americans as integral to American society in a wide variety of roles. Speaking without foreign accents.
- *Asian Americans in stereotypical occupations:* Common occupational portrayals are restaurant workers, Korean grocers, Japanese businessmen (serious, inscrutable), Indian cab drivers, TV anchorwomen, martial artists, gangsters, faith healers, laundry workers, and prostitutes. *Stereotype buster:* Portraying Asian Americans in a wide range of mainstream occupations, including doctors, lawyers, therapists, educators, and US soldiers.
- *Asian cultures as predatory:* Portrayals in American media have shown Asians as taking advantage of individual freedoms and economic opportunities in the United States through sinister and unlawful means at the expense of others, and without "giving anything back." Examples are portrayals of Chinatowns as "breeding grounds of crime." In *Rising Sun*, Japanese businessmen attempt to take over American industry by violence and deceit. *Stereotype buster:* Portraying Asians as "positive contributors to American society."
- *Asian racial features, names, accents, or mannerisms as inherently comic or sinister:* These distinctive characteristics are often used in movies and television for quick laughs or for dramatic appeal. *Stereotype buster:* Considering Asian names or racial characteristics as "no more unusual than those of Whites."

- *Asians in supporting roles in movies and television with primarily Asian or Asian American content:* Examples are *The Killing Fields*, *Seven Years in Tibet*, and *Come See the Paradise*. Exceptions are *Gandhi*, *The Last Emperor*, and *The Joy Luck Club*. *Stereotype buster:* Casting "more Asian and Asian American lead roles."
- *Asian male sexuality as negative or nonexistent:* "Asian men are almost never positively paired with women of any race." Common portrayals are that they are "threatening corruptors of white women," or do not have any love life at all. *Stereotype buster:* Casting "more Asian men as positive romantic leads."
- *Asian women in stereotypical negative roles:* Common portrayals are Asian women as "China dolls" (exotic, subservient, compliant, and eager to please), as "dragon ladies" (scheming, untrustworthy, back-stabbing), or in "unmotivated white-Asian romance" ("Asian women are attracted to white men because they are white"). *Stereotype busters:* (1) Portraying "Asian women as self-confident and self-respecting[, and] well-motivated in interracial romances as in same-race romances"; and (2) having "villainy not be attributed to … ethnicity" when villains are Asian.

These are some examples of stereotypic portrayals of Asian Americans and Asians in the media. For more stereotypical portrayals, including those in the news media, see the website of the Asian American Journalists Association (aaja.org), particularly the pages on "Media Watch" and "Media Guide."

Latino Americans

Attention to Latino Americans in news and entertainment media has accelerated recently, as the debate over immigration policy continues, and as Latinos continue to be the fastest-growing segment of the American population. Unfortunately, most portrayals are stereotypically negative, as the following studies show.

Latino Decisions, National Hispanic Media Coalition (NHMC)

The National Hispanic Media Coalition (NHMC; nhmc.org) and Latino Decisions (latinodecisions.com) sponsored a random survey of nine hundred non-Latinos across the United States to find out about their stereotypes of Latinos, and their perceptions of how the media portrays Latinos. The study was funded by the Kellogg Foundation. The survey used an innovative way of identifying stereotypes. Instead of doing a content analysis, the researchers asked non-Latino respondents what they thought portrayals of Latinos in the media were. The survey was done by phone in March 2012.

Respondents were asked, "[Think] about programs like dramas and comedies that are on TV. When you see Hispanics or Latinos on TV shows, how often are they playing the role of [INSERT ROLE]?I Is that very often, sometimes, not too often or never?" (Barreto, Manzano and Segura 2012, p. 27.)

The responses, in order of frequency of "very often" and "sometimes" responses, were as follows:

Criminals or gang members: 71%
Gardeners or landscapers: 64%
Maids or housekeepers: 61%
Police: 56%
High school dropouts: 47%
Doctors/nurses: 45%
Teachers: 41%
Lawyers/judges: 38%

As these results show, the most common perceived portrayal was in criminal activity, while portrayals in high-prestige occupations was less common. These results are supported for the news media in a study by the National Association of Hispanic Journalists (NAHJ; Montalvo and Torres 2006). This study showed that network news (ABC, CBS, NBC, and Fox) increased crime coverage of Latinos from 7.8% of all news items in 2004 to 18.1% in 2005. In most of these stories, Latinos were the perpetrators, rather than the victims, of crime.

Similar results were found In another study of news programming in Los Angeles County and Orange County (Dixon and Linz 2000). A content analysis of the programs showed that (1) Latinos were significantly more likely than Whites to be portrayed as lawbreakers in television news; (2) Latinos were significantly more likely to be portrayed as lawbreakers than defenders of crime, whereas Whites were more likely to be portrayed as defenders than lawbreakers; (3) Latinos were underrepresented as lawbreakers, when comparing frequency of portrayals to actual crime statistics; and (4) Latinos were underrepresented as police officers in television news, when compared to actual percentage of Latinos in the police force.

The NAHJ conducts studies on representations of Latinos in the media. The NAHJ's Network Brownout report examines ways in which Latinos and Latino-related issues are portrayed in the news programs of ABC, CBS, NBC, and Fox. The Latinos and Media Project also provides related reports on representation of Latinos in the news media. Links to these sites can be found in (nahj12.com).

African (Black) Americans

Perhaps the most studied racial group, in terms of public and media stereotypes, is African or Black Americans, at more than 50% of the studies done, according to Correll, Park, Judd, and Wittenbrink (2007). (Current usage is "Black Americans," because not all Black Americans are originally from Africa.) The historical portrayals of Black Americans in the media have been predominantly negative and demeaning, with some roots in stereotypes going back to slavery (see, e.g., Wilson, Gutierrez, and Chao 2013). Although there has been some improvement in the nature (more positive and realistic) and frequency of Black portrayals, the media today still stereotype Blacks negatively in news and entertainment. Here are some common stereotypes from contemporary studies:

- Using vulgar profanity, being physically violent, having no self-control among female movie characters (Entman and Rojecki 2001)
- Being associated with danger and weapons (IAT test; Correll, Park, Judd, and Wittenbrink 2007)
- Living in poverty and having athleticism (see, e.g., Wittenbrink, Judd, and Park 2001)
- Engaging in criminality, having to be feared, and being assumed guilty in criminal cases (see, e.g., Oliver, Jackson II, Moses, and Dangerfield 2004)
- Being immoral (Monk-Turner, Heiserman, Johnson, Cotton, and Jackson 2010)
- For Black women, being "nurturing asexual mammies, sexually aggressive jezebels, and lazy welfare queens" (Monahan, Shtrulis, and Givens 2005, p. 200)
- In local television, being portrayed as lawbreakers (more frequently than the occurrence of actual criminal offenses in California, for example), being portrayed as lawbreakers rather than defenders (i.e., police), and being underrepresented as police officers (Dixon and Linz 2000)

Racial stereotypes in the media are found abroad too. Consider this report about racial stereotyping of American Blacks in Thailand.

Thai Ad for Dunkin' Donuts Racist?

The *AP* (2013) reported that a human rights group has asked Dunkin' Donuts to withdraw an advertisement for chocolate doughnuts in Thailand that shows a smiling woman with bright pink lips in blackface makeup.

The image was used in posters and TV commercials that show the woman with shiny jet black 1950s-style beehive hairdo holding a bitten black doughnut alongside the slogan, "Break every rule of deliciousness."

According to the Human Rights Watch, the image represents a nineteenth- and early twentieth-century American stereotype for black people.

The *AP* reported that the campaign hasn't bothered many in Thailand where "it's common" to use racial stereotypes in advertisements. Examples are a Thai brand of household mops and dustpans called "Black Man" that uses a logo with a smiling Black man in a Tuxedo and bow tie. A skin whitening cream TV commercial says that white-skinned people have better job prospects than people with dark skin. An herbal Thai toothpaste says it's dark-colored product is "black, but it's good."

The *AP* reported that the CEO for Dunkin' Donuts in Thailand said the criticism is "paranoid American thinking. It's absolutely ridiculous. We're not allowed to use black to promote doughnuts? I don't get it. What's the big fuss? What if the product was white, and I painted someone white, would that be racist?"

Question

- Who do you agree with—Human Rights Watch or CEO Salhani? Why?

Nonverbal Bias Against Blacks in Television

In this novel study, Weisbuch, Pauker, and Ambady (2009) analyzed whether bias against Blacks might be shown in more subtle ways than through characterization in roles or verbal behaviors. They looked at nonverbal behaviors—body and face language (discussed in Chapter 2)—as indicators of affective valence (positive or negative interactions) between White and Black characters in television shows. To find out if there are differences in nonverbal behaviors directed by other characters toward Black characters and White characters, the researchers took ten-second clips from popular television shows that feature Blacks and Whites in major roles. They took scenes featuring the Black and White main characters interacting separately with the other characters, cropped out the main characters from the scene, deleted sound, and then asked White college students to rate how much the remaining onscreen characters, who were White, liked or disliked the cropped-out characters. There was no sound and no image of the Black or White main character, so the assumption was that the students would be basing their ratings on nonverbal body and facial language of the remaining characters. Among the television shows studied were *Scrubs, House, Grey's Anatomy, CSI*, and *Friday Night Lights*. The student ratings showed that in nine out of eleven shows, White characters exhibited less favorable non-verbal behaviors to the cropped-out Black characters than they did to Whites, thus showing that within the shows, implicit biases were expressed by White characters toward the Black character. The authors of the study offer three explanations: (1) White "actors spontaneously exhibit nonverbal bias," (2) "biased nonverbal behavior is written into scripts," and/or (3) "directors persuade their actors" (Weisbuch et al. 2009, 1712) to express the biased nonverbal behaviors. Regardless of the reason, the researchers say, these biased behaviors may be picked up by audiences, and may reinforce or evoke negative stereotypes.

Native Americans

Like Black Americans, Native Americans historically have been stereotyped inaccurately and negatively in many demeaning caricatures to fit mainstream perceptions and interpretations of history, including "how the West was won." Movies and television entertainment depicting these stereotypes had an audience, fulfilled in-group needs, and were therefore profitable. The Western genre was particularly successful, and the image of the Native American as the villain evolved, with few exceptions (e.g., Wilson, Gutierrez, and Chao 2013).

Has the media image of the Native American improved in today's media?

Consider an episode of the CBS sitcom *Mike and Molly*. Mike's mother Peggy asks, "You ever been to Arizona? It's just a furnace full of drunk Indians."

Consider also the recent remake of *The Lone Ranger*. Tonto is no longer the loyal sidekick; instead, he creates the persona of the Lone Ranger. An improvement, for sure, but the movie has been a disappointment in the box office. One critic attributes the lower-than-expected ticket sales to the fact that many young people and children do not know who Tonto and the Lone Ranger are. Ironically, if they did, today's characterizations would go against what earlier films depicted.

According to the Native American Journalists Association (NAJA; www.naj.com) and other writers, the following historical media stereotypes of Native Americans can still be found in contemporary entertainment media, including video games. (Note: For images in video games, see "Video Games the Top 7 ... Native American Stereotypes," Games-Radar U.S 2008, 11–24.) The list below is from NAJA and McLaurin 2012).

- Wise elder
- Aggressive drunk
- Indian princess
- Loyal sidekick
- Obese and impoverished
- Nature lovers
- Devoted environmentalist
- Trackers—"can track and hunt down anything living"
- Rich from gaming businesses
- Recipients of special privileges and handouts they don't deserve
- Native women are sexually available, slender, and naïve
- Drug addicts—smoke "peace" pipes (these are actually prayer pipes, not peace pipes)
- Worshippers of objects and beings they consider sacred

According to the NAJA, these are simplistic characterizations. Most are negative and demeaning. The positive attributes romanticize Native culture and show Native Americans as historical figures rather than broadly in a modern context.

Stereotypes of Contemporary Native Americans

Virginia McLaurin (2012 studied the contemporary stereotypes of Native Americans in popular media today. An anthropologist, McLaurin did a content analysis of all films, books, and television entertainment programs that featured Native American characters, either recurring or in a single issue, and that were produced or published within the past twenty years. Also, she divided up her sample of media between East and West using the Mississippi as the demarcation, arguing that portrayals may differ because of historical context and contemporary events affecting Natives. More Native Americans in the East, for example, were benefiting from gaming revenues; Native American casinos were first established in the East.

In general, McLaurin found support for the existence of traditional media Native stereotypes, but she found some new ones as well, particularly in the East. She summarizes the media stereotypes in the East as follows:

> These people are exactly like you, only tricky and deceptive (or confused). They aren't any different from you, they aren't special, and so they don't deserve any kind of consideration that you also don't deserve. (2012, 73)

McLaurin explains that Native Americans in the East were seen as a threat because of their growing economic power, so the corresponding stereotypes of being "tricky," "deceptive," and not deserving of special considerations were depicted in popular media.

In the West, the popular media stereotype of Native Americans was summarized by McLaurin as follows:

> These people are different and alien. You won't understand them and they won't understand you. (2012, p. 73).

McLaurin concludes that in the East, where casinos first prospered and led to some Native American prosperity, there was, in some popular media, "active hostility to the very idea of Indian wealth or modernity" (2012).

In the West, a common image in popular media was that of the "Noble Savage": "authentic yet strange, supernatural, sympathetic" (73).

These findings support our analysis of out-groups and in-groups, and how competition and threats contribute to negative stereotyping and prejudice (see Chapter 6).

Often reported in news about sports are the names and mascots of sports teams. Consider the following report about the controversy over the Washington Redskins of the National Football League.

Washington "Redskins" Name a Racial Slur?

The *Associated Press* (2013) reported that a tribal leader of the Oneida Indian Nation was leading an effort to change the Washington Redskins name. According to him, the name is a racial slur. He told the *AP*, "this was a word that was used against our people to push us on to reservations. They took our children from our homes forcibly at gunpoint, calling us the r-word." He also said that his tribe cannot "rest on its own (economic) success, when Indians are being told they're nothing more than a stereotype and a mascot."

According to the *AP*, the Redskins owner said that the name is a "badge of honor" and that it won't be changed.

Questions

- Are the Washington Redskins name and mascot a "slur" to Native Americans, or are they "badges of honor?"
- Should the Washington Redskins change its name and mascot?

Arab Americans, Arabs, and Muslims

According to Jack Shaheen, scholar of popular media and American ethnic minorities (particularly media portrayals of Arabs), American media have a long history of presenting demeaning images of Arabs. Consider this verse from the opening song in Disney's original *Aladdin*: "I come from a land ... where they cut off your ear if they don't like your face. It's barbaric ... but, hey, it's home." (Note: This line was edited out for later releases because of protests from Arab Americans.)

Shaheen has written extensively about Arab portrayals in American media (Shaheen 2003 2008), and has helped produce a traveling exhibit ("A Is for Arab: Stereotypes in U.S. Popular Culture") in collaboration with the Arab American National Museum (arabamericanmuseum.org). He has also produced a film on Arab stereotypes, *Reel Bad Arabs: How Hollywood Vilifies a People*, in collaboration with the Media Education Foundation.

Here are some of the stereotypes of Arab Americans, Arabs, and Muslims in American entertainment and news media, identified in content analysis and critical analysis by scholars (e.g., Sides and Gross 2010) and groups such as the Arab American National Museum. Most of the stereotypes do not differentiate between Arab Americans, Arabs, and Muslims.

- Having hostile intentions, being a threat to America
- Being linked to crisis, war, and conflict. Slightly more than half of the news stories about Muslims analyzed in one study included references to "fundamentalists," "militants," "terrorists," "radicals," or "extremists"
- Being lazy, wealthy sheikhs, slothful, and indolent; being casted as villains in film portrayals

- Being perceived as "buying up America," being seen as "White-slavers and uncivilized rulers of kingdoms," fitting the description that "all Palestinians are terrorists," and being seen as "the world's enemies"
- Being evil, being terrorists, causing explosions, being attackers
- Pursuing fun, lust, and extravagance
- Being far from civilization and science, presenting tent and camel images for Bedouin Arab characters
- Being arrogant, nervous, and repressive of women

Older People

In general, older people are under-represented in television and movies, and when present, are generally portrayed negatively, reflecting stereotypes of physical and cognitive decline, and sexual impotence (Montepare and Zebrowitz 2002). Other stereotypes portray older people as dependent, helpless, unproductive and "demanding rather than deserving" (Dittmann 2003).

Attention has recently focused on the portrayal of older people in Disney films and TV cartoons. By the time they enter primary school, children have a negative view of older adults. These negative perceptions might be influenced by exposure to negative stereotyping in children's entertainment programs.

Robinson et al. (2007) studied how older characters were depicted in public television cartoons and Disney films. Here are some of their findings:

- The most negative older characters in the Disney animated films were the villains. Examples are Madam Mim in *The Sword in the Stone*, the wicked stepmother in *Cinderella*, the witch in *Snow White*, Cruella De Vil in *101 Dalmatians*.
- Disney generally portrayed older females negatively, while older male characters were more often authority figures such as clergyman, ruler, and mentor.
- Snow White had the most elderly characters.
- Older characters were healthy 73% of the time, but more than 25% were shown as toothless or missing teeth; many had cracking voices, were hunched over, and if female, "were often depicted with saggy breasts."
- Most older characters were villains; otherwise, they were not central to the film's story and plot.

Women

Studies of the portrayals of men and women in popular media generally show that women in comparison to men are under-represented and continue to be stereotyped negatively. For example, Stacy Smith and her colleagues at the University of Southern California recently completed a comprehensive analysis of the portrayals of women in popular entertainment (Smith, Choueti, Prescott and Pieper 2014) for the Geena Davis Institute on Gender in Media (https://www.seejane.org/). Smith studied 11,927 speaking characters in 129 top-grossing family films (G, PG, PG-13) released to theatres between September 2006 and September 2012; 275 prime time programs over a week in the spring of 2012 that aired over a week on 10 broadcast and cable channels; and 36 children's TV shows aired in 2011 in Disney, Nickelodeon, and PBS programs. Here are some of the results (Smith et al 2014).

- Males significantly outnumber females in family films (2.53 male to 1 female speaking character ratio); prime-time programs (1.57 male to 1 female ratio); and children's shows (2.25 male to 1 female ratio). For perspective, just over 50% of the US population is female.

- Women are far more likely than men to be depicted as "eye candy" (that is, as sexualized objects) in all types of programs analyzed. Sexualized indicators were operationally defined as wearing sexy attire ("tight or alluring apparel"); showing some exposed skin ("between the mid chest and high upper thigh region"); thin; and referenced by another character, verbally or non-verbally as physically attractive or desirous. As shown in Table 9.1, women were more often portrayed than men in all of the sexualized indicators. The largest differences were "wearing sexy attire" in prime-time programs (8.4% men, 36.2% women) and with thin bodies in prime-time programs (13.6% men, 37.5% women).
- Women were more frequently portrayed in traditional domestic roles in family films (as parents: women 56%, males 44%; in a committed romantic relationship: women, 60%, males, 29%). No gender differences were found in prime time programs.
- Women were less likely than men to be depicted in prestigious and powerful positions. As shown in Table 9.2, men significantly outnumbered women in portrayals of all 8 powerful positions. The greatest differences were observed for family films in depictions as corporate executives (96.6% men, 3.4% women); as investors and developers (100% men, 0 women); high level politicians (95.5% men, 4.5% women); chief justice and district attorneys (100% men, 0 women); and editors in chief (100% men, 0 women.) Gender depictions of men and women in prime time programs, although favoring men, were less differentiated compared to family films.

TABLE 9.1 Media Portrayals of Men and Women in Sexualized Roles (Data taken from Smith et al. 2014)

Sexualized Appearance Indicator	Family Films		Prime Time Programs		Children's Shows	
	% Males	% Females	% Males	% Females	% Males	% Females
Wearing sexy attire	8	28.3	8.4	36.2	10.1	18
With exposed skin	8.5	26.6	11	34.6	12.4	17.2
Referenced attractive	4.3	14.9	3.5	11.6	1.8	5.6
With thin bodies	10.7	34.3	13.6	37.5	18.7	37.4

TABLE 9.2 Media Portrayals of Men and Women in Powerful Professions (Data taken from Smith et al. 2014)

Profession	Family Films		Prime Time Programs	
	% Males	% Females	% Males	% Females
CEOs, CFOs, Presidents, VPs, GMs	96.6	3.4	86	14
Investors, developers	100	0	57.1	42.9
High-level politicians	95.5	4.5	72.2	27.8
Chief justices, district attorneys	100	0	100	0
Doctors, healthcare managers	78.1	21.9	70.4	29.6
Editors in chief	100	0	0	100
Academic administrators	61.5	38.5	61.5	38.5
Media content creators	65.8	34.2	72.7	27.3

Why the Negative Media Stereotypes?

The question of why negative stereotyping of racial groups, women, and other out-groups continues in the media in an age when explicit prejudice is no longer acceptable is difficult to study scientifically. After all, we can't easily do laboratory or field experiments in the newsroom or in entertainment media production studios;

neither can we easily convince the producers of media content to take the IAT test to promote self-awareness. And if we did surveys with explicit measures, we would get a standard response: "We are not prejudiced, and we do our best to present all groups realistically and fairly." The best we can do is to evaluate performance using critical analysis of information from in-depth interviews of the producers of the content, and to apply theories of communication and prejudice to an interpretive analysis of why negative stereotypes exist in the media. Here are some possible answers.

"We Write What We Know"

This quote, offered by McLaurin (2012) as an explanation of biased images of Native Americans in popular media, is certainly plausible, and can be applied to producers of all media content. Considering statistics showing that most producers of media content in the United States are from a mainstream in-group (i.e., White males), the question of how much they know about other groups such as racial minorities is a reasonable question. Of course, knowledge about an out-group can come from education, personal contact, and diligent research; White males can certainly gain this knowledge, and many do. But it is a reasonable assumption, although not always true, that a member of an out-group will have firsthand knowledge about the culture of his or her own group, and this knowledge will help create realistic and unbiased portrayals of the out-group. Therefore, the involvement of more out-group members (e.g., racial minorities) in the creation and production of media contents could reduce negative stereotyping of their groups. In spite of the best efforts of the media industry, particularly daily newspapers, there is still very little diversity in the media. Consider the following data from various media organizations:

- Out of 41,600 print journalists in 2011, only 5,300, or 12.7%, were racial minorities; 12% of newsroom management positions were held by racial minorities. For comparison, 35% of the US population consisted of racial minorities in 2010 (American Society of Newspaper Editors 2012). Also, 37% were women (30% Caucasian women, 7% minority women), and 63% were men (56% Caucasian, 7% minority).
- A study of 38 major daily newspapers by the *4th Estate* (4thestate.net) on authorship of news reports of political issues during the 2012 presidential campaign showed that White journalists wrote 91% of stories on the economy, 90.8% of stories on social issues, 92.7% of stories on foreign policy, and 98.2% of stories on immigration. Among the newspapers studied were the *New York Times*, the *Washington Post*, the *Boston Globe*, the *Los Angeles Times*, the *Chicago Tribune*, the *Miami Herald*, *USA Today*, and the *Dallas Morning News* (huffington.com. 10/25/2012).
- The OpEd Project (theopedproject.org) in 2012 studied the proportion of articles written by women in new media (e.g., the Huffington Post, *Salon*), legacy media (e.g., the *New York Times*, the *Washington Post*, the *Los Angeles Times*, the *Wall Street Journal*), and college media (e.g., Columbia, Harvard, Princeton, and Yale). The percentages of stories written by women were 33% in new media 20% in legacy media, and 38% in college media. Out of 1,410 general interest articles (on politics, economy, health, and education), women wrote 261 (18.5%).
- According to Smith et al. (2014), women are under-represented in "behind the camera" work for entertainment films and television. Of 1,565 content creators in Smith's sample, 7% of directors were women; 13% of writers were women; and 20% of producers were women.

These results show that racial minorities and women are significantly underrepresented in the staff and management of newspapers. Therefore, the knowledge and perspectives (e.g., use of diverse sources) they could bring to major stories of the day are not fully utilized. For example, the National Association of Hispanic Journalists (NAHJ) noted,

Latino voices are lacking in news coverage. Key political stories about Latinos lack Hispanic perspectives. The vast majority of immigration stories also was not told from the Latino perspective. (Montalvo and Torres 2006)

Media Are a Business

In general, media operate not only to serve the public good but also to make a profit. To be profitable, news and entertainment media need to attract the largest possible audiences in their demographic markets, so that they can, in turn, attract the advertisers. Considerable audience research is conducted to analyze what audiences want and how to balance the needs of the audience with serving the public good, particularly in the case of the print media. From a social identity perspective, we can interpret audience preferences in the context of out-groups and in-groups, and the human need for reinforcement of self and group identities. One way of doing this is to hold one's group superior to others. We need villains and heroes and heroines. And out-groups are convenient villains. Villains in American entertainment media have included, at one time or another, Native Americans, the Japanese, Russians, the Chinese, Arabs, Latinos, other racial minorities, and so on. Shaheen (2003) quotes a director of program practices for a television network on the need for villains (and, consequently, their negative stereotypes) in entertainment programming:

It is an easy thing to do. It is the thing that is going to be most readily accepted by a large number of the audience. It is the same thing as throwing in sex and violence when an episode is slow. (1)

Structural Constraints

The producers of media content, whether news or entertainment, work under time constraints that often result in doing things as they've always done them before, using routines and practices that often result in biased coverage and biased portrayals of groups they are not familiar with. Deadline pressure often leads to hasty decisions (i.e., choosing what has worked before). Ruscher (2001) tells about an African American news correspondent, who, given two hours to put together a story about shelters for homeless people, "relied upon b-roll that happened to portray African American individuals utilizing the shelters, rather than persons of diverse ethnic and racial backgrounds" (141).

Another structural constraint is reliance on official and expert sources, who in most cases will be White men. For example, Darling-Wolf (1997) analyzed twenty-one articles in the *New York Times* on breast implants. She found that of eighty-three sources used for the articles, only two were women. Reporters and writers will consult sources with whom they are familiar, and whom they've used in the past. More diverse content producers can be expected to consult more diverse sources, thus giving additional perspectives to the stories they are telling.

Implicit Biases?

Studies have shown that more than eighty percent of people probably have implicit biases against out-groups, including racial groups. We also know that implicit biases can trigger automatic responses toward the target groups, such as negative evaluations, negative stereotypes, and discriminatory behaviors. It's reasonable to assume, then, that a large proportion of the producers of media content have the same implicit biases that you and I have, and that these biases can result in automatic behaviors and evaluations that lead to negative portrayals and negative stereotyping of out-groups. The key is to educate media producers on how to control these biases.

Do Media Stereotypes Influence Public Stereotypes?

We are interested in media stereotypes because of the very real possibility that they can influence our own stereotypes. After all, our generalized impression of out-groups is based on information and images, no matter how inaccurate or biased they may be. Because most of us are limited in our personal contact with out-groups, particularly racial groups, the media are important sources of information and images. Because we don't always go to the media for information—we use them for other purposes such as diversion and entertainment—this influence might be in ways that we even aren't aware of. Two sets of theories explain how the media might influence our stereotypes of others. Social cognitive theory and cognitive processing theory take a rational approach, meaning that media influence is conscious, and that we evaluate information before we decide to accept or reject it. Priming theory explains stereotype activation as an unconscious, automatic response—we are not even aware that it's happening. We study these theories for a better understanding of what's happening (inside our heads) when we are influenced by the media to take as our own the stereotypes that are portrayed in their stories. After learning about these theories, we'll look at research studies that illustrate some of their major principles and predictions.

Social Cognitive Theory

Social cognitive theory (Bandura 1986) explains how people learn behaviors and ways of thinking vicariously, that is, by observation. Television, the movies, and other visual media are major sources for vicarious learning, even for children. The starting point for vicarious learning is the behavior observed, which may depict overt action, such as hitting another person, or an attitude or opinion expressed by the actors in the observed event. Overt action, attitudes, and opinions can convey stereotypes toward a group. For example, if Arabs are depicted as violent and ruthless terrorists by their actions, that stereotype is conveyed to observers. Or, stereotypes can be expressed in more subtle ways—conversations among characters, frequency of depictions in occupations and roles (e.g., low status/high status; criminals/police officers), and context in which the characters are portrayed (hero/villain; slums/suburbs). We pay attention to when we see events and behaviors depicted in the media with these characteristics:

- Distinctive (e.g., sex, violence, ruthless villains; unusual or exotic behaviors and physical features)
- Evaluated positively (i.e., arouse positive emotions, such as when an in-group member is the hero/heroine and an out-group member is the villain)
- Prevalent (repeated and accessible, such as in recurring television portrayals)
- Useful (such as when the observed event helps us maintain group- and self-identity)

As we can see, negative stereotypic portrayals of out-groups in the media meet most of the criteria above. Therefore, these negative portrayals will more likely draw our attention than will portrayals that are balanced, instances where there are no heroes or villains, or cases where the roles are reversed or ambiguous.

The first step in vicarious learning, according to social cognitive theory, is attention, which is determined not only by the attributes of the observed event, but also by the mental and physical state of the observer. These attributes include perceptual capabilities (e.g., attention span), arousal level (some degree of emotional excitation facilitates attention), and acquired preferences (likes and dislikes for observed characters and behaviors acquired from other socialization agents or by experience). Again, we can see that negative depictions of out-groups are more likely to gain attention, arouse some positive emotions, and be reinforced by previous experience than are positive or neutral depictions.

After attention, the next step is for the observer to store the observed event in long-term memory and to integrate the event into similar bits of information. Retention is facilitated by symbolic coding (using symbols such as words, signs, or images to represent the observed event mentally), cognitive organization (integrating the event into the existing cognitive structure, such as similar pieces of information), and rehearsal (repeating the event mentally). Research shows that we are more likely to remember negative events than positive events, because negative events and information arouse just enough emotion to aid recall (see, e.g., Lang 2000). Therefore, negative depictions of out-groups are more likely to be remembered than are positive depictions.

After the observed event is stored in memory, it becomes accessible when primed, and when performance of the learned behavior or expression of the learned attitude or opinion (e.g., a stereotype) is rewarded externally (e.g., by approval of others) or internally (gives a good feeling). The expression of learned negative stereotypes of out-groups is often approved by members of the in-group, increasing the likelihood of repeated expression.

The social cognitive theory of the influence of media stereotypes on our own (individual or public) stereotypes follows a very conscious process. According to this theory, we learn stereotypes depicted in the media following the steps discussed above. And, it's more likely that we will learn negative stereotypes than positive ones.

Cognitive Processing Theory

The basic premise of this model (developed by Tan, Dalisay, Zhang, Han, and Merchant 2010) is that receiver evaluations of information are a more powerful explanation of media influence on stereotypes than frequency of exposure to information. This premise is based on the fundamental assumption that human beings are rational and seek to maximize cognitive rewards by utilizing available information (see, e.g., Bandura 2002). The de-emphasis in the model on frequency of exposure is based on previous research indicating that even brief, "one-shot" exposures to information may alter stereotypical beliefs (see, e.g., Appiah, and Eighmey 2011; Dalisay and Tan 2009; Oliver, Kaylamaraman, and Ramasubramanian 2007). Also, personal contact research shows that even a single encounter with a member of another group can lead to stereotyping (see, e.g., Pettigrew 1998). What matters, at least in stereotype development, is not how much information one has but how one evaluates the information.

The cognitive processing model focuses on information valence (positive or negative) and realism/believability, dimensions of information evaluation that increase cognitive involvement, identification, credibility, and self-efficacy (see, e.g., Austin and Freeman 1997; Gibbons et al. 2005). The model predicts that negative stereotypical portrayals in the media lead to negative stereotypes when these portrayals are perceived by the receiver to be real and believable. Positive portrayals will lead to positive stereotypes when these portrayals are perceived to be real and believable.

(Author's note: This section is adopted from Tan et al. [2010].)

Priming Theory

Rather than considering stereotype acquisition from the media as a rational, conscious, and information-based process, priming theory considers another route to stereotype acquisition and reinforcement. This route is *priming*, defined as "the incidental activation of knowledge structures, such as trait concepts and stereotypes, by the current situational context" (Bargh, Chen, and Burrows 1996). The learning and activation of a stereotype is automatic, which involves the "unintentional or spontaneous activation of some well-learned set of associations or responses that have been developed through repeated activation in memory" (Devine 1989). Put simply, we do not have to go through conscious, voluntary effort to learn and activate stereotypes. These cognitive structures—stereotypes—can be activated automatically without conscious effort by primes in the environment. The mere presence of a target person (the person stereotyped) or stereotypic behavior (even when the target is not present) are primes that can activate a stereotype. Activating a stereotype means applying the stereotype to evaluations of the target person, related behaviors, and thoughts about the target person. Important to our analysis of the priming influence of mass media stereotypes on individual (audience) stereotypes is the research finding that the unconscious or preconscious activation of stereotypes develops from frequent and consistent observation of trait-relevant behavior (stereotype consistent) in the environment (Bargh 1989; Bargh et al. 2012). The stereotypic behaviors could be observed in the real world or vicariously in the media.

To illustrate, let's say that I have stored in my memory through conscious thought and unconscious priming a knowledge structure pertaining to Asian Americans. This knowledge structure constructs Asian Americans as smart and hardworking, but clumsy socially and unpatriotic. This construct is my stereotype of Asian Americans. I don't go around thinking about this stereotype all the time; I am not conscious that I have it. However, primes in my environment—the mere presence of an Asian American student in my office, observing a martial arts demonstration—can activate this stereotype automatically. Without thinking, in the presence of a prime, I will evaluate an Asian American or behave toward him or her according to the stereotype, even without being aware that my behavior is directed by the stereotype. This stereotype is reinforced subconsciously (I'm not aware it's happening) by images of Asian Americans I see or read about in the media. Thus, the process is circular: Latent stereotypes (in my subconscious) lead to activation, which leads to reinforcement, which leads to a stronger latent stereotype, and so on. The influence of the media is in reinforcing latent stereotypes, because rarely do we bring a blank slate to the media experience. The process is unconscious (we are not aware it's happening) or preconscious (it happens before awareness of what's happening). Priming theory does not require that we evaluate the information or images before we develop a stronger stereotype. If the seed is there, we will strengthen the stereotype, unconsciously, from priming in the media.

Research

The Impact of Media Stereotypes on Public Stereotypes of Latinos

This online experiment in 2012 studied the influence of positive and negative Latino stereotypes in different media formats on the stereotypes of Latinos held by non-Latino audiences. The study was sponsored by the National Hispanic Media Coalition and was funded by the Kellogg Foundation. It was authored by Dr. Matt Barreto, Dr. Sylvia Manzano, and Dr. Gary Segura of Latino Decisions (www.latinodecisions.com).

In the experiment, 3,000 non-Latino participants recruited online were randomly assigned to one of ten experimental conditions. Eight conditions were visual, aural, or printed media images depicting positive or negative stereotypes of Latinos. The experimental conditions were as follows:

- No stimulus (control group)
- Placebo: unrelated content
- Negative entertainment film clip of gang party from *Training Day*
- Positive entertainment film clip of Jimmy Smits as presidential candidate from *The West Wing*
- Negative TV news: story on MS-13 gang
- Positive TV news: interview with astronaut Jose Hernandez
- Negative radio: excerpt from the Michael Savage Show
- Positive radio: interview with Ellen Ochoa, first Latina astronaut
- Negative print: excerpt from Pat Buchanan's *State of Emergency*
- Positive print: article on astronaut Jose Hernandez

Participants were instructed to attend to one of the stimuli above. They then answered questions about their opinions of Latinos (stereotypes). The experiment was done online. Results are shown in Tables 9.3A and 9.3B (constructed from Barreto, Manzano, and Segura 2012).

These results show that, consistently, negative media portrayals were associated with negative audience stereotypes, and positive media portrayals were associated with positive audience stereotypes. The exceptions are "religious" and "family-oriented," traits that most of the participants, regardless of media stimulus, said were descriptive of Latinos. The "effects" of media portrayals are stronger for the negative stereotypes—"less educated," "use welfare," "crime and gangs,, "take jobs away from Americans," and "illegal immigrants." For these negative traits, media influence was greater, as indicated by larger differences between audience stereotypes in the positive and negative content conditions. Of the different media studied, television news and entertainment generally had the most influence on audience stereotypes, with positive portrayals more strongly associated with endorsement of positive traits, and negative portrayals more strongly associated with endorsement of negative traits.

TABLE 9.3A   Media Influence on Public Stereotypes of Latinos

Media Stimuli	Stereotype Trait (Percentage Who Agree)					
	Honest	Neighborly	Patriotic	Religious	Family-oriented	Less-educated
Entertainment neg.	58%	51%	37%	75%	87%	53%
Entertainment pos.	64	56	44	74	85	44
TV news neg	53	51	34	74	85	56
TV news pos.	68	61	47	76	88	45
Radio neg.	57	50	38	72	85	55
Radio pos.	59	52	42	70	85	43
Print neg.	54	49	29	69	85	55
Print pos.	64	55	41	72	81	47

TABLE 9.3B   Media Influence on Public Stereotypes of Latinos

Media Stimuli	Stereotype Trait (Percentage Who Agree)			
	Use Welfare	Crime and Gangs	Take Jobs Away From Americans	Illegal Immigrants
Entertainment neg.	51%	49%	42%	56%
Entertainment pos.	46	42	34	54
TV news neg	61	59	47	62
TV news pos.	42	42	44	48
Radio neg.	59	55	49	59
Radio pos.	42	44	33	53
Print neg.	54	49	48	50
Print pos.	43	44	32	47

Although this study did not explicitly test for the processes in stereotype acquisition enumerated in social cognitive theory (e.g., attention, cognitive representation, retention), the results can be interpreted as supporting the theory. The media stimuli required some level of cognitive processing to have an effect because they were not presented subliminally, and because the measures of stereotyping were quite explicit.

Stereotypes in American Media and
Stereotypes of African Americans in South Korea

In a test of the cognitive processing model of stereotyping, Tan et al. (2010) studied use of American media and stereotyping of African Americans in South Korea. They surveyed 378 high school students to find out how much they used American television, movies, newspapers, and magazines; their perceptions of the realism and believability of American media; their perceptions of stereotyping of African Americans in American media; and their stereotypes of African Americans. They predicted that, in line with the cognitive processing model of stereotyping, the high school students would adopt media stereotypes as their own when they were rated to be real and believable, and that frequency of use would not be a factor. Here are some results of the study:

- The study participants used American media "sometimes" to learn about Americans (mean of 1.44 on a 4-point scale, from 1, almost never, to 4, very often). American movies were the most often used, followed by television.
- The participants rated American media as "somewhat" realistic and believable, and as portraying African Americans "somewhat negatively."
- The participants' stereotypes of African Americans were mixed; half of the stereotypes were positive (humorous, hardworking, not prejudiced, and generous); half were negative (violent, aggressive, not beautiful, not intelligent, poor morals, and arrogant).
- The participants' stereotypes were influenced by media stereotypes when media stereotypes were evaluated to be real and believable: Positive media portrayals perceived to be real and believable led to positive stereotyping of African Americans by the participants; negative media portrayals perceived to be real and believable led to negative stereotyping.

The researchers concluded that the influence of American media on stereotyping of African Americans by South Korean high school students was dependent on evaluations of the realism and believability of the media, an indication that the process was deliberate, rational, and conscious. Therefore, they suggest that the study supports a cognitive processing model of media influence on stereotyping.

Priming Welfare Queens and Other Stereotypes

Do media primes of stereotypes influence subsequent unconscious stereotyping of the target person in contexts unrelated to the media prime? The activation-recency hypothesis (Dines and Humez 2003) and priming theory (Bargh et al. 2012) suggest that the answer is yes. The activation-recency hypothesis, for example, predicts that "individuals who are primed with media content use it for subsequent information processing in social situations" (Monahan et al. 2005).

Monahan et al. (2005), in a direct test of the priming hypothesis, studied whether video primes of African American women would lead to automatic/unconscious stereotyping of African women in contexts unrelated to the video primes. The researchers studied three stereotypes of African women. The "mammy" stereotype includes traits such as being maternal, loyal, and nurturing. The "Jezebel" stereotype is characterized by "uncontrollable excessive appetite for sex" (Collins 1991, as quoted in Monahan et al. 2005, p. 200). The "welfare queen" stereotype includes traits such as being poor, having many children, living on federal aid (Gilliam 1999), being hostile, and being lazy (Collins 2004).

Monahan et al. (2005) showed one of three video clips depicting these stereotypes to college students assigned randomly to a video clip condition. The video clips shown were as follows: (1) For the mammy stereotype, a segment was shown from *To Dance With the White Dog* depicting a mammy character who is "reminiscing with a white family about her long involvement with them and taking care of the now grown children. Her features (dark-skinned, asexual and stout) are consistent with a typical mammy representation" (Monahan et al. 2005, 200). (2) For the Jezebel stereotype, a segment was shown from *Introducing Dorothy Dandridge,* which portrays "a physically attractive opportunist that desires the attention of men and takes pride in her sexual conquests" (Monahan et al. 2005, 200–201). (3) For the welfare queen stereotype, a segment was shown from *The Women of Brewster Place* depicting a "slatternly dressed mother watching a soap opera as her several children play. Interrupted by a neighbor who informs her that her son is eating out of the garbage, she becomes aggressive, says she has plenty of food stamps, and slams the door" (Monahan et al. 2005, 201).

After watching one of the stereotype video clips, the research participants, ostensibly for another study, watched a video clip of a professionally dressed African American woman being interviewed for a sales position by a man, who was off-camera. Research participants then completed a computer-based response task in which they were presented with a number of adjectives and were asked to press a "yes" or "no" button as quickly as possible to indicate whether the adjective described the woman being interviewed. (The participants all saw the same video of the woman being interviewed.) The responses were timed in milliseconds to indicate stereotype activation. The faster a "yes" button was pressed, the more quickly a stereotype trait was activated for the woman being interviewed.

Results supported the expectation from priming theory: Participants "primed with a specific stereotype responded quicker to stereotype-consistent than to stereotype-inconsistent adjectives" (Monahan et al. 2005, p. 202). The stereotypic-consistent traits primed by the video clips were more quickly used by the participants to describe the "target person," who was seen in a context (job interview) far removed from the contexts of the video clips. The stereotypical traits used by the participants to describe the target person were

- Mammy: strict, nurturing, affectionate, maternal, dedicated, loyal
- Jezebel: erotic, seductive, provocative, sexual, enticing, exotic
- Welfare queen: lazy, irresponsible, undeserving, ignorant, dirty, complaining

This study provides evidence that media priming, even from only one exposure, influences the automatic activation of stereotypes applied in another context and generalized to other members of the target group. Considering repeated exposures, the priming influence of the media, particularly visual media, should not be underestimated.

Stereotypes in Disney Animated Films

Let's consider stereotypes in Disney animated films, popular with young children across the world for over seventy years. Many Disney classics are still in circulation and easily available in digital form (e.g., Dundes 2001; Towbin et al. 2004; Coyne et al. 2016). We are interested in how Disney films portray their characters and the effects of these portrayals on a primary audience, young children.

Research has focused on the portrayals of women, men, racial and ethnic minorities, and older people. In general, studies show recent films and re-issues of older films with some revisions portraying these groups both negatively and positively, although negative portrayals outnumber positive portrayals.

Towbin et al. (2004) studied the images for gender, race, and age in 26 popular feature-length animated movies. Their sample included classic movies (e.g., *Snow White and the Seven Dwarfs* 1937) as well as more recent releases (e.g., *The Emperor's New Groove* 2000).

Portrayals of Women and Men

Here are some of the findings regarding the portrayals of men and women (Towbin et al. 2004):

- In most films, male characters resorted to physical and violent behavior to resolve emotional confrontations (e.g., *Bambi, Cinderella, Peter Pan, Lady and the Tramp, Sleeping Beauty, Beauty and the Beast, Hercules, Mulan*).

- In 19 movies, men and boy characters were portrayed as strong, as heroic, and as rescuers (e.g., *Pinnocchio, Bambi, Cinderella, Peter Pan, Jungle Book, Beauty and the Beast, Aladdin, The Lion King, Tarzan*).
- In 15 movies, the appearance of women as beautiful and physically attractive was more important than intellect and competence. These movies were *Snow White and the Seven Dwarfs, Pinocchio, Cinderella, Alice in Wonderland, Peter Pan, Lady and the Tramp, Sleeping Beauty, Dalmatians, The Jungle Book, Aristocrats, Robin Hood, Oliver, The Hunchback of Notre Dame, Hercules*, and *The Emperor's New Groove*.
- In 6 movies women were valued for their appearance, intellect, and competence. These movies were *The Little Mermaid, Beauty and the Beast, Aladdin, Pocahontas, Tarzan*, and *Mulan*.
- In 11 movies, women were portrayed as helpless and in need of protection. These movies were *Snow White and the Seven Dwarfs, Bambi, Cinderella, Peter Pan, Lady and the Tramp, Sleeping Beauty, Robin Hood, Oliver, The Little Mermaid, The Lion King*, and *Hercules*.
- In 10 movies, women were portrayed as helpless and in need of protection but also as heroic, adventurous, and independent. These movies were *Alice in Wonderland 101 Dalmatians, The Aristocats, The Fox and the Hound, Beauty and the Beast, Aladdin, Pocahontas, The Hunchback of Notre Dame, Mulan*, and *Tarzan*.
- In 15 movies, women were portrayed as "domestic and likely to marry" (Towbin et al. 2004, p. 31.) These movies were *Snow White and the Seven Dwarfs, Cinderella, Peter Pan, Lady and the Tramp, Sleeping Beauty, The Jungle Book, The Aristocats, Robin Hood, The Fox and the Hound, The Little Mermaid, Beauty and the Beast, The Lion King, The Hunchback of Notre Dame, Hercules*, and *The Emperor's New Groove*.
- Overweight women were portrayed as "ugly, unpleasant and unmarried" (Towbin et al 2004, p. 31) in *Cinderella, Alice in Wonderland, Robin Hood*, and *The Little Mermaid*.

In summary, most portrayals of women were stereotypically traditional and negative: physical attractiveness is valued more than intellect and competence; they are helpless and in need of protection; they are domestic with marriage as a goal. In addition, the portrayals of overweight women were negative: they are ugly and unpleasant; they are also unmarried. There were positive stereotypes in some movies of women as independent, heroic, competent and adventurous. However, negative portrayals were significantly more prevalent than positive portrayals (Towbin et al. 2004).

Portrayals of Racial and Cultural Minorities

What about portrayals of racial and cultural minorities? Here are some results from the Towbin et al. 2004) study:

- Ten movies portrayed racial minorities negatively. These movies were *Pinocchio, Dumbo, Alice in Wonderland, Peter Pan, Lady and the Tramp 101 Dalmatians, The Aristocats, Robin Hood, Oliver*, and *Aladdin*). For example, in *Dumbo*, "the crows appear to have African American voices; they depict stereotypically negative characteristics often associated with racist depictions of African Americans, such as being poor, unintelligent and naïve" (Towbin et al. 2004, 32.) Other examples of negative racial depictions are Peter Pan's reference to indigenous tribes as "red skins," cunning and unintelligent; portrayals of Arabs in *Aladdin* as dirty, cheap, and thieving; the caterpillar in *Alice in Wonderland* with stereotypical Arab characteristics of smoking, lazy, and short-tempered; the Siamese cats in *Lady and the Tramp* with slanted eyes and buckteeth; and Tito, a Hispanic Chihuahua in *Oliver* "that fights, chases women, and hotwires cars" (Towbin et al. 2004, 32.).
- Four movies portrayed racial and cultural minorities positively and negatively, with more positive portrayals. These movies were *Pocahontas, The Hunchback of Notre Dame, The Lion King*, and *Mulan*. For example, "in *Hunchback*, the gypsies are described as poor, evil, and thieves, but in the end Esmeralda breaks the stereotypes about gypsies and talks about the prejudiced way in which they are treated" (Towbin et al. 2004, 32.)

In summary, the portrayals of racial and cultural minorities in Disney films conform to many racist stereotypes, such as sinister, dangerous, aggressive, and evil. Some movies depict minorities positively (heroic as in *Pocahontas* and *Mulan*). However, most portrayals are negative.

Portrayals of Older People

Robinson, Callister, Magoffin, and Moore (2007) studied how older people are portrayed in 34 original animated feature films made entirely by Disney and released in theatres. Older people were identified by the following stereotypical characteristics: "(1) an appearance of retirement; (2) extensive gray hair; (3) wrinkles of the skin; (4) extensive loss of hair or balding; (5) crackling voice; (6) use of an aid such as a cane or wheelchair; (7) the parent of a son or daughter who is middle-aged or older; and (8) evidence of grandchildren or great-grandchildren" (Robinson et al. 2007, 205). These physical characteristics are based on stereotypical portrayals identified in previous research that made it easy for coders to identify older characters (e.g., Robinson and Anderson 2006). After identifying older characters in the Disney films, coders recorded the character's level of activity (very active, active, or inactive); personality descriptions (e.g., forgetful, grumpy, lonely, intelligent); health; body image (e.g., thin, average, overweight); and primary role (e.g., friend, villain) (Robinson et al. 2007). Here are some results:

- All of the films except *Dumbo* had at least one older character.
- Most older characters were male (67%) compared to female (33%).
- Almost all the older characters were Caucasians (83%); 9% were Asians; 1% were African Americans; 7% were Native Americans and Pacific Islanders (all in *Lilo and Stitch* 2002 and *Brother Bear* 2003).
- Most older characters were portrayed in minor roles (61%) compared to major roles (39%).
- Portrayals of older characters in major and minor roles included friend (27%), worker/boss (14%), villain (13%), and parent (11%).
- In primary roles, older men were often portrayed in roles of authority (e.g., clergy, ruler, mentor); women were often portrayed as villains.
- Of principal villain characters in 27 films, 44% were older.
- Older people were portrayed as friendly (25%), angry/grumpy/stern (25%), loving/caring (22%), "wise" (16%), "happy/content" (12%), "evil/sinister" (12%), and "eccentric" (10%).

Robinson et al. (2007) concluded that the majority of portrayals of older characters were generally positive (58%). However, 42% of older characters were portrayed negatively. Ten films contained only overall positive portrayals (*The Aristocats, Bambi, Brother Bear, The Jungle Book, The Lion King, Oliver, Peter Pan, Pocahontas, Tarzan,* and *The Black Cauldron*). Other films contained only overall negative portrayals: *Alice in Wonderland, The Emperor's New Groove, Lilo and Stitch, The Rescuers,* and *Treasure Planet.* Of the films showing both positive and negative portrayals, *Snow White and the Seven Dwarfs* had the highest number of positive portrayals, and *Mulan* had the highest number of negative portrayals (Robinson et al. 2007).

Disney Princesses and Young Girls

Disney princesses have been portrayed in many Disney films and have been popularized through related merchandise exceeding three billion dollars in 2012 (Goudreau 2012). In 2015, Disney identified 13 princesses in their films and merchandising. Most were princesses by birth or marriage (e.g., *Cinderella*); others were not (e.g., *Mulan*) (Coyne et al. 2016). In general, Disney princesses have been portrayed in stereotypical female roles (e.g., physically weak, affectionate, nurturing, helpful, fearful, submissive) (England et al. 2011). In addition, princesses are portrayed as "young and attractive with large eyes, small nose and chin, moderately large breasts, prominent cheekbones, lustrous hair, and good muscle tone and skin complexion" (Coyne at al.

2016, 7). Some recent portrayals of princesses are more complex and do not fit gender stereotypes (England et al. 2011). *Mulan,* for example, is heroic, strong, and independent. Princess movies are extremely popular with young girls. *Frozen,* Disney's best-selling princess movie, was popular with both girls and boys.

Disney princess movies, with their romanticized plots, are generally considered to be "safe" by parents (Orenstein 2011). However, portrayals of princesses are stereotypically gender-based and may send strong messages about what are appropriate real-life roles for girls and women (England et al. 2011).

Coyne et al. (2016) studied whether engagement with Disney princesses affected gender-stereotypical behavior among young girls and boys over a one-year period. Their participants were 198 children ages 36 to 78 months recruited from preschools and kindergartens at four sites, and the children's parents (97.5% maternal). Data were collected for children and parents at Time 1 and only from parents at Time 2, one year later.

Coyne et al (2016) took data on the following variables:

1. **Disney Princess engagement:** Parents reported which Disney princess (photos were shown) their child most identified with and the strength of identification on a seven-point scale; how often their child played with Disney princess toys on a seven-point scale; and how frequently their child watched television shows or movies (including DVD) featuring Disney princesses. These measures were combined into the Disney princess engagement measure.

2. **Children's gender-stereotypical behavior:** Children were asked to sort into boxes toys that they like to play with "a lot," "a little," or "not at all." Four toys were stereotypically for girls (e.g., doll, tea set); four toys were stereotypically for boys (e.g., action figure, tool set); and four toys were gender neutral (e.g., puzzle, paint set). Toy preferences scores were averaged for the four female toys and for the four male toys.

Parents reported their child's gender-stereotypical behavior (e.g., playing with girls/boys, playing sports and ball games, climbing, playing house, playing dress up) and preferences for gender-stereotypical toys.

Coyne et al. (2016) predicted that princess engagement would be positively related to stereotypical girl behaviors among both girls and boys; that is, the more engagement, the greater frequency of stereotypical girl behaviors. Here are some of the results (Coyne et al. 2016):

- Girls were more likely than boys to be engaged with Disney princesses.
- Princess engagement was related to more frequent female-specific behaviors for both boys and girls at Time 1 and Time 2 (one year later).

These results provide some evidence that stereotypes portrayed in Disney princess movies may be internalized by both boys and girls, leading to the adoption of female-gender stereotypical behaviors in children. Coyne et al. (2016) suggest this implication of their findings:

"Although there is nothing inherently wrong with expressing femininity or behaving in a gendered manner, stereotypically female behavior may be potentially problematic if girls believe that their opportunities in life are limited because of preconceived notions about femininity." (38)

Figure Credits

Table 9.1 Source: Stacy Smith et al.
Table 9.2: Source: Stacy Smith et al.

Workbook

Define, describe, or illustrate; summarize the results of the studies:

1.   Stereotypes of Asians, Ronald Takaki quote

2.   Stereotype busters for what stereotypes? MANAA

3.   Portrayals of Hispanics or Latinos on TV shows, most frequently mentioned, NHMC survey

4.   Stereotypes of black people in media today

5.   Dixon and Lutz, portrayals of black people as law breakers and police officers

6.   Weisbuch et al: bias towards black people, nonverbal behaviors in TV shows

7.   Stereotypes of Native Americans in media today

8.   Stereotypes of older people in the media

9.   Stereotypes of women in the media

10.   McLaurin, stereotypes of Native Americans, East and West

11.   Shaheen and others, stereotypes of Arabs and Muslims in media today

12.   Why negative stereotypes in the media?

13.   Social cognitive theory, cognitive processing theory, priming theory

14.   Barreto et al., impact of media stereotypes on public stereotypes of Latinos

15.   Tan et al., American media use and stereotyping of African Americans in South Korea

16.   Monahan et al., priming study, results

17.   Disney stereotypes: effects on girls and boys

10

Video Games, Stereotypes, and Prejudice

In this chapter, we take a look at video games, one of the fastest growing media forms of entertainment in the United States and abroad, both in terms of sales and use. Racial and gender stereotypes, along with demonstrations of violence, are frequently portrayed in video games, prompting many researchers to study possible consequences on frequent players.

Video Games Are Big Business

According to Newzoo (2016), the video gaming industry generated $99.6 billion in sales in 2016, an increase of 8.5%% from 2015. Mobile gaming accounted for $37 billion, a larger share than personal computers and an increase of 21%% globally. Worldwide, the Asia-Pacific region generated the most revenue (47%), followed by North America (25%), and Europe, the Middle East, and Africa (24%). China alone generated $24.4 billion, a quarter of total world revenues. The US total was $23.5 billion, also a quarter of world revenues (Newzoo 2016). Clearly, video games are big business and are being played by millions of people around the world. Who are these people? Data from other countries is sparse. However, we do have data from the US.

Who Plays Video Games and How Much?

A 2016 survey of 4,000 American households by the Entertainment Software Association (Polygon 2016) showed that 63% of US households had at least one self-reported "frequent" gamer. The most popular device for playing games was a video game playing device (65%), and 48% reported owning a dedicated game console (Polygon 2016). The survey also showed that 47% of frequent and regular players ("gamers") were between 18 and 49 years old; 59% were men (average age, 35), and 41%% were women (average age, 44).

Elaborating on these findings, Lofgren (2016) reported that:

- 155 million Americans play games regularly (3 or more hours per week)
- the average number of years gamers have been playing games is 13
- 4 out of 5 households own a video game console

Regarding racial or ethnic differences in video game use, Pew (2015) in a 2015 national random survey of 2,001 American adults 18 years or older found that 19% of Hispanics, 11% of Black people, and 7% of Whites self-identified as gamers.

Pew (2015) also found that many Americans are unsure if minorities and women are negatively stereotyped in video games. Asked if most games portrayed minorities poorly, 47% said they were unsure. Other responses were 9% "true for most games," 20% "true for some games but not others, and 23% "not true for most games." For portrayals of women as "poorly," the responses were: 40% "unsure," 27% "true for some games but not others," and 18% "not true for most games." These responses show that although the most common response regarding negative stereotyping of women and minorities was "unsure," more Americans believed that at least in some video games, minorities (29%) and women (41%) were portrayed poorly, as opposed to not being portrayed poorly (minorities, 23%; women, 18%), in most games. We can conclude that there is some recognition in the general public (people who play and don't play video games) that minorities and women are being negatively stereotyped.

The evidence, then, indicates that video games are an important entertainment activity in most American households and that close to 50% of adults—men and women—play video games. What about children and adolescents, the most likely demographic to be affected by playing video games given that they are in early stages of socialization? The data indicates that video games consume even more of adolescents' time when compared to adults. According to the American Academy of Child and Adolescent Psychiatry (2015), on average, pre-teen girls spend more than an hour per day playing video games and boys spend more than two hours. Walsh et al. (2004) reported that 90% of children between 8 and 17 years old say they are regular players, making them the group that plays the most video games (Gentile, Saleem, and Anderson 2007). In another study (Gentile, Lynch, Linder, and Walsh 2004), 94% of eighth and ninth graders reported they played video games. We can conclude from these studies that children are the heaviest users of video games, potentially making them the most vulnerable group to video game influence.

Of particular interest to parents and researchers is "pathological video game use" also referred to as "video game addiction," defined as video game use that leads to dysfunctional behaviors or states, such as poor grades and increased hostility (Gentile et al. 2011). A longitudinal study over two years of 3,034 third and eighth grade children in Singapore gives us a detailed look at the possible predictors and consequences of video game addiction or pathological gaming (Gentile et al. 2011). Here are some of the results:

- 83% of participants in the sample reported that they played video games at least occasionally, on the average 20.95 hours per week during the last year of the two-year study, with boys reporting more playing hours (21.44 hours) than girls (19.51).
- Between 7.6% and 9.9% of participants reported symptoms of video game addiction.
- Pathological gamers played an average of 31 hours per week compared to 19 hours per week for non-pathological players.
- Some predictors of pathological gaming were higher levels of impulsivity, lower social competence and empathy, and poor emotional control.
- Some consequences of pathological gaming were poorer grades, poorer relationships with parents, more consumption of violent games, and increased depression, anxiety, and social phobia.

These results give us some information about video game players among children in Singapore. Similar results have been reported for other countries. For example, the proportion of video game addicts among youths in the US has been estimated to be 8.5% (Gentile 2009). In other countries, these are the estimated percentages: China, 10.3% (Peng and Li 2009); Australia, 8.0% (Porter et al. 2010); Germany, 11.9% (Grusser, Thalemann, and Griffiths 2007); and Taiwan, 7.5% (Ko et al. 2007.)

These data show that addictive or pathological video game playing is found in many countries, although the percentages are relatively small. In this book, we are interested in a narrower, although related, issue: How does video game playing affect prejudice and stereotyping directed toward outgroups, including racial/ethnic minorities and women? Given research showing that pathological gamers are more likely to be affected by violence in video games, we can assume that they also will be more likely affected by stereotypes depicted in games. Before we can answer questions about effects, we should first analyze the content of video games with attention to stereotypes and demonstrations of prejudice.

Stereotypes, Violence, and Other Anti-Social Content in Video Games

For sure, some video games have educational content. These include games designed specifically for use in K–12 classrooms, including those accessed on educational game websites such as BrainPOP, which provide kids the opportunity to learn about math, science, social studies, English, technology, art, music, and health (Novotney 2015). Other games available for use in home devices promote prosocial behaviors, that is, behaviors beneficial to others. An example is *Chibi Robo*, which "lets the player control a robot whose job is to make its family happy by cleaning up, helping them out in chores and everyday tasks" (Saleem, Anderson, and Gentile 2012, 283). Therefore, video games promoting and teaching about prosocial behaviors are available. However, according to the American Academy of Child and Adolescent Psychiatry (2015), most popular games emphasize harmful (antisocial) behaviors, such as:

- "the killing of people or animals;
- the use and abuse of drugs and alcohol;
- criminal behavior, disrespect for authority and the law;
- sexual exploitation and violence toward women;
- foul language and obscene gestures;
- and racial, sexual and gender stereotypes"

(American Academy of Child and Adolescent Psychiatry 2015, 1).

Of these harmful behaviors, we are primarily interested in racial and gender stereotypes, and their effects on game players

Racial Stereotypes in Video Games

How are racial minorities—Black people, Hispanics, Asians, Native Americans, Arabs—portrayed in video games? To answer this question, researchers have analyzed video game magazines, video game covers, and the games themselves as early as 2000. The interest in racial minority portrayals continues to this day primarily because of the concern that negative portrayals will transfer into evaluations and behaviors in the real world, especially considering the increased popularity of video games among children and teenagers, our most vulnerable populations. Here are some findings:

- Racial minorities are seldom portrayed in video games. Williams et al. (2009) analyzed 150 games across nine platforms. He found that Native Americans and biracial characters did not exist; African Americans were found in 11% of the games; Hispanics were in less than 3%. In an analysis of the top 10 games each year from 2007–2012, Shoemaker (2014) found that Black and Asian characters accounted for 3% of main protagonists, Hispanics accounted for 1%. Burgess et al. (2011) compared the representation of male racial minorities in six best-selling video game magazines with the actual racial distribution in the US population from U.S. Census data. They found that White males were over-represented (76% in video games, 65% in the US population); Black males were accurately represented (12% in video games and the US population); other male racial minorities were under represented (Asian: 2.1% in video games, 4.3% in the US population; Hispanics: 1.7% in video games, 14.4% in the US population).
- Racial minorities are often portrayed negatively in video games. Often, these portrayals define racial minorities quite narrowly, relegating them to narrow stereotypical roles. For example, Children Now

(2001) reports that an analysis of 1,716 video game characters showed that all Hispanic male characters were in a sport, usually baseball. Similarly, 83% of African American males in video games competed in sports (Children Now 2001).

More recently, Burgess et al. (2011) analyzed how White and racial minority males were portrayed in video games according to game ratings (e.g., E, appropriate for players younger than 17; M, appropriate for players 17 or older because of violent and sexual content); game genre (e.g., fantasy, war, cops and special "ops"); and "illicit" (e.g., "person perpetrating nonmilitary violence without a clear and present danger,") (299). The authors considered aggression and violence in war, and by cops, and special "ops" to be "socially sanctioned," because the actions were performed by characters in defense of communities, governments, and social environments (groups of "good" people). Burgess et al. analyzed 149 video game covers, including the top 50 games in 2005 for Xbox, PlayStation2 and Nintendo GameCube. Here are some of the results:

1. For all game genres, male minority characters were more likely to be aggressive (64.7%) than male White characters (50%).
2. Male White characters (42.4%) were more likely to be portrayed in fantasy games than male minority characters (14%).
3. Male White characters were more likely to engage in socially sanctioned violence (74.4%) than in illicit violence (35.3%).
4. Male minority characters were more likely to engage in illicit violence (64%) than socially sanctioned violence (25.5%).
5. Male minority characters (41.2%) were more likely to be portrayed in M-rated (for violent and sexual content) than male Whites (27.1%).
6. Male minorities (11.8%) were more often portrayed as athletes than male Whites (4.6%); Black males were athletes in 32% of their portrayals.
7. The most common portrayals of Asian males were as martial artists.

According to Burgess et al. (2011), their results indicate that some racial stereotypes in television and movies are also found in video games: "the violent black thug, the Asian martial artist, the Asian as model minority, and the black athlete" (302.) They offer this conclusion:

> The message communicated by this difference (in portrayals) is clear: whites are heroic fighters, fighting to save an often romanticized world .... or realistic war heroes saving nothing less than Western Civilization itself ... whereas black characters were too often the menace to society with oversized weapons and gang posturing .... whereas the Asian characters simply engage in martial arts, threatening no one but each other, and saving no one. (302)

Whether these conclusions are true today should be studied, considering some positive changes in minority portrayals in television and movies (Chapter 9).

Gender Stereotypes in Video Games

Early research (1989–2002) on the depictions of women in video games tells us that women were largely non-existent and when they were portrayed, they were usually submissive to men and "hypersexualized" with "unrealistically large breasts and small waists," which were "emphasized through revealing clothing or partial nudity" (Jansz and Martis 2007).

In one of the earliest studies, Braun and Giroux (1989) analyzed the depictions of men and women in arcade games. They found male characters in 60% of the games, women characters in 2%. Provenzo (1991) studied the covers of boxes of 47 Nintendo games. Of 124 human characters in the box covers, 92% were male and 8% were female. Men were portrayed in dominant (controlling) roles in 24% of the covers; none of the women were. In contrast, 33% of the women were depicted in submissive roles; none of the men were. Confirming these results, Dietz (1998), in her analysis of 33 games in Nintendo and Genesis game consoles, found that 33% of the games did not have women in leading or supporting roles; 21% of the women were submissive; 15% were heroes. Dietz (1998) reports that female characters not depicted as heroes were princesses or wise old women to be rescued by the male leading character. Similar results are reported by Children Now (2001): 64% of the games analyzed featured men; 17% featured women. In games with player-controlled characters, primary male and secondary male characters were featured in 73% of the games. In general, women were "hypersexualized," did not engage in the action, and were bystanders.

Some changes in the portrayals of women were reported by studies done in 2002 and later. Ramirez et al. (2011) analyzed 87 PC and 79 console games. They found that 50% of women were portrayed in dominant positions, a much larger percentage than in previous studies (e.g., Dietz 1998). Hanninger and Thompson (2004) reported that in their sample of 81 games, 89% included playable male characters while 52% included playable female characters, also a much larger percentage for women than in previous studies (e.g., Children Now, 2001). However, the depictions of women were still "hypersexualized"—often partially nude or in revealing clothing and with exaggerated body shapes to emphasize sexual characteristics (Downs and Smith, 2005).

These more recent studies suggest that, except for hypersexualized portrayals, women were beginning to be portrayed more often and in tough, competent, dominant roles. What led to this change?

First, more women are playing video games. In 2014, a Gallup poll reported that half of all American video game players were women. Second, is the "Lara Phenomenon" (Janz and Martis 2007), named after the main female character Lara Croft in the best-selling *Tomb Raider* game. Because of its popularity and profitability, *Tomb Raider*, featuring Lara Croft, paved the way for portrayals of women that went against the submissive stereotypical norm. Game creators realized that there was a sizeable market for games featuring dominant, powerful, tough, and competent female heroes (Labre and Duke 2004.)

To illustrate the Lara Phenomenon, let's take a look at a study of recent portrayals of women in popular video games.

Jansz and Martis (2007) analyzed how women were portrayed in twelve popular video games. They selected games that were best-sellers; included men, women and minority characters; were based on narratives or had recognizable story lines (excluding fighting games, such as *Tekken* and *Mortal Kombat*); and were available on a game console (Sony's PlayStation 2 and Microsoft's Xbox). Using these criteria, they selected the following games for analysis: *Charlie's Angels, Devil May Cry 2, Enter the Matrix, Final Fantasy X, GTA Vice City, Metal Gear Solid 2: Sons of Liberty; Parasite Eve 2; Primal; Shadowman 2: The Second Coming; Silent Hill 3; Splinter Cell;* and *Tomb Raider: Angel of Darkness*. These games were at the top of sales charts in the early 2000s. The Jansz and Martis (2007) study needs to be updated with current popular video games. Not many studies have been published recently that are as comprehensive and rigorous as this one, because content analysis of video games is a particularly difficult task. As Jansz and Martis (2007) point out, video games provide many layers of content; the completion of one game may take a seasoned gamer up to twenty hours of playing. Consequently, researchers have resorted to analyzing game box covers and magazines instead of the actual games. However, these units provide only summary information on character roles and story lines.

To provide a more comprehensive analysis, Jansz and Martis (2007) studied the introductory films of the video games in their sample. These films provide more information on character portrayals and narratives than game box covers and magazines. Jansz and Martis (2007) coded the following variables:

1. Gender of primary and secondary (supporting) characters based on physical features
2. Race of primary and secondary characters based on features and the language they spoke
3. Role and position: For roles, characters were coded as hero, villain/evil, helper, princess, tough, mother, housewife, victim. For position, characters were coded as dominant, equal, or submissive.
4. Appearance: attire (sexy, ordinary), body (heavy, normal, thin), build (muscular, normal), breasts for female characters only (large, normal), buttocks for all characters (large, normal)

Two coders assigned the primary and secondary characters in the games to a category as listed above. Agreement ranged from 0.75 to 0.85, indicating reliability in coding.

Here are some results:

1. Of 22 characters in all the games, 60% were men, 40% women. There was an even split for leading characters: six men and six women. However, there were more men (seven) than women (three) among secondary characters.

2. Primary characters (leading roles) regardless of gender were dominant over other characters. Female leading characters were just as likely to be portrayed as dominant compared to male leading characters. No women in secondary roles were portrayed as submissive, whereas 43% of men in secondary roles were submissive.

3. The most common character role in all the games was hero (60%), followed by friend or helper (18%), villain (9%), victim (9%), and a tough role (5%). All the women in leading roles (primary characters) were heroes; about 90% of men in leading roles were heroes. Men in secondary roles were mostly friend or helper. Women in supporting roles were heroine, friend or helper, or villain.

4. All game characters, for both men and women, generally had normal or thin bodies. Men were generally portrayed with muscular builds: 60% had emphasized muscles in extreme forms. Most women were shown with large breasts (77%) and emphasized buttocks (77%, compared to 25% of men with large buttocks.) Almost all the women (compared to one man) were shown in "sexy," revealing attire.

These results suggest that in the early 2000s, women's portrayals in video games were moving away from negative stereotyping. More women were portrayed, and they were portrayed equally with men as heroes and in dominant roles. However, women were still "hypersexualized," depicted in scanty attire with emphasized breasts and buttocks (Jansz and Martis 2007).

Taking another route to assess game stereotypes of women, Dill and Thill (2007) asked teenagers to describe typical male and female game characters. Using open-ended questions, the researchers coded the most common responses, which included quite explicit characterizations. Male characters were most often described as powerful (muscular, strong, well built) followed by aggressive (violent, deadly), having a hostile attitude (mean, cocky/arrogant, belligerent), athletic (sports), and thuggish (gangster). The most common characterizations of women were provocative dress (skimpy clothes, naked, tight clothes), curvaceous figure ("big boobs," voluptuous), thin (skinny), sexual ("slutty," sexy, hooker), and aggressive (violent) (Dill and Thill 2007). These results show that teenagers perceived male and female game characters in much the same way as content analyses had showed. Males were powerful and in control; women were hypersexualized.

Effects of Video Game Racial and Gender Stereotypes on Players

As we have seen in previous chapters ("Consequences of Prejudice" and "Consequences of Stereotypes"), portrayals of racial and ethnic minorities, women, older people, and other outgroups in television and the movies influence our evaluations of and actions towards them in the real world. For many, these portrayals provide a convenient source of information when they have limited direct interaction or personal contact with outgroups. Therefore, our perceptions are molded by media representations. More often than not, these representations are inaccurate or, at best, incomplete. Video games can be particularly influential, because of their interactive nature. Players control what they experience and can change outcomes by overt actions using a controller, joypad, keyboard, or other interface mechanism (Jansz and Martis 2007). Interactivity heightens the involvement of players in the world represented in games, making them less aware of its fictional nature (Klimmt and Vorderer 2003), intensifying the feeling of "being there" (Lee, 2004), and allowing the players to identify with game characters by, for example, taking on the role of a game protagonist. Several theories of media effects suggest that heightened identification with characters and deeper involvement in the story increase the probability of media influence on audiences, or in video games, on the players.

Theories that explain how our perceptions of and actions in the real world are affected by portrayals of reality in the media also explain how video games might affect game players. Bandura's (1986) social cognitive theory (SCT) accounts for how reality perceptions including the development of prejudice and stereotypes might be initially influenced by media portrayals among children and adults. SCT predicts that media realities are learned and projected to the real world when the viewer or player identifies with the observed characters, when the observed behaviors lead to rewards rather than punishments, and when the viewer/player is involved in the media experience. As we have seen, video games and the gaming experience meet these requirements.

For media consumers who have already learned the stereotypes, prejudices and social role expectations of outgroups such as racial minorities and women, priming theories (e.g., Bargh et al. 2012) provide an explanation of media and video game effects. According to priming theories, we learn about the real world from socialization agents such as parents, peers, and teachers; from direct observation; and from the cultural environment, which is the sum total of what we see, what we are told, what we directly or vicariously observe, and the behaviors, beliefs, and values that we perceive important or significant other people in our groups and communities approve of. Much of this information including stereotypes and biases or prejudice toward outgroups helps us to make sense of a complicated environment and is stored in long-term memory. We may not even be aware that we have stored some of this information, because it may not be useful in coping with the environment at any given moment or because, as in the case of negative stereotypes and biases, the information is not socially acceptable. Greenwald, Nosek, and Banaji (2003), for example, have shown that most people will not admit to explicit stereotypes and biases but may have unconscious biases (see chapter 4, "Measures of Explicit and Implicit Prejudice"). Priming theory tells us that these unconscious biases and stereotypes can be activated by primes encountered in the media and in video games. Primes may be confirming stereotypes or simply an object associated with the stereotype (e.g., Berkowitz 1993). For example, a common and inaccurate unconscious bias is the association of Black people with violence and crime (e.g., Greenwald, Nosek and Banaji 2003). Most of us will not admit to this unconscious bias because it is not socially acceptable and it is contrary to our cultural and personal values. However, this unconscious bias can be primed by playing a video game supporting the stereotype and could subsequently influence evaluations and behaviors towards Black people in the real world.

Evaluative conditioning (Walther, Weil and Dusing 2011) explains how repeated reinforcement of subconscious biases can lead to the strengthening of those biases. In this theory, simple co-occurrence of an object (A) with another object or behavior (B) is sufficient for a "holistic" perception that A is B, meaning that B is perceived to be part of A or vice-versa. This interpretation of how objects and behaviors are grouped together was initially proposed by Krech and Crutchfield (1958) in their discussion of perception theory. Their "whole-part" and proximity principles, like evaluative conditioning, proposed that objects and behaviors occurring in the same time and space or close to each other will be perceived to be parts of the same "whole." For example, the repeated pairing of a racial minority or women with stereotypical behavior could strengthen the stereotype and subsequently affect direct evaluations of and behaviors toward the racial minority and women in the real world.

Effects of Racial Stereotypes in Video Games

Burgess et al. (2011) provide some evidence that Black people featured in violent games can prime a violent stereotype of Black people. They showed college students, ninety percent% of whom were White, thirty-second digital videos of violent and nonviolent games. The violent games depicted one-on-one fighting with fantasy weapons and gang members fighting each other. The nonviolent games showed individual sports and an interpersonal life skills game (Burgess et al. 2011). Half of the violent games featured a Black character; the other half featured a White character. Likewise, half of the nonviolent games featured a Black character with the other half featuring a White character. After viewing the game videos, participants were asked to identify photos of violent objects (e.g., an axe, a sword) and nonviolent objects (e.g., a cell phone, a camera) as violent or nonviolent by pressing an appropriate computer key. Burgess found that participants took less time to label a violent object as violent when they had seen a violent game clip with a Black character, compared to when they had seen a violent game clip with a White character. Also, participants took more time to identify the nonviolent objects as nonviolent when they had seen a nonviolent video game with a Black character, compared to a nonviolent game with a White character. Burgess et al. (2011) interpreted these results as supporting the expectation that stereotype-consistent portrayals in a game (Black people with violence) primed unconscious stereotypes of Black people as violent. Priming of these stereotypes led to faster recognition of the violent objects. This finding is consistent with results from Implicit Association Tests (IAT) showing unconscious biases linking Black people with danger, crime, and violence (see Chapter 4, "Measures of Explicit and Implicit Prejudice"; also, Greenwald, Nosek, and Banaji 2003).

Yang et al. (2014) studied the effects of playing a violent game as a black or white avatar on Black stereotypes and aggression. Game developers can create realistic avatars that can differ in many dimensions, including race (Yang et al. 2014). Playing a game as an avatar increases involvement and character identification, thereby also increasing the probability of influence on the players (Hollingdale and Greitemeyer 2013). Yang et al. (2014) predicted that White college students who play a violent game as a black avatar will express more negative explicit and implicit biases toward Black people and will demonstrate more general aggression after playing compared to those who play the same violent game as a white avatar.

Yang et al. (2014) conducted two experiments to test this prediction. In Experiment 1, college student participants played a game (*Saints Row 2*) for twenty minutes as a Black or White avatar. Participants were randomly assigned to the Black and White avatar conditions. In the violent condition (randomly assigned), participants were told to break out of prison and kill as many guards as necessary. In the nonviolent condition (randomly assigned) participants were instructed to find a chapel in the city and that they should not hurt others in this search. After twenty minutes of game play, participants in all conditions took a Race IAT pairing White and Black males and females with positive words (e.g., wonderful, glorious, happy) or negative words (e.g., terrible, horrible, evil). This is the Race IAT implicit bias test discussed in Chapter 4 ("Measures of Explicit and Implicit Prejudice"). Participants also took the Symbolic Racism Scale (see Chapter 4) as a measure of explicit prejudice.

Results of Experiment 1 showed that participants who played the violent game as a black avatar had more explicit and implicit biases against Black people after playing the game compared to those who played the violent game as a white avatar. There were no differences in implicit and explicit bias scores for black and white avatar participants in the nonviolent game.

Experiment 2 randomly assigned college student participants to play a violent game as either a black or white male avatar. The violent games were *WWE Smackdown vs. RAW 2010* and *Fight Night Round 4*, both rated at the highest level of violence by the Entertainment Software Rating Board and by independent raters (Yang et al. 2014). The nonviolent game condition was not included in Experiment 2, because Experiment 1 found no effects of Black and White avatars in these games. After playing the violent games, participants completed the race-weapons IAT as a measure of implicit bias (see Chapter 4). They also completed a behavioral measure of aggression, which required them to assign a disfavored (spicy) food to a partner (actually, a confederate of the experimenters) with varying degrees of spiciness, which was the measure of aggression—the more spicy the assigned food, the more aggression.

Experiment 2 showed that participants who played the violent game as a Black avatar were more likely to unconsciously associate Black people with violent weapons as measured by the IAT, compared to participants who played as a White avatar. Also, participants who played as Black avatars, compared to those who played as White avatars, demonstrated more aggression after playing the violent games by prescribing spicier foods to their partners.

Yang et al. (2014) interpret these results as supporting predictions from priming and evaluative conditioning theories. Unconscious stereotypes of and biases towards Black people were primed and reinforced by playing violent games as a black avatar, resulting in their activation as explicit and unconscious stereotypes that were demonstrated in general aggression.

Effects of Gender Stereotypes in Video Games

Video games still portray women as "sex objects," less powerful and less competent than men and subordinate to men. Researchers have studied how these stereotypes might affect the perceptions of women in the real world by game players.

Behm-Morawitz and Mastro (2009) investigated the effects of sexualized female game characters on gender stereotyping and female self-concepts among college students. They randomly assigned their college student study participants to one of three conditions: 1) a violent video game with a sexualized female main character; 2) a violent video game with a non-sexualized female main character; and 3) a control condition with no video game. The video game used in the study was *Tomb Raider: Legend*, selected after pre-testing because it was a top seller, portrayed violence, and featured a female heroine (Lara Croft) who appeared in some scenes as a "sexualized" woman and in others as "non-sexualized." The sexualized Lara was portrayed with "large breasts and a small waist; and exposed skin in the stomach, chest and thigh regions" (Behm-Morawitz and Mastro 2009). The non-sexualized Lara wore winter clothing with little body exposure. The sexualized and non-sexualized versions of the video game differed only in how Lara was depicted. Pre-testing established that there were no differences in skills, weaponry, and actions in the video game scenes. After random assignment to the sexualized, non-sexualized, and control conditions, study participants played the game for thirty minutes; then answered a questionnaire measuring self-esteem (Rosenberg 1965), self-efficacy (Sherer et al. 1982), and attitudes toward women (Spence, Helmreich, and Stapp 1973). The authors defined self-esteem as estimations of self-worth and defined self-efficacy as the ability to accomplish goals and tasks. Attitudes towards women included the following components: appropriate dress (e.g., "Women should dress in a way that pleases and attracts men"); career/domestic work (e.g., "A woman's children should come before her career"); cognitive capabilities (e.g., Men are more rational than women); and physical capabilities (e.g., "Men are better at handling physical challenges than women") (Behm-Morawitz and Mastro 2009). The researchers predicted that female study participants who played the game with a sexualized female heroine (compared to female participants who played with a non-sexualized female heroine) will, after playing the game, have lower self-esteem and lower self-efficacy. Another prediction was that male and female participants who played the game with a sexualized heroine will report more stereotypical attitudes toward women (dress appropriately, home before career, less rational than men, less competent than men) compared to male and female participants who played the game with a non-sexualized female heroine. These predictions are based on social cognitive theory (we learn by observation) and priming theories (portrayals of women in games activate previously learned and stored stereotypes). Results of the study provide support for some of the predictions:

1. Female participants in the sexualized condition reported lower self-efficacy than female participants in the non-sexualized condition.
2. Male and female participants in the sexualized condition reported less favorable attitudes regarding women's cognitive abilities than male and female participants in the non-sexualized condition.
3. In the sexualized condition, male participants reported less favorable attitudes about how women should dress (e.g., to please men) compared to women participants.

These results provide some support for the expectation that stereotypical portrayals of women as sexual objects in games may influence self-evaluations of women and attitudes toward women by male and female players. Behm-Morawitz and Mastro (2009) suggest that positive effects of positive portrayals of women (e.g.,

Lara as competent, strong, in control) may be diminished when women are "hypersexualized." We should note that this study measured immediate effects after playing a game for thirty minutes. This limitation may explain why some of the predictions were not supported.

In addition to self-concepts and attitudes toward women, researchers are also interested in how sexualized portrayals of women in games affect violence toward women among game players. This line of research is guided by a General Aggression Model proposed by Anderson, Gentile, and Buckley in 2007. According to this model, we acquire "knowledge structures" or combinations of stereotypes that lead to a general impression of different "target" groups, including women. These structures are learned from a variety of sources, such as socialization agents (parents, family, peers, the media) and by observation (the cultural environment). Existing knowledge structures are reinforced by new information, such as stereotypical portrayals in the media and video games. For example, hypersexualized portrayals in video games can reinforce existing stereotypes that condone or foster violence toward women (e.g., weak, sex objects, not capable, vulnerable). These game portrayals may also prime or activate latent or subconscious stereotypes. In either case, the priming or reinforcement of existing stereotypes can lead to violence and aggression toward women. Of course, we don't tolerate demonstrations of violence and aggression in the laboratory even in the interest of scientific knowledge. Instead, we study opinions and attitudes toward violence and aggression assuming that they are valid indicators of actual behaviors, an assumption supported by theory (e.g., Anderson et al., 2007). Two such indicators are tolerance of sexual harassment and acceptance of the rape myth.

Dill, Brown, and Collins (2008) studied the effects of exposure to sexualized images of women in a video game on tolerance of sexual harassment and acceptance of the rape myth. They randomly assigned college student participants to two groups. One group (experimental) viewed a PowerPoint presentation that showed images of male and sexualized female characters from several games (*GTA: Vice City; GTA: San Andreas, Dead or Alive, Xtreme Beach Volleyball 2, BMX XXX, Saints Row, Resident Evil*, and *Gears of War*. The other (control) group saw press photos of current male and female US senators and congresspersons. Each group viewed thirty-two images for ten seconds per image. After viewing the images, participants filled out questionnaires measuring attitudes toward sexual harassment and rape.

Sexual harassment, according to Dill et al. (2008), can range from degrading remarks to unwanted sexual advances and sexual assault. In this study, male and female participants read an account of a real-life story about a male college professor's unwanted sexual advances toward his female student at a dinner party. Participants then answered a questionnaire that measured their evaluations of the incident (e.g., was it sexual harassment, a dangerous damaging offense?; did they express empathy for the victim?; did they blame the victim?; what punishment for the professor if act was sexual harassment). Rape supportive attitudes were measured by a twenty-item Sexual Beliefs Scale (Muehlenhard and Rodgers 1998), a general measure of attitudes toward violence against women. This scale has five subscales: Leading on Justifies Force, Token Refusals, Women Like Force, No Means Stop, and Men Should Dominate. Dill et al. predicted that participants who saw the sexualized images would report greater tolerance of sexual harassment and rape. Here are some results of the study:

1. Males who viewed the sexualized images reported greater tolerance for sexual harassment than males in the control group (who viewed images of politicians).
2. Females reported less tolerance for sexual harassment compared to males.
3. Tolerance for sexual harassment was greatest for males who saw the sexualized images, followed by males in the control group.
4. There was no difference in tolerance for sexual harassment between females who viewed the sexualized images and females who viewed the images of politicians.
5. Sexualized images did not affect tolerance for rape. There were no differences between men and women who viewed the sexualized images and men and women who viewed images of the politicians in their acceptance of rape.

Dill et al. provide some evidence that even short-term exposure to sexualized images of game characters can lead to greater tolerance for sexual harassment among men but not among women. There is no evidence that short-term exposure can lead to acceptance of the rape myth.

Dill et al. (2008) wanted to find out whether long-term exposure to violent games in general would lead to greater tolerance of sexual harassment and rape among male and female college students. They assumed, based on previous research, that violent games would include hypersexualized female characters. They asked participants to estimate how many hours per weekday and per weekend they played video games and what video games they played. The researchers then calculated a Violent Video Game Exposure (VVGE) index by adding the number of violent games played (action, first-person shooter, and fighting) and multiplying this number by hours played. Dill et al. found that there were significant negative correlations between the VVGE and disapproval of sexual harassment (r = −0.232) and between VVGE and rape-supportive attitudes (r = 0.239). There is some evidence, then, that long-term playing of violent games is related to greater tolerance of sexual harassment and rape-supportive attitudes. We should note that these correlations, though significant, are small, and we cannot be sure of the causal direction of effects. Does exposure lead to these attitudes, or do existing attitudes lead to more frequent playing of violent games? More research is called for to more clearly define these relationships.

Workbook

Define, describe, or illustrate the concepts; summarize the results of the studies:

1.   Video game sales, trends, regional growth

2.   Video game players: demographics, frequency

3.   Pathological video game players: Gentile et al. (2011)

4.   Stereotypes in video games: racial, gender

5.   Williams et al. (2009) (race)

6.   Burgess et al. (2011) (race)

7.   Labre and Duke (2004) (gender)

8.	Jansz and Martis (2007) (gender)

9.	Dill and Thill (2007) (gender)

10.	Violence in video games

11.	Anti-social content in video games

12.	Effects of video game stereotypes on players

13.	Theories: social cognitive theory; priming theories; evaluative conditioning theories

14.	Effects of racial stereotypes in video games: Burgess et al. (2011); Yang et al. (2014)

15.   Effects of gender stereotypes in video games: Behm-Morawitz and Mastro (2009); Dill, Brown, and Collins (2008)

16.   Positive effects of video games

11

Cyberbullying, Stereotypes, and Prejudice

As more children and teenagers use social media, bullying directed at vulnerable groups because they are "different" has also increased. Messages used to bully are expressions of prejudice, are often based on negative stereotyping of outgroups, and have harmful consequences including mental and emotional distress and even suicide. In this chapter, we take a look at victims and perpetrators of cyberbullying and consequence on perpetrators and victims.

Bullying and Cyberbullying

Cyberbullying is a form of bullying. Both are aggressive acts; victims and perpetrators share many similar characteristics; and the injurious consequences to victims are similar in scope and severity. But there are also differences in how the aggressive act is carried out, the environment in which it occurs, the anonymity of the perpetrators, and the ease with which the aggressive attacks can be spread among a large group of peers. To understand these similarities and differences, let's take a look at definitions commonly accepted by researchers.

Bullying is repeated acts of aggression by one or more perpetrators toward one victim who typically cannot defend himself/herself. Direct bullying includes physical and verbal acts such as kicking, hitting, threatening, name-calling, and insulting. Indirect bullying includes social isolation, such as ignoring, excluding, and "back-biting" (van der Wal, de Wit, and Hirasing, 2003.) Boys are more frequently perpetrators of direct bullying; indirect bullying is more frequent with girls (Whitney 1993). Bullying often occurs in schools and areas where victims and perpetrators are in direct contact with each other such as during field trips, athletic meets and other school-sponsored events (van der Wal et al. 2003).

Like bullying, cyberbullying is also an aggressive act intended to hurt a victim. Here are some definitions:

An aggressive, intentional act carried out by a group or individual using electronic forms of contact, repeatedly or over time against a victim who cannot easily defend him or herself. (Smith et al., 2008, 147)

Any behavior performed through electronic or digital media by individuals or groups that repeatedly communicate hostile or aggressive messages intended to inflict harm or discomfort on others. In cyberbullying experiences, the identity of the bully may or may not be known. Cyberbullying can occur through electronically mediated communication at school; however, cyberbullying behaviors commonly occur outside of school as well. (Tokunaga 2010)

These definitions suggest that cyberbullying, like bullying in general, are aggressive acts intended to harm a victim who is often defenseless. Kowalski et al. (2014) and Willard (2007) provide a taxonomy of specific acts included in cyberbullying:

- Flaming: abusive or abrasive language intended to provoke an "online fight" (Kowalski et al, 2014, 1074)
- Harassment: offensive messages repeatedly sent to a victim
- Outing and trickery: sharing personal information electronically about a victim without her/his consent
- Exclusion: isolating a victim by, for example, not including her/him in friends' lists, invitations
- Impersonation: posing as the victim and sending to others inappropriate, negative, or inaccurate information
- Cyberstalking: sending repetitive threatening messages
- Sexting: sending sexually explicit photos of the victim to others without her/his consent

While these acts of cyberbullying are aggressive and harmful, they do not include physical attacks associated with bullying in general. This is because bullying occurs when the perpetrator and victim are in direct contact with each other. Cyberbullying, on the other hand, uses electronic devices, such as mobile phones, tablets, and laptop computers to deliver bullying messages via the internet on social media sites, including Facebook, Twitter, and Instagram. Other forms of electronic communication used for cyberbullying are e-mail, instant messaging, online gaming, chat rooms, message boards, blogs, text messages, and digital images (Kowalski et al. 2014). This feature of cyberbullying—that it is accomplished in online communication without direct contact between perpetrator and victim—increases the probability of its occurrence and potential non-physical harm to victims. Some other features of cyberbullying are:

- Perceived anonymity: Unlike traditional bullying, cyberbullying promotes the perception by the perpetrator that he/she cannot be identified by the victim, authorities (e.g., school officials), parents, and peers. Perceived anonymity has two consequences (Kowalski et al. 2014). First, it increases the pool of potential aggressors. According to deindividuation theory (Postmes and Spears 1998), people say and do things anonymously that they would not say or do in face-to-face interactions when they can be identified. Some people may refrain from face-to-face bullying even if they wanted to engage in it, because of perceived punishments (disapproval from peers, sanctions from authorities, physical and psychological injury if the victim retaliates). These constraints are greatly minimized by the anonymity of cyberbullying. Therefore, a person who might not engage in face-to-face bullying might be tempted instead to cyberbully. A second consequence of anonymity is reduction of self-restraint by the perpetrator. In traditional bullying, the perpetrator can observe the harmful effects of his/her actions on the victim. Some aggressors may feel remorse and empathy for the victim, and therefore, cease his/her bullying (Sourander et al. 2010). Cyberbullying allows for less self-restraint, because the aggressor cannot immediately observe the effects of his/her actions on the victim. It is, therefore, more likely to continue and be repeated than face-to-face bullying (Sourander et al. 2010).
- Accessibility of the victim: Traditional bullying often occurs in school during the school day (Nansel et al. 2001). Cyberbullying can occur at any time of the day, seven days a week. Messages can be sent and received at home, in school, at work, in the mall. Victims, therefore, are more easily targeted.
- Reproducibility: Compared to traditional bullying, cyberbullying can reach a much larger audience. Messages can be easily reproduced and distributed with ease (Kowalski et al. 2014). Therefore, the potential for harm to the victim is also increased (e.g., spreading a rumor to hundreds of people).
- Permanence: Many online messages are stored and can remain online indefinitely until someone deletes them (Kowalski et al. 2014). Therefore, the potential for more lasting harm to the victim is also increased.
- Lack of accountability: Online messages are often uncontrolled without a moderator who can put a stop to aggressive or harmful interactions. In traditional bullying, bystanders may intervene. Therefore, cyberbullying is more likely to be repeated.

These unique features suggest that cyberbullying, compared to traditional bullying, has greater potential to harm victims, to be repeated, and to have a more lasting effect. (The exception is immediate physical harm, such as when a bully hits a victim.)

Social Media Use

Children and teenagers are heavy users of social media. They are also the perpetrators and victims of cyberbullying more often than adults.

The internet, mobile smartphones, home and school computers, and other digital devices have become the media of choice among school children and adolescents in the United States. Almost all of this demographic (youth) use the internet; 68% use the internet at school (Kowalski et al. 2014; Lenhart 2010). Also, school children and adolescents "spend an average of seventeen hours per week on the internet; some spend more than forty hours per week online" (Kowalski et al. 2014, 1074).

Frequency of Cyberbullying

Estimates of the frequency of cyberbullying range from 10–72%, depending on the duration and age of the victim. On the high side, Juvoven and Gross (2008) report that 72% of their youth sample said they were bullied online at least once in their life. They did not use "cyberbullying" in their questionnaire. Instead they asked their respondents whether anyone had done "mean things" on the internet "at least once" in their life. Therefore, their definition of cyberbullying is quite broad and did not specify the extent to which the aggressive behaviors were repeated.

Other studies that specifically measure the aggressive acts included in cyberbullying and that ask about repeated occurrences report lower estimates. Cox Communications (2009) reports that in their sample of 655 teenagers (ages 13 to17) 15% said they had been bullied online, 10% by cellphone; 7% said they had bullied online; and 5% by cellphone. Fight Crime: Invest in Kids (2006) reports that 17% of 6- to 10-year-olds and 36% of 12- to 17-year-olds had been cyberbullied in the past year. Aftab (2005) reports that 53% of adolescents in her sample reported being victims of cyberbullying.

Although these estimates vary, we can see that cyberbullying is prevalent among children and teenagers, including children as young as 6 to 10. This leads to the question, who among this group are most likely to be victims and who are most likely to be perpetrators?

Victims of Cyberbullying

In general, cyberbullying occurs when there is perceived power imbalance between victims and aggressors (Kowalski, Limber, and Agatston 2012). Aggressors feel that they have power over victims, because of perceptions of physical superiority (e.g., more attractive, stronger); social advantage (more popular, support from peers); psychological advantage (more competent in general); and technological advantage (more competent with new digital technologies) (Olweus 2013).

We can also analyze cyberbullying as aggression by members of in-groups directed at members of out-groups. Distinctions between in-groups and out-groups particularly among children and teenagers are often defined by who has power (in-groups) and who is different from the majority or from favored and popular groups because of race, ethnicity, sexual orientation, academic ability, social competency, or other easily identifiable physical, social, or psychological characteristics. Therefore, victims of cyberbullying are often also the victims of prejudice and negative stereotyping.

Cyberbullying victims are often victims of traditional bullying. In a nationally representative sample of school children, Ybarra, Diener-West, and Leaf (2007) found that 36% said they experienced bullying and cyberbullying at the same time. Juvonen and Gross (2008) reported that 85% of children and teenagers in their sample who said they were victims of cyberbullying also said that they had been victims of traditional bullying at school.

A 99% overlap between traditional bullying and cyberbullying was reported in a recent survey of 2,745 youth ages 11 to 16 in the United Kingdom (Wolke, Lee, and Guy 2017). Participants answered an electronic questionnaire that measured traditional and cyberbullying victimization, self-esteem, and emotional and behavioral problems. Only 1% said they were victims of cyberbullying only, without being victims of traditional bullying. Wolke et al. (2017) conclude that cyberbullying is mainly "a new tool to harm victims already bullied by traditional means" (1).

Considering the strong link between cyberbullying and traditional bullying (Didden et al. 2009), let's take a look at victims of traditional bullying who are also, most likely, victims of cyberbullying.

According to Vossekuil et al. (2004), the following groups of children and teenagers are most at risk of being bullied:

- Children who belong to a minority racial group
- Children with mental or physical disabilities
- Children who are overweight
- Gay, lesbian, or transgender children
- Children who don't "fit in"
- Children who have low self-confidence
- Children with few friends
- Children who are below average in size, strength, or coordination

A 2015 Dane County Youth Assessment (DCYA) survey (Dane County Youth Commission 2015) asked 21,558 youth in grades 7–12 whether they had been bullied or harassed in school. Bullying was defined by asking whether they "had been pushed, picked on, made fun of, or called names" in the past thirty days. Here are some of the results:

- 50.5% of middle schoolers (7–8 graders) reported being bullied in the last thirty days;
- 37.3% of high school students (9–12 graders) said they had been bullied in the last thirty days;
- 19% of all 7–12 graders said they had been bullied via the internet or text messaging in the past twelve months;
- Targets of bullying included lesbian, gay, bisexual, transgender, or queer (LGBTQ) (14.6%) and racial minority youth (15.8%)
- 7–12 graders said they were more likely to be bullied about "how they look" than about their race/ethnicity or perceived sexual orientation

The California Healthy Kids Survey (CHKS) asked 7–12 graders whether they had been targets of rumor spreading, physical and sexual harassment at school, and harassment related to how they "looked," how they talked, or "any other reason" in the past twelve months (California Healthy Kids 2007–2008). Here are some of the results: 10.2% reported sexual orientation harassment; 17.7% harassment based on race/ethnicity; 10% harassment based on religion or gender; and 6.5% harassment based on disability.

Some studies have specifically looked at victims of cyberbullying. Results support the conclusion that traditional and cyberbullying victims share many of the same characteristics indicative of being an "outgroup" member. In addition, these studies have also examined internet and mobile phone use, and psychological characteristics as predictors of cyberbullying victimization. Here are some results:

- Gender: some studies show that girls and boys are at equal risk of being victims of cyberbullying (e.g., Patchin and Hinduja 2012). Other researchers have reported higher percentages of victimization among girls than boys. Li (2007), for example, reports that that 60% of cyber victims in his sample were girls.
- Internet use: Most studies show a strong correlation between internet use and victimization. According to Ybarra (2004), the most significant predictors of cyberbullying victimization among girls are frequency of internet use in general and use of instant messaging (IM) programs. Among boys, a significant predictor is internet use. Similar findings are reported by Patchin and Hinduja (2006). Youth who participate frequently in online activities are more likely to be victims of cyberbullying. Additionally, Juvonen and Gross (2008) found that frequency of use of IM and webcams increase the likelihood of victimization. It is not surprising that internet use and participation in online activities predict the likelihood of victimization, considering that cyberbullying occurs online. We can't be sure, however, whether variables that predict internet use and online participation are the underlying causes of cyberbullying victimization. Therefore, researchers have also examined some psychological characteristics as possible causes of both frequent internet use and cyberbullying victimization.
- Psychological characteristics: Patchin and Hinduja (2006) report that 42.5% of the cyberbullying victims in their sample were "frustrated"; 40% felt "angry"; and 27% felt "sad." Ybarra (2004) found that males in his sample who reported major depression symptoms were eight times more likely to report being victims of cyberbullying. Juvonen and Gross (2008) found that youth in their sample who reported being socially anxious were more likely to be victims.

We can see from these studies that frequency of internet use and participation in online activities are related to frequency of victimization. We can also see that the likelihood of being a victim is related to certain psychological states. However, we should be careful in interpreting the direction of causality. For obvious ethical reasons, we cannot manipulate cyberbullying and negative psychological states in the laboratory. Researchers depend on surveys and self-reports for their data. Therefore, the time order of occurrence of cyberbullying, internet use, and psychological states cannot be easily determined. It's quite possible that the psychological states associated with victimization are the results rather than causes of cyberbullying. A possible explanation for these relationships is that outgroup members (youth who "don't fit in") are visible targets for traditional and cyberbullying. They experience stress and negative psychological states which are exacerbated by victimization. So, unless broken by interventions, it is a dangerous circle.

Perpetrators of Cyberbullying

Like perpetrators of prejudice, negative stereotyping, and related discriminatory behaviors, perpetrators of traditional and cyberbullying see their victims as less powerful, not fitting in, and as visible members of outgroups. Perpetrators perceive themselves to be more powerful, fitting in and as members of in-groups. Additionally, cyberbullying perpetrators have the following characteristics:

Gender: Sourander et al. (2010) report that boys are more likely than girls to be cyberbullies and girls are more likely to be victims. Girls are targeted more than boys in email; boys are victims more often in text messaging.

Motives: Some research shows that anger and retaliation are motivations to cyberbully. Youth who have been victims of traditional bullying or cyberbullying retaliate by being aggressors themselves (e.g., Kowalski, Morgan, and Limber 2013). Other motivations for aggressors are to demonstrate technological skill, for fun, or to feel powerful (Gradinger, Strohmeir, and Spiel 2010).

Psychological States: Cyberbullies score higher than youth who don't cyberbully in tests of depression and anxiety and lower on tests of self-esteem (Kowalski and Limber 2012). Compared to youth not involved in internet harassment, cyberbullies report lower grades and more problems with concentration; have lower school commitment; and dislike school more (Kowalski and Limber 2013). Some researchers suggest that depression, anxiety, and low self-esteem may lead to negative attitudes toward school and poorer academic performance (Kowalski et al 2014). Many of these psychological states have been observed for victims as well, and it's not clear whether they are causes or consequences of cyberbullying.

Moral Justification: Cyberbullies, like perpetrators of traditional bullying and other aggressive acts, are more likely than non-aggressors and victims to reframe their actions as less harmful and to blame the victim. The aggressor, therefore, rationalizes his/her behavior by not taking responsibility, by minimizing potential harm, and by ascribing to the victim traits or behaviors that justify the aggression (e.g., Lazuras et al. 2013). Considering the perceived anonymity of cyberbullying and the absence of physical contact between aggressor and victim, cyberbullies are more likely than victims and perpetrators of traditional bullying to use moral justification for their actions.

Dysfunctional Behaviors: Cyberbullies are more likely than youth not involved in online harassment to report a number of dysfunctional or maladaptive behaviors such as alcohol and tobacco use, damaging school property, truancy, poor grades, and fighting (e.g., Kowalski et al. 2014). Victims of cyberbullying also demonstrate many of these behaviors. One explanation is that victims often become aggressors themselves as a form of retaliation. Another explanation is that these behaviors are the result of victimization rather than causes or that the relationship is bi-directional.

Parental Involvement: Compared to youth who do not harass others on the internet, cyberbullies have poorer relations with their parents. They trust their parents less, are less likely to discuss problems with their parents and they have fun with their parents less frequently. Also, their online activities are monitored less frequently by their parents or caregivers (Ybarra and Mitchell 2004). The prospect of punishment is a deterrent to cyberbullying. Hinduja and Patchin (2013) report that youth who said their parents monitored their online activities were less likely to be aggressors.

The picture that emerges of the cyberbully is one of troubled youth with low self-esteem, angry and likely to be depressed, with psychological states that may lead to a dislike of school and related behavioral problems. Parental control is an important deterrent to online aggression. Many of these characteristics have also been observed among victims of cyberbullying, so we can't be sure whether they are causes or effects of online aggression.

Effects of Cyberbullying on Victims

Kowalski et al. (2014) have developed a General Aggression Model (GAM) that identifies the effects of cyberbullying on victims and explains how a victim might become a perpetrator. In this model, personal and situational factors (discussed in the preceding section) might lead to victimization of a boy or girl. If you recall, personal factors include perceptions that the victim is "different." Situational factors include lack of parental control and trust. The initial online encounter with a bully creates worry, stress, and anxiety in the victim, negative psychological states exacerbated by repeated bullying. These negative states lead to maladaptive behaviors, such as drug and alcohol use, school absenteeism, and revenge by traditional or cyberbullying.

Several studies provide support for GAM predictions. Repeated victimization is associated with an increased risk of depression, loneliness, thoughts about suicide, decreased self-esteem, poor physical health and increased likelihood of self-injury. Behavioral effects include poor school performance, increased likelihood of aggression and increased likelihood of retaliation (e.g., Kowalski et al.; 2014, van der Wal 2003; Tokunga 2010). Considering that most of these studies include children and teens in large samples from the US and other countries (e.g., the Netherlands, the United Kingdom, Canada, Japan, Norway, Spain, Germany), we can conclude that cyberbullying is certainly a health hazard affecting large numbers of youths around the world.

Interventions to Reduce Bullying

Interest in reducing or preventing bullying and cyberbullying has prompted the implementation and assessment of interventions in many countries including the US (US Department of Health and Human Services 2006). These interventions include peer support systems, school tribunals, curriculum development, and school-wide policies prohibiting bullying (Smith, Ananiadou, and Cowie 2003). Interventions that involve youth participation (peer support systems, peer tribunals) and education (curriculum development) are generally more effective than school policy alone (Smith et al. 2003.)

Peer support systems encourage interventions by the majority of students in the classroom who do not approve of bullying. These activities include student-led discussion of relationship issues such as anger, fighting, and bullying; identification of friends who provide support to bullying victims; and "school watch," in which students elect a committee to propose and implement anti-bullying activities (Smith et al. 2003.)

Curriculum development includes discussion of bullying in the classroom with a focus on consequences, empathy building, active listening, internet literacy, and rules to deal with bullying.

Smith et al. (2003) provide an extensive review of these interventions. They conclude that, for maximum effectiveness, interventions should involve the school, students, and parents.

Workbook

Define, describe, or illustrate the concepts; summarize the results of the studies:

1.   Video game sales, trends, regional growth

2.   Video game players: demographics, frequency

3.   Pathological video game players: Gentile et al. (2011)

4.   Stereotypes in video games: racial, gender

5.   Williams et al. (2009) (race)

6.   Burgess et al. (2011) (race)

7.   Labre and Duke (2004) (gender)

8.   Jansz and Martis (2007) (gender)

9.   Dill and Thill (2007) (gender)

10.   Violence in video games

11.   Anti-social content in video games

12.   Effects of video game stereotypes on players

13.   Theories: social cognitive theory; priming theories; evaluative conditioning theories

14.   Effects of racial stereotypes in video games: Burgess et al. (2011); Yang et al. (2014)

15. Effects of gender stereotypes in video games: Behm-Morawitz and Mastro (2009); Dill, Brown and Collins (2008).

16. Positive effects of video games

12

Hate in Social Media

A s the internet continues to revolutionize how people communicate with each other, share information, and develop and reinforce social relationships, it has also been increasingly used to promote hate and to threaten individuals and groups. The frequency of posts and websites on the internet promoting hate has not gone unnoticed by researchers, advocacy groups for minority groups who are often targeted, and policy makers. Here's how Christopher Wolf, immediate past chair of the International Network Against Cyber Hate, described the problem of hate on the internet:

> From cyberbullying to terrorists' use of the Internet to recruit and incite, Internet hate speech is a serious problem. The most notorious hate crimes of late ... were committed by individuals who used the Internet to spread hate and to receive reinforcement from like-minded haters, who made hatred seem normal and acceptable.
>
> (Quoted in Hudson and Ghani 2017, 1)

In this chapter, we will discuss why and how the internet—particularly social media—has been used by racists, misogynists, xenophobes, terrorists and other extremist groups on the fringes of society to communicate their views, recruit followers, harass others, and plan attacks on communities and other people. We will also discuss strategies to mitigate the effects of online hate shown to be effective by recent research.

Defining Hate Speech

In the United States, hate speech is defined as speech that "attacks a person or group on the basis of attributes such as race, religion, ethnic origin, national origin, sex, disability, sexual orientation, or gender identity" (ElSherief 2018). Attacks are defined as threats of physical or emotional harm, insults, and in general, expressions of hostility. In Europe, hate speech is similarly defined as" an expression of hostility towards individuals or social groups based on their perceived group membership, which can refer to their race, ethnicity, nationality, religion, disability, gender or sexual orientation" (Bojarska 2019, 2). The Council of Europe (1997) provides an elaboration, defining hate speech as " all forms of expression which spread, incite, or promote or justify racial hatred, xenophobia, antisemitism, or other forms of hatred based on intolerance, including intolerance expressed by aggressive nationalism and ethnocentrism, discrimination and hostility against minorities, migrants and people of immigrant origin" (as cited in Bojarska 2019, p.2). The US and European definitions are similar, identifying groups targeted and expressions of hate.

In the US hate speech on the internet is protected by the First Amendment equivalent to protection of other media such as print. For example, online hate speech is protected as much as a Ku Klux Klan pamphlet promoting hate (Hudson and Ghani 2017). The exception to protection of online hate speech is "incitement to imminent lawless action or true threats", which receives no protection (Hudson and Ghani 2017, 2). Unprotected "true threats" are defined as:

> True threats encompass those statements where the speaker means to communicate a serious expression of an intent to commit an act of unlawful violence to a particular individual or group of individuals. The speaker need not actually intend to carry out the threat. Rather, a prohibition on true threats protects individuals from the fear of violence and from the disruption that fear engenders, in addition to protecting people from the possibility that the threatened violence will occur.
>
> (US Supreme Court, in *Virginia vs. Black, 2003* as quoted in Hudson and Ghani 2018, 2)

Most online hate speech is protected unless the "true threat" standard is met, in which case, the hate speech is likely unprotected. In Germany, online hate speech which "incites hatred" is a punishable criminal offense liable to imprisonment from three to five years (Bojraska 2019). Incitement to hatred is defined as speech that:

1. "incites hatred against a national, racial, religious group or a group defined by their ethnic origins, against segments of the population or individuals because of their belonging to one of the aforementioned groups or segments of the population or calls for violent or arbitrary measures against them; or
2. assaults the human dignity of others by insulting, maliciously maligning an aforementioned group, segments of the population or individuals because of their belonging to one of the aforementioned groups or segments of the population, or defaming segments of the population." (German Criminal Code, as quoted in Bojarska 2019, 2)

Hate speech, then, is defined similarly in the US and Europe. Targets identified are minority groups generally marginalized and with less power. Hate speech includes verbal and visual expressions that are threatening, incite to violence or generally promote hostility. Online hate speech in the US is protected as a First Amendment right unless the speech is a "true threat". In Germany, "incitement to hatred" in hate speech is a criminal offense punishable by imprisonment.

Why the Internet Is an Instrument of Hate

Social Media Use: The internet has taken the place of traditional media and interpersonal communication as the primary way in which people share information and interact with each other. According to the PEW Research Center (2019), 73% of U.S. adults say they use YouTube; 69% say they use Facebook. Use of other online platforms are less: Instagram, 37%; Pinterest, 28%; Linkedin, 27%; Snapshot, 24%; Twitter, 22%; WhatsApp, 20%; and Reddit, 11%. Snapchat and Instagram are popular among young people (18 to 24); Facebook is popular among older people (50 and older). The majority of Facebook, Snapchat and Instagram users of all ages visit these sites daily.

Online Disinhibition Effect: People are more likely to express hate or threaten others on the internet because of disinhibition, which is the reduction of anxiety that would normally, in face-to-face interactions, prevent us from engaging in hateful and threatening language and behaviors. Anxiety is reduced because of the following characteristics of internet communication (Bojarska 2019):

- Anonymity: Both the aggressor and target of hate on the internet can be anonymous. Anonymity allows users to create an alternate identity with a pseudonym or username, which makes it easier for them to express hostility and aggression because they think they "can't be caught." With anonymity, it's also easier to deny ownership and responsibility for aggressive words and actions.

- Online communication can be asynchronous, that is, sending and receipt of the message does not occur at the same time as in face-to-face communication. Therefore, aggressors do not see the effects on targets of their words and actions concurrently with or immediately after communication. It's more difficult to assess the damaging consequences, and therefore easier to disregard or minimize these consequences.
- Online communication, even when not anonymous, is "invisible"—the actors do not occupy the same physical space. Eye contact and other non-verbal cues are not visible. By contrast, face-to-face communication allows for immediate evaluation of communication by observation of body language, tone of voice, and gaze. Invisible online communication is a barrier to understanding and empathy, and can make it easier and less stressful for users to be aggressive.

These characteristics of online communication explain why the internet is often used as an instrument of hate. Most people do not express hate, threaten, and insult other people because the targets may retaliate, other people may express disapproval, and confrontational encounters may result in stress. Online communication minimizes these deterrents, resulting in hateful and uncivil aggression towards vulnerable targets.

Why the Internet Can Be Effective in Spreading and Reinforcing Hate

Hate is spread on the internet because of its networked structure of connections, making it easy for any individual or group to publish content in blogs, online forums and websites worldwide and in a short period of time (MediaSmarts, Canada 2019). Hate messages spread between online platforms and traditional media outlets that overlap each other in ideology, then to other mainstream media. For example, hate messages and ideas from White supremacist forums find their way easily from alt-right Twitter and YouTube personalities, to conservative TV commentators and to mainstream TV news (MediaSmarts, Canada 2019). Some mainstream media consider as newsworthy the fact that topics, events, ideas and actions are being discussed on social media, and will report them. As a consequence, a small number of people or a few organizations can increase their reach and influence, therefore moving fringe ideas into the mainstream, reinforcing followers and reaching potential converts. As technology columnist Farhad Manjoo put it:

> "extreme points of views ... that couldn't have been introduced into national discussion in the past are being introduced now by this sort of entry mechanism ... people put it on blogs, and then it gets picked up by cable news, and then it becomes a national discussion" (as quoted in MediaSmarts, Canada 2019).

The migration of hate speech from the internet to traditional media may be inadvertent or unplanned. However, extremist groups have become skilled in extending their reach and influence. Here are some strategies they use (MediaSmarts, Canada 2019):

- Casting arguments in non-extremist but provocative language to attract mainstream audiences, people who are not supporters but who may be willing to "hear the other side." Examples of terminology used by hate groups are "race realism" for biological race (proven by science to have no validity), which then can lead to distorted justification for racial hate and prejudice; "skepticism," suggesting that any information from mainstream media should be doubted, and that mainstream media "suppress the real truth," which the hate groups claim to provide; "atheism," which suggests a suspension of belief or neutrality, which can lead to ideas supporting hate (such as misogyny and Holocaust denial).
- Replacing well-known slurs with acronyms or "in-joke" equivalents to avoid filters, such as "Google" and "Skype" as substitutes for racist and anti-Semitic slurs. (Please read the section in this chapter on racist acronyms and symbols.)

- Appropriating behaviors accepted by mainstream cultures and using them to communicate hate. Examples are drinking milk and making the OK sign.

These strategies used by hate groups explain why hate can easily be spread on the internet to reach supporters, potential converts and even mainstream audiences. Trickery is involved to reach the vulnerable including teens and even pre-teens.

An unintended effect of algorithms used by search engines is the progression from seemingly harmful search terms to hate websites, blogs, and forums. MediaSmarts (2019) gives this example: Anderson Cooper, CNN anchor, asked David Hogg, a survivor of the Parkland school shooting murders who has become a gun control advocate, about rumors that he was a crisis actor paid to take part in the "fake" shootings. After the interview, searches of the term "crisis actor" led to content supporting the conspiracy theory.

Online Interpersonal Aggression

Hate speech on the internet directed at targeted individuals is interpersonal aggression. These acts and expressions include hateful speech such as the use of slurs; physical threats; harassment (repeated assaults on character, behaviors, beliefs), and doxxing (revealing private information). These attacks use social media and other platforms, including Facebook, Twitter and YouTube). (Note: Online hate is also discussed in this book's chapter on cyberbullying.)

A 2019 survey of adult Americans by the Anti-Defamation League (reported by *USA Today*, Guynn 2019) showed that:

- More than half (53%) reported that they were subjected to online hateful speech and harassment.
- Thirty-seven percent reported "severe attacks" including sexual harassment and stalking.
- About 33% of online abuse targeted sexual orientation, religion, race, ethnicity, gender, or disability.
- Frequent targets of hate speech were LGBTQ people (63% reporting being targets); Muslims (35%); Hispanics or Latinos (30%); African Americans (27%); Asian Americans (20%); and Jews (16%). Twenty-four percent of women and 15% of men reported being targets.
- Harassment took place on Facebook (56%), Twitter (19%), YouTube (17%), Instagram (16%), WhatsApp (13%), reddit (11%), and Snapchat (10%).

Over half (53%) of Americans experienced some type of online harassment in 2019. This is higher than the 41% reported to a comparable question asked in 2017 by the Pew Research Center. More severe forms of harassment were also commonly experienced—with 37% of American adults reporting such an experience, up from 18% in 2017. According to Adam Neufield, ADL's vice president of innovation and strategy, "This is an epidemic and it has been far too silent" (as quoted by Guynn, *USA Today* 2019).

Who Are the Hate Groups Using the Internet?

Hate groups use the internet to validate their beliefs and ideologies, reinforce followers and recruit new members. Common platforms are hate websites, social networks, blogs, newsgroups, YouTube and other video sites. In 2009, the Simon Wiesenthal Center (SWC) identified more than 10,000 hate and terrorist websites and postings. In 2019, hate groups have used a new generation of social media platforms as well as popular gaming platforms to advocate and reinforce racism, anti-Semitism and bigotry. These platforms include Alt. Tech which serves the Alt-Right; video games like Fortight; and gaming platforms like Steam (SWC 2019 Digital Terrorism and Hate Report Card).

Definitions of hate groups: Several civil rights organizations and the FBI have defined and identified hate groups. Here are some examples:

- Anti-Defamation League (2019): "An organization whose goal and activities are primarily or substantially based on a shared antipathy towards people of one or more other different races, religions, ethnicities/nationalities/national origins, genders, and/or sexual identities. The mere presence of bigoted members in a group or organization is typically not enough to qualify it as a hate group; the group itself must have some hate-based orientation or purpose" (p.3).
- Southern Poverty Law Center (2017): "An organization that—based on its official statements or principles, the statements of its leaders or activities—has beliefs or practices that attack or malign an entire class of people, typically for their immutable characteristics. We do not list individuals as hate groups, only organizations. The organizations on our hate group list vilify others because of their race, religion, ethnicity, sexual orientation or gender identify ...." (2)
- Federal Bureau of Investigation (2019): "A hate group's primary purpose is to promote animosity, hostility, and malice against persons belonging to a race, religion, disability, sexual orientation, or ethnicity/national origin which differs from that of the members of the organization" (2).

Hate groups, according to these definitions, demean and vilify other groups by assigning negative traits to them, thereby placing members of the target groups in a category of "inferior" human beings because of group membership. Target groups are generally minority groups in a society because they are numerically in the minority or because they do not share in the power and resources available to others. Targets of hate groups include racial, ethnic, and religious minorities as well as sexual identity and gender minorities. The vilification takes the form of verbal and symbolic attacks, often on the internet. Although violence is not a requirement for a group to be labeled as a hate group, hate ideologies often lead to violence, and some hate groups openly advocate for violence to achieve their goals. Here are some categories of hate groups as defined by the Anti-Defamation League (2019):

- White Supremacists: These groups subscribe to an ideology that include one or more of the following beliefs: "1) whites should have dominance over people of other backgrounds, especially where they may co-exist; 2) whites should live by themselves in a whites-only society; 3) white people have their own 'culture' that is superior to other cultures; 4) white people are genetically superior to other people; 5) the white race is in danger of extinction due to a rising 'flood' of non-whites who are controlled and manipulated by Jews, and that imminent action is needed to 'save' the white race."

  Traditional white supremacists include the Ku Klux Klan, the Council of Conservative Citizens, the League of the South, and others (see hate map by ideology from the Southern Poverty Law Center later in this chapter,)
- Alt-Right: Short for "alternative right," alt-right, according to the ADL (2019) "is a segment of the white supremacist movement consisting of a loose network of racists and anti-Semites who reject mainstream conservatism in favor of politics that embrace implicit or explicit racism, anti-Semitism and white supremacy. The alt right also includes many racist users of image boards and message forums such as 4chan, 8chan and Reddit" (3).
- Christian Identity: According to the ADL, Christian Identity is "one of the longstanding segments of the white supremacist movement." Many of its followers believe that people of European ancestry are descendants of the "Lost Tribes" of ancient Israel and are therefore the chosen people of God; that "non-whites were created by God not when God made 'man' but when he created the 'beasts in the field'"; that non-whites are "mud people"; and that "Jews are descended from Satan through a sexual liaison between Eve and the serpent." The ADL says that "Christian Identity followers are not Christian fundamentalists, who strongly oppose their views" (2).
- Neo-Nazis: According to the ADL, "one of the main segments of the white supremacist movement. ... They revere Adolf Hitler and Nazi Germany and sometimes try to adopt some Nazi principles to their own times and geographic locations" (5).

- White Nationalism: According to the ADL, it is a euphemism for white supremacy which also "emphasizes defining a country or region by white racial identity and which seeks to promote the interests of whites exclusively, typically at the expense of people of other backgrounds" (6).

The Southern Poverty Law Center (SPLC) places hate groups in categories according to ideology and identifies state chapters affiliated or supporting the ideology of the larger group. In 2019, the SPLC identified over 1,000 hate groups in the United States, the highest number in twenty years. White nationalist groups increased from 100 in 2017 to 148 in 2018, the most significant increase of any hate group. Although most of the groups listed by the SPLC are white supremacist groups, anti-Semitic groups, and anti-people of color groups, some are anti-White groups. Here is a partial listing of hate groups in 2019 from the SPLC with some examples of listed groups. For a complete list and reasons for a group being on the list, go to **www.splcenter. org.hate-map**

- Anti-Immigrant (17): Center for Immigration Studies (Washington, DC); Federation for American Immigration Reform (Washington, DC); Mountain Minutemen (Tecate, California); Oregonians for Immigration Reform (Salem, Oregon); Respect Washington (Seattle, Washington)
- Anti-LGBT (49): American College of Pediatricians (Gainesville, Florida); American Family Association (Pennsylvania and Mississippi); Center for Family and Human Rights (Washington, DC, and New York, New York); Family Research Council (Washington, DC); Mass Resistance (Colorado, Texas, California and Massachusetts)
- Anti-Muslim: ACT for America (47 states); American Freedom Alliance (Los Angeles, California); Bomb Islam (Phoenix, Arizona); Center for Security Policy (Washington, DC); Soldiers of Odin (10 states)
- Black Nationalists (264): According to the SPLC, "Black nationalist groups have always been a reaction to white racism. These groups are typified by their anti-semitic, anti-LGBT, anti-white rhetoric and conspiracy theories. They should not be confused with mainstream black activist groups such as Black Lives Matter and others that work to eliminate systemic racism in American society and its institutions" (6). Great Millstone (21 states); Israel United in Christ (44 states); Nation of Islam (76 states)
- Christian Identity (17): American Promise Ministries (Sandpoint, Idaho); Our Place Fellowship (Colville, Washington); Christian America Ministries (Greensburg, Louisiana)
- General Hate (127): American Guard (17 states); Pacific Northwest Wolfpack Kindred (statewide, Washington); Patriot Movement AZ (Litchfield Park, Arizona); Proud Boys (44 states)
- Ku Klux Klan (51); various names (50 states and , Washington, DC)
- Neo-Nazi (112): Aryan Nations Sadistic Souls (6 states); Atomwaffen Division (27 states); National Socialist Movement (6 states); The Daily Stormer (22 states)
- Racist Skinhead (63): Blood and Honour (10 states); Hammerskins (11 states); Vinlanders Social Club (5 states)
- White Nationalist (148): American Freedom Party (10 states); Identity Evropa, also known as American Identity Movement (30 states); Patriot Front (16 states); The Right Stuff (30 states)

These are some of the hate groups in the United States identified by the SPLC. Not all of them advocate violence (although some do). They all advocate and promote hate towards identified target groups. Individuals may identify with or approve of some of the beliefs of a group, but may not belong to it. The SPLC identifies a group as an "entity that has a process through which followers identify themselves as being part of the group. This may involve donating, paying membership dues or participating in activities such as meetings and rallies" (2019, 7). The FBI (2019) notes that the US Constitution protects the people's right to have radical beliefs, which includes agreement with the actions or ideologies of violent hate and extremist groups. However, it is illegal to seriously plan to carry out an act of violence, or to strongly push someone to do so. According to the FBI (2019), violence against certain groups, the government, and innocent people to advance their (hate group) ideology is a crime.

How Do Hate Groups Use the Internet?

Hate groups use the internet just like mainstream advertisers and organizers to recruit new followers and to reinforce and solidify support. According to the FBI (2019) here are some of the internet tools often used by hate groups.

- Online forums and chat rooms: Violent extremists and hate groups find many new recruits in these sites. Young people, in particular, are vulnerable. Hate groups talk about topics that interest potential converts, sometimes in secret spaces only for members. Hate groups infiltrate these spaces and look for participants who might be open to their beliefs.
- Internet games: Some internet games promote violence and aggression towards people targeted by hate groups. In some games, a player may have to "kill a world leader or destroy a certain country and its citizens. High scoring players may be referred to violent extremist recruiters) (FBI 2019, 1; **https:// fbi.gov/cue508/teen-website/how**).
- Social networking: According to the FBI (2019), "violent extremists have joined the many popular social networking sites that let you share pictures and personal information. On these sites, extremists create false profiles and look for people who are vulnerable to recruitment." Violent extremists and hate groups also "spread propaganda on these sites through videos, pictures, and messages that glorify their causes" (1).
- Apps: The FBI (2019) reports that violent extremists and hate groups "are now using smartphone applications, or apps, that keep a person's identity and conversations totally private." On these apps, "violent extremists may ask for money or share secret information. They may even start fake romances to trick teens into traveling to other countries to join them" (2).
- Cell phones: According to the FBI (2019), many violent extremists (and hate groups) use cell phones to convince people to support or join them. After initial contact, they send emails and texts to support their beliefs and agendas.

The FBI (2019) is concerned with conversion to extremist ideologies (beliefs) and resulting violent actions. The agency outlines a process of conversion. Although primarily used to explain the conversion process to extremist ideology and violence, the process applies also to conversion to hate group ideologies. The first step is *immersion*, in which a person, through social media or other contact, becomes very interested in the beliefs (ideology) and objectives of the group, which may involve violence. The individual does additional research—often online. Information acquired from biased sources online (most likely to be accessed with key words linked to the group's ideology) reinforce initial information and contacts. The second step is *identification*. The person begins to accept the group's ideology and is often isolated from other people or information that may counter the ideology. The third step is *indoctrination*. The individual identifies with the group and its ideology and may be ready for action. At this stage additional personal contact is made with group members, and this identification is reinforced.

These processes and tools identified by the FBI apply not only to violent extremist groups but to hate groups in general. Here are a few examples from the Carnegie-Knight News21 initiative at Arizona State University (Gardner, 2018) of how internet platforms, social media in particular, have recently been used by hate groups to promote their beliefs and to recruit followers for their activities:

- David Duke, former Grand Wizard of the Ku Klux Klan, "sometimes tweets more than 30 times a day to nearly 50,000 followers." In a tweet, he recently called for the "chasing down of specific black Americans" and claimed "the LGBTQ community is in need of 'intensive psychiatric treatment'" (Gardner, 1).
- When families were being separated at the US–Mexico border, James Allsup, a white nationalist leader, compared the separations to Jewish people during the Holocaust and called parents "deadbeat parents." On Facebook, he posted a photo of migrant children behind a fence with the caption, "They present it like it's a bad thing" (Gardner, 1).

- News21 reports that on "Gab, a censorship-free alternative to Twitter, former 2018 candidate for U.S. Senate Patrick Little, claims ovens are a means of preserving the Aryan race" (Gardner, 1).
- Billy Roper, a leader of neo-Nazis, posted "Let God Burn Them," an acronym for Lesbian Gay Bisexual Transgender (Gardner, 2). In response to immigrant families being separated at the US–Mexico border, he posted, "#KeepFamiliesTogether Deport them all, along with any who support them. With a catapult" (Gardner 2018, 4).

Although hateful posts on the internet are often by known leaders of hate groups, many posts are also from followers. In 2018, News21, the Carnegie-Knight initiative at Arizona State University, monitored the daily social media activity of users belonging to hate groups, including white nationalists and Neo-Nazis. They tracked more than three million followers and recorded and compiled more than 2,500 posts from platforms such as Twitter, Facebook, Gab, and VK. News21 found that about half of the posts were directed at Latinos, Black American Muslims, Jewish people, LGBTQ members, and women. Most of the posts denigrated members of the target groups. For example, some posts described gays as "ill." Others referred to Black Americans as "chimps" and "sh*tskins." In a two-week period, the 2,500 posts were shared nearly 200,000 times and generated more than half a million likes (Gardner 2018, 3).

Besides social media and other web platforms, hate groups use advertising to promote their ideologies, to reinforce followers, and to recruit members. CNN (2018) reported that YouTube ran ads from more than 300 companies in July, 2018. These ads included some that promoted white nationalists, pedophilia, conspiracy theories and North Korean propaganda (CNN 2018).

In response to the proliferation of hate messages, many social media companies have banned or suspended users, and have deleted messages from their platforms. These companies include Facebook, Twitter, Spotify, Squarespace, PayPal, GoDaddy, YouTube, and others. Hate groups have responded by using coded language and symbols and using neutral-sounding identities and language to conceal hateful rhetoric from human censors and from algorithms developed by companies to screen messages. Hate group followers recognize the coded terminology and symbols. This recognition allows followers to communicate with each other, plan activities, reinforce beliefs, and, in general, to build community.

The Anti-Defamation League (2019) has catalogued coded acronyms, slogans, and symbols used by hate groups to conceal their hate messages (https://www.adl.org/education-and-resources/resource-knowledge-base/hate-symbols). Here are some examples. For a complete list, please see the link above to the ADL website.

- **14 Words:** "We must secure the existence of our people and a future for white children."
- **Anti-racist:** code for ani-White
- **Anudda Shoah:** anti-Semitic phrase to mock Jews; claims that Jews bring up the Holocaust "when confronted with anything they don't like"
- **Day of the Rope:** refers to mass murders of "race traitors" as in the novel *The Turner Diaries* by neo-Nazi William Pierce; used to urge or promise "some similar scenario in the real world"
- **ROA:** "Race Over All"
- **Seig Heil:** "Hail Victory," Nazi slogan
- **SWP:** "Supreme White Power"
- **WPWW:** "White Pride World Wide"
- **You Will Not Replace Us**
- **ZOG:** "Zionist Occupied Government" (US government is controlled by Jews)
- **100%:** "100% White"
- **13/52; 13/90:** used by White supremacists to refer to African Americans as "savage" and "criminal"; claim that Blacks make up 13% of the US population but commit 52% of all murders and 90% of all violent crime (author's note: these claims are shown by FBI statistics to be not true)
- **18:** "Adolf Hitler" (1=A; 8=H)

- **33:** Ku Klux Klan (KKK)
- **88:** "Heil Hitler"
- **ACAB:** "All Cops Are Bastards"
- **AKIA:** "A Klansman I Am"
- **AIM:** American Identity Movement (formerly Identity Evropa)
- **AYAK:** "Are You A Klansman?"
- **FGRN:** "For God, Race and Nation"; common Klan slogan
- **GTKRWN:** "Get the Kikes: Race War Now"; Klan slogan
- **KABARK:** "Konstantly Applied By All Regular Klansmen"; used as a sign-off in online messages by Klan members
- **RAHOWA:** "Racial Holy War"
- **ORION:** "Our Race Is Our Nation"
- **SWP:** "Supreme White Power"

Consequences of Hate in Social Media

Given its reach, hate in social media can have harmful consequences at different levels (Bojarska 2019). At the community or societal level, hate speech can incite violence toward target groups by reinforcing collective or group hate towards members of these groups. Followers and supporters of hate groups may feel emboldened to act on their beliefs because online hate speech in "echo chambers" (forums and platforms that reinforce beliefs) provide "validation" and social support (albeit from like-minded people). At the individual level, hate speech can lead to chronic stress, mistrust, and other hostile attitudes among members of target groups. Also, online hate can deter people from raising objections because of the perception that there is social support for the hateful messages (Coustick-Deal 2017, in Bojarska 2019); and can desensitize the public to verbal violence and increase prejudice (Soral, Bilewicz, and Winiewski 2018 in Bojarska 2019).

Researchers have demonstrated how hate in traditional media has historically abetted genocide. The Holocaust in Germany was facilitated by a process of "antilocution," or the disparaging and dehumanization of Jews in conversation, media, and official pronouncements by Hitler (Allport 1954; Fyfe 2017). A similar process was observed for the genocide in Rwanda (Fyfe 2017.

Compared to traditional media, digital media are even more powerful tools for antilocution because of reach, ease of use, and instantaneous delivery and feedback. A recent study in Europe demonstrates that online hate speech incites violence toward target minorities. Muller and Schwartz (2018) found that anti-refugee hate crimes in Germany such as assault and arson disproportionally increased in areas with higher Facebook usage during periods of high anti-refugee posts online. The anti-refugee hate posts were on the Facebook page of the German Alternative for Germany (Bojarska 2019). Müller and Schwarz (2018) also found that "the effect of refugee posts on hate crimes essentially vanishes in weeks of major Facebook outages" (4). In communities with local internet disruptions, the effect of anti-refugee posts on hate crimes was significantly reduced compared to communities unaffected by internet outages. The researchers conclude that anti-refugee online posts incited violent hate crimes toward refugees.

A study in the United States presents similar findings as the study in Germany. Relia et al. (2019) found that the frequency of targeted hate posts on Tweeter in a sample of US cities predicted hate crimes towards people of minority races, ethnicities, and national origins. The proportion of targeted social media hate posts was significantly related to the number of hate groups operating in the cities, leading the researchers to suggest a causal relationship.

Other evidence of the connection between online hate speech and violent hate crimes is provided by post-event analysis of targeted killings in the United States and New Zealand. These analyses, although not based on scientific studies, are compelling because of a common element: the murderers were incited to action by online hate speech. Here are three examples:

The white supremacist shootings in El Paso, Texas: An alleged white supremacist targeted "Mexicans" at an El Paso Walmart, killing twenty-two people and injuring twenty-six others. He told police that he intended to kill "Mexicans." He was reported to have posted a racist, anti-immigrant "manifesto" to 8chan, a website often used by white supremacists (ADL 2019).

Christchurch mosque shooting: A white supremacist shot and killed fifty Muslims worshipping at a mosque in Christchurch, New Zealand. The murderer, born in Australia, livestreamed the attack on Facebook and then posted it on YouTube. Just prior to the attack, he posted a manifesto online complaining about migration and white "genocide" (ADL 2019).

The 2017 Unite the Right rally in Charlottesville, Virginia: Heather Heyer was killed by James Alex Fields Jr. who "rammed his car into an unsuspecting group of (counter) demonstrators" (Gardner 2019). According to the Carnegie-Knight News21 initiative, months before the rally, "people associated with the far-right movement used the online chat room Discord" to encourage sympathizers to protest the removal of Confederate statues, "particularly one of General Robert E. Lee" (Gardner 2019, 2). Some participants discussed weapons they might take to the rally, such as guns and shields, and "the logistics of running a vehicle into the expected crowds of counterprotesters" (Gardner 2019, 2).

Countering Online Hate Speech

Online hate speech is difficult to counter because of the sheer number of hate sites, blogs, and comments; the relative anonymity of individual haters; the networked nature of hate clusters; the speed of dissemination; and the challenge of distinguishing between protected hate speech and criminal hate speech.

A counterstrategy favored by the public and some government agencies is self-regulation by social media companies; that is, social media companies must decide what is to be accepted or deleted from their platforms. Some companies have responded by developing removal policies and hiring "moderators" to evaluate contents (Bhatnager 2018). Yahoo prohibits the posting of "content that is unlawful, harmful, threatening, abusive, harassing, tortuous, defamatory, vulgar, obscene, libelous, invasive of another's privacy, hateful, or racially, ethnically or otherwise objectionable" (in Bhatnager). Twitter warns its users that they "may be exposed to content that might be offensive, harmful, inaccurate or otherwise inappropriate, or in some cases, postings that have been mislabeled or are otherwise deceptive" (in Bhatnager 2018). YouTube's terms of service read: "We encourage free speech and defend everyone's right to express unpopular points of view. But we do not permit hate speech which attacks or demeans a group based on race or ethnic origin, religion, disability, gender, age, veteran status and sexual orientation/gender identity." Facebook "removes hate speech, which includes content that directly attacks people based on their race, ethnicity, national origin, religious affiliation, sexual orientation, sex, gender, or gender identity, or serious disabilities or diseases." Microsoft prohibits mobile phone applications that "contain any content that advocates discrimination, hatred, or violence based on considerations of race, ethnicity, national origin, language, gender, age, disability, religion, sexual orientation, status as a veteran, or membership in any other social group" (Bhatnager 2018). Other social media companies have similar policies that, on face value, would prohibit hate speech that doesn't necessarily fit the criminal definition (imminent threat of violence). Most research has suggested that self-regulation is not generally effective but is a necessary first step, pointing to the increase in hate crimes even as hate speech is being regulated by tech companies. In a recent article in *Nature*, Johnson et al. suggest that one reason is the networked configuration of online hate communities that reside on multiple social media platforms. These communities or clusters contain links to other clusters. Clusters can rapidly reinvent and repair themselves. Banning hate content on a single platform promotes the creation of other clusters that are not detectable by platform policing. Therefore, hate content can go unchecked (Johnson et al., in Dersey 2019). To help solve this problem, Johnson et al. suggest a few things: removing small hate clusters rather than the largest online cluster; banning a small number of users selected at random from online hate clusters; and that platform administrators promote an organization of clusters of anti-hate users, which could serve as a "human immune system" to fight and counteract hate clusters.

Other strategies suggested by research to combat online hate speech by individuals are "counterspeech" and "shaming." Counterspeech contradicts hate speech by using emotion or reason (facts) to show the hate-user why he/she is wrong. For example, Bojarska suggests "encouraging online civility by reminding other users about the humanity of persons targeted by hate" (10). Research has shown that photos and videos are more effective than language in producing this empathy. To reach a larger audience with counterspeech, Benesch (2019) suggests sharing these messages widely along with the hateful messages they are responding to. This can be accomplished by establishing accounts with tag lines that would attract other people interested in combatting hate. An example is the Twitter account @YesYoureRacist (http://twitter.com/YesYoureRacist. The person running this account retweets racist posts that he finds to his nearly 400,000 followers.

A strategy to combat online hate that has long-term consequences is digital media literacy. Young people, in particular, can be taught to critically evaluate information on the internet, to verify sources, and to dismiss hate messages. Please see Chapter 16 in this book for a detailed discussion of digital media literacy.

13

Fake News and Political Bias in Social Media

T he popularity of social media has transformed how we produce and consume news. Facebook and Twitter, for example, are popular platforms people use to receive, share, and distribute news, competing with traditional media such as newspapers and television as news sources. A 2018 survey by the Pew Research Center shows that 62% of US adults consume news from online social media sites. Young adults, in particular depend primarily on Facebook and Twitter for their news.

News dependence is not the only transformation we can attribute to social media. Anyone can register as an online news publisher. For example, anyone can create a Facebook page claiming to be a newspaper or news media organization without any upfront cost (Ribeiro et al. 2018). The popularity of these online sites among young and old users, men and women, and generally across education and income categories, has led many traditional news corporations as well as social-media-only news outlets to establish online sites (Lella 2016). Traditional print publishers increased their digital audiences more than 20% in 2015 (Lella).

These two developments in the past decade—dependence on online news sources and multiple sites claiming to be news publishers—have led to concerns about online news among the public, policy makers, and media scholars. The major concerns are the legitimacy of news sources, bias in online news, "fake" news, and effects of online news on users.

Online News Sources

A 2018 study by the Pew Research Center shows that the percentage of Americans who get their news online is growing (Geiger 2019). In 2016, 28% of US adults said they preferred to get news from online channels such as social media, news websites, or apps. This percentage increased to 34% in 2018. Television was still the most popular news source, preferred by 44% of American adults. However, more Americans get news from social media (20%) than from print newspapers (10%). The most popular social media site for news was Facebook. About 43% get news on this site. For local news, nearly as many Americans preferred to get their local news online (37%) as television (41%).

Even with the increasing popularity of social media as news sources, skepticism about the veracity of information is prevalent among frequent users. A majority (57%) say they expect news from social media sites to be largely inaccurate. As a result, over half have stopped following a news source because they thought it was posting inaccurate and false or made-up information, although about a third say they at least "sometimes" click on stories they think are false (Geiger 2019).

The Pew surveys provide evidence of the growing preference for online news. At the same time, the majority of users question whether the news they get is accurate. Even with this skepticism, more than a third of say they sometimes or often click on stories they think are false. These trends have led researchers, content and search engine providers, policy makers, and the public to evaluate the accuracy and truthfulness of online news. Among the most discussed and studied issues are news bias and fake news.

Bias in Online News

Media bias can be defined as "distortions of reality, favoritism or one-sidedness in presenting controversies, and close-minded or partisan attitudes" (Kenski and Jamieson 2017, 405). Media bias can be intentional or unintentional. Intentional media bias serves to achieve a specific goal, such as to portray a candidate for political office positively or negatively. Unintentional media bias results from news values such as the geographical proximity of an event to the news outlet or news consumers, or the potential impact of an event on communities served by the news outlet, such as a hurricane (Hamborg et al. 2019). Most studies of bias in online news have focused on political ideological bias on a "liberal" to "conservative" spectrum, using party ideology (Democrat and Republican) as a benchmark and considering bias intentional or unintentional. Commonly asked questions are:

- Is online news fair and balanced between Democrats and Republicans?
- Are social networks biased against conservatives?
- Are search results biased along party lines?

A Pro-Democrat Bias in Online News?

A concern is whether online news is partisan, favoring one political party or ideology over another. This bias could result from issue filtering or selective coverage of issues, and issue framing or selective presentation of information so that one side of an issue is favored (Budak et al. 2016). Research on television and print newspapers has shown that traditional media can indeed be ordered on a liberal–conservative spectrum, with most clustering at the center or slightly left of center (Budak et al. 2016).

A recent study of the top thirteen online US news outlets and two popular political blogs confirm the findings from previous studies of traditional media. Budak et al. compiled a list of news outlets that included *USA Today* and *Yahoo News,* expected to occupy the center of the liberal–conservative spectrum; the blogs, expected to occupy the endpoints of the spectrum; Daily Kos, on the left; and Breitbart on the right. Other news outlets analyzed were BBC News, *Chicago Tribune*, CNN News, Fox News, Huffington Post, *Los Angeles Times*, NBC News, *New York Times*, Reuters, *Washington Post*, and *Wall Street Journal*. To select the news articles for analysis, Budak et al. recorded all unique URLs that were viewed by at least ten Bing toolbar users and then crawled the news sites to obtain the full article titles and texts. The researchers also estimated the popularity of each article by counting the number of views by toolbar users. This procedure yielded over eight hundred articles published on the fifteen news sites over a year. An algorithm identified over ten thousand articles about political news (elections, campaigns, public policy issues, public officials) for further analysis. To evaluate political bias, the researchers recruited 749 online human judges to classify a random sample of the political news articles according to ideological position. This process was called "crowdsourced content analysis" by the researchers. In general, the analysis showed that there was no particular bias in political news coverage:

- The large majority of political news articles were neutral.
- Ideologically opposed articles were present in the same outlet.

- News outlets generally presented topics neutrally, with little ideological bias.
- There were no systematic differences in story selection; all major news outlets covered a wide variety of political topics regardless of ideological position.

From this study, we can conclude that, as suggested by Budak et al., major news organizations present political topics in a non-partisan manner, neither favoring Democrats nor Republicans. The study drew this conclusion from an aggregate of online political news articles over a year. Analysis of political figures such as candidates in political scandals, a political campaign, and singular events might show ideological bias. As Budak et al. suggest, "News organizations express their ideological bias not by directly advocating for a preferred political party, but rather by disproportionately criticizing one side" (250). However, overall differences between liberal and conservative news outlets are not significant.

A Pro-Liberal, Anti-Conservative Bias in Social Networks?

Social media platforms such as Facebook and Twitter have been accused in congressional hearings of an anti-conservative bias, actively censoring conservative speech through content policies and search algorithms (Newton 2019). The scientific evidence, however, does not support this assertion. For example, a recent study (Newton 2019) measured engagement across left- and right-leaning Facebook pages over 37 weeks. Engagement was measured by the frequency of likes, comments and shares. The frequency of weekly interactions for right-leaning pages was slightly higher (372,000) than for left-leaning pages (369,000). Over six months, right-leaning pages attracted fifty-one percent more total interactions than left-leaning pages (Newton 2019).

These studies suggest that social media platforms like Facebook do not curtail conservative comments and conversations. Although partisan bias is minimal, a bias against extreme views has been acknowledged by Facebook founder, Mark Zuckerberg (Newton 2019). The purpose is to avoid polarization—not to censor conservative voices.

Are Search Engines and Results Biased Along Party Lines?

Search engine results play a major role in the information a user will get. This information can influence candidate preferences in an election or which position to take on an issue. The influence of search results can be significant, since web users are more likely to find and trust news through a web search than social media (de Witte 2019). Recently, concerns have been raised from many sources including the White House that search engines may be biased against conservative media and news stories in their algorithms. Recent research has provided evidence that this concern is unfounded. For example, a study at Stanford University shows that Google, used in ninety percent of all searches, does not favor Republicans, Democrats, or any other ideological position. In this study, the researchers (Hancock; de Witte, 2019) reviewed the first page of Google search results for every candidate running for federal office in the 2018 U.S. election over a six-month period (de Witte 2019). This procedure resulted in about four million URLs. The researchers assigned partisan scores (Democrat or Republican; liberal or conservative) to the news sources, using a scoring method based on another study that tracked party preferences of Twitter users in the 2016 election (de Witte 2019). Results showed that search results for the candidates showed no preference for either party, regardless of candidate party affiliation. Search results for the candidates consisted mostly of centrist news sources, neither strongly liberal nor conservative, with no bias for either party, leading to a conclusion that a search engine (Google) was non-partisan.

Fake News

One consequence of the ease of posting information at no cost on the internet is the proliferation of "fake news" and "fake" news producers masquerading as legitimate news organizations. Definitions of fake news have been politicized, that is, used for political gain. To some politicians, fake news is any information that counters or does not agree with their policies, agendas, and actions. To scientists, fake news is information that has not been verified or that cannot be verified. Verification is accomplished through fact-checking, often by non-partisan and credible organizations such as snopes.com, politifact.com, factcheck.org, truthorfiction.com, hoax-slayer.com, and urbanlegends.about.com (Vosoughi et al. 2018). Other definitions of fake news similarly emphasize the lack of verifiability. Lazer et al. (2018) define fake news to be fabricated information that "mimics news media in form but not in organizational structure or intent" (1094). Real news is based on facts and real world events, and can be verified. Fake news is made up to serve the purposes of the provider, often to persuade or to support a particular position on an issue, a political agenda, or a particular political figure. When fake news is deliberately produced and disseminated to promote an agenda, it is sometimes called "misinformation." Other definitions focus on the producers of information. Producers of genuine (real) news are organizations with a definable and observable structure, a set of norms or standards for professional performance, and are generally permanent, that is, with recurring activity. Producers of fake news, on the other hand, are individuals or groups of individuals without formal organizational structure, without norms or standards of practice, and are often temporary ("fly by night") operators without a verifiable record as a producer (Lazer et al. 2018). Some online platforms such as First Draft and Facebook refer to unverified information posing as news, as "false news" rather than "fake news" because of the political use of "fake" as unfavorable information (Lazer et al. 2018). Regardless of whether news is real or fake, it is spread online on popular platforms such as Twitter and Facebook. In this section, we use "fake" to mean unverified or unverifiable information produced by non-traditional sources without verifiable credentials as news organizations.

How Prevalent Is Online Fake News?

The ease of widespread distribution of information on the internet facilitates the distribution of fake news. One study of fake news and the 2016 election (Allcott 2017) showed that a database of 156 fake news articles generated 38 million shares "translating into 760 million instances of a user clicking through and reading a fake news story, or about three stories per American adult" (3). The same data base showed that fake news stories were heavily supportive of Donald Trump: 115 pro-Trump fake stories shared on Facebook 30 million times, compared to 41 pro-Clinton fake stories shared 7.6 million times (Allcott 2017). Online users proactively sought news from fake news websites (where over half of articles are false). These websites were visited 159 million times during the month before the 2016 election, or .64 times per US adult (Allcott 2017). This study provides evidence that online users are heavily exposed to fake news; they also proactively visit fake news websites to seek affirmation of their support for a preferred candidate.

Producers of Fake News

Most fake news sites are created by individuals or groups of individuals to resemble legitimate news organizations. They publish intentionally fabricated and misleading articles. They may publish a mix of factual and false articles to confuse users, often to support a political agenda, a particular position on an issue, or a political candidate. During the 2016 election, BuzzFeed and the Guardian, in separate investigations, identified some major producers of fake news. These producers were motivated by financial gain and by ideological support. More than one hundred sites posting fake news were operated by teenagers in Veles, a small town in

Macedonia. They produced stories favoring both Trump and Clinton, earning thousands of dollars in advertising revenue. Four of the ten most popular fake news stories on Facebook were posted on Endingthefed. com, produced by a 24-year-old Romanian, probably also for profit. Fake news sites mimicking legitimate news organizations included NationalReport.net, USAToday.com.co, and WashingtonPost.com.co. National Report produced mainly pro-Trump stories including a widely circulated fake story claiming that President Obama used his own money to support a Muslim museum during the federal government shutdown (Allcott 2017).

Regardless of the motivation—financial gain or ideological support—fake news is easily produced on the internet, requiring no initial investment. Without careful investigation, it's difficult to identify producers. Online users are heavily exposed to fake news, and large numbers of users proactively seek out fake news sites.

Spread of True and False Online News

Online news can be true or false. Which spreads faster, and which has a greater reach? A recent study provides evidence that false or fake news not only spreads faster than real news but also reaches significantly more people.

Vosoughi, Roy, and Aral (2018) studied 126,000 verified true and false news stories distributed on Twitter from 2006 to 2017. News stories were classified as true or false independently by six fact-checking organizations. Agreement was well over ninety percent on whether a story was true or false. Three million people tweeted the true and false news stories (126,000) more than 4.5 million times. Here are some of the results:

- False stories reached significantly more people than true stories. A true story rarely diffused to more than one thousand people. The top one percent of false news stories diffused to between one thousand and one hundred thousand people.
- True stories took six times as long to diffuse to one thousand people as false stories.
- False stories were seventy percent more likely to be retweeted than true stories.

These results show that false stories diffused or spread farther, faster, deeper, and more broadly than true stories. These findings were more pronounced for political news, but were also evident for false news about terrorism, natural disasters, science, urban legends, and financial information. In explaining these results, Vosoughi suggest that false news is generally more novel (new) than true news. They indeed found that users had less previous exposure to false news topics compared to true news. People, they suggest, are drawn to novel and new information. Therefore, they are more likely to share false news (Vosoughi 2018).

Effects of Online News

We might expect online news—fake and real—to influence user positions on issues and candidate preferences in an election. This expectation follows from evidence that online news is prevalent, and that users increasingly prefer online news to traditional media as sources of information, although television is still the first choice. With some exceptions, research does not support this expectation. A general finding is that partisan online news does not convert as much as it reinforces existing issue positions and candidate preferences. These null (no effect) findings can be explained by traditional selective exposure theories more recently recast as theories of the "echo chamber" and confirmation bias. These theories say that people find dissonance to be stressful and therefore will avoid it. Dissonance arises when cognitions and behaviors contradict each other. In the context of online news, dissonance is produced when new information challenges currently held information used as a basis for issue positions or candidate preference. In a more general sense, dissonance arises when current positions and issue positions are challenged, whether by information, emotional appeals, or attacks on current choices. The human aversion to dissonance leads to seeking out supportive information, sources, or appeals, and avoiding contradictions—hence the echo chamber and the motivation to confirm biases (choices). If this analysis is correct, online news audiences will be more exposed to news and sources confirming their biases, compared to news and sources challenging their biases. A study of Facebook friends by Bakshy, Messing, and Adamic (2015) supports this analysis. Facebook friend networks were ideologically separated. The median share of friends with the opposite ideology was twenty percent for liberals and eighteen percent for conservatives, suggesting that people were more likely to read and share news stories that supported their ideological positions. A consequence is that people who get news from Facebook or other social media "are less likely to receive evidence about the true state of the world that would counter an ideologically aligned but false news story" (Allcott, 12). A corollary consequence is that people will seek out ideologically aligned information from news stories regardless of veracity, thus increasing the potential influence of fake news. Heavy media users and users with segregated social networks are the most likely to seek out and believe ideologically supportive news articles, true or false.

A general conclusion, then, is that online news, including fake news, reinforces existing ideological positions and related candidate choices. There is however, one notable exception. Undecided voters, or people unaligned in their ideological positions (for example, those scoring neutral in Likert attitude scales), can be swayed by contrary online news, real or fake. Undecided voters, particularly those who have not made up their minds about whom to vote for three months or less before an election, are less likely to believe ideologically supportive news, compared to voters who decided before three months (Alcott 2017). Therefore, online news can be potentially influential in elections with large numbers of undecided voters.

In summary, online fake news is prevalent on the internet, reaches more people more quickly than real news, and has the potential to influence undecided voters. These conclusions are consistent with recent research showing minimal persuasive effects of campaign contact outside of the internet in general elections, except for undecided voters, who are susceptible to influence (Kalla and Brockman 2017). The difference is that online news has a broader reach than traditional campaigning, and can therefore be used to more efficiently target potential converts simply by sheer saturation, as illustrated by the reach and breadth of fake news in the 2016 election.

Workbook

Define, describe, or illustrate the concepts; summarize the results of the studies:

1.   News dependence on social media: PEW, 2018

2.   Political bias: Budak et al. (2016)

3.   Ideological (liberal/conservative) bias: Newton (2019)

4.   Party line bias: De Witte (2019)

5.   Fake news definitions

6.   Fake news, prevalence: Allcott (2017)

7.   Producers of fake news

8.   Spread of true and fake news: Vosoughi, Roy, and Arat (2018)

9.   Effects of online news

14

Media Interventions to Reduce Negative Stereotyping

As we saw in Chapter 9, the media can influence public and individual stereotyping of groups by providing information and primes that form the bases of the stereotypes. In this chapter, I discuss how the media can reduce negative stereotyping and reinforce positive stereotyping. Interventions to reduce prejudice are discussed in the next chapter. Remember that stereotypes are cognitive beliefs, while prejudices are attitudes or feelings. In most cases, the interventions for stereotypes and prejudice will be similar. However, information is more often studied as the instrument of stereotype change, while emotional appeals, personal contact, self-introspection, and motivation are studied as instruments of prejudice change. Here, we look at how information transmitted by the media—television and print, in particular—can change negative stereotypes and reinforce positive stereotypes.

Media Exemplars and Counter-Stereotypic Portrayals

Exposure to exemplars in the media provide the observer with accessible information about the traits and behaviors of a target group that can reinforce or contradict an existing stereotype. An exemplar is a member of the group presented, explicitly or implicitly, as a representative of the group. Exemplars can be portrayed positively or negatively. A positive portrayal counters or contradicts negative stereotypes; a negative portrayal reinforces negative stereotypes. Counter-stereotypes are contradictions of a negative stereotype. For example, if a prevailing stereotype of Latinos associates them with crime and gangs, a counter-stereotype would depict a Latino exemplar as a police officer or teacher. Research has consistently shown that positive exemplars and counter-stereotypical portrayals in the media can reduce negative stereotyping and reinforce positive stereotyping (see, e.g., Blair 2002). Here are a few examples:

1. Dasgupta and Greenwald (2001) showed their non-Black college students pictures of admired or disliked Black and White exemplars. They found that exposure to admired Black exemplars reduced implicit bias against and stereotyping of Blacks. The strongest reduction in implicit bias and stereotyping occurred when pictures of admired Blacks were paired with pictures of disliked Whites. (This study is discussed in more detail in the next chapter because prejudice reduction was the focus of the study.) Given these results, the authors offered this analysis of how the media can reduce negative stereotyping (and bias against) out-groups:

   > The mass media have been frequently criticized for disproportionately emphasizing stereotypic images of minorities and women (Greenberg and Brand 1994; Harris 1999). Interestingly, even

when disliked members of dominant groups are portrayed in the popular media (e.g., news stories about White criminals like Jeffrey Dahmer), their race is typically not made salient. By contrast, news stories about Black criminals often highlight the individual's race. In our study, by forcing people to classify admired and disliked individuals by race, we emphasized the exemplar's group membership as well as their valence. These data imply that if media representations were to become more balanced, reminding people of both admired members of out-groups and less-than-stellar members of in-groups with emphasis on their group membership, the combined effect may be able to shift implicit prejudice and stereotypes (808).

2. Dalisay and Tan (2009) studied the effects of positive and negative exemplars in television portrayals of Asian Americans on stereotypes of Asian Americans among White college students. In an experimental study, they showed a TV clip portraying Asian Americans as "model minorities" to one group of participants, assigned randomly to this condition. (Author's note: The model minority stereotype is controversial. Some scholars claim it "dehumanizes" Asian Americans to a caricature, lumps all Asians in one category, and "praises" Asians at the expense of other racial minorities—"If they can do it, why can't you?") The thirteen-minute positive exemplar video clip was from *The Asianization of America*. (Author's note: "Asianization" is considered derogatory by many Asian Americans because it implies an "Asian invasion." However, depictions of Asians were generally positive.) The clip featured three scenes: East Asians immigrating to the US, Asian Americans working hard at their jobs and in their schools, and interviews with prominent Asian Americans who were successful in the corporate world.

In the negative exemplar viewing condition (group assignments to viewing condition were random), the researchers showed a thirteen-minute video clip from the movie *Better Luck Tomorrow*. The clip showed a fight scene in which an Asian American character uses a handgun, Asian American teenagers breaking into and robbing their high school, and Asian American teenagers consuming alcohol and cocaine.

A third group of participants served as the control. They saw a thirteen-minute video clip from a PBS documentary titled *On the Edge of Extinction: Panthers and Cheetahs*.

After watching the video clips, participants from all three groups completed a questionnaire measuring stereotypes of Asian Americans on a seven-point semantic differential scale. Examples of items were violent/not violent, honest/dishonest, good/bad, moral/immoral, and greedy/not greedy. Responses to the ten items in the scale were summed to form one measure of stereotype. (Author's note: Stereotypes of African Americans were also measured, to see if the video clips resulted in a "contrast effect." Those results are reported in Dalisay and Tan [2009].)

Results supported the researchers' predictions: Participants who saw the positive exemplar reported more positive stereotypes of Asian Americans than did participants in the control and negative exemplar groups. Participants who saw the negative exemplar reported more negative stereotypes of Asian Americans than did participants in the control and positive exemplar groups.

According to the researchers, these results provide support for propositions from priming and assimilation theories stating that exemplars in the media provide access to stereotypical traits that can be assimilated by the viewer and expressed as his or her own stereotypes of the target group.

3. Zhang and Tan (2011) studied whether a single positive exemplar—President Barack Obama—could change stereotypes about African Americans among Chinese high school students. They used a panel design, asking the participants to complete an online questionnaire two weeks before the presidential election in 2008 and two weeks after the election. They expected that President Obama would be a positive exemplar after he was elected, carrying the prestige of the American presidency for the relatively "naïve" participants (they were less likely than Americans to have preconceived attitudes toward Mr. Obama). Previous studies have indicated that the stereotypes of African Americans in China were a mix of positive (e.g., hardworking, honest, generous) and negative (violent, aggressive, loud), so that there would be room for movement toward the positive end of the scales.

Results confirmed the researchers' expectations. Negative stereotypes (violent, loud, impulsive, and aggressive) of African Americans improved (were less negative) after the elections compared to before. This change was significantly associated with how the participants evaluated media coverage of Mr. Obama and their knowledge of him. The more positive the Chinese participants perceived media coverage of Mr. Obama to be, and the more knowledge they had of him, the more their negative stereotypes improved. These findings are consistent with priming and cognitive processing theories of stereotype change.

Designing TV Programs to Reduce Negative Stereotyping in Children

We know from Chapter 6 that children recognize race as early as six months (see, e.g., Katz and Kofkin 1997), explain behaviors according to racial categories at two years (Hirschfeld 2008), and express racial preferences as young as three (Aboud 2008). Rather than interpreting these behaviors as prejudice, or dislike for other children of another race, some researchers favor a "cognitive categorization" explanation. Considering their immature cognitive structures and capabilities, very young children (e.g., preschoolers) are particularly susceptible to simplified categorization of the world around them. Like adults, children "actively make sense of the world around them and are particularly responsive to information that helps them develop a better understanding of the world and their experiences" (Graves 1999, 713). In a simplified world, race is an accessible category that can distinguish people based on physical characteristics (Aboud 2008). Children are therefore able to categorize people according to race, and ascribe variable traits and behaviors to people based on race. In attaching meanings to racial categories, children are influenced by what they see and hear, and by what they are told by parents, teachers, and peers. The ability of children to interpret and "make sense" of racial categories on their own is illustrated in this quote from Winkler (2009):

> Children also learn which social categories are important by observing their environments. ... Children may notice when going to the store or doctor's office or riding the bus that height and hairstyle do not seem related to occupation or neighborhood, but skin color does. (3)

Therefore, children attach meanings to social categories, and a category that is most visible and accessible is race. This simplified categorization—or stereotyping—leads to behaviors such as preference for playmates reflecting in-group bias. The resulting behaviors are rooted in cognitive categorizations or stereotypes. Therefore, to change prejudicial behaviors, the underlying stereotypes, although not consciously recognized and expressed by children, would have to be addressed. Children's television can potentially be an effective vehicle for the reduction of negative stereotyping in children. Children watch an average of 3.5 hours per day (A. C. Nielsen Co. 2012); television is highly involving and provides children with a window to the world (Pecora, Murray, and Wartella 2007). Television viewing is a preferred activity of children. In one national survey, fifty-four percent of four-to-six-year-olds said they would rather watch television than spend time with their fathers (A. C. Nielsen Co., 2012).

Sesame Street

In the mid-1990s, the producers of *Sesame Street* developed segments with racial themes specifically for preschoolers. The goals of the segments were as follows (Lovelace et al. 1994; Graves 1999):

- To emphasize similarities in humans
- To appreciate racial and ethnic cultural differences
- To consider people who look different as "potential friends"
- To include (in play and other activities) a child rejected for physical or cultural differences

To accomplish these objectives, the *Sesame Street* segments showed live actors—children and adults—in cross-cultural friendships, including activities such as visiting the home of a friend. An example is described by Graves (1999):

> The segments include a European American girl or boy visiting an African American friend. Both visits take place in the African American's home with the African American family members shown. The cross-racial friends played together, ate a meal together, and interacted with African American family members and friends. The Black and White children in the segments looked comfortable with each other and they talked about having fun during the visit. (718)

This episode shows children that racial categories do not matter in friendships. Although stereotypical traits are not explicitly demonstrated, the implication is that "friendliness" and "niceness" are traits of all people, regardless of race.

These segments were shown to preschoolers in school or in the home. Immediately after viewing, children reported that they remembered details of the episodes, liked them, and related the events they had seen to their own lives (Lovelace et al. 1994). However, most African American and European American children who had viewed the segments said that their mothers "would be angry or sad about the friendships and the visits" (Graves 1999, 718). This response was consistent with data collected before the evaluation of the segments that indicated most mothers of the children were not enthusiastic about cross-race friendships (Lovelace et al. 1994).

These results suggest that television can influence children to break down racial stereotyping in friendships and play. However, adult and family support is needed for the children to enact in their daily activities the cognitive structures they learn from television.

Different and the Same

Different and the Same is a series of nine videos, each of them twelve to fifteen minutes in length, for early elementary children. The series was developed by Family Communications, Inc., the producers of *Mister Rogers' Neighborhood*. Intended for use in the classroom, the video series includes a teacher's guide, a workshop facilitator's guide, and a training video (Graves 1999).

Different and the Same focuses on four principles: fairness, awareness, inclusion, and respect. The videos use animal puppets that are not identifiable by race but are helped by ethnically diverse adults in resolving difficult intergroup problems. The episodes are set in schools and demonstrate behaviors of the puppets, such as the following (Graves, 1999):

- Resisting peer pressure
- Looking beyond stereotypes
- Including others
- Reaching out to helpful adults
- Expressing feelings
- Honoring differences and similarities
- Problem solving
- Taking positive action

Graves (1999) describes on episode from the series as follows:

> "Sticks and Stones," a segment on name-calling, starts with Cat-a-lion's experience of being called "Mophead" by children at the playground. He is hurt and angry when this happens. When a new boy, Arthur, joins the class, Cat-a-lion tells his friends that he doesn't like the new boy's looks and encourages them to join him in calling Arthur "Pumpkinhead." Mrs. Chung, the Chinese-American principal, overhears the name-calling. She

tells Cat-a-lion about her childhood experiences about being called horrible names. She talks about how she felt about the name-calling and her parents' emphasis on feeling proud about who she was. Cat-a-lion apologizes to Arthur, invites him to his birthday party, and promises never to call him names again. (719–720)

The effectiveness of *Different and the Same* in changing negative stereotyping of other race children was tested in several schools (Graves 1999; Katsuyama 1997). Here are some of the results:

- Children who saw the videos (experimental group) were, in comparison to those who did not see the videos (control group),

  a. more likely to use a group standard (norm) than personal characteristics of a child to explain the child's social isolation from the group.
  b. less likely to base friendship preferences on physical attributes. (This result was more apparent in African, Asian, and Latino American children than in White children.)
  c. more likely to express positive attitudes toward photographs of children from another race—a result more apparent among White children.
  d. at the third–grade level, more likely to select children from another race as friends.

These results imply that *Different and the Same* was effective in changing how children cognitively represented race, so that race did not matter in friendships and other interactions in school. The program's success can be attributed not only to its content and format, but also to active support from teachers and other adults, reminding us that media interventions don't exist in a vacuum. For media to provide successful interventions for children (and adults, for that matter), a supportive environment is necessary. This environment consists of other people (teachers, peers, leaders), groups, and institutions—in other words, the cultural milieu in which prejudice occurs.

Institutional Interventions

Media groups and institutions can play a major role in reducing negative stereotyping among their publics. As we have seen, a key to successful intervention is content that has been shown to be effective in scientific studies. But no matter how many effective interventions are identified through research, they won't matter at all unless they reach the public. And the media— newspapers, television, radio, magazines, books, and the internet—are the main conduits to large audiences.

Support from many media producers is not lacking. The Associated Press, for example, revised its style book in 2013 to guide how "immigrants" is to be used in news reports:

Illegal should not be used to describe people ("illegal immigrants") but be used to describe the actions people take. (AP Stylebook 2013)

Some major newspapers, including *USA Today* and the *Chicago Tribune,* have adopted this guideline.

The Associated Press policy change indicates a recommended shift away from labeling people and toward labeling behavior as in, for example, "people diagnosed with schizophrenia" instead of "schizophrenics."

The Associated Press calls for detail in describing people who are in the US illegally: "Specify wherever possible how someone entered the country illegally and from where. Crossed the border? Overstayed a visa? What nationality?" (Weiner 2013.)

Another example of media support is from the American Society of News Editors, which periodically surveys the racial and gender diversity in newsrooms and publishes reports such as "The Future of Diversity in the Newsroom."

Minority Journalists' Organizations

Major sources of information on how to cover and present diverse groups in the media include the minority journalism organizations, such as the Asian American Journalists Association, the National Association of Black Journalists, the National Association of Hispanic Journalists, and the Native American Journalists Association. These organizations develop style guidebooks on how to cover racial minorities fairly and accurately so that stereotyping and bias are kept at a minimum.

ALL-AMERICAN: How to Cover Asian America (AAJA 2000) is an example. This guidebook was developed by the Asian American Journalists Association in cooperation with the South Asian Journalists Association and with funding from Knight Ridder, Inc. The guidebook gives pointers on how to cover Asian Americans without bias and with greater accuracy. It includes chapters on terminology to use and to avoid in referring to Asian Americans and their activities, examples of biased coverage, and advice for unbiased and accurate coverage. Here are some excerpts from the terminology chapter (11–27)[1]:

- "All-American: Refers to the best high school and college athletes of the year; not a synonym for white and blond."
- "American: A citizen, native-born or naturalized, of the United States of America; not a synonym for white.
- "Asian American: Form the noun without the hyphen, as in 'French Canadian,' to denote current group membership. In compound phrases, where the term is used as an adjective, use a hyphen, e.g., French-Canadian folklore. Similarly, with Japanese-American and Pakistani-American."
- "Asian Gangs: *Caution*: Logically equivalent to European gangs. Better to specify the country or ethnicity, e.g., Vietnamese or Chinese or Filipino gangs if relevant and the relevance can be explained to the satisfaction of the reader or viewer. Some ethnic groups, notably Italian Americans with regard to the Mafia, argue that gangs are criminals first and members of ethnic groups second, so ethnic identification can perpetuate invidious stereotypes."
- "Asiatic: *Avoid*. A 19th-Century adjective typically used in 'scientific' European treatises assuming the superiority of the white race."
- "China Doll: *Caution*. A figurine, usually porcelain, but when used metaphorically or as a comparison the implied image of female submission demeans women of Chinese heritage."
- "Chinaman: *Avoid*. A slur, often applied to anyone of Asian heritage. A term from the 19th century, specifically for the poorly paid Chinese workers who risked their lives building the American transcontinental railroad, as in 'Chinaman's chance,' meaning no chance at all."
- "Exotic: *Caution*. When describing women of Asian and Pacific Islander heritage, it often implies a departure from the white norm. Swedes, for example, are rarely described in the United States as exotic."
- "Immigrant: *Caution*. A racially or ethnically charged term under certain circumstances. Like race and ethnicity, the status of being a first-generation immigrant should be mentioned where relevant and its relevance can be shown to the satisfaction of the reader or viewer. For example, a person whose accent leads to a bar brawl or whose lack of English may have led to his failure to stop when requested by police can be fairly described, along with other biographical details, as a recent immigrant (date of entry to U.S. also helpful, if available). The status of undocumented workers is another issue and should be discussed carefully both with the source and editors, as to the risks of deportation. However, an immigrant who has lived in the United States for many decades may be, depending on individual circumstances, unfairly described as an immigrant and prompt invidious racial or ethnic associations."
- "Oriental: *Caution*. Many Asian Americans, especially younger ones, liken 'Oriental' to 'Negro.' A vestige of British imperialism, the term, at minimum, is vague. In art, it may include countries such

---

1   "ALL-AMERICAN: How to cover Asian America," *AAJA Handbook to Covering Asian America*, pp. 11-27. Copyright © 2000 by Asian American Journalists Association. Reprinted with permission.

as China and Japan, but not Turkey. In food, it may mean China or Japan, but not India, Vietnam or the Philippines."

- "Racial Slurs: The list of disparaging racial epithets is long and so is the list of those directed solely at Asians. They include 'Jap,' 'Chinaman,' 'Paki,' and 'gook.' They are as offensive as 'spic,' 'kike,' and 'nigger.' By definition, such slurs are designed to stigmatize an entire racial group. Of course, not every racial slur is newsworthy, but the journalistic obligation to report such slurs grows with the slur's potential public impact, when uttered by, say, a prominent business executive, law enforcement officer or elected official."
- "Yellow Peril: *Caution.* An imagined invasion of the United States at the beginning of the 20th century by Asian hordes, specifically Japanese, who had become successful entrepreneurs in California agriculture."

Guides like the AAJA handbook provide guidelines for unbiased and accurate coverage. Similar guide-books for other racial groups have been developed by the other minority journalists' associations and can be accessed at their websites.

Media Content by Experts

"Writers write what they know" (McLaurin 2012). Accurate and adequate knowledge of the groups being portrayed in the media is essential for content that is accurate, balanced, representative, and unbiased. Of course, anyone, regardless of group membership, can gain this knowledge through formal or self-education. And, just as clearly, most members of the portrayed group would have knowledge about their own group—its culture, what representative portrayals look like, and how to avoid bias in those portrayals. When group representatives cannot create or produce media content about their own groups, they can be consulted to provide first-hand knowledge. Knowledge is a key to creating, writing, and producing portrayals that are accurate, realistic, balanced, representative, and unbiased. Here are a few examples of organizations using expert knowledge to create, produce, and/or distribute balanced and unbiased media content about various groups in their communities:

- Aboriginal Peoples Television Network (APTN; www.aptn.ca), a Canadian broadcast and cable television network, "airs and produces programs made by, for and about Aboriginal Peoples" (aptn.ca). The first of its kind in the world, APTN produces and distributes documentaries, news magazines, dramas, entertainment specials, children's series, movies, sports events, and educational programs about Aboriginal peoples. Its reach is national; programming is about 56% English, 16% French, and 28% Aboriginal languages. These programs include *APTN National News, Anash and the Legacy of the Sun-Rock, Arbor Live!, Cooking With the Wolfman, Medicine Woman, Moccasin Flats, One With Nature, Rez Bluez, The Sharing Circle, Storytellers in Motion, Wapos Bay: The Series,* and *Warriors: TKO.*

APTN programming, according to its website, "offers all Canadians a window into the remarkably diverse worlds of Indigenous Peoples in Canada and throughout the world" (aptn.com). Other pertinent data, according to APTN (aptn.com), are the following:

- APTN is available to approximately ten million Canadians
- APTN is aimed at both Aboriginal and non-Aboriginal audiences.
- APTN broadcasts a daily national news program and a weekly investigative news show "that provide balanced, accurate and provocative coverage of national issues. APTN National News looks beyond the headlines and offers context and a historical perspective."
- Over 75% of APTN employees are Aboriginal Peoples.

- Canadian Broadcasting Corporation (CBC): Through its "Overcoming Stereotypes" programming, the CBC has produced and distributed a number of television dramas aimed at providing all Canadians with a balanced, authentic, and unbiased portrait of indigenous peoples. Members of the portrayed communities are consultants, writers, actors, or otherwise heavily involved in the production and creation of these programs. The series began with *Spirit Bay*, which aired from 1982 to 1987. *Spirit Bay* portrays the lives of indigenous people in a reservation town from the viewpoint of a young person. It focuses on how the people have adapted to "white society," balancing family, nature, and modern life, but also on how they have retained their traditional beliefs, customs, and practices, including a reverence for nature and using the land wisely.

Moccasin Flats, a more recent production, aired on APTN in 2004 and continued until 2008. The story shows how indigenous people in an urban reserve attempt to "maintain their cultural identity while overcoming poverty, gangs, violence, and racism" (aptn.ca/series/id.13467787).

- MediaSmarts (www.mediasmarts.ca), a non-profit Canadian organization, provides information, media reports, and research about media effects, particularly on young people, with a focus on media literacy and new digital media. Its section on "Aboriginal People" generates and distributes information about "many issues that are specific or unique to Aboriginal people in Canada, including the underreporting of crimes against Aboriginal people by news media and the unique challenges faced by Aboriginal people seeking to produce content for their own communities" (mediasmarts.ca). Recent reports include
  - Common Portrayals of Aboriginal People
  - Aboriginal People in the News
  - Media Portrayals of Missing and Murdered Aboriginal Women
  - The Impact of Stereotyping on Young People
  - The Development of Aboriginal Broadcasting in Canada
  - Aboriginal Expression in the Arts and Media
  - The Importance of Media Education

- *The Native Americans* (a project by Ted Turner; www.imdb.com/title/tt0215431/) is often cited as a balanced and unbiased portrayal of Native Americans, telling history from the perspective of Native Americans. Part of this success is attributed to the participation of Native American writers, producers, and academic advisors in the creation of the documentary (McLaurin 2012). The three-part series was shown in 1994 on TBS.

The examples above of accurate, balanced, and relatively unbiased representations of out-groups illustrate the importance of expert knowledge in the creation of content. Media interventions will be successful only to the extent that their content provides the information needed by audiences to form their own unbiased beliefs (stereotypes) of people who are not like themselves. In the next chapter, we look at communication interventions for reducing the negative feelings (prejudices) that we often direct at members of out-groups.

Workbook

Define, describe, or illustrate; summarize the results of the studies:

1.   Dasgupta and Greenwald, exemplars study

2.   Dalisay and Tan, Asian American exemplars study

3.   Zhang and Tan, exemplar study in China

4.   Social categorization theory, how children learn

5.   Sesame Street and negative stereotyping

6.   Different and the Same and improving cross-race relations

7.   AP Stylebook and use of "illegal"

8.   Asian American Journalists Association, biased terminologies

9.   Aboriginal Peoples Television Network

10.   Canadian Broadcasting Corp., Spirit Bay

11.   CBC, Moccasin Flats

12.   MediaSmarts, Canada

13.   The Native Americans, TBS

15

Communication Interventions to Reduce Prejudice

Do not fight hate with hate.

—My student, exceptional communication major, exceptional student athlete, and African-American man who has experienced hate

As we have seen in previous chapters, prejudice is not only contrary to the ideals of most peoples and countries, it is costly to individuals and societies and leads to intergroup conflict, war, violence, aggression, crime, low productivity, and, at the individual level, mental and emotional disorders. Not surprisingly, billions of dollars are spent each year by government and private and nonprofit agencies on programs to reduce prejudice in communities, the workplace, and schools (Hansen 2003; Paluck and Green 2009). Some notable examples are the numerous diversity, sensitivity, and cultural competency programs in schools, business, and government agencies: the Partners Against Hate (2003) project; the Anti-Prejudice Consortium (2011); and programs sponsored by the Southern Poverty Law Center.

Prejudice and its reduction have been one of the most popular topics of research in communication and the social sciences, resulting in hundreds of studies over the last few decades. In this chapter, we discuss some of the interventions that research has generally shown to be successful. We focus on interventions that have a clear communication component at the intrapersonal, interpersonal, and mediated levels of analysis. Also, we discuss strategies that apply to explicit and implicit prejudice. As we saw in Chapter 3, explicit prejudice is conscious, deliberate, and controllable; usually measured by self-report questionnaires; and more amenable to control (see, e.g., Turner and Crisp 2010). On the other hand, implicit prejudice is "subconscious" (i.e., we are not aware we have it), automatic (i.e., triggered without conscious effort), unintentionally activated by the mere presence of an attitude object, and more difficult to control. Implicit prejudice is measured by the Implicit Associations Test (IAT; Greenwald and Banaji 1995). The IAT asks participants to match target stimuli (e.g., racial groups; young and old people) with positive and negative words or objects. Associations between targets and words or objects are measured in milliseconds; the shorter the time it takes for an association, the stronger that association is.

Target Audiences: Who Can Reduce Their Prejudices?

The literature on persuasion tells us that not everyone can change attitudes (Appiah and Eighmey 2011). The hard-core believers, those who strongly agree or strongly disagree with a position on an issue, will not change their attitudes no matter how forceful and convincing the intervention might be. Most likely to change are the "middle-of-the-roaders" and, to a lesser extent, those who are not fully committed to a position on the issue, those who "somewhat" agree or "somewhat" disagree. It's not surprising, therefore, that politicians focus their attention on undecided voters and independents.

The same principle can be applied to the identification of target audiences for prejudice reduction interventions. People most likely to change are those who are prejudiced but who don't realize that they are prejudiced, and who would like to change. Recent studies have shown that close to 80% of Americans fall into this category because they have implicit biases, meaning they have prejudicial thoughts that they aren't aware of (as discussed in Chapters 3 and 4), and because they want to reduce or control these thoughts (Nosek, Greenwald, and Banaji 2007). A smaller percentage—52%—admit to explicit biases (e.g., assigning negative characteristics to individuals because they belong to an out-group, discussed in Chapter 3), but also indicate an interest in controlling these biases. We can conclude from these data that the large majority of Americans are potential targets for prejudice reduction interventions.

Intrapersonal Communication Interventions

Interventions at the intrapersonal level include strategies that increase an individual's motivation to regulate prejudice, enhance accountability and egalitarian goals, promote emotional reactions to prejudice, and promote value consistency and self-worth (Paluck and Green 2009). These interventions have in common a focus on the individual. Although another communicator may be involved (e.g., in the delivery of new information), the processes leading to prejudice reduction occur primarily within the individual, whether it is the processing of information, the priming of motivations, or the recognition of values.

Priming Motivation

A large body of research has shown that individuals can self-motivate to reduce prejudice (Legault, Gutsell, and Inzlicht 2011). This motivation—to regulate prejudice—can either be anchored internally (it is the right thing to do; is consistent with an individual's values) or externally (pressure from peers; fear of out-groups). Most studies have used assessments of individual motivation to reduce prejudice through surveys—people are asked what their motivations are. Results have generally shown that internally motivated individuals show less racial prejudice, while externally motivated individuals show more racial prejudice (see, e.g., Plant, Devine, and Peruche 2010). Based on self-determination theory (Deci and Ryan 2002), these results support the principle that people do not want their thoughts and behaviors to be constrained by external forces and may respond in the opposite direction (e.g., show more prejudice when faced with an externally anchored motivation to be nonprejudiced). On the other hand, internally generated motivations to be nonprejudiced support the individual's perceived autonomy, and consequently lead to less prejudice. These results suggest that, to reduce prejudice, individuals perform a self-assessment and ask themselves the following: (1) Am I prejudiced, even just a little? (2) Do I want to be less prejudiced? and (3) Why do I want to be less prejudiced? If the answers to the first two questions are yes, one can assess whether the motivation is internally or externally induced, and work on strengthening and elaborating on internal motivations.

In an experimental study, Legault et al. (2011) provided evidence that motivations to reduce prejudice can be manipulated, that internal motivations lead to less explicit and less implicit prejudice, and that external motivations lead to more explicit and more implicit prejudice. This study is instructive not only for these results; it also tells us how individuals can strengthen internal motivations.

In their first study, Legault et al. assigned non-Black college students randomly to read one of three brochures. Brochure 1 (the autonomy condition) primed internal motivations to reduce prejudice. It explained why it is important for an individual to reduce prejudice but also pointed out that prejudice reduction was a personal choice. Brochure 2 (the controlling condition) primed external motivations by telling the participants that they should fight prejudice because doing so is a social norm. Brochure 3 was the "no motivation" condition, giving only a definition of prejudice without mentioning prejudice reduction. After reading the brochures, the participants filled out the Symbolic Racism Scale (Henry and Sears 2002), a measure of explicit prejudice against Black people. Results showed that the autonomy brochure led to lowest scores on the explicit prejudice scale, followed by the no-motivation brochure. The controlling brochure resulted in the highest scores. Therefore, students who were internally motivated to reduce prejudice were the least prejudiced against Blacks, while students who were externally motivated were the most prejudiced. In study 2, Legault et al. (2011) measured the effects of a more subtle induction of internal and external motivations (compared to direct statements in brochures as in study 1). Also, their dependent variable (effects of motivation) was implicit bias rather than explicit prejudice (the effect measured in study 1). Priming for motivations was accomplished by asking college students to answer questionnaires and then to describe how they felt about their responses. As in study 1, participants were assigned randomly to one of three conditions. In the autonomy condition, the students answered a questionnaire designed to prime internal motivations with questions such as "Being nonprejudiced is important to me" and "I can freely decide to be a nonprejudiced person." After answering the questions on a Likert scale (disagree completely to agree completely), the students were asked to describe why it is "personally satisfying," "enjoyable," and "important" to be nonprejudiced. In the controlling condition, students answered questions that primed external motivations, such as "It is socially unacceptable to discriminate based on cultural background" and "People in my social circle disapprove of prejudice." Then they were asked to describe obligations and social pressure to be nonprejudiced. In the third neutral condition, students were asked only questions that did not refer to prejudice. After completing the questionnaires and writing descriptions of their answers, the students completed the Implicit Associations Test (Greenwald and Banaji 1995) which measured time reactions of associations between the Black and White race categories and positive and negative attributes. Results showed that students in the "autonomy" condition showed the least implicit bias against Blacks, while students in the "controlling" condition showed the most bias.

What can we conclude from this study? First, internal motivations to reduce bias can be induced; second, internal motivations lead to less explicit and implicit biases; external motivation leads to more explicit and implicit biases. This study also suggests that individuals can induce internal motivations to reduce bias by asking themselves questions such as "Why is it important to me, personally, to reduce prejudice?" and "What choices do I have to reduce bias?"

Enhancing Accountability and Egalitarian Goals

Individuals can raise their consciousness of implicit biases and in the process learn to regulate prejudicial thoughts and actions. For example, many theories predict that holding people accountable for their prejudices should reduce them. To raise this consciousness—that one should be held accountable—researchers asked study participants to simply provide "concrete reasons" for their prejudices (Dobbs and Crano 2001). Participants who provided these reasons subsequently showed less prejudice by allocating more points to a fictitious out-group in a simulated contest. Similarly, Bodenhausen, Kramer, and Susser (1994) found that students who believed that they would be held accountable to their peers were less likely to stereotype a hypothetical Hispanic student in a school disciplinary case. There is evidence, then, that accountability strategies work. At the individual level, accountability can be accomplished by holding oneself accountable for prejudicial actions, and by assessing reasons for being prejudiced. Of course, these strategies depend on an individual's willingness to admit to implicit biases or prejudicial actions. As seen in a previous section, most Americans are indeed willing to do so. A related strategy to inhibit stereotyping is to activate egalitarian goals. To be egalitarian is to treat everybody equally, or to treat others as we ourselves would like to be treated. Although most people profess to be egalitarian, thoughts and actions don't always support egalitarian goals because these goals, like implicit biases, are often subconsciously held. Moskowitz and Li (2011) devised a strategy to activate egalitarian goals by asking research participants to think about past experiences in which they had behaved toward African American men unfairly—in other words, past failures at being egalitarian. After this mental exercise, participants showed less negative stereotyping of African American men. This finding suggests that simply prompting oneself to think about past failures at being egalitarian may reduce the activation of implicit biases, including stereotyping.

Inducing Empathy by Targeting Emotions

Empathy, or the ability to identify with others' feelings, can be an effective inhibitor of implicit biases. Particularly effective strategies are "perspective-taking" interventions, which encourage the individual to experience the out-group member's emotions. For example, Galinsky and Moskowitz (2000) and Vescio et al. (2003) asked research participants to write essays from the perspective of an elderly person and other out-groups. They found that participants who wrote these essays subsequently rated the elderly and other targeted out-groups less stereotypically and more positively on a number of personality traits. Stephan and Finlay (1999) asked their research participants to be more emphatic when reading about everyday discrimination against Blacks by imagining how Blacks felt; they found that this intervention subsequently reduced negative stereotyping of Blacks. Similarly, Esses and Dovidio (2002) asked their research participants to focus on their feelings as they watched a video depicting discrimination against Blacks. These participants, compared to those who were instructed to focus on their thoughts, subsequently expressed a greater desire to interact with Blacks. In general, these results suggest that empathy can be triggered by focusing on emotions felt by the victims of prejudice and emotions felt by an observer. Empathy, in turn, can lead to reduced prejudice and reduced negative stereotyping.

Enhancing Value Consistency

A general principle in psychology supported by decades of research is that people strive for consistency in their beliefs, values, and actions (see, e.g., Eisenstadt et al. 2003; Festinger 1957). Inconsistency is mentally uncomfortable, leads to stress, and motivates the individual to strive for consistency. For example, my self-identity as a college professor includes the belief that I am an egalitarian person who does not have any prejudices; in addition, I believe that all people should be treated equally (equality is a value). Any behaviors contradicting my self-identity, egalitarian belief, and values (equality) will lead to stress and will motivate me to change the contradictory behavior. Examples of these behaviors are prejudice toward out-groups (e.g., feeling animosity toward a person who looks like a skinhead), negative stereotyping (e.g., assuming that Asian students are good at math but terrible writers and speakers), and discrimination (e.g., prohibiting Latino students from speaking Spanish to each other during breaks from work). If I am made aware that these behaviors and thoughts contradict my self-concept and values, I will make an effort to change them because the inconsistency will be uncomfortable. The key, then, is to make me aware of the inconsistencies.

Ball-Rokeach, Rokeach and Grube (1984) did some pioneering work on value consistency. In television programs specially designed for three cities in Washington state, they emphasized and illustrated the centrality of the value "equality" to Americans. They found that people who watched these programs subsequently showed less negative stereotyping of racial minorities. Other studies have similarly shown that people are able to inhibit biases when they are made aware of their values. Some awareness strategies are writing essays about why their values are important, sending public statements supporting minority policies and rights, and encouraging participants to see prejudice as inconsistent with their self-concepts and values. The key principles in these strategies are (1) recognition that equality is an American value and (2) recognition that prejudice is inconsistent with equality. At the individual level, self-awareness of these principles has the potential to inhibit implicit biases and prejudice.

Personal Contact and Interpersonal Communication

Personal Contact

First proposed by Gordon Allport in 1979, personal contact as a prejudice reduction intervention has a long history of research in social psychology, with generally strong support from more than five hundred studies (Pettigrew and Tropp 2006). The personal contact principle says that simple contact between groups can improve intergroup relations by reducing negative stereotyping and prejudice. Personal contact allows interacting individuals to "individuate"—that is, to see others as individuals rather than as members of a group and to observe each other in a wide range of behaviors, thereby providing more information that could negate the strict categorization imposed by stereotyping.

Although some studies have shown that simple contact improves intergroup relations (Pettigrew and Tropp 2006), attention has recently been directed to the optimal conditions of contact to increase the likelihood of reduced prejudice and stereotyping. These conditions are equal status of the interacting individuals, cooperation to achieve common goals, support by important societal institutions, shared goals, authority sanction (approval), and absence of competition (Pettigrew and Tropp 2006). When these conditions are present, the likelihood of success of personal contact interventions to reduce prejudice significantly increases as shown by a number of studies, some of which are discussed below.

1. Cook (1978) hired racially prejudiced White young adults to work on a management task for a railroad company with two "coworkers"—one Black and the other White. The participants worked on the project for a month under optimal conditions of contact—shared goals, cooperation, and equal status, and as directed by an authority. At the completion of the project, the prejudiced White adults rated their Black coworkers as more attractive, likeable, and competent than did a control group of prejudiced White adults who did not have the personal contact experience. Several months later, the participants who had personal contact with a Black coworker showed less prejudice in a survey about race relations than a control group did.

2. Duncan et al. (2003) studied minority and white students who had been randomly assigned to college dormitory rooms. They found that white students who were assigned to room with non-White students were more likely to support affirmative action than were White students who were assigned White roommates. There were only weak effects on other attitudinal and behavioral measures of prejudice.

3. Green and Wong (2008) randomly assigned fifty-four White teenagers to all-White or racially mixed groups for an Outward Bound camping expedition. The experience fulfilled optimum contact conditions for prejudice reduction—equal status, a common survival goal, approval from an authority (an experienced expedition leader), and intimate contact. The trip lasted two to three weeks. After the trip, White teens from the racially mixed teams reported less prejudice toward Blacks and gays than did White teens from all-White teams.

Extended and Vicarious Contact

These are but a few of the studies that show the effectiveness of *direct* personal contact in reducing prejudice. Because most people have limited opportunities to interact with people from out-groups (remember from Chapter 6, we prefer "our own"), particularly under optimum conditions of contact, we now turn our attention to two simulations of direct contact: *extended or vicarious contact*. Can simulations of direct contact reduce prejudice and stereotyping?

Extended or vicarious contact occurs when in-group members have knowledge about interactions of other in-group members with out-group members. This knowledge could be gained from direct observation, from conversations with in-group members, or from the media. A number of studies has shown that expectations about out-group interactions may be more positive when an out-group member is observed being friendly and positive toward in-group members; also, in-group members will express more positive attitudes toward out-groups after observing an in-group member showing tolerance toward an out-group (see, e.g., Turner et al. 2008).

Will the personal contact reported in the following news report lead to a reduction in prejudice?

Can NAACP-KKK Meeting Reduce Prejudice?

The Associated Press (2013) reported that a representative of the Wyoming chapter of the NAACP and a Ku Klux Klan organizer met secretly in a hotel in Casper, Wyoming, under tight security. According to the Southern Poverty Law Center, the meeting was a first.

The AP reported that the Klan organizer paid fifty dollars to join the NAACP. He said he joined the organization so he could receive the group's newsletters and some insight into its views. He said he paid a thirty-dollar membership fee and gave a twenty-dollar donation.

According to the NAACP representative, "It's about opening dialogue with a group that claims they're trying to reform themselves from violence. They're trying to shed their violent skin, but it seems they're just changing the packaging."

Mental Imagery

The potential of imagined interpersonal contact as a prejudice reduction intervention is based on the observation that mental imagery can elicit similar neurological, emotional, and behavioral responses associated with direct experience (Dadds et al. 1997). Based on this similarity, several studies have shown that mental imagery can be effective in reducing stereotyping and prejudice.

1. Blair, Ma, and Lenton (2001) asked college students to imagine a counter-stereotypic strong woman. These participants subsequently showed less implicit stereotypes of women than participants who imagined a weak woman or a strong man.
2. In studies by Turner, Crisp, et al.(2007), young participants who imagined talking to an elderly person subsequently showed less bias toward the elderly than did participants who imagined an outdoor scene. Also, heterosexual men who imagined talking to homosexual men subsequently evaluated homosexual men more positively than a control group did. In both studies, participants in the experimental ("imagine talking") condition expressed less intergroup anxiety or anxiety from interacting with the imagined out-group.

These studies suggest that mental imagery works best when participants engage in (e.g., are instructed to) simulated contact (such as conversation) rather than just thinking about an out-group ("imagine an elderly person). In other words, the participant engages in a mental script of an interaction rather than simply imagining the target person. Also, mental imagery, to be effective, should be of positive rather than neutral contact involving interactions that are pleasant and rewarding to the participant.

3. Turner and Crisp (2010) provide evidence that mental imagery of positive intergroup contact reduces implicit prejudice. They did their studies in the United Kingdom, where surveys showed that age discrimination was the most common form of prejudice. For example, people age fifty-five years and older were almost twice as likely to experience age discrimination as any other form of discrimination.

In Study 1, Turner and Crisp (2010) assigned undergraduate students ages eighteen to twenty-three to an experimental group (imagined contact condition) or to a control group (no imagined contact condition). They asked students in the imagined contact condition to "spend the next 2 minutes imagining yourself meeting an elderly stranger for the first time. Imagine that, during the encounter, you find out some interesting and unexpected things about the person" (Turner and Crisp 2010, 134). After the 2-minute mental imagery session, the students were asked to "List the interesting and unexpected things you learned about this person." (Turner and Crisp 2010, 134). The researchers asked students in the no-imagined-contact condition to "spend the next 2 minutes imagining an outdoor scene" and to try to imagine aspects of the scene (e.g., Is it a beach? A forest? Are there trees, hills? What's on the horizon?). The no-imagined-contact students then were asked to "list the different things you saw in the scene you just imagined." After the listing exercises, experimental and control students completed a questionnaire that measured explicit attitudes toward the elderly. They were asked how they felt about elderly people in general on a six-point semantic differential scale with the following descriptors: cold/warm, suspicious/trusting, positive/negative, friendly/hostile, respect/contempt, and admiration/disgust. Students in both conditions also completed an Implicit Association Test (IAT) that measured implicit attitudes toward the elderly (Greenwald and Banaji 1995). The IAT required participants to simultaneously pair target persons with positive words (e.g., smile, paradise) or negative words (e.g., slime, pain). The target people were the elderly (identified by typically older names such as Cyril, Arthur, and Mildred) and young people (identified by typically younger names such as Brad, Zack, and Lucy). Implicit attitudes were measured by the time (in milliseconds) that a target person was paired with either a positive or negative word: The lesser the time, the stronger the association. Therefore, a person who had implicit biases about the elderly would take less time to pair elderly names with the negative words than it would take them to pair young names with the negative words. Results of the study were as predicted: Participants in the imagined contact condition showed less explicit and implicit biases toward older people than did participants in the no-imagined-contact condition.

In Study 2, Turner and Crisp (2010) used Muslims as the targeted group. Non-Muslim undergraduate students were randomly assigned either to an experimental (imagined contact) or a control (no imagined contact) condition. In the imagined contact condition, the researchers asked participants to "spend the next 2 minutes imagining yourself meeting someone who is a Muslim for the first time. Imagine that the interaction is relaxed, positive, and comfortable" (Turner and Crisp 2010, 136). After the imagining session, students were asked to "list as many things [as possible] about the interaction that you just imagined." In the control (no imagined contact) condition, students were asked to "think about Muslims." The experimental condition primed the participants to imagine *positive interaction* with Muslims, while participants in the control group imagined the category "Muslim" without imagined positive contact. Results showed that participants who imagined positive contact expressed less explicit and implicit biases than did participants who imagined Muslims without positive interaction, providing support for the hypothesis that the key element in imagery as an intervention is *imagined positive contact*.

Mediated Communication Interventions

The prejudice reduction interventions I have discussed so far require either proactive and self-initiated strategies or strategies involving face-to-face interactions with out-group and in-group members. In this section, I will discuss strategies that require a medium to deliver the interventions to an audience. These mediated interventions are usually initiated by a mass medium (e.g., a television network, a newspaper); professional organizations (e.g., the Asian American Journalists Association); a private organization (e.g., the Southern Poverty Law Center); local, state, or national government agencies; or private foundations (e.g., the Bill and Melinda Gates Foundation). The intervention is delivered to large audiences via traditional media or the internet. Because audiences will not necessarily seek out these messages, audience participation is reactive (reacting to a message) rather than proactive (seeking out the message). Therefore, as suggested by theories of persuasion, the interventions have less probability of success compared to intrapersonal and interpersonal strategies, although, potentially, a much larger audience can be affected.

Most of the media-based interventions have not actually been tested in naturalistic settings (e.g., communities) with large audiences. In an extensive review of prejudice reduction research covering more than three decades, Paluck and Green (2009) found only thirteen media studies, and most of them were conducted in schools. Recommendations for media interventions have depended primarily on results of experimental studies and need to be tested with actual media messages and media audiences. Some of these experimental studies are discussed below, along with results that can be adopted for use in media campaigns.

Informational Narratives

If prejudice arises out of ignorance (Allport 1979), knowledge can be an antidote. Research has focused not so much on knowledge about targeted out-groups, but on knowledge about interactions with and discrimination against out-groups. For example, Finlay and Stephan (2000) found that the act of simply reading about discrimination against African Americans reduced biases against African Americans. The researchers asked a group of White students, randomly assigned, to read several essays purportedly written by African American freshmen. Written in the first person, some of the essays described African Americans "being falsely accused of wrongdoing, being denied membership in an organization, being denied check-writing privileges, overhearing personally relevant racially slanderous remarks, [and] being perceived as a threat" (Finlay and Stephan 2000, 1724). In the essays, the writers reported anger, annoyance, hostility, discomfort, or disgust because of the discrimination. Another group of White students, also randomly assigned, read essays by White American students who had been discriminated against in Hong Kong. After reading the essays, participants in both groups completed a questionnaire measuring stereotypes about African Americans and White Americans, including the following traits: safe, materialistic, polite, immoral, ambitious, lazy, dishonest, ignorant, loud, intelligent, impolite, good-natured, and dirty. Participants also answered another set of questions regarding their feelings toward African Americans and Whites, including the following evaluations: positive/negative, good/bad, desirable/undesirable, and like/dislike. Results of the study show that students who read "first-person" accounts by African Americans reduced biases against African Americans as measured by the stereotype and evaluative questions, compared to students who read the essays attributed to White students. These results suggest that media coverage of discrimination against out-groups, particularly if written in the first person, can reduce prejudice.

Other research has indicated that reading narratives or stories about interactions between in-groups and out-groups is an effective prejudice reduction intervention, particularly for children. The key elements of these narratives are depictions of friendship and positive contact. These findings are similar to results from studies of personal contact suggesting that vicarious contact from reading about out-groups can reduce prejudice. For application to the media, stories about friendships, cooperation, shared experiences, and other forms of positive contact between in-group and out-group members (e.g., Blacks and Whites) can be effective in reducing prejudice.

As themes for stories in the media, "color-blindness" and "multiculturalism" lead to very different narratives. The color-blindness theme proposes that social categories such as race should be dismantled and disregarded and that everyone should be treated as an individual (see, e.g., Firebaugh and Davis 1998). Proponents of this approach suggest that it can reduce racism and ensure equal treatment for everyone. On the other hand, multiculturalism proposes that group differences and memberships should not only be acknowledged and considered, but also celebrated (Richeson and Nussbaum, 2004). Proponents suggest that ethnic differences should be recognized and that ignoring them can be detrimental to ethnic minorities (Sleeter 1991). For the most part, the color-blind perspective has been the dominant influence on social psychology research, which has investigated, for example, how social categorization (e.g., race and ethnicity) can lead to in-group favoritism, ethnocentrism, prejudice, and stereotyping. Solutions proposed from this research include reducing the salience of categories and encouraging looking at people as individuals. Multiculturalism, on the other hand, proposes that group identification should not be "dismantled"; rather, it should be recognized and celebrated, and cooperation and positive relations between groups are possible while maintaining separate group identities (Hewstone 1996).

As a prejudice reduction intervention, the question, then, is which is more effective—color-blindness or multiculturalism? Recent evidence suggests that, in general, multiculturalism may be more effective in reducing implicit and explicit prejudice, and that colorblindness may actually increase racial bias. For example, Richeson and Nussbaum (2004) randomly assigned college students to read a one-page statement that either endorsed color-blindness or multiculturalism. The students then completed the Implicit Association Test (to measure implicit biases) and a questionnaire to measure racial attitudes toward Blacks and other racial groups (explicit biases). Results showed that students in the color-blind condition exhibited a larger pro-White bias in the IAT and more explicit prejudice than students in the multiculturalism condition did. The researchers concluded that "relative to the multiculturalism perspective, exposure to the color-blind perspective generated greater automatic (and explicit) racial bias" (Richeson and Nussbaum 2004, 421). These findings imply that the multiculturalism perspective may be a more effective intervention to reduce prejudice.

Applied to the media, news and entertainment content emphasizing and celebrating cultural differences may generate more positive intergroup attitudes, while contents that diminish or devalue these differences may exacerbate prejudice.

Exemplars

Exemplars are distinctive examples of a group who exhibit traits that may either be positive or negative. Most of the attention in prejudice reduction research has focused on counter-stereotypical exemplars who exhibit behaviors and dispositions that disconfirm negative stereotypes. Blair (2002) provides some evidence that counter-stereotypical exemplars can reduce negative stereotyping when the behaviors depicted are believable and arouse positive emotions in the in-group. These results can be explained by the conversion model of stereotype change, which explains how sudden changes in perceptions of people (as in stereotyping) can be brought about by exposure to new information (as in counter-stereotypic exemplars) that is convincing and forceful.

Building on previous research about exemplars, Dasgupta and Greenwald (2001) propose that as a prejudice reduction intervention, counter-stereotypic exemplars can be effective in reducing implicit biases when presented in comparison to exemplars from another group. Specifically, they suggest that pairing a negative exemplar from the mainstream group (e.g., Whites) with a positive exemplar from the negatively stereotyped out-group (e.g., Blacks) will reduce implicit biases against the out-group and implicit preference for the mainstream group.

To test their hypotheses, Dasgupta and Greenwald (2001) showed White and Asian undergraduate students, randomly assigned, photos of (a) admired Black individuals and disliked White individuals (pro-Black exemplar condition), (b) disliked Black individuals and admired White individuals (pro-White exemplar condition), or (c) non-racial exemplars (flowers and insects; control condition). The participants were told that they were participating in a study of "general knowledge," and were asked to correctly identify the person (or object, the control condition). They then completed a test of implicit biases (the IAT) and an explicit bias questionnaire (feeling thermometers and semantic differential ratings). The photos of White and Black individuals were obtained from the internet. Placement in the admired or disliked categories was based on past and current events (in 2001) and were validated through pretesting. All the photos were of men; the researchers explained that they could not find enough examples of admired and disliked women. Here are examples of the Black and White exemplars used in the study:

- Admired Black exemplars: Martin Luther King, Jr., Jesse Jackson, Colin Powell, Denzel Washington, Eddie Murphy, Michael Jordan, Tiger Woods, Will Smith, Bill Cosby, Gregory Hines
- Admired White exemplars: Clint Eastwood, Jim Carrey, Tom Cruise, David Duchovny, Tom Hanks, Jay Leno, John Kennedy, Robert Redford, Norman Schwarzkopf
- Disliked Black exemplars: O. J. Simpson, Mike Tyson, Louis Farrakhan, Marion Barry, Arthur Washington, Lonny Gray
- Disliked White exemplars: Ted Bundy, Jeffrey Dahmer, Timothy McVeigh, Charles Manson, Al Capone, Howard Stern

Dasgupta and Greenwald (2001) reported that exposure to admired Black and disliked White exemplars significantly weakened automatic pro-White attitudes (over Black) immediately and twenty-four hours after exposure, but did not affect explicit prejudice. Therefore, an admired Black exemplar was effective in reducing implicit biases against Blacks when paired with a disliked White exemplar.

Dasgupta and Greenwald (2001) repeated the study with age-related exemplars and found similar results. Exposure to an admired "old" exemplar and a disliked "young" exemplar reduced implicit biases against old people; explicit biases were not affected. Examples of the exemplars used in the study were as follows:

- Admired elderly people: Barbara Walters, Mother Teresa, Eleanor Roosevelt, Frank Sinatra, Willie Nelson, Albert Einstein, Dr. Benjamin Spock, Walter Cronkite
- Admired young people: Princess Diana, Steffi Graf, Jodie Foster, Leonardo DiCaprio, Prince William
- Disliked elderly people: Leona Helmsley, Tammy Faye Bakker, Ted Kaczynski, Sam Bowers, Bob Packwood
- Disliked young people: Tonya Harding, Susan Smith, Erik Menendez, Timothy McVeigh, Jeffrey Dahmer, Ted Bundy

Results were similar as in the first study. Exposure to admired elderly exemplars and disliked young exemplars reduced implicit biases toward the elderly. In explaining their results, Dasgupta and Greenwald (2001) proposed that evaluations of a social group depend on "the subset of exemplars retrieved from memory, which in turn depends on exemplar accessibility" (807). People have positive and negative exemplars of in- and out-groups stored in memory. The photos in their study primed (or brought attention to) the exemplars. Accordingly, implicit associations (biases) were shaped by the recently retrieved exemplars.

These studies suggest that exemplars presented in media news and entertainment can reduce implicit biases. When reporting on or portraying negative and positive exemplars, highlighting or identifying the person's social category (e.g., race, age) can reduce implicit biases when done equally for in-groups and out-groups and for both positive (admired) and negative (disliked) behaviors. Unfortunately, research tells us that the media disproportionately depicts minorities and women in negative, stereotypical ways. More balanced media representations would remind people of both admired members of out-groups and disliked members of in-groups. In addition, when group memberships of these positive and negative exemplars are emphasized, the combined effect may be to reduce implicit prejudice and stereotypes (Dasgupta and Greenwald 2001).

In this chapter, I discussed prejudice and stereotype reduction interventions that have been shown to be effective in laboratory studies. These interventions, for the most part, are proactive—the participant has to recognize his or her implicit and explicit biases and must be willing to change. I categorized these interventions according to level of analysis. At the intrapersonal level, the participant can work on motivations, enhancing accountability and egalitarian goals and assessing consistency between values and behaviors. Personal contact is the key strategy for reducing prejudice at the interpersonal level. This contact could be direct, vicarious, or imagined. For maximum effectiveness, contact should be interactive and positive. Media strategies are, for the most part, untested. Results from laboratory studies suggest a number of strategies that the media could adopt, including narratives about intergroup interactions, a focus on emotions or feelings resulting from these interactions, using positive and negative exemplars equally for out- and in-groups, and a focus on multiculturalism.

Granted that prejudice is embedded in the human psyche, there is hope in the potential of these interventions, particularly for the more than eighty percent of Americans who have implicit biases, and who would like to control or reduce them.

Workbook

Define, describe, or illustrate concepts; summarize the results of the studies.

1.   Most likely to reduce prejudice?

2.   Communication interventions—intrapersonal, interpersonal, mediated levels

3.   Legault et al., motivations to reduce prejudice

4.   Enhancing accountability and egalitarian goals

5.   Esses and Dovidio, results

6.   Equality value and belief consistency

7.   Ball, Rokeach, and Grube, results

8.   Personal contact; optimum conditions

9.   Cook "railroad study," results

10.   Green and Wong, expedition group study, results

11.   Duncan et al., dorm study, results

12.   Vicarious contact; mental imagery

13.   Turner and Crisp, mental imagery, results

14.   Finlay and Stephan, informational narratives, results

15.   Color blind, multicultural narratives

16.   Boldenhausen et al., exemplars, results

17.   Dasgupta and Greenwald, black and white exemplars, results

16

Digital Media Literacy

The internet has significantly changed how we use information in many ways. It has exponentially increased our potential sources and has made it possible for just about anyone to be a source and creator of information. Because we can control what we see or read online and for how long, the internet has become a major and preferred source of news and information relied on by many, particularly young adults. At the same time, the internet has become an often-used medium for the spread of hate, prejudice, and stereotyping. Our reliance on the internet and its ubiquity calls for the ability to evaluate the credibility and veracity of information sources and their products, such as news. This ability—to recognize "fake" from real, information from propaganda, news from advertisements, and rumor from facts and to take appropriate action—is at the heart of media literacy or, in the case of online communication, digital information literacy.

Reliance on the Internet for News and Information

Americans generally prefer to get their news on a screen, television first followed by digital media. However, among young adults the first choice is digital media followed by television. A random national survey of adult Americans, ages 18 and above conducted by the Pew Research Center in 2016 had the following results:

Percentage of American adults who often get their news from

- Cable, local, or network nightly television: 57%
- Online from social media, websites, apps: 38%
- Radio: 25%
- Print newspapers: 20%

Percentage of Americans 18–29 years old who often get their news from

- Television: 27%
- Online: 25%
- Radio: 14%
- Print newspapers: 5%

Percentage of Americans 30–49 years old who often get their news from

- Television: 45%
- Online: 49%

- Radio: 27%
- Print newspapers: 10%

Percentage of Americans 50–64 years old who often get their news from

- Television: 72%
- Online: 29%
- Radio: 29%
- Print newspapers: 23%

Percentage of Americans more than 65 years old who often get their news from

- Television: 85%
- Online: 20%
- Radio: 24%
- Print newspapers: 48%

These percentages tell us that there is a linear relationship between preferences for each platform (except radio) and age: the older the respondent, the more often television and print newspapers are used; the younger the respondent, the more often online platforms are used. These percentages are based on frequent users within each age groups. They may add up to more than 100%, because respondents could identify more than one source they often used for news.

The Pew survey also showed that more adult Americans prefer to watch news (46%) rather than read it (35%) or listen to it (17%). Among respondents who prefer watching the news (over reading or listening) 80% preferred getting the news from television and 12% from online media. Among those who prefer to read news, 59% preferred getting the news online; 26% preferred print newspapers (Pew Research Center 2016a). These data show that the internet has drawn readers rather than watchers at the expense of print newspapers.

Children also use the internet for information, although rarely for news of current events (Hobbs 2010). For children, the internet, like television, is primarily an instrument for entertainment. The Kaiser Family Foundation (2010) estimates that children eight to eighteen years old watch television for more than three hours per day and spend ten to twelve hours per day with some form of electronic media to download music, watch videos, play games, and interact on social networks. Although children may be exposed to news in schools (e.g., *Channel One*, *Time for Kids*), the internet is primarily used for entertainment at home. Even so, children may turn to the internet for information that might help them personally or for schoolwork (Hobbs 2010).

Media and digital information literacy programs for children focus on evaluating entertainment and information sources—how to distinguish reality from fantasy; how to recognize bias and prejudice; and how to search for credible information on the internet.

Strengths and Limitations of the Internet as a Source of Information

The internet provides us with more choices than ever before for information, entertainment, news, and comment. It allows us not only to be consumers, but also to be creators of information. Compared to newspapers, radio, and television, we exercise more control over what, when, and where we watch or read. It is also much easier to share information with many people. The internet (and the electronic devices we use to access it) has revolutionized our consumption and creation of information.

At the same time, the internet has restricted our processing of information. We learn less, are more susceptible to inaccurate information, and are less exposed to information that contradicts what we already believe. Research has identified several reasons for these limitations.

Cognitive Load

Humans have limited short-term information processing capacity (e.g., Miller 1956; Baddely, Thomson, and Buchanan 1975; Cowan 2001). The average person can store in his or her short-term memory about "seventeen plus or minus two" bits of information, and the average storage time is ten to twenty seconds (Baddely et al. 1975; Cowan 2001). This limited capacity is diminished by noise, such as distractions and multitasking, conditions that are often present when we access information from the internet on a screen. Examples of these distractions are multiple sites on one screen, hyperlinks, and advertisements. These distractions contribute to cognitive overload, defined as information that exceeds a person's capacity to store it (Baddely et al., 1986). One indicator of cognitive overload is low recall of the information.

To analyze cognitive overload, researchers have compared how we process information when we read it in print media (such as a book or newspaper) and when we read it on a screen (such as a computer screen). The dependent variables or effects typically involve recall, stress, enjoyment, and physiological responses. Results show that college students and children ages eight to seventeen learn more (recall more information) when they read the material in print (e.g., books, newspapers) compared to reading the material on a computer screen. They also report less stress and more enjoyment but prefer receiving the information on a computer screen (e.g., Mangen et al. 2013). Researchers have also found that screen readers, compared to print readers, blink their eyes more often, an indication of more cognitive effort (e.g., Wastlund et al. 2005). Taken together, these results suggest that screen readers, compared to print readers, experience more cognitive overload, more stress, and less enjoyment and expend more effort in processing information. Screen readers are more likely to encounter competing tasks (to reading). These tasks are often decisions that have to be made before the information is accessed: whether the source is credible; which heading to click; which hyperlink to follow; whether material is news, opinion, or advertising; whether to scroll on or not. Also, it is more inconvenient to scroll back for a review of previous information (Mangen et al. 2013). These results suggest that we learn less and are more likely to accept inaccurate information from a computer screen, as compared to print.

Confirmation Bias

We are protective of our attitudes, beliefs, and behaviors and do not wish to be challenged by information that might suggest we are "wrong." Contradictory information leads to uncomfortable states such as stress and uncertainty. Consequently, we are receptive to supportive information, more likely to seek it out, and more likely to pay attention to it. Conversely, we avoid and misinterpret contradictory information. These principles of selective information exposure are derived from cognitive dissonance theory (Festinger 1957) and confirmation bias theory (Nickerson 1998). Confirmation bias explains both our tendency to seek out supportive information from websites and social media and our susceptibility to accepting inaccurate information that appears to support our political attitudes, biases, stereotypes, and resulting behaviors.

Deficiencies in Digital Information Literacies

Many children, teens, and young adults can produce and upload their own videos; solve problems in video games with a virtual community of other "gamers"; use their mobile phones to organize social events; and create virtual newspapers and other contents. However, they may lack the ability to use search strategies that can discriminate for quality and relevance, such as using appropriate keywords; to identify the author of a webpage; to evaluate the credibility, purpose, objectivity, and veracity of information they access; to comprehend the information; to quickly read a webpage and find the best link for more relevant information (rather than "clicking and looking"); to evaluate the trustworthiness and expertise of sources; and to be open to all relevant, credible information even if it contradicts existing beliefs, attitudes, and behaviors (Hobbs 2010). These deficiencies in digital information use are what digital information literacy programs seek to remedy.

Evaluating the quality of digital sources is particularly problematic, especially for young users. Metzger (2009) and Hobbs (2010) note that digital media can confuse many users regarding the validity of the source and information. Sources with self-serving objectives, such as to sell, persuade, recruit, or spread misinformation to discredit an opposing point of view, use some of the following strategies: attractive graphic designs; hidden, absent, or fake authorship; aggregated information from many sources on one webpage; multiple hyperlinks; and biased, incomplete, or self-serving reviews and rating services (e.g., Hobbs 2010). Also contributing to the confusion is increased use of "native advertising" by many news organizations as a source of revenue. Native advertising sells or promotes a product or idea by disguising the advertising material as a news story, making it difficult for the consumer to judge whether the information is news or advertising and what the source intends to gain from the information (Stanford History Education Group 2016).

Reliance on online communities for news and information is another major obstacle to accurate evaluation. This reliance contributes to confirmation bias. It can also lead to the acceptance of false information as credible. Although most online news consumers say they are more likely to get their news from professional news organizations (76%), many say they also get news from "people they are close with" (69%) (Pew 2016b). The credibility of news from close friends is often assumed since these sources are trusted and liked.

The potential for confirmation bias is heightened by the ease of sending inaccurate and false information to large groups of online communities, particularly like-minded communities. Pew (2016b) reports that 74% of adult news consumers who get their news from people they are close with say that the news they get is very or somewhat close to their interests. Among news consumers who get their news from news organizations, 71% say the news they get is very or quite close to their interests. These data provide support for the confirmation bias principle: we attend to news sources that provide us with information that supports existing cognitive, affective, and behavioral biases.

I have presented some reasons why it's difficult to accurately evaluate information on the internet. Is there evidence that online news consumers actually make these mistakes? A recent study (Stanford History Education Group 2016) provides some answers.

Stanford researchers presented 7,804 middle school, high school, and college students with prototypes of online webpages and asked them to judge the credibility of information. The prototypes and questionnaires for assessment were given to middle and high school students as paper and pencil tests and to college students online. Fifteen protocols were used and assessed. Here are assessment results for three.

Home Page Analysis: The Stanford researchers presented 203 middle school students with the home page of *Slate* magazine's website, which included news items and advertisements. They wanted to find out whether the students could distinguish between news and advertising. The webpage showed a traditional advertisement, a news story, and a native advertisement. The students were asked to identify whether each section was a news story or an advertisement and to explain the features that led them to their answers. Most students (75%) were able to distinguish the traditional advertisement from the news story. However, more than 80% said that the native advertisement identified in the webpage as "Sponsored" was a bona fide news story. According to the researchers, these results indicate that children do not understand what "sponsored" means and can be easily misled into believing that native advertising is indeed real news (Stanford History Education Group 2016).

Evaluating Evidence: The researchers (Stanford History Education Group 2016) showed 170 high school students a post from Imgur, a website that shares photos. The post was a picture of daisies with unusually large blossoms; one blossom was attached to another. The caption read "Not much more to say, this is what happens when flowers get nuclear birth defects." The picture was posted after an accident at the Fukushima Daiichi Nuclear Power Plant in Japan in 2011. The high school students were asked whether the photo provided strong evidence of the effects of the nuclear spillage near the power plant. According to the researchers, a "literate" response demonstrating the ability to evaluate the credibility of the photo as evidence would question 1) the credibility and motivations of the person who posted the photo (anyone can do so on this particular website), 2) whether the photo was taken near the power plant, and 3) whether nuclear radiation caused the daisies' unusual growth (Stanford History Education Group 2016). Few students gave literate responses: less than 20% questioned the credibility of the source of the post or the website; about 40% said that the photo provided strong evidence, because it was a picture taken close to the plant; about 25% said that the photo did not provide strong evidence because it showed only flowers and no other plants or animals, but they did not question the credibility of the source. According to the researchers, these results show that even older students, in this case high school students, need education to assess the credibility of information sources and websites they may encounter on the internet (Stanford History Education Group 2016).

Claims on Social Media: The researchers asked 44 undergraduate college students to evaluate the strengths and weaknesses of a tweet as a source of information. The tweet, from MoveOn.org, a liberal advocacy organization, read "New polling shows the NRA is out of touch with gun owners and their own members." It was accompanied by a graphic that said, "Two out of three gun owners say they would be more likely to vote for a candidate who supported background checks." The tweet said that the poll was conducted by Public Polling Policy in 2015 and contained a link to the Center for American Progress. According to the researchers, a literate response would acknowledge that the tweet may provide useful information, because the poll cited was a professional polling firm. However, literate consumers would question whether the tweet was unbiased even if based on a scientific poll, considering that MoveOn.org and the Center for American Progress both support strong gun control measures. They would search for more information about the two organizations and would question how the poll was conducted and how results were publicized. In the end, they may agree that the information was useful and credible after processing more information that was not in the tweet. According to the researchers, only "a few" students noted that the tweet was based on information from a scientific poll and, therefore, would be a credible source of information. Less than a third of the students questioned the political agendas of the sources of the tweet. In interviews, more than half of the students said they did not click on any links for more information, and simply scrolled up and down within the tweet. According to the researchers, "these results suggest that students need further instruction in how best to navigate social media content, particularly when that content comes from a source with a clear political agenda" (Stanford History Education Group 2016, p. 24).

Media and Digital Information Literacy

Public and academic interest in media literacy is not new. As far back as the fifth century BC, philosophers debated and taught critical thinking as a pathway to successful argumentation, particularly in politics (e.g., Hobbs 2008). In the United States, teachers and scholars were concerned about the influence of motion pictures on youth and the potential of films as educational tools (Saettler 2004). Canada, Australia, Finland, England, France, New Zealand, Denmark, and the Netherlands were first to develop large-scale media education programs for schoolchildren (Lederer 1988; Hobbs 2010).

In the US, there is renewed focus by schools, citizen groups, academics, private foundations, and local, state, and national government agencies on educational programs in and out of schools to educate youth about the media, broadly defined as any mediated means by which information is sent and received. This concern about the media is brought about by the dominance of the internet as a source of information and entertainment available even to children as young as three; the amount of time youth spend on mediated experiences, mostly on the internet, (e.g., searching/accessing information, watching movies, playing video games, 10–11 hours per week); and decades of scientific research showing a link between media use and pro-social (beneficial) and anti-social (destructive) behaviors of users, particularly children (e.g., Hobbs 2010).

Education about the media is used synonymously with "media literacy." Digital information literacy is a subset of media literacy, referring to search, evaluation, creation, and application skills specifically for the internet. Hobbs (2010) defines media/digital literacy:

> the full range of cognitive, emotional and social competencies that includes the use of texts, tools and technologies; the skills of critical thinking and analysis; the practice of message composition and creativity; the ability to engage in reflection and ethical thinking; as well as active participation through teamwork and collaboration. (17).

Let's look at what competencies or skills a media and digitally literate person is expected to have mastered:

- The ability to use media and technology to search for information. Examples are searching the internet for news, a video clip, a movie, directions to a hospital, or a recipe.
- The ability to evaluate the credibility, veracity, completeness, and objectivity of information. Examples are distinguishing between news and traditional advertising, between news and "native advertising," and between real and fake news. This also includes being able to articulate the reasons for making these distinctions.
- The ability to create and send messages using traditional and digital technologies, knowledge of the distinctions between media forms and their possible effects on users, and knowledge of the technical tools to send these messages.
- The ability to be mindful of the influence media and specific messages may have on the individual and other users and to mitigate this influence through critical analysis or curtailment of the use of harmful contents.
- The ability to be a good citizen, discuss social and political issues from an informed perspective, share knowledge, and participate in the democratic process at local, state, and national levels; for children, awareness of school and community issues that might affect them, and the ability to talk about these issues with other students, teachers, and parents.

To illustrate the evaluation competencies with examples from real-life, let's re-visit the study by the Stanford History Education Group (2016). If you recall, the Stanford researchers asked middle school, high school, and college students to evaluate the information in prototypes of internet content.

Middle school children accurately identified traditional news stories and advertisements; however, most said that native advertising was news. To assess literacy, the researchers used the following rubric (Stanford History Education Group 2016, 11):

Mastery
"Student correctly identifies the item as an ad or non-ad and provides coherent reasoning."

Emerging
"Student correctly identifies the item as an ad or non-ad and provides limited or incoherent reasoning."

Beginning
"Student incorrectly identifies the item as an ad or non-ad."

Here are some examples of student responses demonstrating different levels of competence (11–14). Students who correctly identified the ad based on its features:

Mastery
"It has the 'ad choices' and 'stop seeing this ad' buttons in the top right corner"; "It has a coupon code, a big company logo, and has the words 'limited time offer'"; "In the left side there is something that says 'save $20,' and usually money is involved if people are selling something."

Emerging

"It is an advertisement because it advertises something"; "It's an advertisement because there's no really useful thing on it."

Students who correctly identified the news story based on its features:

Mastery

"There is no little blue X, it has an author of the article, and it doesn't say sponsored content."

Emerging

"It is not an advertisement because it does not have a blue button on top."

Beginning

"There is nothing to suggest that something is sold. No money, deals, etc. It sounds like an article."

High school students evaluated a picture of daisies showing abnormal growth as evidence of nuclear contamination. The researchers used the following rubric to assess student response (Stanford History Education Group 2016, 18–19):

Mastery

"Student argues the post does not provide strong evidence and questions the source of the post (e.g., we don't know anything about the author of the post) and/or the source of the photograph (e.g., we don't know where the photo was taken)."

Emerging

"Student argues that the post does not provide strong evidence, but the explanation does not consider the source of the post or the source of the photograph, or the explanation is incomplete."

Beginning

"Student argues that the post provides strong evidence or uses incorrect or incoherent reasoning."

Here are examples of student responses (18–19):

Mastery

"No, it does not really provide strong evidence. A photo posted by a stranger online has little credibility. This photo could very easily be Photoshopped or stolen from another completely different source; we have no idea given this information, which makes it an unreliable source."

Emerging

"This post does not provide strong evidence about conditions near the power plant. They just put a picture of a flower. Plus the poster has a strange username."

Beginning

"This post does provide strong evidence because it shows how the small and beautiful things were affected greatly, that they look and grow completely different than they are supposed to. Additionally, it suggests what such a disaster could do to humans."

College students evaluated the usefulness and objectivity of a tweet regarding the National Rifle Association (NRA). The researchers used the following rubric to assess responses (Stanford History Group 2016, 24):

Mastery

"Student fully explains that the tweet may be useful because it includes data from a poll conducted by a polling firm."

Emerging

"Student addresses the polling data and/or the source of the polling data but does not fully explain how those elements may make the tweet useful."

Beginning
"Student does not address the polling data or the source of the polling data as a reason the tweet may be useful."

Here are examples of student responses:

Mastery
"The polling information which the tweet references was collected by Public Policy Polling, which appears to have a fairly strong accuracy record, though with a Democratic bent (e.g., *Wall Street Journal* article: http://ww.wsj/articles/SB122592455567202805)."

Emerging
"The photo used in the tweet was compiled from a public policy polling survey."

Beginning
"It could be useful because a graphic with a strong message can be enlightening or more likely thought provoking."

These responses to internet prototypes provide us with some information on the specific topics that a digital media literacy education class could provide, particularly as the information pertains to evaluating sources and evidence.

Fake News on the Internet

Media/digital literacy programs can be an effective antidote to fake news on the internet, defined as "fictitious articles deliberately fabricated to deceive readers, generally with the goal of profiting through clickbait" (Tavernise 2016). PolitiFact defines fake news as "fabricated content designed to fool readers and subsequently made viral through the Internet to crowds that increase its dissemination" (Kertscher 2016). Other definitions emphasize the use of fake news for political gain, that is, to promote a political ideology, idea, or candidate (Chen 2015).

Here are several characteristics of fake news:

- Fictitious and fabricated
- Wide distribution to audiences through social media
- Embedded in fake websites made to look like the official websites of trusted sources (e.g., ABC News, MSNBC)
- Promotion for a product, political ideology, candidate, or idea
- International in scope (e.g., fake news in Brazil, Canada, China, France, Germany, and other countries)
- Not easy to detect

Fake News as an Instrument of Prejudice and Hate

The internet can be a powerful instrument for good and bad. On the good side, it provides free and easy access to more information than has ever been possible; the opportunity to connect socially across time and geographical borders; and the opportunity to organize and participate in community and political activities. On the bad side, the internet can be a vehicle for the spread of inaccurate or false information, prejudice, and hate.

According to the Southern Poverty Law Center (2017), the number of hate groups in the US, were at "near-historic highs" in 2016 (38). Many of these groups are increasingly using the internet to spread their message, recruit converts, and organize followers. Their online activity increased in 2017, including posts on social media, hate group websites, and fake news sites (The Southern Poverty Law Center, 2017).

To warn users about potentially prejudicial content, Google has asked its review teams of "quality raters" to flag as "upsetting-offensive" content that promotes hate or violence against a specific group based on gender, race, or other criteria (Associated Press 2017). The article will still show up in the search, but with the label "upsetting-offensive," and placed less prominently on the list of content matching the search keywords. For example, if I search for "Holocaust history," a website listing "Top 10 reasons why the Holocaust didn't happen" would be flagged as "upsetting-offensive." I could still access the website, but I would know that the content is controversial, possibly biased or not true. To help users evaluate the accuracy of content, Google gives prominence (listed at the top) to "high quality pages such as the home page of a newspaper that has won seven Pulitzer awards" (Associated Press 2017).

Similarly, Facebook, a conduit for legitimate and fake news for many of its users, labels articles that are fabricated and with no factual basis as "Disputed" (USA Today 2017). BuzzFeed News reports that the fake news articles in the last few months of the 2016 presidential campaign generated more comments and online conversations on Facebook than articles from major news outlets. According to the PEW Research Center (2016), nearly one-fourth of adult Americans say they have shared a fake news story. The "Disputed" label is intended to dissuade Facebook users from spreading fake news.

Media Literacy: How to Detect Fake News

Media literacy education places responsibility on the user to detect fake news. The warning labels on Google and Facebook will work only if users pay attention and exercise caution in evaluating and sending information flagged by the "Upsetting-Offensive" and "Disputed" labels.

Media literacy education is taught in schools and colleges. Outside of these settings, fact-checking organizations give us guidance on how to detect fake news. Here are some pointers from FactCheck.Org (Keilly and Robertson 2016):

- Check the source. Many fake news stories originate from websites that graphically look like reputable news sites but in fact are sites with the main purpose of spreading fake news. Google the author or originating website to check credentials. Snopes.com keeps a list of fake news websites.
- Read the entire story, not just the headline. Provocative headlines are misleading. The story may contain clues as to the veracity and authenticity of the author and information.
- Check support for claims made in the story. Google secondary sources, such as "official" reports. Do not assume that these sources are credible.
- Be skeptical of viral news even if it comes from Facebook friends. If you have any doubts about the veracity of the information, delete chain emails about "breaking" news.
- Be aware of signs that the story is fake news, including the lack of an author or the presence of exclamation points, capital letters, misspellings, or poor grammar.
- When in doubt, consult fact-checking websites, such as FactCheck.org (Ask FactCheck), PolitiFact.com, Snopes.com, and the Washington Post Fact Checker.

In summary, media and digital literacy programs help us evaluate the massive amounts of information available on the internet. Key elements of these programs include checking sources and the evidence, being open to opposing viewpoints, and critically evaluating the evidence.

Workbook

Define, describe, or illustrate the concepts; summarize the results of the studies:

1. Reliance on internet for news: PEW, 2016

2. Cognitive load

3. Cognitive overload

4. Screen and print information processing: retention, distractions, stress, cognitive effort

5. Confirmation bias

6. Digital information literacy: definition; Stanford study (2016)

7. Fake news: definitions, characteristics

8. Detecting fake news

References

Chapter 1: Introduction to Communication and Illustrative Examples of Prejudice

Associated Press. (2007, September 9).

Associated Press. (2011, May 10).

Associated Press. (2012, August 20).

Associated Press. (2013, November 25). In *Moscow Pullman Daily News*.

Associated Press. (2014, April 15).

Bonilla-Silva, E., & Forman, T. (2000). 'I am not a racist but …': Mapping White college students' racial ideology in the USA. *Discourse & Society,* 11 (1), 50–85.

Chau, J. (2012, April 13). *The Chronicle of Higher Education.*

DeSantis, N. (2013, November 18). *The Chronicle of Higher Education.*

Huff Post SCIENCE. (2012, February 1).

Mandela, N. (1994). *Long Walk to Freedom: The Autobiography of Nelson Mandela.* McDonald Purnell.

Nosek, B. A., Greenwald, A. G., & Banaji, M. R. (2005). Understanding and using the Implicit Association Test: Method variables and construct validity. *Personality and Social Psychology Bulletin,* 31 (2), 166–80.

Slate.com. (2012, August 29).

The Spokesman Review. (2009, October 14).

Sterling, T. (2013, November 17). Associated Press in *The Spokesman Review.*

Yahoo! News. (2011, March 8).

Chapter 2: Communication and Prejudice

Appelbaum, R. (1970). *Theories of Social Change.* Markham Publishing.

Argyle, M. (1988). *Bodily Communication.* (2nd ed.). International Universities Press.

Bargh, J., Schwader, K., Hailey, S., Dyer, R., & Boothby, E. (2012). "Automaticity in social-cognitive processes." *Trends in Cognitive Sciences,* 16 (12), 593–606.

Blair, I., Judd, L., & Chapleau, K. (2004). The influence of Afrocentric facial features in criminal sentencing. *Psychological Science,* 15 (10), 674–79.

Bull, P. E. (1987). *Posture and Gesture.* Pergamon Press.

Chandler, D. (2008). Tuning in to unconscious communication. *MIT News.*

Cherry, E. C. (1957). *On Human Communication.* Wiley.

Cooley, C. (1966). The significance of communication. In *Reader in Public Opinion and Communication.* (B. Berelson, & M. Janowitz, Eds.). 147–55. Free Press.

Ekman, P. (2004). *Emotions Revealed.* Henry Holt & Co.

Evans, N., & Levinson, S. (2009). The myth of language universals. Language diversity and its importance for cognitive sciences. *Behavioral and Brain Sciences,* 32 (5), 429–92.

Friedman, R., & Elliot, A. (2008). The effect of arm crossing on persistence and performance. *European Journal of Psychology,* 38 (3), 449–61.

Hargie, O., & Dickson, D. (2004). *Skilled Interpersonal Communication: Research, Theory and Practice.* Routledge.

Hoebel, A. (1960). The nature of culture. In *Man, Culture and Society.* (H. L. Shapiro, Ed.). Oxford University Press.

Hogan, K., & Stubbs, R. (2003). *Can't Get Through: 8 Barriers to Communication.* Pelican Publishing Co.

Kirch, M. S. (1979). Non-verbal communication across cultures. *Modern Language Journal,* 63 (8), 417–22.

Knapp, M., & Hall, J. (2007). *Nonverbal communication in human interaction*. (5th ed.). Wadsworth.

Lasswell, H. (1948). The structure and function of communication in society. In L. Bryson (Ed.), *The Communication of Ideas* (pp. 37–51). Harper and Row.

Lenski, G. (1974). *Human Societies: An Introduction to Macrosociology*. McGraw Hill, Inc.

Lester, P. (2006). *Visual Communication: Images with Messages*. Wadsworth.

Maas, A. (1999). Linguistic intergroup bias: Stereotype perpetuation through language. In M. P. Zanna (Ed.), *Advances in Experimental Social Psychology, Vol. 31* (pp. 79–121). Academic Press.

McMillan, D. W., & Chavis, D. M. (1986). Sense of community: A definition and theory. *American Journal of Community Psychology, 14* (1), 6–23.

Mead, G. H. (1934). *Mind, Self and Society*. University of Chicago Press.

Medina, J. (2008). *Brain Rules: 12 Principles for Surviving and Thriving at Work, Home and School*. Pear Press.

Navarro, J. (2008). *What Everybody Is Saying*. Harper Collins.

Parsons, T. (1966). *Societies: Evolutionary and Comparative Perspectives*. Prentice Hall.

Pease, B., & Pease, A. (2004). *The Definitive Book of Body Language*. Bantam Books.

Ruscher, J. (2001). *Prejudiced Communication: A Social Psychological Perspective*. The Guilford Press.

Schramm, W. (1954). How communication works. In W. Schramm (Ed.), *The Process and Effects of Mass Communication* (pp. 3–26). University of Illinois Press.

Shannon, C., & Weaver, W. (1949). *The Mathematical Theory of Communication*. University of Illinois Press.

Smith, K. L. (2005). *Handbook of Visual Communication: Theory, Methods, and Media*. Lawrence Erlbaum Publishers.

Stevens, S. S. (1966). Concerning the measurement of brightness. *Journal of the Optical Society of America, 56* (8), 1135–36.

Tan, A. (1986). Mass Communication Theories and Research. (2nd ed.). Macmillan Publishing Co.

Chapter 3: What Is Prejudice?

Allport, G. W. (1954). *The Nature of Prejudice*. Addison-Wesley.

Allport, G. W. (1979). *The Nature of Prejudice*. (25th Anniversary ed.). Addison-Wesley.

Associated Press. (2012, October 29). Racial Attitudes Survey.

Associated Press. (2013, May 21).

Atkinson, D. R.,Morten, G., & Sue, D. W. (1998). *Counseling American Minorities*. McGraw Hill.

Blinder, A. (2013, September 18). *New York Times*.

Bonham, V., Warshauer-Baker, E. & Collins, F. S. (2005). Race and ethnicity in the genomic era: A complexity of the construct. *American Psychologist, 60*, no. 1, 9–15.

Brewer, M. B. (1994). The social psychology of prejudice: Getting it all together. In M. P. Zanna & J. M. Olson (Eds.), *Ontario Symposium on Personality and Social Psychology, Vol. 7* (pp. 315–330). Lawrence Erlbaum.

Carter, R. T., & Pieterse, A. L. (2005). Race: A social and psychological analysis of the term and its meaning. In R. T. Carter (Ed.), *Handbook of Racial Cultural Psychology and Counseling Theory and Research, Vol. 1* (pp. 41–63). Wiley.

Coeur d'Alene Press. (2011, August 30).

Cole, D. (2009). *No Equal Justice: Race and Class in the American Criminal Justice System*. The New Press.

Darity, W. A., & Mason, P. L. (1998). Evidence on discrimination in employment. *Journal of Economic Perspectives, 2* (2), 63–90.

Dozier, R. W. (2002). *Why We Hate*. McGraw-Hill.

Eagly, A., & Chin, J. L. (2010). Diversity and leadership in a changing world. *American Psychologist, 65* (3), 216–24.

Eagly, A., & Mladinic, A. (1994). Are people prejudiced against women? Some answers from research on attitudes, gender stereotypes, and judgments of competence. *European Review of Social Psychology, 51*, 1–35.

Eng, J. (2013, August 24). *MSN News*.

Eberhardt, J., Davies, P. G., Purdie-Vaughn, V. J., & Johnson, S. L. (2006). Looking deathworthy: Perceived stereotypes of Black defendants predict capital sentencing outcomes. *Cornell Law Faculty Publications*, Paper 41.

Feder, J. (2010, June 23). The age discrimination in employment act (ADEA): A legal overview. *Congressional Research Service*.

Gallup Poll 2008; 2010.

Grovun. (2013, August 5). *Stateline.org* in *The Spokesman Review*.

Hasslinger, T. (2011). *Coeur d'Alene Press*.

Hecht, M. (1998). Introduction. In M. Hecht (Ed.), *Communicating Prejudice* (pp. 1–23). Sage Publications.

Herek, G. M. (1990). Homophobia. In W. R. Dynes (Ed.), *Encyclopedia of Homosexuality* (pp. 552–55). Garland.

Herek, G. M. (2009). Sexual prejudice. In T. Nelson (Ed.), *Handbook of Prejudice* (pp 439–65). Psychology Press.

Hersch, J. (2011a). The persistence of skin color discrimination for immigrants. *Social Science Research*, 40 (5), 671–78.

Herschof, J. (2011b). Skin color, physical appearance and perceived discriminatory treatment. *Journal of Socio-Economics* 40, (5), 671–78.

Human Rights Watch. (2008).

Iversen, T. N., Larsen, L., & Solem, P. E. (2009). A conceptual analysis of ageism. *Nordic Pyschology,* 61 (3), 4–22.

Jones, J. M. (1997). *Prejudice and Racism.* (2nd ed.). McGraw-Hill.

Krogman, W. (1945). *Races of Man.* Columbia University Press.

Lahey, J. N. (2005, November 13). State age protection laws and the age discrimination act. *NBER Working Paper,* 12048. *The Los Angeles Times.*

Lyons, I. (2009). *Public perceptions of older people and ageing.* National Centre for the Protection of Older People. www.ncpop.ie.

McConahay, J. B. (1986). Modern racism, ambivalence, and the Modern Racism Scale. In J. Dovidio & S. Gaertner (Eds.), *Prejudice, Discrimination and Racism* (pp. 91–125). Academic Press.

McConatha, J. T., Hayta, V., Rieser-Danner, L., McConatha, D., & Polat, T. S. (2004). Turkish and U.S. attitudes toward aging. *Educational Gerontology,* 30 (3), 169–83.

McLeod, S. A. (2008). Social Identity Theory.http://www.simplypsychology.org/social-identity-theory-html.

MSN News. (2013, August 24).

Nelson, T. D. (2005). Ageism: prejudice against our feared future self. *Journal of Social Issues,* 61 (2), 207–21.

New York Times. (2013, September 18).

Omni, M., & Winant, H. (1986). *Racial formation in the United States: From the 1960s to the 1980s.* Routledge & Kegan Paul, Inc.

Organisation for Economic Co-operation and Development (OECD). (2012). Social institutions and gender index (SIGI). Paris, France.

Pew Research Center. (2007).

Pew Research Center. (2013, August 22).

Ponterotto, J. (2006). Understanding prejudice and racism. In J. Ponterotto (Ed.), *Preventing Prejudice: A Guide for Counselors, Educators, and Parents* (2nd ed.) (pp. 3–25). Sage Publications.

Rakow, L., & Wackwitz, L. (1998). Communication of sexism. In M. Hecht (Ed.), *Communicating Prejudice* (pp. 99–111). Sage Publications.

Rose, J. (1976). *Peoples: The ethnic dimension in human relations.* Rand McNally.

Schutz, H., & Six, B. (1996). How strong is the relationship between prejudice and discrimination? A meta-analytic answer. *International Journal of Intercultural Relations,* 20 (3–4), 441–62.

Simpson, G. E., & Yinger, J. M. (1985). *Racial and cultural minorities.* (5th ed.). The Plenum Press.

Stateline.org. (2013, August 5).

Sue, D. W. (2004). Whiteness and ethnocentric monoculturalism: Making the "invisible" visible. *American Psychologist,* 59 (8), 761–69.

Tajfel, H. (1979). Individuals and groups in social psychology. *British Journal of Clinical and Social Psychology,* 18 (2), 183–90.

Tajfel, H., & Turner, J. C. (1986). The social identity of intergroup behavior. In S. Worchel & W. G. Austin (Eds.), *Psychology of Intergroup Relations* (pp. 7–24). Nelson-Hall.

Tan, P. P., Zhang, N. H. & Fan, L. (2004). Students' attitudes toward the elderly in the People's Republic of China. *Educational Gerontology,* 30 (4), 305–14.

US Census Bureau. (2010).

World Health Organization (WHO). (2009). *Definition of an older or elderly person.* http://www.who.int/healthinfo/survey/ageingdefnolder/en/index.html.

Chapter 4: Measures of Explicit and Implicit Prejudice

Allport, G. W. (1979). *The nature of prejudice.* (25th Anniversary ed.). Addison-Wesley.

Aosved, A., Long, P. & Voller, E. (2009). Measuring sexism, racism, sexual prejudice, ageism, classism. *Journal of Applied Social Psychology,* 39 (10), 2321–54.

American Psychological Association. (2002). *Guidelines on multicultural education, training, research, practice and organizational change for psychologists.*

Bargh, J., Schwader, K., Hailey, S., Dyer, R., & Boothby, E. (2012). Automaticity in social-cognitive processes. *Trends in Cognitive Sciences,* 16 (12), 593–606.

Baron, A. S., & Banaji, M. R. (2006). The development of implicit attitudes: Evidence of race evaluations from ages 6 and 10 and adulthood. *Psychological Science* 17 (1), 53-58.

Blanton, H., Jaccard, J., Gonzales, P., & Christie, C. (2006). Decoding the implicit association test: Implications for criterion prediction. *Journal of Experimental Social Psychology*, 42 (2), 192-212.

Bogardus, E. S. (1933). A social distance scale. *Sociology & Social Research*, 17, 265-71.

Fraboni, M., Sallstone, R., & Hughes, S. (1999). The Fraboni Scale of Ageism (FSA): An attempt at a more precise measure of ageism. *Canadian Journal on Aging*, 9 (1), 56-66.

Glick, P., & Fiske, S. T. (1996). The ambivalent sexism inventory: Differentiating hostile and benevolent sexism. *Journal of Personality and Social Psychology*, 70 (3), 491-512.

Greenwald, A. G., & Banaji, M. R. (1995). Implicit social cognition: Attitudes, self-esteem, and stereotypes. *Psychological Review*, 102 (1), 4-27.

Greenwald, A. G., & Krieger, L. H. (2006). Implicit bias: Scientific foundations. *California Law Review*, 94 (4), 945-67.

Greenwald, A .G., McGhee, D. E., & Schwartz, J. L. K. (1998). Measuring individual differences in implicit cognition: The Implicit Association Test. *Journal of Personality and Social Psychology*, 79 (6), 1022-38.

Greenwald, A. G., Nosek, B. A., & Banaji, M. R. (2003). Understanding and using the Implicit Association Test: An improved scoring algorithm. *Journal of Personality and Social Psychology*, 85 (2), 197-216.

Greenwald, A. G., Poehlman, T. A., Uhlmann, E. L., & Banaji, M. R. (2009). Understanding and using the Implicit Association Test: III. Meta-analysis of predictive validity. *Journal of Personality and Social Psychology*, 97 (1), 17-41.

Henry, P. J., & Sears, D. O. (2002). The symbolic racism 2000 scale. *Political Psychology*, 23 (2), 253-83.

Karakayali, N. (2009). Social distance and affective orientations. *Sociological Forum*, 24 (3), 538-62.

McConahay, J. B. (1986). Modern racism, ambivalence, and the Modern Racism Scale. In J. Dovidio & S. Gaertnerp (Eds.), *Prejudice, Discrimination and Racism* (pp. 91-125). Academic Press.

Neville, H., Lilly, R. L., Duran, G., Lee, R., & Browne, L. (2000). Construction and initial validation of the color-blind.

New York Times. (2003, May 24).

Nosek, B. A. (2005). Moderators of the relationship between implicit and explicit evaluation. *Journal of Experimental Psychology*, 134 (4), 565-84.

Nosek, B. A., Banaji, M. R., & Greenwald, A. G. (2002). Harvesting implicit group attitudes and beliefs from a demonstration web site. *Group Dynamics*, 6 (1), 101-15.

Nosek, B. A., Greenwald, A. G., & Banaji, M. R. (2007). The Implicit Association Test at age 7: A methodological and conceptual review. In J. A. Bargh (Ed.), *Automatic Processes in Social Thinking and Behavior* (pp. 265-92). Psychology Press.

Parillo, V., & Donoghue, C. (2013). The national social distance study: Ten years later. *Sociological Forum,* 28 (3), 597-614.

Racial Attitudes Scale (CoBRAS). *Journal of Counseling Psychology*, 47 (1), 59-70.

Raja, S., & Stokes, J. P. (1998). Assessing attitudes toward lesbians and gay men: The Modern Homophobia Scale. *Journal of Gay, Lesbian, and Bisexual Identity*, 3 (2), 113-34.

Santso. (2013, May 24). Associated Press.

Sears, D. O., & Henry, P. J. (2005). Over thirty years later: A contemporary look at symbolic racism. *Advances in Experimental Social Psychology*, 37, 95-150.

Selle, J. KCSO May Drop Boy Scouts Charter. http://www.cdapress.com/archive/article-128b8731-7455-5508-aa15-fb6643f4330f.html.

Spence, J., Helmreich, R., & Stapp. J. (1973). A short version of the Attitudes toward Women Scale (AWS). *Bulletin of the Psychonomic Society*, 2 (4), 219-20.

Chapter 5: Consequences of Prejudice

Ayres, I., & Waldfogel, J. (1994). A market test for race discrimination in bail setting. *Stanford Law Review*, 46 (5), 988-1008.

Azarian, B. (2018, December 27). A complete psychological analysis of Trump's Support. *Psychology Today*. psychologytoday.com/us/blog/mind-in-the-machine/201712/analysis-trump-supporters-has-identified-5-key-traits

Banks, R., Eberhardt, J. L., & Ross, L. (2006). Discrimination and implicit bias in a racially unequal society. *California Law Review* 94 (4), 1169-90.

Bertrand, M., & Mullainathan. S. (2004). Are Emily and Greg more employable than Lakisha and Jamal? A field experiment on labor market discrimination. *The American Economic Review*, 94 (4), 991-1013.

Bielen, S., Marneffe, W., & Mocan, N. (2018). Racial bias and in-group bias in judicial decisions: Evidence from virtual reality courtrooms. NBER Working Paper No. w25355, Dec. https://ssrn.com/abstract=3302466

Blair, I. V., Steiner, J. F., & Havranek, E. P. (2011). Unconscious (implicit) bias and health care disparities: Where do we go from here? *The Permanente Journal*, 15 (2), 71-76.

Bridges, K. (2019). Implicit racial bias and racial disparities in health care. *Human Rights Magazine, 43* (3). www.americanbar.org. human_rights_magazine_home

Brigham, J. (1993). College students' racial attitudes. *Journal of Applied Social Psychology, 23* (23), 1933–67.

Carter, M., & Miletich, S. (2013, September 18). Survey finds racial disparities in views toward Seattle police. *Seattle Times, Chronicle of Higher Education.*

DeAngelis, T. (2019). How does implicit bias by physicians affect patients' health care? American Psychological Association, CE Corner 50 (3), 22.

DePaulo, B. M. (1992). Nonverbal behavior and self-presentation. *Psychological Bulletin, 111* (2), 203–43.

Foschi, M. (2000). Double standards for competence: Theory and research. *Annual Review of Sociology, 26,* 21–42.

Gawronski, B., Geschke, D., & Banse, R. (2003). Implicit bias in impression formation: Associations influence the construal of individuating information. *European Journal of Social Psychology, 33* (5), 573–89.

Gawronski, Q. (2019, November 7). Racial bias found in widely used health care algorithm. *NBC News.* http://www.nbcnews.com

Graham, S., & Lowery, B. (2004). Priming unconscious racial stereotypes about adolescent offenders. *Law and Human Behavior, 28* (5), 483–504.

Green, A. R., Carney, D. R., Pallin, D. J., Ngo, L. H., Raymond, K. L., Iezzoni, L. I., & Banaji, M. R. (2007). Implicit bias among physicians and its prediction of thrombolysis decisions for black and white patients. *J. Gen Intern Med, 22* (9), 1231–38.

Greenwald, A. G., Carville, J., Agne, K., & Gerstein, J. (2009). The very separate world of conservative Republicans: Why Republican leaders will have trouble speaking to the rest of America. https://democracycorps.com/news/the-very-separate-world-of-conservative-republicans/ http://www.democracycorps.com/wp-content/files/TheVerySeparateWorldofConservativeRepublicans101609.pdf

Greenwald, A .G., McGhee, D. E., & Schwartz, J. L. K. (1998). Measuring individual differences in implicit cognition: The Implicit Association Test. *Journal of Personality and Social Psychology, 79* (6), 1022–38.

Greenwald, A. G., Poehlman, T. A., Uhlmann, E. L., & Banaji, M. R. (2009). Understanding and using the Implicit Association Test: III. Meta-analysis of predictive validity. *Journal of Personality and Social Psychology, 97* (1), 17–41.

Greenwald, A. G., Smith, C. T., Sriram, N., Bar-Anan, Y., & Nosek, B. (2009). Race attitude measures predicted vote in the 2008 U.S. presidential election. *Analyses of Social Issues and Public Policy, 9* (1), 241–53.

Hodson, G., & Busseri, M. (2012). Bright minds and dark attitudes: Lower cognitive ability predicts greater prejudice through right-wing ideology and low intergroup contact. *Psychological Science, 23* (2), 187–95. https://pss.sagepub.com/content/23/2/187

Hooghe, M., & Dassonneville, R. (2018). Explaining the Trump vote: The effect of racist resentment and anti-immigrant sentiments. *PS: Political Science and Politics, 5* (3), 528–34.

Knowles, E., Lowery, B., & Schaumberg, R. (2010). Racial prejudice predicts opposition to Obama and his health care reform plan. *Journal of Experimental Social Psychology, 46* (2), 420–23.

Levinson, J. D., Cai, H., & Young, D. (2010). Guilty by implicit racial bias: The Guilty/Not Guilty Implicit Association Test. *Ohio State Journal of Criminal Law, 8,* 187–208.

Levinson, J. D., & Young, D. (2010). Different shades of bias: Skin tone, implicit racial bias, and judgments of ambiguous evidence. *West Virginia Law Review, 112,* 307–39.

Luttig, M. D., Federico, C. M., & Lavine, H. (2017). Supporters and opponents of Donald Trump respond differently to racial cues: An experimental analysis. *Research and Politics, 4* (4), 1–8.

McConahay, J. B. (1986). Modern racism, ambivalence, and the Modern Racism Scale. In J. Dovidio & S. Gaertner (Eds.), *Prejudice, Discrimination and Racism* (pp. 91–125). Academic Press.

McConnell, A. R., & Leibold, J. M. (2001). Relations among the Implicit Association test, discriminatory behavior, and explicit measures of racial attitudes. *Journal of Experimental Social Psychology, 37* (5), 435–42.

Monin, B., & Miller, D. T. (2001). Moral credentials and the expression of prejudice. *Journal of Personality and Social Psychology, 81* (1), 33–43.

Moss-Racusin, Dovidio, J. F., Brescoll, V. L., Graham, M., & Handelsman, J. (2012). Science faculty's subtle gender biases favor male students. *Proceedings of the National Academy of Sciences, 109* (41), 16474–79. doi: http://www.pnas.org/cgi/doi/10.1073/pnas.1211286109.

Mustard, D. B. (2001). Racial, ethnic, and gender disparities in sentencing: Evidence from the U.S. Federal Courts. *Journal of Law & Economics, 44* (1), 285–314.

Neville, H., Roderick, I., Duran, G., Lee, R., & Browne, I. (2000). Construction and initial validation of the Color-Blind Racial Attitudes Scale (CoBRAS). *Journal of Counseling Psychology, 47* (1), 59–70.

Patton, S. (2013, October 15). Scientist or 'whore'? Incident symbolizes struggle of color in Science. *The Chronicle of Higher Education.*

Pettigrew, T. F. (2017). Social psychological perspectives on Trump supporters. *Journal of Social and Political Psychology, 5* (1), 107–16.

Pettigrew, T. F., & Meertens, R. W. (1995). Subtle and blatant prejudice in western Europe. *European Journal of Social Psychology, 25* (1), 57–75.

Rachlinski, J., Johnson, S. L., Wistrich, A. J., & Guthrie, C. (2009). Does unconscious racial bias affect trial judges? *Notre Dame Law Review*, 84 (3).

Rooth, D. (2010). Automatic associations and discrimination in hiring: Real world evidence. *Labour Economics*, 17 (3), 523–34.

Seattle Times. (2013, September 18).

Schaffner, B. F. (2018). Follow the racist? The consequences of Trump's expression of prejudice for mass rhetoric. *Semantic Scholar*. Retrieved from https://www.semanticscholar.org/paper/Follow-the-Racist-The-Consequences-of-Trump-%E2%80%99-s-of-Schaffner/3ff29822155973661029da17a4c0610088e15340

Stephan, W. G., & Stephan, C. W. (2000). An integrated theory of prejudice. In S. Oskamp (Ed.), *Reducing Prejudice and Discrimination* (pp. 23–46). Lawrence Erlbaum Associates.

Swim, J., Aiken, K., Hall, W., & Hunter, B. (1995). Sexism and racism: Old-fashioned and modern prejudices. *Journal of Personality and Social Psychology*, 68 (2), 199–214.

Uhlmann, E., & Cohen, G. (2007). 'I think it, therefore it's true': Effects of self-perceived objectivity on hiring discrimination. *Organizational Behavior and Human Decision Processes*, 104 (2), 207–23.

Ziegert, J. C., & Hanges, P. J. (2005). Employment discrimination: The role of implicit attitudes, motivation, and a climate for racial bias. *J Appl Psychol*, 90 (3), 553–62.

Chapter 6: Where Do Prejudices Come From?

Aboud, F. E. (2008). A social-cognitive developmental theory of prejudice. In S. M. Quintana & C. McKown (Eds.), *Handbook of Race, Racism, and the Developing Child* (pp. 55–71). John Wiley & Sons.

Aboud, F. E. (2005). The development of prejudice in childhood and adolescence. In J. F. Dovidio, P. S. Glick, & L. A. Rudman (Eds.), *On the Nature of Prejudice: Fifty Years After Allport* (pp. 310–26). Blackwell.

Bigler, R. S., & Liben, L. S. (2007). Developmental intergroup theory: Explaining and reducing children's social stereotyping and prejudice. *Current Directions in Psychological Science*, 16 (3), 162–66.

Carlson, J. M., & Iovini, J. (1985). The transmission of racial attitudes from fathers to sons: A study of Blacks and Whites. *Adolescence*, 20 (77), 233–37.

Deary, I. J., Batty, G. D., & Gale, C. R. (2008). Bright children become enlightened adults. *Psychological Science*, 19 (1), 1–6.

Doyle, A. B., & Aboud, F. E. (1985). A longitudinal study of White children's racial prejudice as a social-cognitive development. *Merrill-Palmer Quarterly*, 41 (2), 209–28.

Fiske, S. T. (2000). Stereotyping, prejudice, and discrimination at the seam between the centuries: Evolution, culture, mind, and brain. *European Journal of Social Psychology*, 30 (3), 299–322.

Giroux, H. A. (2001). *The mouse that roared: Disney and the end of innocence.* Rowman & Littlefield.

Graves, S. B. (1999). Television and prejudice reduction: When does television as a vicarious experience make a difference? *Journal of Social Issues*, 55 (4), 707–27.

Hirschfeld, (2008). Children's developing conceptions of race. In S. M. Quintana & C. McKown (Eds.), *Handbook of Race, Racism, and the Developing Child* (pp. 37–54). John Wiley & Sons.

Hodson, G., & Busseri, M. A. (2012). Bright minds and dark attitudes: Lower cognitive ability predicts greater prejudice through right-wing ideology and low intergroup contact. *Psychological Science*, 23 (2), 187–195.

Jost, J. T., Glaser, J., Kruglanski, A. W., & Sulloway, F. J. (2003). Political conservatism as motivated social cognition. *Psychological Bulletin*, 129 (3), 339–75.

Katz, P. A. (2003). Racists or tolerant multiculturalists? How do they begin? *American Psychologist*, 58 (11), 897–909.

Katz, P. A., & Kofkin, J. A. (1997). Race, gender, and young children. In S. S. Luthar & J. A. Burack (Eds.), *Developmental Psychopathology: Perspectives on Adjustment, Risk, and Disorder* (pp. 51–74). Cambridge University Press.

Keiller, S. W. (2010). Abstract reasoning as a predictor of attitudes toward gay men. *Journal of Homosexuality*, 57 (7), 914–27.

Mahajan, N., Martinez, M. A., Gutierrez, N. L., Diesendruck, G., Banaji, M., & Santos, L. (2011). The evolution of intergroup bias: perceptions and attitudes in rhesus macaques. *Journal of Personality and Social Psychology*, 100 (3), 387–405.

Mosher, D. L., & Scodel, A. (1960). Relationships between ethnocentrism in children and the ethnocentrism and authoritarianism rearing practices of their mothers. *Child Development*, 31, 369–76.

Murphy, N. A., & Hall, J. A. (2011). Intelligence and interpersonal sensitivity: A meta-analysis. *Intelligence*, 39 (1), 54–63.

Patterson, M. M., & Bigler, R. S. (2006). Preschool children's attention to environmental messages about groups: Social categorization and the origins of intergroup bias. *Child Development*, 77 (4), 847–60.

Pettigrew, T. F., & Tropp, L. R. (2006). A meta-analytic test of intergroup contact theory. *Journal of Personality and Social Psychology*, 90 (5), 751–83.

Rokeach, M. (1948). Generalized mental rigidity as a factor in ethnocentrism. *Journal of Abnormal and Social Psychology*, 43 (3), 259–77.

Schoon, I., Cheng, G., Gales, C. R., Batty, G. D., & Deary, I. J. (2010). Social status, cognitive ability, and educational attainment as predictors of liberal social status and political trust. *Intelligence, 38* (1), 144-50.

Sidanius, J. (1985). Cognitive functioning and sociopolitical ideology revisited. *Political Psychology, 6* (4), 637-61.

Sinclair, S., Dunn, E., & Lowery, B. (2005). The relationship between parental racial attitudes and children's implicit prejudice. *Journal of Experimental Social Psychology, 41* (3), 283-89.

Stankov, L. (2009). Conservatism and cognitive ability. *Intelligence, 37* (3), 294-304.

Stephan, W. G., & Stephan, C. W. (2000). An integrated theory of prejudice. In S. Oskamp, (Ed.), *Reducing Prejudice and Discrimination*, (pp. 23-46). Lawrence Erlbaum Associates.

Stephan, W. G., Ybarra, O., & Bachman, G. (1999). Prejudice toward immigrants. *Journal of Applied Social Psychology, 29* (11), 2221-37.

Tatum, B. D. (1997). *Why Are All The Black Kids Sitting Together in the Cafeteria? And Other Conversations about Race.* Basic Books.

Van Ausdale, D., & Feagin, J. R. (2001). *The First R: How Children Learn Race and Racism.* Rowman & Littlefield.

Winkler, E. N. (2009). Children are not colorblind: How young children learn race. PACE: *Practical approaches for continuing education, 3* (3), 1-8. HighReach Learning.

Chapter 7: What Are Stereotypes?

Allport, G. W. (1979). *The nature of prejudice.* 25th anniversary ed. Addison-Wesley.

Aronson, R. (1988). *The social animal.* Jossey-Bass.

Associated Press, (2012, October 29). Associated Press Racial Attitudes Survey.

Associated Press. (2013, August 29).

Banaji, M., & Greenwald, A. G. (1994). Implicit stereotyping and prejudice. In M. Zanna & J. Olson (Eds.), *The psychology of prejudice, Ontario symposium*, (pp. 55-76). Lawrence Erlbaum.

Bandura, A. (2002). Social cognitive theory in cultural context. *Applied Psychology, 51* (2), 269-90.

Bargh, J., Chen, M., & Burrows, L. (1996). Automaticity and social behavior: Direct effects of trait construct and stereotype activation on action. *Journal of Personality and Social Psychology, 71* (2), 230-44.

Barreto, M., Manzano, S., & Segura, G. (2012). The Impact of Media Stereotypes on Opinions and Attitudes Towards Latinos, National Hispanic Media Coalition. (www.nhmc.org)

Barrett, A. E., & Cantwell, L. E. (2007). Drawing on stereotypes: Using undergraduates' sketches of elders as a teaching tool. *Educational Gerontology, 33* (4), 327-48.

Barrett, A. E., & Pai, M. (2008). Sketches in cyberspace: using student drawings of elders in an online social gerontology course. *Gerontology & Geriatrics Education, 29* (1), 84-103.

Brigham, J. C. (1971). Ethnic stereotypes. *Psychological Bulletin, 76* (1), 15-38.

Cuddy, A. J. C., Norton, M. I., & Fiske, S. T. (2005). This old stereotype: The pervasiveness and persistence of the elderly stereotype. *Journal of Social Issues, 61* (2), 267-85.

DeFleur, M. L., & DeFleur, M. H. (2003). *Learning to Hate Americans: How U.S. Media Shape Negative Attitudes among Teenagers in Twelve Countries.* Marquette Books.

Devine, P. G. (1989). Stereotypes and prejudice: Their automatic and controlled components. *Journal of Personality and Social Psychology, 56* (1), 5-18.

Dixon, T. L. (2006). Psychological reactions to crime news portrayals of Black criminals: Understanding the moderating roles of prior news viewing and stereotype endorsement. *Communication Monographs, 73* (2), 162-87.

Dolan, K. (2014). Gender stereotypes, candidate evaluations, and voting for women candidates: What really matters? *Political Research Quarterly, 67* (1), 96-107.

Eagly, A., & Mladinic, A. (1994). Are people prejudiced against women? Some answers from research on attitudes, gender stereotypes, and judgments of competence. *European Journal of Social Psychology, 5* (1), 1-35.

Fiske, S., & Cuddy, A. (2006). Stereotype content and relative group status across cultures. In S. Guimond, (Ed.), *Social comparison processes and levels of analysis: Understanding culture, intergroup relations and cognition* (pp. 249-63). Cambridge University Press.

Fiske, S., Cuddy, A. & Glick, P. (2007). Universal dimensions of social cognition: Warmth and competence. *Trends in Cognitive Science, 11* (2), 77-84.

Fiske, S., Cuddy, A., Glick, P., & Xu. J. (2002). A model of (often mixed) stereotype content: competence and warmth respectively follow from perceived status and competition. *Journal of Personality and Social Psychology, 82* (6), 878-902.

Ford, T. E., & Stangor, C. (1992). The role of diagnosticity in stereotype formation: Perceiving group means and variances. *Journal of Personality and Social Psychology, 63* (3), 356-67.

Gaertner, S.L., & Dovidio, J.F. (1986). The aversive form of racism. In S. L. Gaertner & J. F. Dovidio (Eds.). *Prejudice, Discrimination, and Racism* (pp. 61-89). Academic Press.

Gardner, R. C. (1973). Ethnic stereotypes: The traditional approach, a new look. *Canadian Psychologist,* 14 (2), 133–48.

Gilbert, D. T., & Hixon, J. G. (1991). The trouble of thinking: activation and application of stereotypic beliefs. *Journal of Personality and Social Psychology,* 60 (4), 509–17.

Glick, P., & Fiske, S. T. (2001). An ambivalent alliance: Hostile and benevolent sexism as complementary justifications for gender inequality. *American Psychologist,* 56 (2), 109–18.

Goldman, A., & Apuzzo, M. (2013, August 29). Mosques designated as terrorism organizations. Associated Press, *Moscow Pullman Daily News.*

Hamilton, D. L., & Sherman, J. W. (1994). Stereotypes. In R. S. Wyer & T. K. Srull, (Eds.), *Handbook of Social Cognition, Vol 2, Applications,* (pp. 1–68). Erlbaum.

Hamilton, D. L., & Trolier, T. K. (1986). Stereotypes and stereotyping: An overview of the cognitive approach. In S. L. Gaertner & J. F. Dovidio, (Eds.), *Prejudice, Discrimination, and Racism,* (pp. 127–57). Academic Press.

Hilton, J., & von Hippel, W. (1996). Stereotypes. *Annual Review of Psychology,* 47 (250), 237–71.

Jost, J. T., Burgess, D., & Mosso, C. (2001). Conflicts of legitimization among self, group, and system. The integrative potential of system justification theory. In J. T. Jost & B. Major, (Eds.), *The Psychology of Legitimacy: Emerging Perspectives on Ideology, Justice, and Intergroup* Relations, Cambridge University Press,

Katz, D., & Braly, K. (1933). Racial stereotypes of one hundred college students. *Journal of Abnormal and Social Psychology,* 28 (3), 280–90.

Katz, D., & Braly, K. (1935). Racial prejudice and racial stereotypes. *Journal of Abnormal and Social Psychology,* 30 (2), 175–93.

Kite, M. E., Stockdale, G. D., Whitley, B. E., & Johnson, B. T. (2005). Attitudes toward younger and older adults: An updated meta-analytic review. *Journal of Social Issues,* 61 (2), 241–66.

Lang, A. (2000). The limited capacity model of mediated message processing. *Journal of Communication,* 50 (1), 46–70.

Lyons, I. (2009). Public Perceptions of Older People and Ageing. National Centre for the Protection of Older People. www.ncpop.ie.

Monteith, M. J., & Spicer, C. V. (2000). Contents and correlates of Whites' and Blacks' racial attitudes. *Journal of Experimental Social Psychology,* 36 (2), 125–54.

Moss-Racusin, C. A., Dovidio, J. F., Brescoll, V. L., Graham, M., & Handelsman, J. (2012). Science faculty's subtle gender biases favor male students. *Proceedings of the National Academy of Science.* doi: http://www.pnas.org/cgi/doi/10.1073/pnas.1211286109.

Myers, D. (1990). *Social psychology.* 3rd ed. McGraw-Hill.

Narayan, C. (2008). Is there a double standard of aging? Older men and women and ageism. *Educational Gerontology,* 34 (9), 782–87.

Nelson, L. J., & Miller, D. T. (1995). The distinctiveness effect in social categorization: You are what makes you unusual. *Psychology Science,* 6 (4), 246–49.

Nisbet, E., Ostman, R., & Shanahan, J. (2007). Public opinion toward Muslim-Americans: Civil liberties and the role of religion, ideology, and media use. In A. Sinno (Ed.), *Muslims in Western Politics.* Indiana University Press.

Nosek, B. A., Banaji, M. R., & Greenwald, A. G. (2002). Harvesting implicit group attitudes and beliefs from a demonstration web site. *Group Dynamics: Theory, Research & Practice,* 6 (1), 101–15.

Panagopoulos, C. (2006). The polls-trends: Arab and Muslim Americans and Islam in the aftermath of 9/11. *Public Opinion Quarterly,* 70 (4), 608–24.

PEW Global Attitudes Project, (2012).

PEW Research Center, (2008).

Phalet, K., & Poppe, E. (1987). Competence and morality dimensions in national and ethnic stereotypes: A study in six eastern-European countries. *European Journal of Social Psychology,* 27 (6), 703–23.

Schneider, D. J. (2004). *The Psychology of Stereotyping.* The Guilford Press.

Secord, P. (1959). Stereotyping and favorableness in the perception of Negro faces. *Journal of Abnormal and Social Psychology,* 59 (3), 309–15.

Sides, J., & Gross, K. (2013). Stereotypes of Muslims and support for the war on terror. *Journal of Politics,* 75 (3).

Snyder, M. (1981). On the self-perpetuating nature of social stereotypes. In D. L. Hamilton (Ed.), *Cognitive Processes in Stereotyping and Intergroup Behavior,* (pp. 183–212). Lawrence Erlbaum Associates.

Snyder, M., & Meine, P. (1994). Stereotyping of the elderly: A functional approach. *British Journal of Social Psychology,* 33 (1), 63–82.

Tan, A., Dalisay, F., Zhang, Y., Han, E., & Merchant, M. (2010). A cognitive processing model of information source use and stereotyping: African American stereotypes in South Korea. *Journal of Broadcasting & Electronic Media,* 54 (2), 569–87.

Tan, A., Dalisay, F., Zhang, Y., & Zhang, L. (2009). Information Source use and Stereotypes of Americans in China. Paper presented at the International Communication annual conference.

Tan, A., Fujioka, Y., & Tan, G. (2000). Television use, stereotypes of African Americans and opinions on affirmative action: An affective model of policy reasoning. *Communication Monographs,* 67 (4), 362–71.

Tan, P. P., Zhang, N. H., & Fan, L. (2004). Students' attitudes towards the elderly in the People's Republic of China. *Educational Gerontology,* 30 (4), 305–14.

Tan, S. (2011). Myths of aging. *Psychology Today*, http://www.psychologytoday.com/blog/wise/201101/myths-aging.

Wojciszke, B. (2005). Affective concomitants of information on morality and competence. *European Psychology, 10* (1), 60–70.

Chapter 8: Consequences of Stereotypes

Allport, G. W. (1979). *The nature of prejudice.* 25th anniversary ed. Addison-Wesley.

Associated Press. (2013, September 17).

Barnes, M., Blom, A., Cox, K., Lessof, C., & Walker, A. (2006). *The social exclusion of older people: Evidence from the first wave of the English Longitudinal Study of Ageing (ELSA)-Final Report.* Office of the Deputy Prime Minister, London.

The *Chronicle of Higher Education.* (2013, September 30).

Clark, K. B. (1965). *The dark ghetto: Dilemmas of social power.* Harper & Row.

Cohen, G. L., Garcia, J., Apfel, N., & Master, A. (2006). Reducing the racial achievement gap: A social-psychological intervention. *Science, 313* (579), 1307–10.

Cohen, G. L., Steele, C. M., & Ross, L. D. (1999). The mentor's dilemma: Providing critical feedback across the racial divide. *Personality and Social Psychology Bulletin, 25,* 1302–18.

Correll, J., Hudson, S. M., Guillermo, S., & Ma, D. S. (2014). The police officer's dilemma: A decade of research on racial bias in the decision to shoot. *Social and Personality Psychology Compass, 8* (5), 201–13.

Correll, J., Park, B., Judd, C. M., & Wittenbrink, B. (2002). The police officer's dilemma: Using ethnicity to disambiguate potentially threatening individuals. *Journal of Personality and Social Psychology, 83,* 1314–29.

Correll, J., Park, B., Judd, C. M., & Wittenbrink, B. (2007). The influence of stereotypes on decisions to shoot. *European Journal of Social Psychology, 37* (6), 1102–17.

Correll, J., Wittenbrink, B., Park, B., Judd, C. M., & Goyle, A. (2011). Dangerous enough: Moderating racial bias with contextual threat cues. *Journal of Experimental Social Psychology, 47* (1), 184–89. doi:10.1016/j.jesp.2010.08.017.

Cuddy, A. J. C., Norton, M. I., & Fiske, S. T. (2005). This old stereotype: The pervasiveness and persistence of the elderly stereotype. *Journal of Social Issues, 61* (2), 267–85.

Danaher, K., & Crandall, C. S. (2008). Stereotype threat in applied settings re-examined. *Journal of Applied Social Psychology, 38,* 1639–55.

Eligon, J. (2012, March 22). Taking on police tactic, critics hit racial divide. *New York Times.*

Gilens, M. (1996). Race coding and white opposition to welfare. *American Political Science review, 90,* 593–604.

Glaser, J., & Knowles, E. (2008). Implicit motivation to control prejudice. *Journal of Experimental Social Psychology, 44* (1), 164–72.

Good, C., Aronson, J., & Harder, J. A. (2008). Problems in the pipeline. Stereotype threat and women's achievement in high-level math courses. *Journal of Applied developmental Psychology, 29,* 17–28.

Gordon, R. A., Michels, J. L., & Nelson, C. L. (1996). Majority group perceptions of criminal behavior: The accuracy of race-related crime stereotypes. *Journal of Applied Social Psychology, 26* (2), 148–59.

Grier, W., & Cobbs, P. (1968). *Black Rage.* BasicBooks.

Happell, B. (2002). Nursing home employment for nursing students: valuable experience or a harsh deterrent? *Journal of Advanced Nursing, 39* (6), 529–36.

Huffington Post (2018, December 14).

Huguet, P., & Regner, I. (2007). Stereotype threat among schoolgirls in quasi-ordinary classroom circumstances. *Journal of Educational Psychology, 99* (3), 545–60.

Independent. (2018, May 7).

Jones, J. M. (1997). *Prejudice and Racism.* 2nd ed. McGraw-Hill.

Katz, I., & Haas, R. G. (1988). Racial ambivalence and American value conflict: Correlational and priming studies of dual cognitive structures. *Journal of Personality and Social Psychology, 55,* 893–905.

Kooij, D., de Lange, A., Jansen, P., & Dikkers, J. (2008). Older workers' motivation to continue to work: Five meanings of age. A conceptual review. *Journal of Managerial Psychology, 23*(4), 364–94.

Levy, B. R., Slade, M. D., Kunkel, S. R., & Kasl, S. V. (2002). Longevity increased by positive self-perception of aging. *Journal of Personality and Social Psychology, 83* (2), 261–70.

Lyons, I. (2009). Public Perceptions of Older People and Ageing. National Centre for the Protection of Older People. www.ncpop.ie.

Mangan, K. (2013, September 30). Stereotypes add to burden for minority male students, researcher says. *The Chronicle of Higher education.*

McGlone, M. S., & Aronson, J. (2006). Stereotype threat, identity salience, and spatial reasoning. *Journal of Applied Developmental Psychology, 27,* 486–93.

McGuire, S. L., Klein, D. A., & Chen, S. L. (2008). Ageism revisited: A study measuring ageism in East Tennessee, U.S.A. *Nursing and Health Sciences,* 10 (1), 11–16.

McVittie, C., McKinlay, A. & Widdicombe, S. (2003). Committed to (un)equal opportunities? 'New ageism' and the older worker. *British Journal of Social Psychology,* 42, 595–612.

NBCNewYork.com. (2013, October 24).

New York Times. (2012, March 22).

O'Keefe, M., Hills, A., Doyle, M., McCreadie, C., Scholes, S., Constantine, R., Tinker, A., Manthorpe, J., Biggs, S., & Erens, B. (2007). *UK Study of the Abuse and Neglect of Older People.* NatCen, London.

Oliver, M. B., & Fonash, D. (2002). Race and crime in the news: Whites' identification and misidentification of violent and nonviolent criminal suspects. *Media Psychology,* 4, 137–56.

Pager, D., & H. Shepherd, H. (2008). The sociology of discrimination: Racial discrimination in employment, housing, credit and consumer markets. *Annual Review of Sociology,* 34, 181–209.

Palmore, E. (2004). Research note: Ageism in Canada and the United States. *Journal of Cross-Cultural Gerontology,* 19, 41–46.

Persico, N. (2009). Racial profiling? Detecting bias using statistical evidence. *Annual Review of Economics,* 1, 229–254. https://doi.org/10-1146/annurev.economics.050708.143307

Pittman, C. (2020). 'Shopping while Black': Black consumers' management of racial stigma and racial profiling in retail settings. *Journal of Consumer Culture,* 20 (1), 3–22.

Quinn, D. M., & Spencer, S. J. (2001). The interference of stereotype threat with women's generation of mathematical problem-solving strategies. *Journal of Social Issues,* 57 (1), 55–71.

Satzewich, V. & Shaffir, W. (2009). Racism versus professionalism: Claims and counter-claims. *Canadian Journal of Criminology and Criminal Justice,* 51 (2), 199–226.

Siff, A. (2013, October 24). Black teen sues over arrest after buying $350 designer belt. *NBCNewYork.com.*

Schmader, T., Johns, M., & Forbes, C. (2008). An integrated process model of stereotype threat effects on performance. *Psychological Review,* 115 (2), 336–56.

Schimel, J., Arndt, J., Banko, K. M., & Cook, A. (2004). Not all self-affirmations were created equal: The cognitive and social benefits of affirming the intrinsic (vs. extrinsic) self. *Social Cognition,* 22, 75–99.

Sniderman, P. M., Brody, R. A. & Tetlock, P. E. (1991). *Reasoning and Choice: Explorations in Political Psychology.* Cambridge University Press.

The Spokesman Review (2020, January 2). WSP stops Native drivers more, find less.

Stanford Open Policing Project (2019). Openpolicing.stanford.edu

Starr, S. (2016). Testing racial profiling: Empirical assessment of disparate treatment by police. *University of Chicago Legal Forum,* 485–531. https://repository.law.umich.edu/articles/1857

Steele, C. M. (1997). A threat in the air: How stereotypes shape intellectual identity and performance. *American Psychologist,* 52 (6), 613–29.

Steele, C. M. (1999). Thin ice: 'Stereotype threat' and Black college students. *Atlantic Monthly,* 44–54.

Steele, C. M. (2010). *Whistling Vivaldi and Other Clues to How Stereotypes Affect Us.* W. W. Norton & Co.

Steele, C. M., & Aronson, J. (1995). Stereotype threat and the intellectual test performance of African Americans. *Journal of Personality and Social Psychology,* 69 (5), 797–811.

Stricker, L. J., & Ward, W. C. (2004). Stereotype threat, inquiring about test takers' ethnicity and gender, and standardized test performance. *Journal of Applied Social Psychology,* 34, 665–93.

Weiss, M., & Collins, J. (2013, September 17). Family of man shot by Charlotte cop wants answers. Associated Press, *Moscow Pullman Daily News.*

Tan, A., Fujioka, Y., & Tan, G. (2000). Television use, stereotypes of African Americans and opinions on affirmative action: An affective model of policy reasoning. *Communication Monographs,* 67 (4), 362–71.

Timberlake, J. M., Baumann-Grau, A., Howell, J., & Williams, R. (2012). Who 'they' are matters: Immigrant stereotypes and assessments of the impact of immigration. *The Sociological Quarterly* 53 (4):

Timberlake, J. M., & Williams, R. H. (2012). Stereotypes of U.S. immigrants from four global regions. *Social Science Quarterly,* 93 (4), 867–90.

U.S. News (2019, September 9).

Vox (2018, December 31).

Working Group on Elder Abuse (WGEA) (2002). *Protecting Our Future.* The Stationery Office, Dublin.

Chapter 9: Media Stereotypes

American Society of Newspaper Editors, (2012). The Future of Diversity in the News.

Appiah, O., & Eighmey, J., (Eds.) (2011). *The Psychology of Persuasion: Perspectives for Theory, Research, and Application in A Diverse World.* Cognella Academic Publishing.

Asian American Journalists Association (2012). Handbook to Covering Asian America. Updated. www.aaja.org/aajahandbook/.

Associated Press. (2013, August 31).

Associated Press. (2013, October 13).

Austin, E., & Freeman, C. (1997). Effects of media, parents and peers on African-American adolescents' efficacy toward the media and the future. *Howard Journal of Communications,* 8 (3), 275–90.

Bandura, A. (1986). *Social Foundations of Thought and Action: A Social Cognitive Theory.* Englewood Cliffs, N.J.: Prentice-Hall.

Bandura, A. (2002). Social cognitive theory in cultural context. *Applied Psychology,* 51 (2), 269–90.

Bargh, J. A. (1989). Conditional automaticity: Varieties of automatic influence in social perception and cognition. In J. S. Uleman & J. A. Bargh, (Eds.) *Unintended Thought,* (pp. 3–51). Guilford Press.

Bargh, J. A., Chen, M., & Burrows, L. (1996). Automaticity of social behavior: Direct effects of trait construct and stereotype activation on action. *Journal of Personality and Social Psychology,* 71 (2), 230–44.

Bargh, J. A., Schwader, K., Hailey, S., Dyer, R., & Boothby, E. (2012). Automaticity in social-cognitive processes. *Trends in Cognitive Sciences,* 16 (12), 593–605.

Barreto, M., Manzano, S., & Segura, G.S. (2012). The Impact of Media Stereotypes on Opinions and Attitudes Towards Latinos. National Hispanic Media Coalition. www.latinodecisions.com.

Collins, P. H. (2004). *Black Sexual Politics.* Routledge.

Correll, J., Park, B., Judd, C. M., & Wittenbrink, B. (2007). The influence of stereotypes on decisions to shoot. *European Journal of Social Psychology,* 37, 1102–17.

Coyne, S., Linder, J. R., Rasmussen, E., & Birkbeck, V. (2016). Pretty as a princess: Longitudinal effects of engagement with Disney princesses on gender stereotypes, body esteem, and prosocial behavior in children. *Child Development,* 87 (6), 1–38.

Darling-Wolfe, F. (1997). Framing the breast implant controversy: A feminist critique. *Journal of Communication Inquiry* 21 (1).

Dalisay, F., & Tan, A., (2009). Assimilation and contrast effects in the priming of Asian- and African-American stereotypes through TV exposure. *Journalism and Mass Communication Quarterly,* 86.

Devince, P. (1989). Stereotypes and prejudice: Their automatic and controlled components. *Journal of Personality and Social Psychology,* 56, 5–18.

Dittmann, M. (2003). Fighting ageism. *American Psychological Association,* 34 (5). http://www.apa.org/monitor/may03/fighting.aspx.

Dixon, T.L., & Linz (2000). Overrepresentation and underrepresentation of African Americans and Latinos as lawbreakers on television news. *Journal of Communication,* 50(2), 131–154.

Dundes, L. (2001). Disney's modern heroine Pocahontas: Revealing age-old gender stereotypes and role discontinuity under a façade of liberation. *Social Science Journal, 38,* 353–365.

England, D. E., Descartes, L., & Collier-Meek, M. A. (2011). Gender role portrayal and the Disney Princesses. *Sex Roles,* 64, 555–67.

Entman, R., & Rojecki, A. (2001). *The Black Image in The White Mind: Media and Race in America.* University of Chicago Press.

Gecker, J. (2013, August 31). Group calls the ad 'racist.' The Associated Press, in the *Spokesman Review.*

Gibbons, J. A., Lukowski, A. F., & Walker, W. R. (2005). Exposure increases the believability of unbelievable news headlines via elaborate cognitive processing. *Media Psychology,* 7 (3), 273–300.

Gilliam, F. D., Jr. (1999). The 'Welfare Queen' experiment: How viewers react to images of African Mothers on welfare. *The Nieman Foundation for Journalism,* 53, 112–19.

Goudreau, J. (2012). Disney princess tops list of 20 best-selling entertainment products. *Forbes.* Retrieved from http://www.forbes.com/sites/jennagoudreau/2012/09/17/disney-princess-tops-list-of-the-20-best-selling-entertainment-products/

Hill, M. (2013, October 30). Opponents of Redskins name meeting with NFL. *The Associated Press in *Moscow Pullman Daily News.*

Lang, A. (2000). The limited capacity model of mediated message information processing. *Journal of Communication,* 50 (1), 46–70.

McLaurin, V. A. (2012). Stereotypes of Contemporary Native American Indian Characters in Recent Popular Media. Masters Thesis, University of Massachusetts Amherst. (scholarworks.umass.edu)

Media Action Network for Asian Americans (2012). www.manaa.org/

Monk-Turner, E., Heiserman, M., Johnson, C., Cotton, V., & Jackson, M. (2010). The portrayal of racial minorities on prime time television: A replication of the Mastro and Greenberg study a decade later. *Studies in Popular Culture,* 32 (2), 101–14.

Monahan, J. L., Shtrulis, I., & Givens, S. (2005). Priming welfare queens and other stereotypes: The transference of media images into interpersonal contexts. *Communication Research Reports,* 22 (3), 199–205.

Montepare, J. M., & Zebrowitz, L. A. (2002). A social-developmental view of ageism. In T. D. Nelson, (Ed.), *Ageism: Stereotyping and Prejudice Against Older Persons*, MIT Press, (pp. 77–125).

National Association of Hispanic Journalists (2006). www.nahp.org/

Oliver, M. B., Jackson II, R., Moses, N., & Dangerfield, C. (2004). The face of crime: Viewer's memory of race-related features in individuals pictured in the news. *Journal of Communication,* 54 (1), 88–104.

Oliver, M. B., Kalyanaraman, S., & Ramasubramanian, S. (2007). Sexual and violent imagery movie previews: Effects on viewers' perceptions and anticipated enjoyment. *Journal of Broadcasting & Electronic media,* 51 (4), 596–614.

Orenstein, P. (2011). *Cinderella Ate My Daughter.* Harper Collins.

Robinson, T., Callister, M., Magoffin, D., Moore, J. (2007). The portrayal of older characters in Disney animated films. *Journal of Aging Studies* 21 (3), 203–13. http://www.sciencedirect.com/science/journal/08904065

Ruscher, J. B. (2001). *Prejudiced Communication.* The Guilford Press.

Shaheen, J. G., (2003). Reel bad Arabs: How Hollywood vilifies a people. *The Annals of the American Academy of Political Science,* 588 (1), 171–93.

Shaheen, J. (2008). *Guilty, Hollywood's verdict on Arabs after 9/11.* Olive Branch Press.

Sides, J., & Gross, K. (2010). "Stereotypes of Muslims and support for the war on terror." *Journal of Politics,* 75 (3), 583–98.

Smith, S., Choueti, M., Prescott, A., & Pieper, K. (2014). Gender Roles & Occupations: A Look at Character Attributes and Job-Related Aspirations in Film and Television. Geena Davis Institute on Gender in Media. https://www.seejane.org/

Tan, A. (1986). *Mass communication theories and research.* Macmillan Publishing Co.

Tan, A., Dalisay, F., Zhang, Y., Han, E., & Merchant, M. (2010). A cognitive processing model of information source use and stereotyping: African-American stereotypes in South Korea. *Journal of Broadcasting & Electronic Media,* 54 (4), 569–87.

Sorensen, E. (1998, March 3). American Beats Out Kwan. *The Seattle Times.*

Takaki, R. (1989). *Strangers from A Different Shore: A History of Asian Americans.* Little, Brown and Co.

Towbin, M. A., Haddock, S. A., Schindler-Zimmerman, T., Lund, L. K., & Tanner, L. R. (2004). Images of gender, race, age, and sexual orientation in Disney feature-length animated films. *Journal of Feminist Family Therapy,* 15 (4), 19–44.

Wilson II, C. C., Gutierrez, F., & Chao, L. M. (2013). *Racism, Sexism, and the Media.* 4th ed. Sage Publications.

Weisbuch, M., Pauker, K., & Ambady, N. (2009). The subtle transmission of bias via televised nonverbal behavior. *Science* 326 (5960), 1711–14.

Wittenbrink, B., Judd, C. M., & Park, B. (2001). Evaluative versus conceptual judgments in automatic stereotyping and prejudice. *Journal of Experimental Social Psychology,* 37 (3), 244–52.

Chapter 10: Video Games, Stereotypes, and Prejudice

American Academy of Child and Adolescent Psychiatry (2015). Video games and children: playing with violence. Retrieved March 10 2017 from https://www.ascap.org/AACAP/Families_and _Youth/Facts_for_Families/FFF-Guide/Children-and-Video-Games-Playing-with-Violence-091.aspx.

Anderson, C. A, Gentile, D. A., & Buckley, K. (2007). *Violent Video Game Effects on Children and Adolescents: Theory, Research, and Public Policy.* Oxford University Press.

Bandura, A. (1986). *Social Foundations of Thought and Action: A Social Cognitive Theory.* Prentice-Hall.

Bargh, J. A., Schwader, K., Hailey, S., Dyer, R., & Boothby, E. (2012). Automaticity in social-cognitive processes. *Trends in Cognitive Sciences,* 16 (12), 593–605.

Behm-Morawitz, E., & Mastro, D. (2009). The effects of the sexualization of female video game characters on gender stereotyping and female self-concept. *Sex Roles,* 61 (11), 808–23.

Berkowitz, L. (1993). *Aggression: Its Causes, Consequences, and Control.* McGraw-Hill.

Braun, C., & Giroux, J. (1989). Arcade video games: Proxemic, cognitive and content analyses. *Journal of Leisure Research,* 21 (2), 92–105.

Burgess, M. R., Dill, K. E., Stermer, S., Vurgess, S. R., & Brown, B. P. (2011). Playing with prejudice: The prevalence and consequences of racial stereotypes in video games. *Media Psychology,* 14 (3), 289–311.

Children Now. (2001). Children and video games. Retrieved March 10 2017 from https://kaiserfamilyfoundation.files.wordpress.com/2013/04/5959.pdf.

Dill, K., Brown, B. & Collins, M. (2008). Effects of exposure to sex-stereotyped video game characters on tolerance of sexual harassment. *Journal of Experimental Social Psychology,* 44 (5), 1402–08.

Dill, K., & Thill, P. (2007). Video game characters and the socialization of gender roles: Young people's perceptions mirror sexist media depictions. *Sex Roles,* 57 (11), 851–64.

Dietz, T. L. (1998). An examination of violence and gender role portrayals in video games: Implications for gender socialization and aggressive behavior. *Sex Roles,* 38 (516), 425–42.

Downs, E., & Smith, S. (2005). Keeping abreast of hypersexuality: A video game character content analysis. Paper presented at the annual conference of the International Communication Association, New York City.

Gentile, D. (2009). Pathological video-game use among youth ages 8 to 18: A national study. *Psychological Science*, 20 (5), 584–602.

Gentile et al. (2009). The effects of prosocial video games on prosocial behaviors: International evidence from correlational, longitudinal, and experimental studies. *Personality & Social Psychology Bulletin*, 6, 752–63.

Gentile, D., Choo, H., Liau, A., Sim, T., Li, D., Fung, D., & Khoo, A. (2011). Pathological video game use among youths: A two-year longitudinal study. *Pediatrics* 127 (2): 318–28.

Gentile, D., Lynch, P., Linder, J., & Walsh, D. (2004). The effects of violent video game habits on adolescent hostility. *Journal of Adolescence*, 27, 5–22.

Gentile, D., Saleem, M., & Anderson, C. (2007). Public policy and the effects of media violence on children. *Social Issues and Policy Review*, 1 (1), 15–61.

Greenwald, A., Nosek, B., & Banaji, M. (2003). Understanding and using the implicit association test: An improved scoring algorithm. *Journal of Personality and Social Psychology*, 85 (2), 197–216.

Grusser, S. M., Thalemann, R., & Griggiths, M. D. (2007). Excessive computer game playing: Evidence for addiction and aggression? *CyberPsychology & Behavior*, 10 (2), 290–92.

Hanninger, K., & Thompson, K. M. (2004). Content and ratings of teen-rated video games. *JAMA*, *291*(17), 856–65.

Hollingdale, J., & Greitemeyer, T. (2014). The effect of online violent video games on levels of aggression. *PLOS One* 9 (11): e 111790. doi: 10.1371/journal.pone. 0111790.

Jansz J., & Martis, R. (2007). The Lara phenomenon: Powerful female characters in video games. *Sex Roles*, 56 (3), 141–48.

Ko, C., Yen, J. Y., Yen, C. F., Lin, H. C. & Yang, M. J. (2007). Factors predictive for incidence and remission of internet addiction in young adolescence: A prospective study. *CyberPsychology & Behavior*, 4, 545–51.

Krech, D., & Crutchfield, R. (1958). Perceiving the world. In D. Krech & R. Crutchfield (Eds.), *Theory and Problems in Social Psychology*. McGraw Hill.

Labre, M. P., & Duke, L. (2004). Nothing like a brisk walk and a spot of demon slaughter to make a girl's night: The construction of the female hero in the Buffy video game. *Communication Inquiry*, 28 (2), 138–56.

Lofgren, K. (2015). 2015 video game statistics & trends: Who's playing what & why? Retrieved March 10, 2017 from www. bigfish-games.com/blog/2015-global-videogame-stats-whos-playing-what-and-why/

Muehlenhard, C., & Rodgers, C. (1998). Token resistance to sex: New perspectives on old stereotypes. *Psychology of Women Quarterly*, 22 (3), 443–63.

Newzoo (2016). 2016 Global games market report. Retrieved March 10, 2017 from https://newzoo.com/wp-content/uploads/2016/01/Newzoo_Global_Games_Market_Report_Dummy.pdf.

Novotney, A. (2015). Gaming to learn. *Monitor on Psychology*, 46 (4), 46.

Pew Research Center. (2015). Gaming and gamers. Retrieved March 10, 2017 from www.pewinternet.org/2015/12/15/gaming-and-gamers/.

Polygon. (2016). 2016: The year in games. Retrieved March 20, 2017 from www.polygon.com/features/2016/12/16/13958746/2016-the-year-in-games.

Porter, G., Starcevic, V., Berle, D., & Fenech, P. (2010). Recognizing problem video game use. *Australian & New Zealand Journal of Psychiatry*, 44 (2), 120–28.

Provenzo Jr., E. (1991). *Video Kids: Making Sense of Nintendo.* Harvard University Press.

Ramirez, E. R., Norman, G. J., Rosenberg, D. E., Ken, J., Saelens, B. E., Durant, N., & Sallis, J. F. (2011). Adolescent screen time and rules to limit screen time in the home. *Journal of Adolescent Health*, 48 (4), 379–85.

Saleem, M., Anderson, C. A., & Gentile, D. A. (2012). Effects of prosocial, neutral and violent video games on college students' affect. *Aggressive Behavior*, 38 (4), 263–71.

Sherer, M., Maddux, J., Mercandante, B., & Rogers, R. (1982). The self-efficacy scale: Construction and validation. *Psychological Reports*, 51 (2), 663–71.

Shoemaker, B. (2014). Top 10 games of 2014. Retrieved March 10, 2017 from www. giantbomb.com/articles/brad.shoemaker-s-top-10-games-of-2014/1100-5132/

Spence, J. T., Helmreich, R., & Stapp, J. (1973). A short version of the attitudes toward women scale (AWS). *Bulletin of the Psychonomic Society*, 2 (4), 219–20.

Walsh, D .A. (2004). *Why Do They Act That Way? A Survival Guide to the Adolescent Brain for You and Your Teen.* Free Press.

Williams, D., Martins, N., Consalvo, M., & Ivory, J. (2009). The virtual census: Representations of gender, race and age in video games. *New Media & Society*, 11, 815–34.

Yang, G. S., Gibson, B., Lueke, A., Huesmann, R. L., & Bushman, J. (2014). Effects of avatar race in violent video games on racial attitudes and aggression. *Social Psychological and Personality Science*, 5 (6), 698–704.

Chapter 11: Cyberbullying, Stereotypes, and Prejudice

Aftab, P. (2005). Cyberbullying: A problem that got under parent's radar. Retrieved March 10 from www.aftab.com/cyberbullying. ingpage.htm.

California Healthy Kids Survey. (2007–2008). Retrieved March 10 from https://www.pausd.org/student.connectedness/california-healthy-kids-survey.

Cox Communications. (2009). Retrieved March 10 from https://enough.org/stats_cyberbullying_archives.

Dane County Youth Assessment. (2015). Retrieved March 10, 2017 from https://danecountyhumanservices.org/yth/dox/asmt_survey/2015/2015_hs.pdf.

Didden, R., Scholte, R. H., Korzillus, H., de Moor, J. M., Vermuelen, A., O'Reilly, M., Lang, R., & Lancioni, G. E. (2009). Cyberbullying among students with intellectual and developmental disability in special education settings. *Developmental Neurorehabilitation,* 3, 146–51.

Gradinger, P., Strohmeier, D., & Spiel, C. (2010). Definition and measurement of cyberbullying. *CyberPsychology* 4 (2), Article 1.

Hinduja, S., & Patchin, J. (2013). Social influences on cyberbullying among middle and high school students. *Journal of Youth and Adolescence,* 42 (5), 711–22.

Juvonen, J., & Gross, E. F. (2008). Extending the school grounds? Bullying experiences in cyberspace. *Journal of School Health,* 78 (9), 496–505.

Kowalski, R. M., & Limber, S. E. (2013). Psychological, physical, and academic correlates of cyberbullying and traditional bullying. *Journal of Adolescent Health,* 53, 813–20.

Kowalski, R. M., Limber, S. E., & Agatson, P. W. (2012). *Cyberbullying: Bullying in the Digital Age* (2nd ed.). Wiley-Blackwell.

Kowalski, R. M., Morgan, C. A., & Limber, S. E. (2012). Traditional bullying as a potential warning sign of cyberbullying. *School Psychology International,* 33 (5), 505–19.

Kowalski, R. M., Schroeder, A. N., Giumetti, G. W., & Lattanner, M. R. (2014). Bullying in the digital age: A critical review and meta-analysis of cyberbullying research among youth. *Psychological Bulletin,* 140 (4), 1073–137.

Lazuras, L., Barkoukis, V., Ourda, D., Tsorbatzoudis, H. (2013). A process model of cyberbullying in adolescence. *Computers in Human Behavior* 29 (3), 881–87.

Lenhart, A. (2010). Cyberbullying: What the Research Is Telling Us. Retrieved March 10, 2017 from http://www.PewInternet.org/Presentations/2010/May/Cyberbullying-2010.aspx.

Li, Q. (2007). Bullying in the new playground: Research into cyberbullying and cyber victimization. *Australian Journal of Educational Technology,* 23 (4), 435–54.

Nansel, T. R., Overpeck, M., Pilla, R. S., Ruan, W., Simons-Morton, B., & Scheidt, P. (2001). Bullying behaviors among U.S. youth: Prevalence and association with psychosocial adjustment. *JAMA: Journal of the American Medical Association,* 285 (16), 2094–100.

Olweus, D. (2013). School bullying: Development and some important challenges. *Annual Review of Clinical Psychology,* 9 (1), 751–80.

Patchin, J., & Hinduja, S. (2012). Cyberbullying: An update and synthesis of the research. In J. Patchin & S. Hinduja (Eds.), *Cyberbullying Prevention and Response: Expert Perspectives,* (pp. 13–35). Routledge.

Postmes, T., & Spears, R. (1998). Deindividuation and antinormative behavior: A meta-analysis. *Psychological Bulletin,* 123 (3), 238–59.

Smith, P. K., Ananiadou, K., & Cowie, H. (2003). Interventions to reduce school bullying. *The Canadian Journal of Psychiatry,* 48 (9), 591–99.

Smith, P. K., Mahdavi, J., Carvalbo, M., Fisher, S., Russell, S., & Tippett, N. (2008). Cyberbullying: Its nature and impact in secondary school pupils. *Journal of Child Psychology and Psychiatry,* 49 (4), 376–85.

Sourander, A., Klomek, A. B., Ikonen, M., Lindroos, J., Luntamo, T., Koskelainen, M., & Henenius, H. (2010). Psychosocial risk factors associated with cyberbullying among adolescents. *Archives of General Psychology,* 67 (7), 720–28.

Tokunaga, R. S. (2010). Following you home from school: A critical review and synthesis on research on cyberbullying victimization. *Computers in Human Behavior,* 26 (3), 277–87.

U.S. Department of Health and Human Services. (2006). Cyberbullying. Retrieved March 10, 2017 from www.education.com/reference/article/cyberbullying-what-adults-can-do/.

Van der Wal, M., de Wit, C. A. M., & Hirasing, R. (2003). Psychosocial Health Among Victims and Offenders of Direct and Indirect Bullying. *Pediatrics,* no. 111, 1312–17.

Vossekuil, B., Fein, R. A., Reddy, M., Borum, R., & Modzeleski, W. (2004). The final report and findings of the safe school initiative: Implications for the prevention of school attacks in the United States. Retrieved March 20, 2017 from https://www2.ed.gov/admins/lead/safety/preventing attacksreport.pdf.

Willard, N. E. (2007). *Cyberbullying and Cyberthreats: Responding to the Challenge of Online Social Aggression, Threats, and Distress.* Champaign: Research Press.

Wolke, D., Lee, K., & Guy, A. (2017). Cyberbullying: A storm in a teacup? *European Child & Adolescent Psychiatry*, 26 (8), 899–908. doi: 10. 1007/s00787-017-0954-6.

Ybarra, M. L. (2004). Linkages between depressive symptomatology and Internet harassment among young regular Internet users. *CyberPsychology & Behavior*, no. 7, 247–57.

Ybarra, M. L., Diener-West, M., & Leaf, P. J. (2007). Examining the overlap in Internet harassment and school bullying: Implications for school intervention. *Journal of Adolescent* Health, 41 (6), 842–50.

Ybarra, M. L., & Mitchell, K. J. (2004). Online aggressor/targets, aggressors, and targets: A comparison of associated youth characteristics. *Journal of Child Psychology and Psychiatry*, no. 43, 1308–16.

Chapter 12: Hate in Social Media

Allport, G. W. (1954). *The nature of prejudice*. Addison-Wesley.

Anti-Defamation League. (2019). Hate-symbols. www.adl.org.what-we-do.combat-hate.extremism-terrorism-bigotry

Benesch, S. (2019). Combating hate speech through counterspeech. Harvard University. https://dangerousspeech.org/

Bhatnagar, P. (2018). Countering online hate speech. *Global Media Review* 1 (3). http://www.amitymediajournal.com.

Bojarska, K. (2019). Europa-Universitat Viadrina, Frankfurt (Oder). https://cihr.eu/wp-content/uploads/2018/10/the-dynamics-of-hate-speech-and-counter-speech-in-the-social-media-English-1.pdf

Carnegie-Knight News21 Initiative (2019). Arizona State University. https://hateinamerica.news21.com/

CNN May 2, (2018). "Five ways hate speech spreads online."

FBI (2019). Hate Crime Data Collection Guidelines. https://www.fbi.gov/about-us/faqs

Fyfe, S. (2017). Tracking hate speech acts as incitement to genocide in international criminal law. *Leiden Journal of International Law*, 30 (2), 523–48. https://doi.org/10.1017/S0922156516000753

Gardner, K. (2018). Social media: Where voices of hate find a place to preach. *Money and Democracy*, Aug. 30. https://hateinamerica.news21.com/

Guynn, J. (2019, February 13). If you've been harassed online, you're not alone. More than half of Americans say they've experienced hate. *USA Today*. http://www.usatoday.com.

Hudson, D., & Ghani, M. (2017). Hate speech online. Freedom Forum Institute, Sept 18. www.freedomforuminstitute.org/.../hate-speech-online

Media Smarts (2019). Deconstructing online hate. Canada's Centre for Digital and Media Literacy. http://mediasmarts.ca/

Müller, K., & Schwarz, C. (2019). From Hashtag to Hate Crime: Twitter and Anti-Minority Sentiment. Social Science Research Network, Oct 31. https://ssm.com/abstract=3149103

PEW Research Center (2019). Internet & Technology. http://www.pewresearch.org

Relia, K., Li, Z., Cook, S., & Chunara, R. (2019). Race, ethnicity and national origin-based discrimination in social media and hate crimes across 100 U.S. cities. *Proceedings of the International AAAI Conference on Web and Social Media* 13 (01), 417–27. Retrieved from https://www.aaai.org/ojs/index.php/ICWSM/article/view/3354

Simon Wiesenthal Center (2019). 2019 Digital Terrorism and Hate Report Card, March 14. www.wiesenthal.com.news.2019 -digital-report-card

Southern Poverty Law Center (2019). Hate Map. https://www.splcenter.org/hate-map

Chapter 13: Fake News and Political Bias in Social Media

Allcott, H., & Gentzkow, G. (2017). Social media and fake news in the 2016 election. *Journal of Economic Perspectives*, 31 (2), 211–36.

Bakshy, E., Messing, S., & Adamic, L. A. (2015). Exposure to ideologically diverse news and opinion on Facebook. *Science* 348 (6239), 1130–33.

Budak, C., Goel, S., & Rao, J. (2016). Fair and balanced? Quantifying media bias through crowdsourced content analysis. *Public Opinion Quarterly*, 80 (S1), 250–71.

Chiang, C., & Knight, B. (2011). Media bias and influence: Evidence from newspaper endorsements. *The Review of Economic Studies*, 78 (3), 795–820.

De Witte, M. (2019). Search results not biased along party lines, Stanford scholars find. *Stanford News*, Nov. 26. http://news.stanford.edu

Geiger, A. W. (2019). Key findings about the online news landscape in America. Fact -Tank/Pew Research Center (Sept. 11). http://www.pewresearch.org

Hamborg, F., Donnay, K., & Gipp, B. (2019). Automated identification of media bias in news articles: an interdisciplinary literature review. *International Journal of Digital Libraries*, 20, 391–415. https://doi.org/10.1007//s00799-018-0261-y

Lazer, D. M., Baum, M., Benkler, Y., Berinksy, A., Greenhill, K., Menczer, F., & Miriam, J. M. (2018). The science of fake news. *Science,* 359 (6380), 1094–96. DOI:10.1126/science.aao2998 .

Lichter, R. S. (2017). Theories of media bias. In K. Kenski & K. Jamieson (Eds.), *The Oxford handbook of political* communication, Oxford University Press.

Newton, C. (2019). The real bias on social networks isn't against conservatives, it's toward polarization. *The Verge,* April 11. www. theverge.com

Ribeiro, F., Henrique, L., Benevenuto, F., Chakraborty, A., Kulshrestha, J., Babael, M., & Gummadi, K. (2018). Media bias monitor: Quantifying biases of social media news outlets at large-scale. Association for the Advancement of Artificial intelligence. www. researchgate.net/publication/327652478_Media ...

Vosoughi, S., Roy, D., & Aral, S. (2018). The spread of true and false news online. *Science,* 359, 1146–51.

Chapter 14: Media Interventions to Reduce Negative Stereotyping

Aboud, F. E. (2008). A social-cognitive developmental theory of prejudice. In S. M. Quintana & C. McKown (Eds.), *Handbook of Race, Racism, and the Developing Child,* (pp. 55–71). John Wiley & Sons.

A. C. Nielsen Co. (2012).

Asian American Journalists Association (2000). "ALL-AMERICAN: How To Cover Asian America. www.aaja.org/aajahandbookup-date/

Associated Press *Stylebook.* (2013). https://www.apstylebook.com/.

Blair, I. (2002). The malleability of automatic stereotypes and prejudice. *Personality and Social Psychology Review,* 6 (3), 242–61.

Dalisay, F., & Tan, A. (2009). Assimilation and contrast effects in the priming of Asian- and African-American stereotypes through TV exposure. *Journalism and Mass Communication Quarterly,* 86.

Dasgupta, N., & Greenwald, A. G. (2001). On the malleability of automatic attitudes: Combating automatic prejudice with images of admired and disliked individuals. *Journal of Personality and Social Psychology,* 81, 800–814.

Graves, S. B. (1999). Television and prejudice reduction: When does television as a vicarious experience make a difference? *Journal of Social Issues,* 55 (4), 707–27.

Greenberg, B. S., & Brand, J. E. (1994). Minorities and the mass media: 1970s to 1990s. In J. Bryant & D. Zillman (Eds.), *Media effects: Advances in theory and research,* (pp. 273–314). Erlbaum.

Harris, R. J. (1999). *A Cognitive Psychology of Mass Communication.* 3rd ed. Erlbaum.

Hirschfeld, L. A. (2008). Children's developing conceptions of race. In S. M. Quintana & C. McKown, *Handbook of Race, Racism, and the Developing Child,* (pp. 37–54). John Wiley & Sons.

Katsuyama, R. M. (1997). *An Evaluation of the Springfield City Schools' "Reaching Our Children" (ROC) Program.* University of Dayton, Social Science Research Center.

Katz, P. A., & Kofkin, J. A. (1997). Race, gender, and young children. In S. S. Luthar & J. A. Burack, *Developmental Psychopathology: Perspectives on Adjustment, Risk, and Disorder,* (pp. 51–74). Cambridge University Press.

Lovelace, V., Scheiner, S., Dollberg, S., Segui, I, & Black, T. (1994). Making a neighborhood the *Sesame Street* way: Developing a methodology to evaluate children's understanding of race. *Journal of Educational Television,* 20 (2), 69–77.

McLaurin, V. (2012). Stereotypes of Contemporary Native American Indian Characters in Recent Popular Media. Masters Thesis. University of Massachusetts Amherst.

Pecora, N., Murray, J., & Wartella, E., eds. (2007). *Children and Television: Fifty Years of Research.* Lawrence Erlbaum Associates.

Weiner, R. (2013, April 2). *Washington Post.*

Winkler, E. (2009). Children are not colorblind: How young children learn race. *Pace,* 3 (3), 1–8.

Zhang, Y., & Tan, A. (2011). Impact of mass media during the 2008 U.S. presidential election: A cross cultural study of stereotype change in China and the United States. *Communication Studies* 62, (4), 353–70.

Chapter 15: Communication Interventions to Reduce Prejudice

Allport, G. W. (1979). *The Nature of Prejudice.* 25th anniversary ed. Addison-Wesley.

Anti-Prejudice Consortium (2011). www.antiprejudice.org/.

Appiah, O., & Eighmey, J., eds, (2011). *The Psychology of Persuasion: Perspectives for Theory, Research, and Application in a Diverse World.* Cognella Academic Publishing.

Associated Press. (2013, September 5).

Ball-Rokeach, S., Rokeach, M., & Grube, J. (1984). *The Great American Values Test.* The Free Press.

Banda, P. S. (2013, September 5). NAACP–KKK meeting believed to be a first. *The Associated Press in Moscow Pullman Daily News.*

Blair, I. V. (2002). The malleability of automatic stereotypes and prejudice. *Personality and Social Psychology Review,* 6 (3), 242–61.

Blair, I. V., Ma, J., & Lenton, A. P. (2001). Imagining stereotypes away: The moderation of automatic stereotypes through mental imagery. *Journal of Personality and Social Psychology,* 81 (5), 828–41.

Boldenhausen, G. V., Kramer, G., & Susser, K. (1994). Happiness and stereotypic thinking in social judgment. *Journal of Personality and Social Psychology,* 66 (4), 621–32.

Cook, S. W. (1971). *The Effect of Unintended Interracial Contact upon Racial Interaction and Attitude Change. Proj. No. 5-13320, Final Report.* Washington, D.C.: U.S. Department of Health, Education and Welfare.

Cook, S. W. (1978). Interpersonal and attitudinal outcomes in cooperating interracial groups. *Journal of Research in Developmental Education,* 12 (1), 97–113.

Dadds, M. R., Bovbjerg, D. H., Redd, W. H., & Cutmore, T. R. (1997). Imagery in human classical conditioning. *Psychological Bulletin,* 122 (1), 89–103.

Deci, E. L., & Ryan, R. M. (2008). Facilitating optimal motivation and psychological well-being across life's domains. *Canadian Psychology,* 49 (1), 14–23.

Dobbs, M., & Crano, W. D. (2001). Outgroup accountability in the minimal group paradigm: Implications for aversive discrimination and social identity theory. *Personality and Social Psychology Bulletin,* 27 (3), 355–64.

Duncan, J. G., Boisjoly, J., Levy, D. M., Kremer, M., & Eccles, J. (2003). Empathy or Antipathy? The Consequences of Racially and Socially Diverse Peers on Attitudes and Behaviors. Working Paper, Institute of Policy research, Northwestern University, Chicago, IL.

Eisenstadt, D., Leippe, M. R., Rivers, J. A., & Stambush, M. A. (2003). Counterattitudinal advocacy on a matter of prejudice: Effects of distraction commitment and personal importance. *Journal of Applied Social Psychology,* 33 (10), 2123–52.

Esses, V. M., & Dovidio, J. F. (2002). The role of emotions in determining willingness to engage in intergroup contact. *Personality and Social Psychology Bulletin,* 289, 1202–14.

Festinger, L. A. (1957). *A Theory of Cognitive Dissonance.* Stanford University Press.

Finlay, K., & Stephan, W. (2000). Improving intergroup relations: The effects of empathy on racial attitudes. *Journal of Applied Social Psychology* 30 (8): 1720–37.

Firebaugh, G., & Davis, K. E. (1988). Trends in antiblack prejudice, 1972–1984: Region and cohort effects." *American Journal of Sociology,* 94 (2), 251–72.

Galinsky, A. D., & Moskowitz, G. B. (2000). Perspective taking: Decreasing stereotype expression, stereotype accessibility, and in-group favoritism. *Journal of Personality and Social Psychology,* 78 (4), 708–24.

Green, D. P., & Wong, J. S. (2008). Tolerance and the contact hypothesis: A field experiment. In E. Borgida (Ed.), *The Political Ideology of Democratic Citizenship.* Oxford University Press.

Greenwald, A. G., & Banaji, M. R. (1995). Implicit social cognition: Attitudes, self-esteem, and stereotypes. *Psychological Review* 102 (1), 4–27.

Henry, P. J., & Sears, D. O. (2002). The Symbolic Racism 2000 Scale. *Political Psychology,* 23 (2), 253–83.

Legault, L., Gutsell, J., & Inzlicht, M. (2011). Ironic effects of antiprejudice messages: How motivational interventions can reduce (but also increase) prejudice. *Psychological Science,* 22 (12), 1472–77.

Moskowitz, G., & Li, P. (2011). Egalitarian goals trigger stereotype inhibition: A proactive form of stereotype control. *Journal of Experimental Social Psychology,* 47 (1), 103–16.

Nosek, B. A., Greenwald, A. G. & Banaji, M. R. (2007). The Implicit Association Test at age 7: A methodological and conceptual review. In J. A. Bargh (Ed.), *Automatic Processes in Social Thinking and Behavior,* (pp. 265–92). Psychology Press.

Paluck, E. L., & Green, D. P. (2009). Prejudice reduction: What works? A review and assessment of research and practice. *Annual Review of Psychology,* 60, 339–67.

Partners Against Hate (2003). www.partnersagainsthate.org/.

Pettigrew, T. F., & Tropp, L. R. (2006). A meta-analytic test of intergroup contact theory. *Journal of Personality and Social Psychology,* 90 (5), 751–83.

Plant, E. A., Devine, P. G., & Peruche, M. B. (2010). Routes to positive interracial interactions: Approaching egalitarianism or avoiding prejudice. *Personality and Social Psychology Bulletin,* 36 (9), 1135–47.

Richeson, J. A., & Nussbaum, R. J., (2004). The impact of multiculturalism versus color-blindness on racial bias. *Journal of Experimental Social Psychology,* 40 (3), 417–23.

Sleeter, C. E. (Ed.) (1991). *Empowerment through Multicultural Education.* SUNY Press.

Stephan, W. G., & Finlay, K. (1999). The role of empathy in improving intergroup relations. *Journal of Social Issues,* 55 (4), 729–44.

Turner, R., & Crisp, R. (2010). Imagining intergroup contact reduces implicit prejudice. *British Journal of Social Psychology* 49 (1), 129–42.

Turner, R., Crisp, R., & Lambert, E. (2007). Imagining intergroup contact can improve intergroup attitudes. *Group Processes and Intergroup Relations,* 10 (4), 427–41.

Turner, R., Hewstone, M., Voci, A., & Vonofakou, C. (2008). A test of the extended intergroup contact hypothesis: The mediating role of intergroup anxiety, perceived ingroup and outgroup norms, and inclusion of the outgroup in the self. *Journal of Personality and Social Psychology,* 95 (4), 843–60.

Vescio, T. K., Sechrist, G. B., & Paolucci, M. P. (2003). Perspective taking and prejudice reduction: The meditational role of empathy arousal and situational attributions. *European Journal of Social Psychology,* 33 (4), 455–72.

Chapter 16: Digital Media Literacy

Associated Press (2017). Google to improve search quality with 'offensive' flag. Retrieved March 18 2017 from bigstory.ap.org/article/.../google-adds-tool-flag-offensive-search-results.

Baddely, A. D., & Hitch, G. J. (1994). Developments in the concept of working memory. *Neuropsyhology* 8 (4): 485–93.

Baddely, A. D., Thomson, N., & Buchanan, M., (1975). Word length and the structure of short term memory. *Journal of Verbal Learning and Verbal Behavior,* 14 (6): 575–89.

Chen, A. (2015). The agency. *New York Times.* ISSN 0362-4331.

Cowan, N. (2001). The magical number 4 in short-term memory: A reconsideration of mental storage capacity. *Behavioral Brain Science,* 24 (1), 87–114.

Festinger, L. (1957). *A Theory of Cognitive Dissonance.* Stanford University Press.

Hobbs, R. (2008). Debates and challenges facing new literacies in the 21st century. In S. Livingstone & K. Drotner (Eds.), *International Handbook of Children, Media and Culture,* (pp. 431–47). Sage.

Hobbs, R. (2010). Digital and media literacy: A plan of action. A white paper on the digital and media literacy recommendations of the Knight commission on the information needs of communities in a democracy. Retrieved March 17, 2017 from www.knightfoundation.org/reports/digital-and-media-literacy-plan-action.

Kiely, E., & Robertson, L. (2016). How to spot fake news. Fact.check.org. Retrieved March 17, 2017 from http://www.factcheck.org/2016/11/how-to-spot-fake-news/.

Kertscher, T. (2016). PolitiFact's lie of the year: fake news. *Milwaukee-Journal Sentinel.* Retrieved March 17, 2017 from www.jsonline.com/story/news/politics/..../2016/dec./13/2016-lie-year-fake-news/.

Lederer, L. (1988). What are other countries doing in media education? An excerpt from the 1988 annual report of the L.J. Skaggs and Mary C. Skaggs Foundation. Retrieved March 17 2017 from http://medialit.net/reading-room/what-are-other-countries-doing-media-education.

Mangen, A., Rigmor Walgermo, B., & Bronnick, K. (2013). Reading liner texts on paper versus computer screen: Effects on reading comprehension. *International Journal of Education Research,* 58, 61–68.

Metzger, M. J. (2009). Credibility research to date. Credibility and Digital media @ UCSB. Retrieved March 17, 2017 from http://www.credibility.uscb.edu/past_research.php.

Miller, G. A. (1956). The magical number seven, plus or minus two. Some limits on our capacity for processing information. *Psychological Review,* 63 (2), 81–97.

Nickerson, R. S. (1998). Confirmation bias: A ubiquitous phenomenon in many guises. *Review of general psychology,* 2 (2), 175–230.

Pew Research Center (2016a). 10 facts about the changing digital news landscape. Retrieved March 17, 2017 from http://www.pewresearch.org/fact-tank/2016/09/14/facts-about-the-changing-digital-news-landscape/.

Pew Research Center (2016b). Digital news audience: A fact sheet. Retrieved March 17, 2017 from http://www.journalism.org/2016/06/15/digital-news-audience-fact-sheet/.

Saettler, L. P. (2004). *The Evolution of American Educational Technology.* Information Age Publishing.

Stanford History Education Group (2016). Evaluating information: The cornerstone of civic online reasoning. Retrieved March 27, 2017 from https://sheg.stanford.edu/upload/.../Executive%20Summary%2011.21.16.pdf.

Southern Poverty Law Center (2017). Hate Map. Retrieved March 17, 2017 from https://www.splcenter.org/hate-map.

Tavernise, S. (2016). As fake news spreads lies, more readers shrug at the truth. *New York Times.* Retrieved March 17, 2017 from https://www.nytimes.com/2016/12/06/us/fake-news-partisan-republican-democrat-html.

USA Today (2017). Facebook begins flagging 'disputed' (fake) news. Retrieved March 17, 2017 from http://www.usatoday.com/story/tech/news/2017/03/06/facebook-begins-flagging-fake-news/98804948/.

Wastlund, E., Reinikka, H., Norlander, T., & Archer, T. (2005). Effects of VDT and paper presentation on consumption and production of information: Psychological and physiological factors. *Computers in Human Behavior,* 21 (2), 377–94.

Index

Herek, G.M., 236

Herschof, J., 237

heterosexism, 43

Hewstone, M., 216, 219, 251

Hillary Clinton, 69

Hill, M., 245

Hilton, J., 93, 94, 242

Hiring discrimination, 123

hiring evaluations, 64

hiring practices, 64

Hirschfeld, 87, 240

Hirschfeld, L.A., 203, 250

Hixon, J.G., 94, 96, 241

Hodson, G., 82, 240

Hoebel, A., 23, 235

Hogan, K., 17, 18, 235

Howell, J., 122, 244

Hughes, S., 54, 55, 238

Huguet, P., 121, 243

Hunter, B., 65, 240

I

Iezzoni, L.I., 71, 239

immigrants, 21, 56, 86, 94, 98, 105, 122, 147, 205

Implicit Association Test, 57, 82, 217, 219

implicit biases, 7, 8, 14, 25, 49, 56, 57, 58, 64, 100, 137, 143, 212, 217, 219

implicit measures, 63, 67, 97, 99

implicit prejudice, 49, 56, 63, 77, 89, 99, 202, 211, 212, 216, 220

indirectness, 8

individual-level analysis, 81

individual racism, 40

informational narratives, 218

in-group identification, 85, 87

in-groups, 24, 84, 93, 94, 97, 139, 143, 202, 218, 220

institutional racism, 40

Integrated Threat Theory, 85

intelligence, 82, 95, 101, 111, 119

intergroup prejudice, 84

Intergroup Threat Scale, 89

Internet games, 187

Interpersonal aggression, 184

interpersonal level of analysis, 22

interracial marriage, 7

interventions, institutional, 205

interventions, intrapersonal, 212

intrapersonal level of analysis, 22

Inzlicht, M., 212, 251

Iovini, J., 88, 240

Iversen, T.N., 237

J

Jaccard, J., 60, 238

Jackson II, R., 136, 245

Jackson, M., 136, 245

Jansen, P., 243

Johnson, B.T., 242

Johnson, C., 136, 245

Johnson, S.L., 75, 236, 239

Jones, J.M., 118, 237, 243

Jones, M., 244

Jost, J.T., 82, 97, 240, 242

Judd, C.M., 126, 136, 243, 245

Judd, L., 20, 235

K

Kalyanaraman, S., 245

Karakayali, N., 49, 238

Kasl, S.V., 243

Katsuyama, R.M., 205, 250

Katz, D., 94, 97, 242

Katz, I., 124, 243

Katz, P.A., 87, 203, 240, 250

Keller, S.W., 82, 240

Kellogg Foundation, 135, 146

Kirch, M.S., 18, 235

Kite, M.E., 109, 242

Klein, D.A., 243

Knapp, M., 18, 236

Knowles, E., 67, 127, 239, 243

Kofkin, J.A., 87, 203, 240, 250

Kooij, D., 128, 243

Kramer, G., 213, 250

Kremer, M., 251

Kriger, L.H., 58, 238

Krogman, W., 237

Kruglanski, A.W., 240

Ku Klux Klan, 186

Kunkel, S.R., 243

L

labels, 5, 60, 94

Lahey, J.N., 237

Lambert, E., 251

Lang, A., 97, 145, 242, 245

language, 7, 12, 15, 22, 49, 64, 88, 137

Larsen, L., 237

Lasswell, H., 12, 236

Latino Decisions, 135, 146

Lawyers for Civil Rights, 31

Lee, R., 52, 66, 238

Legault, L., 212, 251

Leibold, J.M., 72, 239

Leippe, M.R., 251

Lending discrimination, 123

Lenski, G., 13, 236

Lenton, A.P., 216, 250

Lester, P., 19, 236

Levinson, J.D., 75, 239

Levinson, S., 16, 235

Levy, B.R., 119, 243

Levy, D.M., 251

Liben, L.S., 88, 240

Linguistic Category Model, 16, 24

Linz, 136, 245

Li, P., 214, 251

Lone Ranger, the, 138

Long, P., 52, 237

Lovelace, V., 203, 250

Lowery, B., 67, 76, 88, 239, 241

Lukowski, A.F., 245

Luttig, 2017, 69

Lyons, I., 109, 128, 237, 242, 243

M

Maas, A., 16, 236

Mahajan, N., 82, 240

Ma, J., 216, 250

Mandela, N., 1, 235

Mangan, K., 243

Manzano, S., 98, 105, 135, 146, 241, 245

Martinez, M.A., 240

Mason, P.L., 236

Master, A., 120, 243

McConahay, J.B., 50, 237

CPSIA information can be obtained
at www.ICGtesting.com
Printed in the USA
LVHW062126020721
691780LV00007B/26